A Reader's Guide to James Merrill's
The Changing Light at Sandover

A Reader's Guide to James Merrill's *The Changing Light at Sandover*

ROBERT POLITO

Ann Arbor
THE UNIVERSITY OF MICHIGAN PRESS

Published in the United States of America by
The University of Michigan Press
Manufactured in the United States of America
∞ Printed on acid-free paper

1999 1998 1997 1996 5 4 3 2

A CIP catalogue record for this book is available from the British Library.

Library of Congress Cataloging-in-Publication Data

A Reader's guide to James Merrill's The changing light at Sandover / [compiled by] Robert Polito.
p. cm.
Includes bibliographical references.
ISBN 0-472-09524-2 (alk. paper). — ISBN 0-472-06524-6 (pbk. : alk. paper)
1. Merrill, James Ingram. Changing light at Sandover.
I. Polito, Robert.
PS3525.E6645C4837 1994
811'.54—dc20 94-7010
CIP

For Mark, Arthur, and Mark

Foreword

It's an old, ongoing story. From prehistory to fairy tales to Henry James's late revery of "The Great Good Place," we read about a hero or heroine faced by an insuperable task—which, however, through some half-magical, wholly unforeseen agency, is accomplished, as it were, overnight. The subtlest of these tasks is perhaps the one in Apuleius, set for Psyche by the jealous Goddess of Love. The poor child is presented with a great heap of different grains and told to sort them according to kind—far more than her clumsy fingers can think of doing. But her friends the Ants unerringly finish the chore by sunrise. While Robert Polito is a poet, not a social insect, and has been at it not for hours but for years, something at once minute and visionary about his labor evokes the industry and organizational skills of Psyche's helpers. To be so thorough, so tidy, and yet so in touch with the underlying sense! I think of the ant colony brought, in a time innocent of ecology, from the Amazon to a trendy New York museum. The habitat appeared intact, yet within weeks every last ant had perished. Had they responded to bad vibes from the Subway? Were their pulses no longer those of Earth's heart? Happily, no such doom awaits this volume. Formic, informative, positively formidable, it will spare the *Sandover* buff hours of rummaging for mislaid "gems," giving him instead leisure for charmed attention to the patterns they form in Mr. Polito's kaleidoscope.

James Merrill

Preface

This book offers a reader's handbook and alphabetical index to *The Changing Light at Sandover.* James Merrill's monumental poem sustains a revisionary attitude toward experience, as the poet and his companion, David Jackson, advance to successively higher levels of spirit guides—Ephraim to Mirabell to the angels and God B—who rework and amend the conceits of their predecessors. These visionary reconsiderations can occur hundreds of pages apart from one another; frequently, too, a subject surfaces long before it is assigned a name (the Research Lab, for instance), or enters the poem under a designation different from its subsequent and common one (as 741 modulates into Mirabell or the 12% into the angels). Gathering together discrete episodes and disparate denominations, the *Reader's Guide* aims to make it easier for the reader to participate in the shifting, self-revising pageant that Merrill designates "the changing light."

Many people befriended this book. I wish to thank all of the writers who permitted me to reprint their original reviews of *Divine Comedies, Mirabell: Books of Number, Scripts for the Pageant,* and *The Changing Light at Sandover* in the section entitled "Responses," but especially, for their additional support and advice, David Lehman, Helen Vendler, and Stephen Yenser. Timothy Peltason of Wellesley College made a crucial suggestion that redirected the manuscript. Publication of this book has been aided by a grant from the Abraham and Rebecca Stein Faculty Publications Fund of New York University, Department of English. At the University of Michigan Press I am very grateful to LeAnn Fields, Eve Trager, the copyediting staff, and Richard Isomaki. I wish to thank Frank Bidart, Lynn Chu, the late Arthur Gold, Glen Hartley, Lloyd Schwartz, and, particularly, Donald Hall, for their many generous actions. I also wish to acknowledge my appreciation to Elizabeth Dickey, Sondra Farganis, Elissa Tenny, Cindy Onore, and my other New School colleagues. My wife, Kristine Harris, contributed her judgment and meticulous handiwork to every page. Finally, I will always be grateful to James Merrill for his generous cooperation—and for his poem.

Contents

Introduction: Sibylline Listening

DANTE'S LUCK LAY IN HIS GULLIBLE
& HEAVENLY WORLD WE MY BOY DRAW FROM 2
SORTS OF READER: ONE ON HIS KNEES TO ART
THE OTHER FACEDOWN OVER A COMIC BOOK.
OUR STYLISH HIJINKS WONT AMUSE THE LATTER
& THE FORMER WILL DISCOUNT OUR URGENT MATTER

—W. H. Auden (*C.L.S.* 147)

Slyly mimicing the quicksilver deviations in tone that he's cooly unraveling, W. H. Auden, the crafty, dauntless spirit-guide of Sandover, focuses the changing light by refracting it through an image-splitting funhouse mirror. But for all their sprightly hocus-pocus, Auden's calculations regarding the likely audience for James Merrill's encounters with the other world anticipate what is most elusive and unprecedented in *The Changing Light at Sandover.* One truism of literary history, at least since the publication of the *Lyrical Ballads,* is that the performances of enduring poets have been so quirky and singular in their ambition to rethink the possibilities of the modern poem that they are initially judged not to be poems at all. As Merrill's trilogy hazarded its final form, ascending from "The Book of Ephraim" through *Mirabell's Book of Number* and on to *Scripts for the Pageant* and the exhilarating coda, "The Higher Keys," the challenges—and the idiosyncracies—spiraled, as if in proportion to the accelerating upsurges of the uppercase type in which he recorded his "ghostwriters." Many flesh-and-blood readers retreated, as confounded as Auden surmised they might be.

Here was a poem that testified increasingly to the plausibility of its occult inspiration, yet set the whole heavenly apparatus spinning amid a domestic chronicle of Merrill's twenty-five years with his companion, David Jackson ("the most convincing description I know of a gay marriage," poet Thom Gunn remarked).[1] Steadily divine *and* homemade, moreover, *Sandover* limned both realms in variable shadings that routinely had the sublime playing leapfrog with the absurd. The poem charted its affinities with the visionary creations of Dante, Blake, and Yeats even as it made room for such popular-priced sci-fi effects as the Ouija board, Atlantis, UFOs, centaurs, and bat-winged angels.

And here was a poet who had once admitted that his early writing often was led on by "some chance phrases, usually attached but not always, not even always attached to a subject," suddenly grappling with "POEMS OF SCIENCE" where (as he acknowledged) "the crisp proliferation of ideas sounds almost like a Shaw preface, not at all the kind of page I could turn out by myself."[2] A poet who had once confessed, "Thus I rarely buy a newspaper or vote"—yet whose fresh stanzas transmitted grave warnings about the perils of atomic fission.

No idler among the baffled was Merrill himself. Introducing selections from the just-completed *Mirabell* during a Morris Gray reading at Harvard in 1977, with his voice catching on each new tangle, he marveled: "Much confusion also to find oneself in a tradition one hadn't thought one belonged to."[3]

More of what Merrill may have been proposing by this notice of his belated crossover to another tradition will be suggested below and in the Afterword to this book. But principally he was remarking his passage from a chiefly lyric poet to one who is preeminently a medium. Finding himself by submitting to and taking on the voices of others, speaking with a composite voice, for *The Changing Light at Sandover* Merrill engaged in what Delmore Schwartz once termed "sibylline listening." Schwartz wrote in his essay "T. S. Eliot's Voice and his Voices":

> [Eliot's] poems are often dominated by a *listening* to other voices—the voices of other poets, in other centuries and countries; the voices of various human beings of differing classes and stations in society, a diversity of beliefs, values, habits of speech, and views of life . . . often the actual substance of a passage is first of all a listening or a quoting . . . . The method of the sibylline or subliminal listener must seem, at first glance, to be no method at all precisely because it is the method which permits all other methods to be used freely and without predetermination; and which allows no particular method to interfere with the quintessential receptivity which opens itself up to any and all kinds of material and subject matter.[4]

Repeatedly in interviews Merrill has dismissed suggestions that in his daily sessions with Jackson the Ouija board served as a mnemonic device, a typewriter, or an instrument, and underscored the quintessential receptivity that Schwartz praised in Eliot: "If anything the keyboard was us. And our one obligation, at any given session, was to be as 'well tempered' as possible."[5]

The Ouija transcriptions hovering behind *Sandover* confront the lyric mode with an insistent polyvocality that conspicuously disdains the authority of any single human speaker. The dissenting, hectoring vocalists who break into the poem could not be more inimical to the formal dazzle and virtuosic verve of previous Merrill. As poet Frank Bidart has evoked one such booming agitator: "I remember when I first heard the demanding, obsessive, unappeased voice of one of the 'sons of Cain' in *Mirabell*—it seemed as if Merrill had let in the static of the universe."[6]

Merrill's own arrangement of his lyric poems in *From the First Nine* (1982) and *Selected Poems 1946–1985* (1992) stresses continuities and foreshadowings, setting *The Changing Light at Sandover* on the pad like a rocket eager to be launched. And just so. But as *Mirabell* demonstrates, "the toy spyglass teaches / That anything worth having's had both ways" (174); and as irresistibly as his ordering of the lyric poems persuades, the reversible perspective prompts a reverse truth: Merrill's trilogy breaks with his lyric past as decisively as the mirror he shatters to free his dead friends, Auden and Maria Mitsotáki, at the conclusion of *Scripts for the Pageant*.

Auden styles Merrill's careering, polyvocal performance "A MAHLER" (301). *The Changing Light at Sandover* is as exquisite and resounding an echo chamber as any symbolist or modernist work. Every stray phrase is like ringing a bell, and even Merrill is driven to acknowledge that it's "Maddening the way / Everything merges and reflects" (415). The poem's legerdemain is legendary, and the poet's aplomb and finish have been extensively cataloged and celebrated. To spotlight *Sandover's* accomplishment against the broader backdrop of English literature, perhaps only George Herbert's *The Temple* comprises so bedazzling a compendium of stanzaic and metrical forms, as Merrill magisterially spins out sonnets, villanelles, Spenserian stanzas, Rubaiyat quatrains, terza rima, Anglo Saxon alliterative meter, and a stunning, crowning canzone.

What's largely escaped notice, though, no doubt because *Sandover* exhibits so much polish, is Merrill's eagerness to engage chance, coincidence, and accident at every level of his aesthetic. The design of the trilogy incorporates the instability and indeterminacy of the self, and probably no other modern poem is simultaneously so shaped and so arbitrary. "Admittedly I err," and "Oh very well then," are the shoulder-shrugging openings of "The Book of Ephraim" and *Mirabell*. Successively chagrined, rueful, resigned, apprehensive, and awed, Merrill makes it clear that he did not *choose* this work, with its almost involuntary entrée to another world.

In the primary organizational schemes of each volume of the trilogy, form literally goes by the board, as the printed symbols on the Ouija board dictate Merrill's design: the alphabet for "The Book of Ephraim," the arabic numerals for *Mirabell*, "Yes & No" for *Scripts for the Pageant*. Given rather than invented, found rather than selected, these compositional devices recall the randomly willful, antisystematic orderings of the surrealists Andre Breton and Francis Picabia, and of their European and American admirers, such as Raymond Roussel in *Impressions of Africa,* Walter Abish in *Alphabetical Africa,* Gilbert Sorrentino in *Splendide Hotel,* Michel Butor in *Mobile,* and even Roland Barthes in his late, alphabetically arranged essays, *A Lover's Discourse* and *Roland Barthes.* Merrill's reliance on his otherworldly transcripts also harks back to the surrealist practice of automatic writing, and to Marcel Duchamp's advocacy of the readymade. Such stratagems exchange the certainties of control for the contingencies of hazard and happenstance.

The Changing Light at Sandover absorbs the dispersals and consolidations of the self into a discontinuous narrative in which characters are continually interrupting or completing one another's lines. The poem fulminates under the pressure of what Mahler once called "ruthless contrapuntal technique," and, like the world it is reproducing, *Sandover* skirts dissolution and collapse. God B instructs JM to "MAKE A V WORK / GIVING BOTH PAUSE AND HOPE" (493), and every page of his trilogy is punctuated by pauses that stall the hopeful flow of the narrative. "The Broken Home," as Merrill himself was the first to note, is the myth that animates both the public and personal histories of *Sandover.* "Eden tells a parable of fission," he writes, "lost world and broken home" (192). His stanzas become slanting, zigzagging rooms in which contending voices vie for, and yield, the floor:

> DJ: For the love of—JM: Peacock *there,*
> There in the realm of no appearances?
> HE APPEARS IN US OUR MINDS (HEARTS) ARE HIS MIRROR
> JUST THE REVERSE OF VAMPIRES, EH ENFANT?
>
> A peacock—hm! Not proud as one, I hope.
> MY DEARS HIS GREAT TAIL SNAPPED SHUT LIKE A FAN
>
> THERE IS A DESIGN AT WORK U ARE NOT BEING PREPARED
> Our lessons can't be finished? WE MUST START
> PUTTING WHAT THE STRAIGHT OLD PAINTERS CALL
> A WASH OVER THEM I SHD THINK MY DEARS
> WE SHALL BATHE THEM IN LIGHT WE SHALL HOLD THEM TO THE
> WINDOW
> TO SEE DENSITY BECOME THE HARMONIC STRUCTURE &
> CHEMISTRY THE ORCHESTRATION & AH SOUL THE HEARING
> Peacock, peacock—
> MAY I ASK A ? DO TEARS PAIN ONE?
> Yes. No. Pain and bless.
> MY EYES BURN RED
> IN THE FEATHERD MASK AS FORMERLY THEY BETRAY MY RACE

Shall we correct that by imagining
Eyes of crystal?
THERE ARE ALAS LIMITS   I HAVE NEVER LOOKD THRU CRYSTAL
Yet you see through us.
NO   O NO   YR SOULS ARE NOT TRANSPARENT   THEY WEAR A VEIL
OF HUMAN EXPERIENCE & THIS I WILL NEVER LIFT.

(157)

Juxtapositions of typography and meter, as earthly and heavenly speakers clash and converge, and the rough pentameter of the human actors skids into and blends with the five stresses of Mirabell's syllabics; rhyming patterns that obliquely square the two worlds (the opening quatrain, for instance, where masculine and feminine endings jostle and fuse); a checkered diction that confounds slang and abstractions, conversational volubility and epigrammatic concision, comic hubbub and visionary music—these are only a few of the feints and dodges that Merrill adopts to stagger his poem. The formal interruption that was heralded in *Sandover's* opening, "Admittedly I err," evolves into a poetics of disruption.

Some of the schisms are violent, as when the bat-angels impose "censorship" on Matt Jackson:

DAVID I WANTED U TO BRING US BACK
TOGETHER   I STILL WANT IT   FIND HER   FIND ME
IN MY NEW LIFE   HER NAME IS
Censorship.

(107)

Others baffle cohesion with Jesuitical cunning. Here the urgency of Maya's disclosure is bent by JM's wandering couplet:

E IS WHISKED
INTO OUR MIDST & THE RECEPTION STARTS
BUT DO U TRULY THINK DEAR FRIENDS DEAR HEARTS
The cup half dancing, Maya no more than we
Knowing, it seemed, what lay in store
OUR PRATTLE HAS NO END BEYOND ITSELF

(73)

Phrases throughout the trilogy are haunted by ghostly, absent endings. In section X of "The Book of Ephraim" a justly celebrated joke on the syllabic lines he's been writing mimes the drama of self and otherness:

The twinklings of

Insight hurt or elude the naked eye, no
Metrical lens to focus them, no kismet
Veiled as a stern rhyme sound, to obey whose wink
Floods with rapture its galaxy of sisters.
Muse and maker, each at a loss without the

—Oh but my foot has gone to sleep!

(85)

The stage directions of *Scripts for the Pageant* embed digressions within digressions, parentheses within parentheses:

Star-map, globe and microscope.
A comfy air of things once used and used.
However, (since this room is both itself
And, with the sly economy of dream,
An entrance hall in Athens (Yes, we're back
Downstairs. . . .))

(320)

But these are ruptures that heal themselves. *Sandover* splits and is stitched back together with such insistent ingenuity that it's easy to overlook the fractures that are not healed, and the losses that are final. The souls destroyed by atomic rays, for example, are irrecoverable. And the closing sections of *Scripts* are among the most formally unsteady and equivocal in the entire poem. In lesson 10, God B traces an X on the Ouija board, which Merrill echoes in a crisscrossing quincunx that shudders under the stress of its fragmentary, incessant questions: "Is it the mark / That cancels, or the letter-writer's kiss? / The X / Of the illiterate? / Fulcrum and consort to our willowy &?" (493–94). Psyche discharges her last speeches in frantic, assymetrical bursts that are as inconclusive as they are wildly punctuated: "LOOK ALIVE! MUCH TO DO! THE SUMMER TO GET UNDER WRAPS! / O RESERVOIR!" (507). The grief and impoverishment that DJ and JM feel after they break the mirror that returns Auden and Maria to earth is enduring and unaccommodated:

But at the heart of each is a pure ache
—Maria, Wystan, George—which time might cure
If there were time in Heaven, or these dead
Weren't so addicted to the loving cup.
Maria, Wystan, George—they've gone, they've gone.

(510)

The breakdown of Merrill's verse into repetitive, spasmodic slivers is matched by other dislocations in the narrative. The "Finale," with its last, long, circuitous sentence fragment and out-of-sequence recapitulation of God B's song, chronologically precedes the segment it follows, "Glimpses of the Future." Merrill's coda also forestalls closure by enacting a circular ending that eternally returns the changed poet and reader to the beginning of the poem for a fresh look at the changing light.

As Stephen Yenser, among other of Merrill's readers, has suggested, *Sandover's* plasticity testifies to Oscar Wilde's Möbius-strip adage that "a truth in art is that whose contradictory is also true." Double dealing determines the shape of Merrill's lines, as well, which typically flex contradiction or detonate puns; omnipresent oxymorons mimic grander oppositions and vacillations. In "The Book of Ephraim" some river stones that DJ and JM name after literary characters they admire are "Pride of (and telling proof against) the clean / Sweep they impel so swiftly they impede" (70). In *Mirabell* salt is "fuel and stabilizer / Of the body electric . . . Raw power and its insulation" (141); bursting cartons in a plastic factory are "bound to enliven *and* muck up the site" (244). In *Scripts* the "&" is simultaneously an open "BRIDGE" and a locked "GATE" (386); the images that an eye sees are also "SCALES" that prevent it from seeing (466); the mirror that links the dead to the living is simultaneously "A STYX OF QUICKSILVER DIVIDING THEM / FROM LIFE-INFECTED DJ & JM" (359). Here George Cotzias discusses his death with JM and Maria:

> YEARS OF RAYS
> HAVING LEFT MY SOUL LIKE A SWISS CHEESE . . .
> Alluding to his work on the disease
> That killed him, or to his saved consciousness,
> Her words of welcome half caress, half mock:
> HOIST WITH YR OWN PETARD I SEE, EH DOC?
>
> (374)

Auden presses home the metaphysical underpinning of Merrill's nonstop paradoxes, which might otherwise be dismissed as a mannerism, by locating duality in the origins of language:

> IN THE BEGINNING MIGHT THE WORD
> (OR FORMULA) NOT HAVE REMAINED UNHEARD
> UNTIL IT HAD ENGENDERED BOTH ITS OWN
> ANTONYM & THE ODD HOMOPHONE?
>
> (341)

As Auden intimates, Merrill's punning is similarly double-edged. Customarily appraised by both partisans and detractors as mere calculation and sleight of hand, his puns instead traffic in linguistic accident ("The lapse that tides us over, hither, yon; / Tide that laps us home away from home," he writes in "The Book of Ephraim"). The puns constitute another species of automatic writing; they're ready-made rifts in the fabric of language. In the coda Maria Callas speaks to the glories of inadvertent wizardry:

> MY BAD EYESIGHT ALONE
> MADE FOR EFFECTIVE TOUCHES IN PERFORMANCE.
> THAT SUDDEN REELING-BACKWARD HALF A SWOON
> IN TOSCA (ACT II) CAUSING HEARTS TO STOP
> CAME FROM WHEN I STUMBLED ON A PROP
> IN DRESS REHEARSAL. LITTLE THINGS LIKE THAT.
>
> (529)

Throughout his trilogy Merrill yields to the sway of language no less than to the demands of his voices. He once described the *Oxford English Dictionary* as "the collective unconscious of the race." A paragraph from the introduction to a volume he selected for the Yale Series of Younger Poets, Pamela Alexander's *Navigable Waterways,* accents the "transactional power" that ripples through his puns and spoonerisms:

> If World War I caused, as we hear tell, the total cave-in of civilization except where it glinted on in the minds of writers like Valery and Joyce, the problem for later generations has been to create works whose resonance would last for more than a season. A culture without Greek or Latin or Anglo-Saxon goes off the gold standard. How, then, to draw upon the treasure? At once representing and parodying our orphic wealth, the lightweight crackle of wordplay retains no little transactional power in the right hands. Of course, it raises—as for that matter did the gold itself—the question of ill-gotten gains. Even today, how many poets and readers choose the holy poverty of some second-hand diction, pure dull "message" in translation from a never-to-be-known original. "There is no wing like meaning," said Stevens. Two are needed to get off the ground.

The lateral leaps of mind that derive "Resistance" from JM and DJ's "resistance" of the bat-angels' communications, "Adam" from "atom," the "twelve powers" of the angels from Mirabell's "12:88 ratio," or the "electrical triggers" in man's brain from the "naked current" owe more to the alchemical "word golf" than Merrill plays out in his recent poem "Processional" ("in three tidy strokes . . . LEAD / Turns (LOAD, GOAD) to GOLD"), than they do to logic or narrative drive. His musings on the "No" or "negative" lessons of *Scripts* epitomize the sidelong gyrations that spur the dynamo:

> Think, before you give
> Way to panic, of what other meanings
> The word "negative" takes on in *Ephraim:*
> X-ray images, or Maya's film
> In which the widow turns into the bride.
> Tricks of the darkroom. All those cameras clicking
> In Venice, on the bridge. For now a new bridge—
> Can it be crossed both ways?—from Yes to No
> Is entering the picture.
>
> (362)

A set piece on *set* intensifies and parodies the prevarications of the grand design:

> Do we get
> The sense of Wystan's "humankind has set
> Idea to Innocence?" Set? AS IN 'SET ONE'S MIND TO'
> 'SET TO MUSIC' 'SET IN MOTION' The word
> Evoking in one swoop tenacity,
> Harmony, resistance—
>
> (441)

Oblique strategies spark and short-circuit *Sandover* because, as Merrill proposes in his *Paris Review* interview with poet J. D. McClatchy, the physical universe is also a pun. "I believe the secret lies primarily in the nature of poetry—and of science too, for that matter—and that the ability to see both ways at once isn't merely an idiosyncracy but corresponds to how the world needs to be seen: cheerful *and* awful, opaque *and* transparent. The plus and minus of a vast, evolving formula."

Even the bravura stylistic moonwalks in *Sandover* flaunt a double-mindedness. Mixing the prearranged and the innovative, the secondhand and the unprecedented, they emanate as antiformal forms. Merrill's "NO ACCIDENT" villanelle delivers a grim, primitive "message" in an exquisite bottle. In "Samos," his ensorcelling canzone, he gambols beyond his models in Dante and Auden by syncopating the recurrent end words with left-handed homophones that scatter the pattern even as they spirit it along. The diametrics of the masque in *Sandover,* which structure so much of the heavenly pageant, break with Renaissance precedent as Merrill simultaneously, rather than successively, stages his "ANTIMASQUE" and "MASQUE." Moreover, the polished lens of the drama is not trained solely on the sovereign; the reversible spyglass also looks on "MANKIND: ALL EYES IN HEAVEN FOCUSED ON / THE MORTAL, SACRED (& EXPENDABLE) THRONE" (491). Again style reciprocates meaning—if the world is a pun, it is also, as Michael says, a "MASQUE" (511).

In Yeats's *A Vision* all conflicts are directed toward synthesis and accord.[7] The question of the corresponding unity of Merrill's design in *Sandover* is perhaps the permanent controversial issue in the writing of critics already sympathetic to the poem. Two of Merrill's most elegant and persuasive admirers, David Lehman and Stephen Yenser, speak for a union of opposites. Lehman writes, "Merrill argues for the affirmative powers of form. *What* it affirms seems secondary to the blessed realization *that* it does; it speaks to the imagination's provisional success in either sensing or willing an order to things while maintaining fidelity to the appearance of disorder, disunity, dispersal."[8] And Yenser: "Unity in duality (or in multiplicity, since dualism propogates) constitutes the poem's fundamental principle, metaphysical and aesthetic alike."[9]

The tense poise of Lehman's and Yenser's phrasing cannot be improved upon. Yet there are pressing matters of emphasis still to be sorted out, and significant cautions that need to be asserted. If *A Vision* was Yeats's final stay against chaos, Merrill's poem is remarkable for the amount of worldly discord, tumult, and pandemonium that it allows in. The degree to which his trilogy is open-ended, indefinite, and undetermined should not be understated. The formidable formal reconciliations of his earlier lyrics must not obscure the suspicions that Merrill registers in *Sandover* regarding this own fluency and control, suspicions that bravely undermine his stylistic rapprochements and untie the knots of his resolve.

He poses the riddle near the center of *Scripts for the Pageant:*

> Oh. Oh yes. The ambiguities . . .
> Resolve them? Wear them on a ring, like keys
> The heroine in James how seldom dares
> Use, on the last page, to open doors?
>
> (399)

But what about that final page? As Yenser points out, the last rhyme in *Scripts* is "Light/NIGHT," and the long sentence that ends that book remains incomplete. Merrill had used the same rhyme words almost one hundred pages earlier for a prayer addressed to the moon and Psyche: "Ripen, Huntress, into matron. Light, / Come full circle through unclouded night" (420). Their reappearance at the conclusion of *Scripts* is no less speculative and unfixed. Approached from one direction, the dovetailing of upper and lower case, and of positive and negative imagery, suggests the ultimate attunement of *Sandover's* two worlds; it accommodates and relaxes the poem's anxieties about nuclear annihilation and the future of the race; and the short closing speech of God B imparts reassurance and certainty. But approached from another direction, the final rhyme is a formal taunt that encodes distance and division; it mimics the destruction of light by Chaos, and the passing of day in "CIPHER NIGHT"; and God B's words are either a harrowing SOS or more static on the galactic radio.

Auden describes the structure of *Scripts* as "2 GOLDEN TRAYS OF 'YES' & 'NO' WITH '&' / AS BRIDGE OR BALANCE" (328). The keen, neutralizing tensions of the ending, the offsetting check and countercheck, may be apprehended as a powerful resolution, in that they reenact the universal dynamics of Resistance. As Merrill remarks after the last lesson in *Scripts,* "Friction made the first thin consomme / Of all we know" (495). Yet a straightforward deconstructionist reading ignores the "ACCIDENTS" that, Michael says, have introduced flutters into the equilibrium. Within the overarching balance of "Yes & No" there are other counterweights that jiggle the scale. What appear to be ecstatic affirmations or final disentanglements prompt fresh doubts and snarls. Michael's glorious fete in "Yes" is followed by God B's hermetic song. "PLAINTIVE? AFFIRMATIVE?" inquires Auden; JM and DJ can answer only by posting their own uncertainties and isolating fears:

> Night. Two phantoms out of Maeterlinck
> Stand on the terrace watching the full moon sink.
> DJ: It's almost as if *we* were dead
> And signalling to dear ones in the world.
> They face it squarely, Wystan and Maria,
> Terror or exaltation or whatever.
> We two are deaf and dumb; they see, they hear.
> They suffer; we feel nothing. We're the dead . . .
> And these were just the lessons that said Yes
> —To what? for up through Michael's magic well
> Eerie undercurrents of distress.
>
> (361)

Psyche's climactic entrance in lesson 5 of "&" is undercut instantly by George Cotzias's question about her relationship to Gabriel. "AREN'T WE BEING A BIT OVERSANGUINE / ABOUT MOTHER N. . . . GABRIEL IS HER SPOILED DARLING. . . . IN G'S VOICE I HEARD / THE HUM THE SUCK THE CONTRADICTING WORD" (416–17). The "LAST RESOUNDING YES" that Psyche bestows on man during her Spenserian revels in the penultimate lesson of "NO" is not as firm as it initially seems. Auden resists DJ and JM's desire to pin her down:

> Nature said Yes to man—the question's settled.

SHE SAYS DEAR BOY E X A C T L Y WHAT SHE MEANS
LOOK IT UP "A last resounding Yes."
LAST? The fête was ending. JM: Or
Because man won't be hearing Yes much more?
AH SHE SETS MEANING SPINNING LIKE A COIN.
HEADS UP? You're asking us? TIP SCALE TO YES
& ALL'S THE GLINT OF QUEEN M(AB)'S ALLEGRESSE.
LEAN TOWARD NO, & NO AMOUNT OF SKILL
WILL KEEP HER IMPS LOCKED UP IN GABRIEL'S SCHOOL.

(492)

Consistent with the strategies of his previous poetry, Merrill steers the inflammatory materials of *Sandover* toward safety. "Mine's for the happy ending," he writes. "Barbarity / To serve uncooked one's bloody tranche de vie . . . / Later, if the hero couldn't smile, / Reader and author could; one called it style" (496). But rigging his affirmation in these clipped, arch idioms—blowing the whistle, as it were, on his stiff upper lip—is virtually to cancel it. Both Auden and Maria betray impatience with JM's formal optimism. Auden preempts his efforts to restate the theme from "The Thousand and Second Night," that "form's what affirms":

MY BOY DON'T QUOTE THIS OLD STICKLER FOR FORM.
WHERE IN ALL THIS IS THE AFFIRMATION?
In the surrender, in the forward motion—
POWER BLAZING ON SHUT LIDS? MIND LAPPED IN WARM
PRIMORDIAL WATERS? Yes, yes! NO NO THIS
INGENUE'S TRUST IN FEELING: NEVER TO THINK?
CHECK UP? ASK QUESTIONS? ONWARD TO THE BRINK,
ANCHOR CUT LOOSE? THAT WAY LIES NEMESIS

(331)

Maria is still more curt as she interrupts JM's reiteration of the angels' bright promises for the future:

JM: Why born? To feed the earthward flow
Of Paradise? That final waterfall
Ephraim first mentioned in—I KNOW, I KNOW

(426)

In *Sandover,* Merrill, like the Sergei of his poem's lost novel, steels himself against "unrelenting fluency." He curses "language's misleading apparatus" (453). And in one of the most disturbing and self-distrusting exchanges in the poem, he exposes the consoling fiction at the heart of the long elegy he is composing:

JM: Though
Hasn't the Board helped us at all to see
Losses recouped? In Wystan and Maria's
Surrender to the minerals and the plants
Those ghastly graveyard facts become a dance
Of slow acceptance; our otherwise
Dumb grief is given words. DJ: Or lies?

(335)

Merrill's writing about the other world prior to *Sandover* brimmed with tidy, paraphrasable epiphanies in which the self and the physical universe served as stable reference points. This is the conclusion of "Voices from the Other World," from *The Country of a Thousand Years of Peace* (1959):

once looked at lit
By the cold reflections of the dead
Risen extinct but irresistible,
Our lives have never seemed more full, more real,
Nor the full moon more quick to chill.

The final sentence of *The Seraglio* (1957), the novel in which he first availed himself of the transcripts that would later figure in "The Book of Ephraim," wrapped up a related insight: "The entire world was real." Both the novel and the poem surveyed the dead from a measured, self-possessed distance. Richard Saez has provided us with a definitive description of Merrill's lyric mode that is consistent with these performances:

> Each poem begins after a physical or emotional crisis has enervated the poet, effecting something like Proust's intensified sensibility after an asthmatic attack. . . . When the focus has narrowed sufficiently to burn through the poet's self-absorption, remaining under their thin gauze of ashes is the poem: a cooling artifice which coalesces and refigures the past.[10]

Subverting the tempering disposition of Merrill's earlier poetry, the trilogy transposes the progression in Saez's metaphor. The fires of *Sandover* are consuming rather than refining; the poem that he writes under the ultimatum of his imperious prompters—"3 OF YOUR YEARS MORE WE WANT WE MUST HAVE POEMS OF SCIENCE"—is itself the crisis, not its banked aftermath. Far from simmering down, *Sandover* advances to exchanges of intenser and more volatile heat.

At once finished and incomplete, stylishly coordinated and agitated by the claims of accident and coincidence, a deep well of echoing effects and a broad avenue of random oddities, *Sandover* crosses the two dominant, if contrary, movements in modern poetry: the romantic/symbolist tradition in which Merrill had always worked, and its discordant rival that, issuing from Rimbaud and the surrealists, Marjorie Perloff has tagged the "poetry of indeterminancy." What Perloff describes as Rimbaud's "mode of undecidability, of literalness and free play" surely has been factored into Merrill's word banks no less than the high modernism of his early mentors, Eliot, Yeats, Valery, and Stevens.[11] Like all "V Work," the poem is a charged composite "cloned" from an explosive crisscrossing of currents.

Sandover, if not the first visionary work to broadcast from a world in tatters, is the first to manifest no nostalgia for a vanished whole. Hazarding the polar uncertainties of modern physics where, as Michel Serres, a French historian of science, remarks, "the real is not cut up into regular patterns, it is sporadic, spaces and times with straits and passes,"[12] the poem steadily resists the pull of a steady center. In section Q of "The Book of Ephraim" Merrill quotes Heinrich Zimmer on the challenges of the divine translation:

> *The powers have to be consulted again directly—again, again and again. Our primary task is to learn, not so much what they are said to have said, as how to approach them, evoke fresh speech from them, and understand that speech. In the face of such an assignment, we must all remain dilettantes, whether we like it or not.* (62)

But threatened, constrained, and fallible, the "powers" in *Sandover* are themselves "dilettantes." Ephraim regrets that "WE ARE OFTEN WEAKER THAN OUR REPRESENTATIVES" (59). Gabriel warns that God B's charter was "LIMITED" (560). Raphael admits "WE ARE INNOCENCE IN THE FACE OF MAN'S ENDEAVORS" (325). *The Changing Light at Sandover* is an approach to the divine, not a Book of Revelations; a way of looking rather than an account of how things look; a disclosing process instead of a disclosure. For both Merrill and his spirit-guides, all bargains are blind:

> WE
> ACCUMULATE THRU YOU A KNOWLEDGE THAT MUST HENCEFORTH BE
> PART OF US IN A REALM BEYOND THE GREAT GOLDFRAMED MIRROR
> ITS SILVER FIELD FILLD WITH THE OBJECTS OF YR ATTENTION
> LIKE A DAILY FEAST & IF YOU HAVE WONDERD WHY WE COME
> & MORE, WHY ONE OF THE WHITE SHD RISK HIMSELF: YR FIELD IS
> YES A KIND OF ANCHOR POINT OF HEAVEN. O SCRIBE, O HAND
> U HAVE PAID YR DUES AGAIN & AGAIN FOR WHO LIVING
> WELCOMES THE DEAD?
>
> (257–58)

Notes

1. Thom Gunn, *The Occasions of Poetry* (San Francisco: North Point, 1985), 146. See "Responses" in this book.
2. All references to James Merrill's *Paris Review* interview in the Introduction and Afterword are to J. D. McClatchy, "The Art of Poetry XXXI," *Paris Review,* 24 (Summer 1982): 185–219. Reprinted in *Writers at Work: The Paris Review Interviews,* sixth series, ed. George Plimpton (New York: Viking Penguin, 1984).
3. James Merrill reading at Harvard, 30 November 1977.
4. Delmore Schwartz, "T. S. Eliot's Voice and His Voices," *The Selected Essays of Delmore Schwartz,* ed. Donald A. Dike and David H. Zucker (Chicago: University of Chicago Press, 1970), 135–40.
5. James Merrill's *Paris Review* interview.
6. Frank Bidart introduced James Merrill in a reading for *Ploughshares,* Cambridge, summer of 1980.
7. See the Afterword for a lengthier discussion of *The Changing Light at Sandover* and *A Vision.*
8. David Lehman, "Elemental Bravery: The Unity of James Merrill's Poetry," in *James Merrill: Essays in Criticism,* ed. David Lehman and Charles Berger (Ithaca, N.Y.: Cornell University Press, 1983), 47.
9. Stephen Yenser, *The Consuming Myth* (Cambridge: Harvard University Press, 1987), 308.
10. Richard Saez, "James Merrill's Oedipal Fire," *Parnassus: Poetry in Review* (Fall–Winter 1974), 172.
11. Marjorie Perloff, *The Poetics of Indeterminacy* (Princeton: Princeton University Press, 1981), vii.
12. Michel Serres, *Hermes: Literature, Science, Philosophy* (Baltimore: Johns Hopkins University Press, 1981), xiii.

A Second Cup: Reader's Guide to *The Changing Light at Sandover*

WHY NOT 2 CUPS?

INDEX A 2ND CUP

POINTS OUT SALIENT PASSAGES

—Mirabell to JM, DJ, and RP
Stonington, Conn.
16 August 1980

Using the Reader's Guide

In addition to the entries that would be expected in any index—names and places—I have compiled a comprehensive listing of the hypotheses and ideas that figure in the "lessons" dictated by Merrill's interlocutors. This conceptual apparatus closely follows the language of the poem ("cloning," "innocence," "negatives," "power," "stripping process," etc.). Crucial citations are signaled by brief quotations from *The Changing Light at Sandover.*

1. Cross-references are indicated by *italics* rather than by the more cumbersome practice of "also see . . . " whenever possible. Thus each of the words that appears in italic type has its own entry in the index. Sometimes, however, the italicized word (or phrase) does not duplicate the entry exactly, but forms a slight variation on it, "*atomic*" for "*atom,*" "*Freud's*" for "*Freud.*"

2. The only significant exceptions to this practice of cross-referencing by italics are the names of the omnipresent speakers in the poem: James Merrill (JM), David Jackson (DJ), W. H. Auden, Maria Mitsotáki, Ephraim, Mirabell, Michael, and Gabriel. Each of these speakers, of course, has his or her own entry in the Reader's Guide.

3. All quotations from *The Changing Light at Sandover* have been regularized as upper- and lowercase prose, without indications of line breaks, stanza breaks, etc.

Abbreviations

E:	Ephraim
E.:	"The Book of Ephraim"
M:	Mirabell
M.:	*Mirabell's Books of Number*
S.:	*Scripts for the Pageant*
C.L.S.:	*The Changing Light at Sandover*
DJ:	David Jackson
JM:	James Merrill
WHA:	W. H. Auden
MM:	Maria Mitsotáki
Gabr.:	Gabriel
Mich.:	Michael

Reader's Guide

ABBA, another name for *God B,* and one of JM's favorite rhyme schemes, 478 (see *design*)

Abel, in the Old Testament, the second son of Adam, slain by his brother Cain (see Genesis 4:2). With *God Biology* is the positive force within the *atom,* 116 (see *myth; scale*); 131; and the *centaurs,* 323

absolute, and "the naked eye," 31, 49, 85; and the "naked current," 84; WHA speaks of "this current sweeping through us," which is identified with the *angels,* 332, 334; see *electricity*

Adam, in the Old Testament, the first man and the progenitor of mankind (see Genesis 2:7). 114; Adam and *Eve* are images for developments in the very nature of *matter,* 115, 116, 121; (see *atomic power; myth; scale*); *atom* is Adam and life and the universe, 118 (see *myth; scale*); and *twins,* 341; 502; 508

"Adonais" (Shelley), 310

Aesop, Greek fabulist of the late sixth century B.C. 52; 139–40

Agatha, Saint, martyr often invoked against fire and diseases of the breast (d. 250). MM works for, 102; and *Luca,* 235, 525, 543, 549; and *Psyche-Chaos,* 404–5; 415; 418; Robert *Morse* calls her "Maggots' folle," 526; 544; 549; 557

age (one assumes upon entering the other world), 16; E's, 16, 27; Maya *Deren's,* 64; WHA's, 87; see *appearances; personification;* the nine *stages*

air, JM linked to the *element* of air, 159, 183; M shares for the first time, 162; *Montezuma* as one of the *Five* is linked to, 164; JM's affinities with air are *Mind* and abstraction, 164; *God B* held safe in air the basic *gene* structures of *Atlantis,* 185; 201; ruled by *Nature,* 230; 271; 294; in "Samos," 369–70; 389; 441; 512

Akhnaton, King of Egypt, original name Amenhotep IV (reigned 1375–58 B.C.). 59; builds a crystal *pyramid,* 126–27 (see *atomic power*); his death, 127, 225, 227–29; *negative* forcefield of his *pyramid* still exerts an influence in the Caribbean, 146 (see *Bermuda Triangle*); M says he "did not get the point," 165; 178; first *cloned* ruler, 179; "the first individual in *history,*" 179; *God B* introduced his religion to, 193; and the *No Accident clause,* 194; as one of the *Five,* 201; with his *twin Nefertiti* first born of the *Five,* and the first *R/Lab soul* 223, 225; *00* was his teacher, 225, 228, 266;

childlessness, 225; and *Thebes,* 225; and the *sun,* 225, 227; with *Nefertiti* "one nature dual to the end," 228 (see *twin*); role in *man's evolution,* 242; as one of the *Five* his *V work* is the *angels' sense* of sight, 337; his *twin Nefertiti,* later *Plato's twin,* 337, 339, 341; later born as *Curie* and *Galileo,* 337; at Mich.'s fete, 356; and the *atom,* 396

Albertine (from Proust's *A la recherche du temps perdu*), 403; see *Proust*

Alençon, François duc d' (1554–84), 16

Alevras, Urania, JM's godchild (b. 1972). 111; 226; a *Muse,* 261; 524–25; see "Verse for Urania" in *Divine Comedies*

Alexander Pope (Quennell), quoted, 61 (New York: Stein and Day, 1970, pp. 185–86); see Alexander *Pope*

Alexander the Great, king of Macedonia (356–23 B.C.). *Cloned* from *Akhnaton,* 179; 180; 402

Alice, see Alice B. *Toklas*

Alison, see Alison *Lurie*

Alpha men, spoken of but not named, 117; WHA refers to "the future's fleshly robots," 196; WHA on "that race using us, *evolving* from us, in that *Paradise,*" 308; George *Cotzias* seems to be describing, 375; WHA's lecture on *earth* seems to touch on them, 393; and *immortality,* 439; and George *Cotzias,* 439; 442; MM terms a race of *gods,* 455–56; "those straight A students," 483; JM's question about *Resistance* in *Paradise,* 511; *Nature* on, "simpler, less wilful being," 512; 523

Amenhotep IV, identified by E as a perfected *soul* who has returned from *stage* nine, 59; see *Akhnaton*

anchor sites (of the *bat-angels' crust world*), "each set at some nerve center of the sacred *earth,*" 121; fourteen in all, 125; illuminated by glowing radiated stones, 125 (see *atomic power*); strained and broke, 134; built and maintained by the *centaurs* after the *bat-angels* subjugated them, 168; attack by the *vegetable* adversary causes them to tear, 168–69; MM compared to, 210; *Ouija* board is an anchor point of *Heaven,* 257; and the *bat-angels'* use of E and Cabel *Stone,* 264–65; WHA says of DJ and JM "anchors at last," 359; radiated stones and the dinosaurs, 453 (see *atomic power*); among the anchor sites: *Avebury; Jerusalem; Peking*

angels, and the "sons of *Abel,*" 131; spoke to *Dante,* the four Apostles, and the transplanted *Jews* (*Buddha; Mohammed*), 133; 140; identified with abstractions, 143; M will guide DJ and JM to, 156; and the *imagination,* 159; and the *12%* that the *bat-angels* are messengers for, 171–72 (see *Mercury*); M says "they seem to come from a calm," 173; after the *bat-angels'* world shattered, the angels "fixed us easily in our place by demonstrating that . . . the calm after our storm was utter *Chaos,*" 173; the *atom* as *metaphor* (116) was a "calling card" from them to DJ and JM, 174; M on the appearance of the *12%,* 192–93; 208; 222; 234; *12%* of *man's soul* entrusted to, 236; messenger angel speaks to DJ and JM in *M.,*

249–50; "we met on this fair field," 257; 260; *God B's* warning to them about *man* ("these are my own darlings"), 261; *oo* and, 266; 269; M's exercises that will prepare DJ and JM to greet Mich., 269–70, 276, 287; 271; 273; Mich. says they reside in the "accumulated *intelligence* in *cells*" (which is also *God B*), 276; unlike the *bat-angels,* are not servants, 276; their creation by *God B* from his "stored *intelligence,*" 293–94; descended on an *arc* composed of the four divine *colors,* 293; *time* does not exist for, 294; fashioned *God B's* children, including the *centaurs* and *man,* 294–95; *man* is the image of, 294; WHA says their names "ring through canyons of *myth,*" 302–3; DJ and JM's first exchange with, 307; WHA on their tone, 308; and the *colors,* 314; *oo* refers to them as "my masters," 317; Mich. implies that there are limits to their knowledge, 323; WHA asks was the putting down of *Chaos* fratricide (if *Chaos* is Gabr.), 323; WHA on the "asexual *imagined* powers we have *personified,*" 327 (see *sex*); WHA speaks of "this current drifting through us," which is identified with the *angels,* 332, 334 (see *absolute; electricity*); JM on their "limpid bel canto phrases," 331 (see *design; language*); the *Five* are their *senses,* 337; 340; the *12%* are the *angels* multiplied by their three natures or *powers,* 345; WHA says, "their powers are in us quite as much as over," 345; JM on catching the "full verve" of their talk by means of the "unmeasurable King James inflections," 346 (see *design*); and the four *elements,* 347; WHA on their reaction to *God B's* first words in the poem, "simply cowed," 349; are the *senses* of *God B,* 350–51; have not heard *God B's* song, 351; say they will touch DJ and JM, 351–52; other Brothers not present at Mich.'s fete, 359; in *God B's* song, 360; do not hear *God B's* song, 361; 383; 388; WHA fears JM's poem is a "whitewash" for the Brothers, 394 (see 398); WHA says that Gabr. is in rank the others' vast superior, 399; *Uni* says they are "kindly," 400; WHA and MM "camouflaged" DJ and JM during the lessons in *S.* because the angels are "terribly strong drink," 414; asked WHA and MM to find a human *language* they could use, 414; WHA on their *language* and style, 414 (see *design*); WHA says their dissension was an act, 414; their relation to *God B* and *Nature* debated by George *Cotzias* and JM, 417; WHA on their teaching style, 420 (see *design; language*); MM on the superiority of their knowledge to E's, 425–26; did they *fall*? 440–41; George *Cotzias* questions their account of *God B's* song, 447; and the thinning process, 449–50 (see *population*); do not punish vagrant *souls,* 452; and *sin,* 454–55; created the creature of the *Chinese* plane in their own image, 459–60; marvel at *man,* who is *shielded* from them, 463; MM as *Plato* is the child of *Nature,* and closest to the angels, 467; 469; *UFOs* are theirs, 477; 543; their "duty" to descend to *earth,* 550–51; are the "*Resisters,*" 551; their *earthly* manifestations, 552–53; are the supreme moments of the *Five,* 552; see *Michael; Gabriel; Emmanuel; Raphael*

animals, *Temerlin's* chimpanzees, 18–21; animal *evolution,* 18; syn-

thesis of human and animal worlds, 20–21; E's story about a Sioux brave exchanging *souls* with a hibernating bear, 45; role in *evolution,* 50–53; use of animal *souls* in the *Research Lab,* 50–53, 117, 140, 145–46, 196, 236, 237, 241; Strato *Mouflouzélis's* past animal life, 50–51; on the etymology of the word, 53 (see *soul*); *bat-angels* accompanied by extinct animal forms, 120 (see *Uni*); ape's role in *evolution,* 133, 236, 241, 251, 269; ratio of animal to human *densities* in DJ and JM's basic formulas, 143 (see *number*); a concern with *time* is a regressive animal trait, 146; *fear* of the *bat-angels* is in the use of *atomic* weaponry now falling into the hands of animal *souls,* 146; 163; JM is not ashamed of his animal nature, 171; animal state of the masses of men, 188; *bat-angels* slip first *soul* into an ape fetus, 236; *bat-angels* use of *12%* of animal *souls,* 237; 260; and the *soul* of the *Firefly woman,* 268; "dull animalistic lives" need *Homer's* and *Dante's* version of *Hell,* 269; and *cells,* 290

antimatter, Gabr. and Mich. had seen that the *bat-angels* were antimatter, 120; its powers "are magnetized by foreign beacons, *black* hands testing the *Greenhouse* pane by pane," 161; the *elements* "keep watch" and "press back" against it, 161 (see *Resistance*); and *evil,* 162; M says it is so far supportive, 187; M asks, does it watch us? 187; and MM, 210; JM asks, "is Gabr. the lord of?" 323; "antigod's antimatter," 460 (see *God A*); antimatter and its *Monitor God,* 476; 494; see *antiworld; matter; twin*

antiworld, compared to *black holes,* 149; is "a Lewis *Carroll* world that keeps pace with ours," 150; *bat-angels* not sure of its relationship to ours ("the original? are we its carbon copy? or: are we in the presence of a *black twin Paradise*"), 150; say they know nothing of it, as *God B* banished it, 151; see *antimatter; Resistance*

Aphrodite, Greek goddess of love and beauty. 225; see *Cupid; Eros; Venus*

Apollo, Greek god of the sun, prophecy, music, medicine, and poetry. Linked to Mich., 473; 538

Apollon Musagète (Stravinsky), 24; see *Stravinsky*

appearances (in the other world), E describes his appearance, 16; DJ and JM attempt to visualize the other world, 16–17; DJ under *hypnosis* sees E, 27; *Maya* in a dream sees E, 44; E's light reveals the *souls* who gather around DJ and JM to each other, 59; *Maya* describes her appearance, 64; countless faces of the Queen of Heaven, 64; WHA's pleasure with his "new prole body," 87; Mary *Jackson* says she "wore a different face" for the children from her past lives, 104; MM says the dead "do not qualify as witnesses except in yr mind's eye," 105; "this riddle of appearances in *Heaven,*" 105; Mary *Jackson* on, 105; E says that the world is with the dead through their *representatives* and their past lives, 105; *bat-angels* describe their appearance, 116; *bat-angels'* appearance described by MM, 117–18; *bat-angels* see DJ and JM at *Avebury,* 125; appearances in heaven

are a fiction, 152; dead see only in the spaces of DJ and JM's *mirrors,* 152–53; M changes into a peacock, 156–57, 180; MM on M: "he appears in us our *minds* (hearts) are his *mirror,*" 157; M says that DJ and JM have "peopled not ideated what has been and is" (to which JM responds, "How can a person not personify?"), 172; 173; MM says that M "had not been visible only his voice," 234; WHA on the messenger *angels'* appearance in *M.,* 250; WHA and MM describe Mich.'s, 285–86, 289, 296–97, 302, 307, 345; WHA says "*God* judges wholly by appearances," 291; WHA describes *00's,* 297; WHA and MM describes *Emmanuel's,* 302; WHA describes *Raphael's,* 307; WHA and MM describe Gabr.'s, 318, 345; JM on working what MM and WHA "see" into *S.,* 319; the appearances of the *Five,* 337–40; WHA on Mich.'s "wordless splendors," 345 (see *language*); WHA and MM describe Mich.'s "*sense* prisms," 357; WHA on *Pythagoras's* appearance, 372; MM describes the *centaurs'* appearance, and *Uni's,* 380; *Psyche's* 407; 429; 437; Robert *Morse* on, 498–99; see *age; personification; senses*

Aquinas, Thomas, Italian Dominican monk, theologian, and philosopher (1225–74). "Thomist structures in *Dante,*" 14; 174

Ararat, highest mountain in Turkey. 253; see *ark*

arc/ark, and *Ouija* board, 5, 253 (see Exodus 37, Numbers 4, Joshua, 3–4); and *language,* 253; and the *minds* of DJ and JM, 253; and *God B* as "the architect," 293, 408; *angels* descend on a beam composed of the four divine *colors,* 293

Arcadia, 152; distinguished from *Paradise* ("Arcadia surrounds us unrealized filling each of us for the length of a love or a thought"), 165; "organic matter *electrically* charged at last produced 3 centers of Arcadian culture," 166 (see *Atlantis*); 180; 184; of *Akhnaton-Nefertiti,* 227; WHA asks, "is not Arcadia to dwell among greenwood perspectives of the mother tongue?" 262 (see *language; poetry*); of the *bat-angels,* 460; 523

Arcadia (Sidney), 152

Archon, in certain Gnostic systems, one of several powers believed superior to the angels. 399; see *Monitor; devils*

Arcimboldi, Giuseppe, Italian painter (1530–93). 268

Ariel (from Shakespeare's *The Tempest*), 523; 554; see Maria *Mitsotáki*

Arnold, Matthew, English poet and critic (1822–88). 178

Artemis, Greek goddess of the hunt and the moon, twin sister to Apollo. *Plenorios* on his temple for, 373

Assyria, an ancient empire of western Asia. 179; 193

Athena, Greek goddess of wisdom and the arts. 296; see *Minerva*

Athens (Greece), house in, 50–51, 430–34, 437, 523, 558; *furnace* breaks down, 53; 98; 99–100; 107; 111; 113; party for WHA, 134; and "Athenian," 158 (see *homosexuality*); 299; 310; 312; 437; 468–69; 482; 500; 506; 513; 523; 558

Atlantis, legendary island in the Atlantic west of Gibraltar, said by Plato to have sunk beneath the sea. With *China,* the first experiments on earth, 121; 136; detailed history of, 166–70, 458–59, 469–71; organic matter *electrically* charged produced three centers of *Arcadian* culture, 166; a smooth green and treeless set of land masses at first, 166–67; appearance of the *centaur*like creatures, 167; the contest with *vegetable* life, 167, 168; *centaurs* invent the *bat-angels* when they need messengers, 167 (see *Mercury); centaurs* evolve, 167; *cloning,* 167; *centaurs'* grave problem is their immortality, 167; *atomic* blast to kill the primitive *centaurs* ("their relics"), 168, 289; *centaurs* then serve the *bat-angels,* building and maintaining the *anchor sites* of their *crust world,* 168, 224; *vegetable* adversary attacks the *anchor sites,* 168, 201; *crust world* tears and shreds, 168–69; *God B* begins to erase all traces of, 169; "the legend of the *centaur* is the last *poetry* of Atlantis," 169 (see *myth*); *centaurs* bred the *bat-angels* as mutant flies and fed them uranium, 169 (see *atomic power*); *bat-angels* saw that they were part of the past the *centaurs* had begun to destroy, 170; when the *bat-angels* destroyed the *centaurs'* primitive immortals, they offended *God B,* 170; *God B* held safe in air the basic *gene* structures of, 185; 199; 201; 224; 289; MM says the *centaurs* were *innocent,* yet they were destroyed, 322–23; WHA says Atlantis was "*idea,* a first pasture to *innocence,* and raped by it," 322; Mich. asks of the *centaurs,* "is among them the perfection of *idea* gone awry?" 323; 325; 327; *Uni* on his life there, 378–80; 384; 415; and the *black* forces, 439; Gabr. on, 458; Gabr.'s fondness for the creature of, 460, 461; 469–70; "Atlantan" troop at *Nature's* fete, 483

atom, see *atomic power*

atomic power, research at *Los Alamos,* 33; JM on, 33, 55–56; *Hiroshima,* 55, 139, 183, 186, 194; destructive effects on the *soul,* 55, 181–82, 183, 185, 207–8, 210, 303–4, 309, 330, 374, 422, 479; nuclear *fire* in *China,* 56; "The droplets atomize. . . . It stops at nothing," 71; MM's *X ray* therapy, 104, 127, 181–82, 183, 207–8, 210–11, 309, 329, 330, 422, (see 324; the *black*); galactic pollen, 112 (see *Rose,* 199, 251); *bat-angels* speak from within the atom, 113; *Adam* and *Eve* are images for developments in the very nature of *matter,* 115; *bat-angels* represent the *negative* force within the atom, 115, 224, 461 (see 396, 398); *Abel* and *God B* represent the positive force within the atom, 116; warring principles produced warring heirs, 116; and *evil,* 116; and *Fermi,* 116 (see epigraph to *M.,* 94); once wrecked the *Greenhouse,* 116; atom is the key, 116 (see 173–74); atom is *Adam* and life and the *universe,* 118 (see *scale; myth*); structures needed to gain *Paradise* are molecular, 118; single contest is the atom, 119; atom glimpsed is a nearly fatal consummation, 119 (see *shield*); *colors* and the inner workings of the atom, 119, 207; is L sided (positive side good, *negative* side "a disappearance an absolute void"), 119 (see 396, 398, and *black holes*); role in the *Fall* of the *bat-angels,* 119–20; atom fused

by the *bat-angels,* 120; atom built the *crust world* of the *bat-angels,* 120 (see *language*); "one atom too many" leads to the destruction of the *crust world,* 120; *bat-angels* broke the ozone layer with a last thrust of atomic fission, 121; *anchor sites* (of *crust world*) illuminated by radiated stones, 125, 134, 168, 264; all energy sources must be kept covered, 126; nuclear energy is the destruction of the atom's *shield,* 126; *Akhnaton's* crystal *pyramid* "hardly a full dress nuclear explosion," 126–27; *East German physicist's* study of "in-space radiant powers," 131 (see the *Five; Montezuma*); *Dante* looked into the atom's eye and saw the potential of *Paradise,* 132; *bat-angels' crust world* composed of materials the atom made nongravitational, 133; radium is the switch of the *bat-angels'* sleeping *power,* 140; *fear* of the *bat-angels'* use of atomic weaponry now falling into the hands of *animal souls,* 146; *negative* forcefield of *Akhnaton's pyramid* still exerts an influence, 146; and *plant souls,* 151; *bat-angels* are atomic, whereas the *centaurs* were *electrically* charged, 167, 169 (see *Atlantis*); *centaurs* wished to destroy their primitive *immortals* and charged the *bat-angels* to use an atomic blast, 168, 289; their ray centers, 168; *crust world* atomically powered, 168; the *centaurs* fed the *bat-angels* uranium, 170; M says that the *metaphor* of the atom was a calling card from the *angels* to DJ and JM, 173–74; and *Democritus,* 178, 391; and the *Greenhouse,* 181; and the *devil,* 181; and the first voice of the *bat-angels,* 181; M says "never suppose the *evil* of earthlife lies in the atom," 182; and arterial structure, 182, 453; appalled JM's principal soul density (*air*), 183; man must become contemptuous of, 183; *losses* among atomic scientists exposed to gamma rays, 185, 186, 260; new *soul* must be formed resistant to the atomic acid, 185; atomic fusion accomplished by the *centaurs* to make the *bat-angels* compared to love and *sex,* 185; plutonium chief link between *bat-angels* and *man,* 185; *bat-angels* feel for gamma rays what *man* feels for *sunlight,* 185; speed of *light, time,* and radiation, 185; atom as a *metaphor* for the talks with M, 191; "*psychic* atom," 191; atom's "precarious inviolability," 191; atom bombs, 193; *sun* is the central atomic *power* of *God B,* 199; is it *galactic* in origin? 199; fuel of the *Pantheon,* 199; *man* tries to sieze and rule, 199; in model of a *DNA* molecule at the *Boston* Museum of Science, 203; DJ and JM's dreams of the atom's heart, 204–7; atom compared to the *soul* by JM, 211; *God B's* use of is both benevolent and chastising, 213; *man's* and the *centaurs'* taking of it is a "Promethean outrage," 213 (see 455–56); and *sun,* 213; and the *metaphors* of the *bat-angels,* 224 (see *language*); atom like JM is "two-minded," 232–33 (see *Yes and No*); "the heavy *elements,*" 236; *Jews* heard the *music* of, and wrote the *Bible,* 243; 244; *bat-angels* plunge deep within the atoms of *man's cells* to implement their *rules,* 247; atom must be returned to the *Research Lab* and uses of *Paradise,* 247; "atomic structures" and the *Ouija board,* 253; 256; certain highly *cloned* scientist *souls* "force boundaries," 260; 261; JM refers to the "atomic forces" that wrecked *Atlantis,* 289; WHA calls Mich. "the

pure photon," 289; WHA on the destruction of his *soul,* 303–4; *Raphael* (*earth*) has the irradiated metals in him, 307; George *Cotzias's* "radiations might cause static in our air," says M, 309; Gabr. is "behind each atom a shadow atom," 329; *Curie* and radium, 337 (see *Akhnaton*); the "shadow riches" of *Raphael* are uranium, 343 (see *black*); and Gabr.'s second nature, *thought,* 344; and George *Cotzias's* lecture on *matter,* 395–98; *white* and *black* forces within, 396, 398; *God B* came on its flutter, 396; 398; 408; 416; 417; 420; 421; 423; 440; the atomic *black* compressed from *time's* reversibility, 452–53; the *idea* of *destruction* that resides both in *man* and the actinides, 453; radiated *anchor* stones and the dinosaurs, 453; *electric* and atomic energies interfused, 453; uranium in *man's* arteries, 453; *natural* and unnatural *power,* 453; Gabr. enacts an atomic test, 456–57, 462; and the *Prometheus* legend, 456 (see 213, 455, *sin*); and the creature of the *Chinese* plain, 458–59; *black* and *white* halves and the *bat-angels* and the *centaurs,* 461 (see *scale*); Gabr. is nuclear commander of the *Greenhouse,* 462; 466; spent *time* in *It* compared by Gabr. to atomic waste, 475; Mich. says, "accidents have begun," 476 (see *No Accident clause*); JM's question about the atom, *history,* and *scale,* 478; 479; George *Cotzias* tells JM (referring to the atom), "'poso akoma' the real motto of your poem," 479; *Tom* (in *The Rake's Progress*) is "our threatened atom," 485; M's "nuclear fire-ache" is quenched during *Nature's* fete, 488; WHA surfaces off Alaska as a vein of pure radium, 511; and Robert *Morse's music,* 530

Auden, Wystan Hugh, English poet and critic (1907–73). 11; his "As I Walked Out One Evening" quoted, 58; *The Rake's Progress,* 81, 106, 303, 370, 481, 484–86, 508, 538, 539; his earthly reaction to JM's communications with E, 87; his pleasure with his "new prole body," 87 (see *age; appearances*); compares *Heaven* to a new machine, 87, 260; *box* in Oxford that he wishes destroyed, 87; 101; Chester *Kallman* on, 106; on the "dreary, deadbang wrong church," 128 (see *religion*); asks to join the seance, 128; on *Faust,* 129; speaks of the *bat-angels* as "information banks" to tap, 129; 130; urges JM to "bear down," 131; party for in *Athens,* 134; introduced to MM by JM, 134–35; quoting *Spenser,* JM calls him "father of forms," 135; praises the *language* of the *bat-angels,* 135; sees "outlines" in what the *bat-angels* say, 136; on the emergence of a *science god,* 137; on *salt,* 141; sees much of *Plato,* 141; *element* is platinum, 142; "flaw" in his work: "mismarriage of lyric to bald farce," 143 (see 164, 308); talent rating is 5.1, 143; on the differences between *Dante's* world and JM's, 147 (see *belief*); it is said that he will shortly return to life, 149; said to be prevented from hearing an early talk with M, 149; 155; as M changes into a peacock, 156–58; wonders if they are prepared for *God B,* 159; on the *imagination,* 159; linked to the *element* of *earth,* 159, 164; on his poetry, 164 (see 143, 308); his "For the Time Being" quoted, 164; on *Arcadia* and *Paradise,* 165; says "is not the moral then as now: be true to something,

true to anything," 170 (see 177); suspicious of the *bat-angels'* change of tone, 175; on Chester *Kallman,* 181–82, 205, 289, 419; his mineral *densities,* 183; on elitism of the *bat-angels'* world, 186; M says he would have been a politician if not a poet, 188; on politics, 189; his *soul* mined by the *bat-angels,* 189; the "hexagonal" pun, 190, 196; compares talks with M to Oxford under *Newman,* 197; asks if *belief* in a life wholly out of his hands is unnatural to man, 198 (see *No Accident clause*); on the "uncloned lives that touch our own," 205; asks why they have been chosen for this seminar, 205–6; describes DJ's dream as a *masque,* 207; asks if "*time* is then the soil of *feeling,*" 209; introduces the *stripping process,* 209; 214; knew about MM, 215; 218; 222; 225; 226; 231; 237–38; 239; suggests that JM transcribe the talk of the *bat-angels* in syllabics, 240 (see *design*); 243; on what JM calls his "posthumous ephemera," 246; 248; on *language* as the poet's church, 252; foresaw an afterlife of arbitration, 252; his "Law Like Love" quoted, 252; on Robert *Graves,* 254; included a poem ("Winter Eve") by Robert *Morse* in *A Certain World,* 255 (see *spoonerisms*); "charmed" by Robert *Morse,* 257; his poem opens the "minimasque," 259 (see *masque*); on the rough drafts of *M.,* 261; on differences between *E.* and *M.,* 261 (see *design*); his "*fact* is is is fable" speech, 262–63 (see *myth;* 303); asks "why E?" for DJ and JM, 263; 271; JM refers to *Miranda's* villanelle (from *The Sea and the Mirror),* 273; on the first visit of Mich., 285–92; says "we were spared our *feelings*" when Chester *Kallman* returns to earth, 289; says God judges wholly by *appearances,* 291; takes up the French, 291–92; on *Strauss,* 292, 355; describes Mich. and *00,* 296–97 (see *appearances*); 300; calls JM's poem "a *Mahler,*" 301 (see *design*); on the protective "human dirt," 300 (see 285; 305–6); 302–3; on joining the *elements,* 303, 309–10, 315; on the destruction of his *soul,* 303–4; Marius *Bewley* says he is the cochairman of *Heaven's* "Athenian" club, 305 (see *homosexuality*); JM's elegy for, 306; on his last decade's work, 308 (see 143, 164); says "we come each to his own nature, not to any universal elevation," 308; on the *Alpha men,* 308; on the *language* and the tone of the *angels,* 308, 414, 420; JM alludes to his "In Praise of Limestone," 310; says that George *Cotzias* is "unique, a one-shot *soul,* his *densities* derived from *Montezuma,*" 312; the limits of his knowledge, 313; asks if *God B* is George *Eliot,* 313; Mich. praises his voice, 317; linked to *Raphael,* 317; his "MEEK" formulation sets out the whole *design* "initially," 318; 319; on Mich.'s first text in *S.,* including *innocence, ideas, Atlantis, sin,* and *Chaos,* 321–23; on the *angels,* the "asexual *imagined* powers we have *personified,*" 327; gives JM the *design* for *S.,* "two golden trays of 'Yes' and 'No' with '&' as bridge or balance," 328 (see Gabr.'s description of *God B,* 322); his "spare our world" speech, 328–29; says "is not *destruction,* much of it, good," 329 (see *white*); his "In Memory of W. B. Yeats" quoted, 331; asks JM "where in all this is the affirmation?" and urges him to "think," "ask

questions," and "plug away," 331–32 (see 394); calls Gabr. "the *universe's* greatest actor," 332; on the "current sweeping through us," 332 (see *absolute, angels, electricity*); on *suicide,* 333; 335; questions Mich.'s versification, 342, 344, 346, 352, 390; his poem on the *Five,* 345; praises JM's poem on the *Five,* 345 (see *design*); says that the *angels'* powers "are in us as well as over," 345; on whether he prefers truth to beauty, 345; on Mich.'s "wordless splendors," 345 (see *language*); says that he and MM did not hear *God B's* voice, but saw JM write the words, 349; 352; his poem to DJ and JM on their anniversary, 353; says that for the first time DJ and JM are not reversed in the *mirror,* 353 (see 354, 358); 354; his poem to *Homer* ("immortal bard, you who created me"), 355; on Mich.'s *sense* prisms and his *memory* of earlier selves and *psyches,* 357 (see *colors*); on *Flagstad,* 358; says of Mich.'s fete and JM, "to each epiphany his own," 359; on the ambiguity of *God B's* song, 361, 362, 363, 365; his poem about *God B,* 365; 378; 381; 383; interrupts Robert *Morse,* 386; 388; his lecture on the *earth,* 391–94; says that the *poet* is most drawn to the concrete, 391; introduces the *Monitor,* 392; fears that JM's poem is a "whitewash for the Brothers," 394 (see 398); 398; says to JM, "one's not my boy brushed by such wings to be of two minds," 399 (see *Yes and No*); says Gabr. is the other *angels'* vast superior, 399; on the *Muses,* 405; calls *Psyche* "Queen Mum," 407; *Psyche* kissed him as he wrote down the title, *Age of Anxiety,* 410–11; 413; MM admits that she and WHA also worked on the first ten lessons of *S.,* 413–15; MM and WHA camouflaged DJ and JM during the lessons in *S.* because the *angels* are "terribly strong drink," 414–15; on how "shapely and distinct . . . those clouds of *myth* used to seem from below," 416; says they should "go out laughing for *God's* sake," 418; on Chester *Kallman's* new life, 419; DJ suggests that he is *Plato,* 420; 421; praises MM as "one of the wonders," 422; on *Yeats's* dictations, 424; 426; on *Plato's* next life, 428; describes *Plato's* defense of Wallace *Stevens,* 428–29; his questions to Gabr. about the *black* forces and *time,* 437–38; says "humankind has set *idea* to *innocence,*" 438 (see 441 for his amplification); says that Gabr. "knows what he's up to and (like *time*) will tell," 442; 448; 452; on *Mohammed,* 453–54, 472; 457; on Gabr. and Mich. as reflections of the "two kinds of critics," 461; persuades JM not to revise his fable in light of new *facts,* 461–62 (see *myth*); JM had hoped he was of the *Five,* 466; 468; 471; on MM's "joy," 472; on *Plato* and *Socrates,* 472–73; *Nature* criticizes his sporting tone, 480; recalls the opening night of *The Rake's Progress,* 481; *The Rake's Progress* plays during *Nature's* fete, 484–90; on *Nature's* last resounding *Yes* to *man,* 492; 494; on what will happen after DJ and JM break the *mirror,* 507; on *number* nine, 509–10; JM on losing him, 510; surfaces off Alaska as a vein of pure radium, 511; 513; M on his predecessor Yan Li, 514; M on his *Homeric densities,* 514; on JM's *V work,* 516; 526; 527

Austen, Jane, English novelist (1775–1817). 383; 386; her *V work,* 524; 546; 559

Avebury (England), 111–12 (see *lenses; scale*); one of the *anchor sites,* 121, 125; *bat-angels* see DJ and JM there, 125

Bach, Johann Sebastian, German composer (1685–1750). 137; 206; 255; 529; see *music*

ballroom (at Sandover), 120; 549; 556–60; see *Sandover*

Bassanio (from Shakespeare's *The Merchant of Venice*), 304; see *Shakespeare*

bats, on the carpet in *Stonington,* 98, 116; on the *wallpaper,* 111, 116; 122; 169; 200; on *Capri* when *Christ* died, 205; see *bat-angels*

bat-angels, are described by E as the *men before mankind,* 56; E describes their sounds, 56; E says they may rule, 56; some have wings, 56 (also 73); issue their ultimatum ("Mind your work, six moons remain"), and press DJ's hand to the board, 73 (see *design; time*); want three more years from JM, 113; *fear* of their *power* stops *Paradise,* 113; speak from within the *atom,* 113; E says, "their presence dims our *stages,*" 113; not *evil* but impatient, 113; "bound to implacable universal wheel," 113; "real order" is "*mind* and *nature* wedded," 113; on their use of *language,* 113, 118–19, 120, 121–22, 144, 146–47, 149–50, 172, 265; their *Fall,* 113, 119, 120, 121, 122, 125, 133–34, 168–69, 171, 253; and *black holes,* 113, 119–20, 149–50; warn *man* against *Chaos,* which they worshiped, 113, 461; once ruled half the *universe,* 114; claim to be the sons of *Cain,* 114, 460; are they *devils*? 114, 192–93, 289; say that the *devil* has been driven out of them into *man,* 114; their tools are *Mind,* words (see *language*), *reason,* and *light,* 114; represent the *negative* potential within the *atom,* 115, 224, 461 (see 396, 398); left the work of *Chaos* when they shed their *feelings,* 115; given a second chance by *God B,* 116; invented the *scribe* and told him "that ancient history" (*Genesis*), 116; describe their *appearance,* 116; are *00* beyond the nine *stages,* 116; are *eternity,* 116; nine *stages* are their *Research Lab,* 116; say to DJ and JM "we are you, you are we, each others' dream," 117 (see *belief*); known as the bad angels, 119; waited on *God B's* left hand, 119; released but did not create an *evil,* 120; created a *crust world* above the *centaurs,* 120, 121, 125–26, 168–69; fused the *atom,* 120; were *antimatter,* 120; no names—names are the invention of the *scribe,* 120; no death, 120; their arrogance and blindness, 120, 168; chose to move on into space and the *crust* shredded and they fell, 120 (see *Fall*); *Divine Comedies* produced through their *cloning,* 121; their *anchor sites,* 121, 125, 134, 168–69 (see *atomic power*); broke the ozone layer with a last thrust of *atomic* fission, 121; *God B* says to them, "out of my sight," and turns to Mich. and Gabr., 121; trust *God B* to take them in again, 121; JM's impatience with their speech, 121–23; MM's defense of them, 122–

23; have no *manners,* 123 (see 130); *anchor sites* illuminated by radiated stones, 125 (see *atomic power*); see DJ and JM at *Avebury,* 125; believed their *crust world* was beyond the reach of *natural* upheaval, 125–26; the handmaidens of *God B* (Geology and Botany) pulled down the *anchors* of their sky platform, 125; say "all energy sources must be kept covered, that is our principal task," 126 (see *atomic power; shield*); called DJ and JM twenty-five years ago, 127; compare DJ and JM's lives to a crystal *pyramid,* 127; their measure is fourteen, 127, 170–71 (see *number*); are DJ and JM's *light,* 127; MM says she is afraid of them, 128; they can use *fire,* 128, 190, 202; WHA says they are like "information banks" to tap, 129; *40070,* 130 (see 125–27); *40076,* 130 (see 124); are messengers, 130, 167, 169–70, 172–73, 185–86, 205, 241, 245, 246, 288 (see *Mercury*); M asks about *manners,* 130 (see 123); during talks with M plus fourteen others are present, 130 (see *number*); on the *universe,* 132–34; use "extra life" *souls* like *Montezuma* for research, 132 (see the *Five*); *Montezuma* believes that they "race for order under orders to save the *Greenhouse,*" 132; read a pattern in the *stars,* 132; believe that *God B's Greenhouse* is among others in the *universe,* 132; heard the signal or song of the *universe* through *Dante* and when the clouds came to put out the flames of their fallen world, 132–34, 363 (see *God B*); WHA praises their *language,* 135; WHA says they speak in "flashing trigonometries," 136 (see *number*); JM's doubts about what he is hearing from them, 136 (see *belief*); have verified the *UFOs,* 136–37; they doubt DJ and JM's doubt, 137; the *12%* is "a dry euphemism for those realms which sky shrouds" from them, 139; direct the *Research Lab,* 140, 145–46; direction of *soul* taken from them when they lost theirs, 140; are programmed, 140; conversations come from *memory* and word banks (see *language*) tapped in DJ and JM, 140; radium is their switch (of their sleeping *power*), 140, 200 (see *atomic power*); on the *carbons,* 141 (see *elements*); on George *Cotzias,* 141–42; metaphor of the blacksmith and the shoe of gold, 144–45 (see *patrons; representatives; souls*); leave to the *patrons* their 3.5 billion *souls,* 145; one small success of their *Research Lab* is the *five,* 145; their use of partial *fictions,* 145–46; daily need five million *souls* (*density* 1: 20,000), and have not half that number, 145; have no sense of *time,* 146, 155, 290, 312; have before them all events concerned with the *Research Lab* for the next three decades, 146, 202; their *fear* is the use of *atomic* weaponry now falling into the hands of *animal souls,* 146; by "nine" they mean that knowledge whereby *souls* from the *Research Lab* will build *Arcadia,* 149 (see *number; Paradise*); their *Paradise* will be on *earth,* 149; describe an *antiworld,* 150–51 (see *antimatter*); seem to have limited knowledge about some matters, 151, 171, 172, 177, 186, 192, 200, 251, 258, 260, 287; use of *plant souls,* 151–52; M says all *power* attracts and must be denied them, 162; as *mirrors* of DJ and JM, 162; say "nerves are our dominion," 163; praise *science,* 163; say they are at home

in the *earth's* molten heart, 163 (see *fire*); on *Paradise* and *Arcadia,* 165; invented by the *centaurs* as messengers to carry their word above the encroaching *vegetable* world, 167; *centaurs* were a "race much superior to them," 167; are *atomic* while the *centaurs* are *electrically* charged, 167, 169, 200; when *centaurs* wish to destroy their primitive *immortals,* they charge the *bat-angels* to use an *atomic* blast, 168; subjugate the *centaurs* and put them to work to build and maintain their *crust world,* 168; *vegetable* adversary attacks the *anchor sites,* which leads to the destruction of the *crust world,* 168–69; lasted at most one thousand years, 169; *God B* begins to erase all traces of them, 169; "like all *soul* or shall we say ex-life force [they] are inextinguishable," 169; began as mutant flies and were fed uranium, 169–70 (see *atomic power*); were the *centaurs'* first success, 169; when the *centaurs* no longer needed messengers they took on other duties (e.g., running heating and lighting plants), 169–70; later sat in the *centaurs'* councils, 170; gradual changes in their size and appearance, 170; saw that they were part of the past the *centaurs* had begun erasing, 170; unlike the *centaurs,* they were not *God B's* creatures, 170; have spent their *eternity* damned, because in slaying the *centaurs' immortals* they offended *God B,* 170; *feelings* were formulas, 170–71 (see *number*); tolerated no life but their own, 170–71; fell for want of obeying their first rule or formula ("obey"), 171; leave certain questions to the *12%,* 171; will stand between the *12%* and DJ and JM, 171; certain subjects are forbidden to them, 172; *God B* must be the first to understand signals from other worlds so *bat-angels* keep them cryptic, 172; have never expressed a thing, 172; *feeling* plays no part in their existence, 172; to their eyes, "these ethical rights and wrongs are so many blanks in (*man's*) canvas," 173 (see *religion*); M says "the calm after our storm was utter *Chaos,*" 173; M says "all is real, the unreal I know nothing of," 174; WHA questions their change in tone, 175; what *man* calls the future, they call reality, 176 (see *time*); *man's* nature is a mystery to them, 177; on *cloning* of rulers, 179; *scribe* becomes their affair, 180; work to *clone cells* so that they can accept radiation, 182 (see *atomic power*); feel for gamma rays what *man* feels for sunlight, 185; plutonium is their chief link to *man* ("we sing in your glands"), 185; *atomic* fission accomplished by the *centaurs* to make them is compared to love and *sex,* 185; JM and WHA discuss their *feelings,* 186; in charge of *soul densities,* 186; M asks, are they watched by *antimatter*?, 187; are the hybrids of the *Research Lab,* 187; mine and *clone* the *souls* of the great *scribes,* 189, 194, 217, 219; are the forces some might accuse of the *devil's* work, 193; imprinted with the *No Accident* formula, 194; one of their *myths* is that from the *galactic Pantheon* came *God B* to build his *Greenhouse,* 199; *myth* of *Prometheus* is their story, 199; numbers never vary, 200; in the *centaurs'* hatcheries, 200; circumvented *God B's* destruction of the *centaurs,* 201; in three decades see solutions to *man's* problems

of pollution and *population,* 201; say MM is "one of us," 208 (see *atomic power; souls*); and the *colors,* 212–19; are the force of *00,* 212; M says no one can reach them directly, 219; their *Research Lab,* 220, 223, 236; more on their use of *language* and *number,* 223–24, 230; M's *00* ancestors represent "the greatest possible *density*" among his kind, 224; will lead DJ and JM to the *12%,* 225; *Nefertiti* is the patron of, 228; M says their penultimate lesson is the end of usefulness, 228; thin, prune, and *clone Nature,* 229; seek licence from *God B* to reveal something of *Heaven* to those *souls* they need back, 229; friendly rival of *Nature,* 231, 247–48; chose *Mind* over *Nature,* 232; 88% of *soul* entrusted to, 236; *Nature* not theirs to use, 236; and the *elements,* 236; their use of the "heavy elements," 236 (see *atomic power*); their use of *salt,* 236; use *12%* of *animal souls,* 237; custodians of the *electrical* nonangelic *12%* in *man,* 238; keep an eye on *man's* body or *Psyche,* 238–39; WHA tells JM they should speak in syllabics, 240 (see *design*); on the talk of *man,* 241; were messengers to whom *God B* gave pass keys to the *mind* of *man,* 241; guided *man's evolution,* 241–42; send a hurricane to DJ and JM, 243–45; are also *Nature's* messengers, 245; believe that "the one unspoken revelation must dwell in the *number five,*" 245; implement a system of *rules,* 246–48; in their *V work* must work at their own level in a complex hierarchy, 246; are *Mercury,* 246, 288; correct *God B's* signals to *man,* 247–48; full mystery of the *S/O/L* kept from, 251, 260; two by two have entered DJ and JM's *minds,* 253; their use of the *Ouija board,* 253; "longstanding experience" of DJ and JM formed their *field,* 253; need spokesmen, 254; Robert *Morse* on their "jargon," 256; "reckless" for them to move into the houses of the living, 257; accumulate knowledge through DJ and JM, 257; can't protect DJ and JM, 258; "pressures" they feel ("we are cattle run through fences"), 260; M on his masters, 264–65; their *anchor sites* and their use of E and Cabel *Stone,* 264–65; spoke to DJ and JM with a composite voice, 265; their *law* of noninterference, 265; M's escapade with the *Firefly woman* who was their first *DNA,* 268; and *Hell,* 269; their challenge is to eliminate *Hell* and make *man* the *clone* of *God B,* 269; WHA says they cannot conceive *man's* easy leap onto the outstretched palm of *God,* 287; cold and heat, like *time,* are nonexistent for them, 290; oversee "*soul* intensities in the *Research Lab*" ("constant rough stuff"), 290; M describes oil as his "ancestors," 300; they work through dreams, 300; belong to Gabr., 314; Gabr. destroyed them, 316; Mich. and Gabr. describe them in their *Research Lab,* 336–40; during *God B's* song, they "clustered round wide-eyed," 363 (see 133, 134, 360, 361); *Pythagoras* on the "faulty readout" of their *12:*88 formula and their *Research Lab* texts, 377; Uni says "they are death," 378; *centaurs* wear the number of their *bat-angel* master, 379; 392; 415; 416; WHA on "bat-politics," 421; 441; Gabr. on, 459–60; and *Cain,* 460; and the *black* forces of *Chaos* in the *atom,* 461 (see *scale*); at *Nature's* fete, 483

Batman, character created by Bob Kane. 288

Beatrice (from Dante's *Divine Comedy*), E identifies her as a perfected *soul* who has returned from *stage* nine, 59; a kind of music *Dante personified* in female form, 132 (see *universe*); 354; MM reveals that she was Beatrice, 468; 479

Beethoven, Ludwig von, German composer (1770–1827). 403; 427; see *music*

belief (in the other world), E and his revelations assessed, 29–32; Reality, Projection, 46; JM notes how much he trusts E, 55, 57; the *god's* own truth or fiction, 63; *Stevens* on *God* and the *imagination,* 66; Maya *Deren* tells DJ and JM that their talk has an end beyond itself, 73; *Jung* on *God* and the Unconscious, 74; JM says to E, "If I fall from a high building, it's your name I'll call," 74; JM on approaching the other world, 111 (see *Zimmer*); JM on his doubt and credulity, 115; *bat-angels* say, "we are you, you are we, each others' dream," 117; JM says, "no opposition graver than between credulity and doubt," 125; *Dante's* strength and that of his time was a fierce credulity, 132–33; JM on "popthink" and his doubts about what he is hearing from the *bat-angels,* 136; JM's doubts answered by the *bat-angels:* "curious that you accept the cup and not the saucer . . . *folie à deux* folie à 2,000,000 what difference?" 137; JM admits he resists "for form's sake . . . deep down . . . we're hooked," 138; *Dante's* "luck lay in his gullible and heavenly world," 147; WHA on the *imagination* ("if MM and I imagine you, you us, and where the powers crisscross we all imagine *741* and then transform him! When the time comes, will our knitted brow produce white wings?"), 159 (see 173; *angels; personification*); *elements* say they are responsible for all of M but his *Mind* ("your *minds* coalesced to form his"), 161; M as a *mirror* to DJ and JM, 162; M says, "all legends are rooted in truth," 162 (see *myth*); "*fear* and doubt put by, though still kept handy," 166; *bat-angels* say that DJ and JM may cast away their chance to meet the *12%* if they are in doubt or *fear,* 171; M is "an impulse only here at the crossroads of our four affections," 173 (see 159; *imagination; personification*); 175; MM on "a way of telling that inspires belief," 206; M on "feathers of proof," 257–58; "doubting Thomas," 262; WHA on (his "*fact* is is is fable" speech), 263 (see 303); JM's *Hell* is doubt, 269; see *Yes and No*

Benson, Edward Frederic, English novelist (1867–1940). His *Lucia* novels cited in connection with Robert *Morse,* 257

Berlioz, Hector, French composer (1803–69). *Les Troyens,* 365

Bermuda Triangle (Caribbean), 146

Bernard, Saint, French monastic reformer and political figure (1091–1153). And *Dante,* 425

Bernhardt, Sarah, French actress (1844–1923). 203 (see *DNA*); 383

Bernini, Giovanni Lorenzo, Italian sculptor, architect, and painter (1598–1680). 264

Betsy, see Beatrice *Merrill,* and then Ellen Prentiss *Cade*

Bewley, Marius, American critic and teacher (1918–73). 72; takes up Mary *Jackson,* 103; his sense of "Athenian," 158 (see *homosexuality*); on *Plato,* 158; 305; 503; 525; 546; 547

Beyle, Marie-Henri (Stendhal), French novelist (1783–1842). 66

Bezelbob, (Note: Beelzebub is the name of the fallen angel in Milton's *Paradise Lost,* next to Satan in power; his name translates from the Hebrew, "Lord of the Flies"). One of the *bat-angels* who speaks in *M.,* 115; 120; 129; see *Bob; furnace*

Bible, M says it is a code of blurred but oddly accurate biohistorical data, 187; 224; "a most inquiring *V work,*" 242–43; the biblical Mich., 285, 289; JM reads *Genesis,* 311; WHA says "these Old Testament names . . . ring many changes on the *Five,*" 341; JM on catching the "full verve" of the *angels'* talk by means of the "unmeasurable King James inflections," 346 (see *design*); 420; see *myth; religion*

black, and the ellipsis at the end of section X in *E.,* 85–86; 150; black hands testing the *Greenhouse* pane by pane, 161, 162; and the *negative, evil* forces arrayed against *God B,* 293; Gabr. is the shadow of his father *God B,* 316; MM says, "I vanished in that black," 329 (see *atomic power; X rays*); Gabr. sits on a black throne, and behind each atom is a shadow atom, 329; Gabr. has known *feelings,* all black, 330; *Raphael's* "shadow riches" are uranium, 343 (see *atomic power*); the "bitter-black *mirror*" and the "ripple within ripple on black water" before *God B's* song, 359–60 (see 361); and the *Monitor,* 392–93; George *Cotzias* on *Resistance* and the black and *white* forces within *matter* and the *atom,* 396–97; 398; *Psyche* identifies *Resistance* with the "dark," 408; 417; WHA's question to Gabr. about, 438; and *time,* 438, 440, 448–52; and *Atlantis,* 439; WHA on the pact between *God B* and the "black beyond black," 440; WHA on "the black of *thought* unthinkable," 440; *Mercury* on, 445; and the "black God" or *God A,* 447; *Mohammed* on, 448–52; "the hourglass in which *time* runs up," 448; *God B* says to *Mohammed,* "you sit on *time* made black," 449; *Mohammed* says, "it calls to us," 450; "the black beyond black is of *time* set running back," 451; and *power,* 451; MM's "Socratic dialogue" on, 452; the "*atomic* black compressed from *time's* reversibility," 452–53; and *destruction,* 453; the *Monitor's* black and *Resistance,* 452; 454; Gabr. says that *time* and *feeling* are "black magics," 455; "*white light,* the *negative* or 'eye' of black," 457; Gabr. says, "We board the lumbering black wagon," 457; and the *destruction* of the creature of the *Chinese* plain, 459; no quarrel between *light* and shadow so long as *substance* stands between them, 460; and the force of *Chaos* in the *atom* represented by the *bat-angels,* 461 (see *scale*); and the face of *man,* 463; 470; and the *It,* 474–

76; *shadow* in the black of *time* reversed in *The Rake's Progress,* 485; M and, 488; *God B* on "the dark force we contain," 493; JM's fall (372) was "a warning from the black transmission case," 497; 498; 499; 504; final rhyme in *S.* is "*Light*/Night," 517; and MM, 523; see *bat-angels*

black holes, 85–86; *negative* energy born when the *bat-angels* fell, 113 (see *Fall*); and the *atom,* 119; and the *antiworld,* 149–50; 186; JM on his own, 187; George *Cotzias's* dream about, 299; and *feelings,* 426; 447; 451; see *black; stars*

Blake, William, English poet and engraver (1757–1827). 27; 178; 215; 250; and the *Rose* tradition, 363; his "Mock on Mock on Voltaire Rousseau" quoted, 391; 407; his "Auguries of Innocence" quoted, 408; *Psyche* perched on his shoulder, 410; 480; 488

Blavatsky, Helena Petrovna, Russian spiritualist and author (1831–91). 136

Blixen, Baroness Karen ("Tania," "Isak Dinesen"), Danish author (1885–1962). 52–53 (see *devotion*); reference to Miss *Malin Nat-og-Dag* (from "The Deluge at Norderney" in *Seven Gothic Tales*), 70; 383

Bob (the furnace man), 91, 131; see *Bezelbob*

body (man's), 87; 147; 238–39; 474; see *Psyche*

Boccaccio, Giovanni, Italian poet, diplomat, and author (1313–75). 298; WHA calls the lessons in *S.* "a closed circle, a Boccaccio," 324

Bohr, Niels, Danish theoretical physicist (1885–1962). 191

Bosch, Hieronymus, Dutch painter (1450?–1516). 318

Boston (Massachusetts), 98; 176; 203; 229; 231

Bottom (from Shakespeare's *A Midsummer Night's Dream*), 480; see *Shakespeare*

box, on *Capri* that *Tiberius* and E wish destroyed, 8; in Oxford that WHA wishes destroyed, 87; the meditation on the phrase "burn the box" and its implications for the writing of *E.,* 87–89 (see *design; fire; memory*); cartons containing transcripts of talks with E removed by thieves, 91; whether to burn these cartons, 91–92

Brave New World (Huxley), 442

Breasted, James Henry, American Egyptologist (1865–1935). His description of *Akhnaton* is cited, 179

Brezhnev, Leonid, Soviet statesman (1906–1982). 193

Brünnhilde (from Wagner's *der Ring des Nibelungen*), quotation from her speech in *Götterdämmerung* (act 1, scene 3), 62; 81; 91; see *Wagner*

Bruno, Temerlin's chimpanzee. 18; 140; see *Temerlin*

Buddha, Gautama, Indian philosopher (563?–483? B.C.). *Angels* spoke to, 133; 426; 441; 442–43; 444; 448; 449; 459; see *religion*

Buddhism, 187; see *Buddha; religion*

Burbank, Luther, American horticulturist (1849–1926), 151–52

bureaucracy, composed of non-Lab souls. Matt *Jackson* on *souls*

who are not special, 108; M on the two kinds of *souls,* 139–40; *bat-angels* leave to *patrons* their 3.5 billion lives, 145; "the great dull bureaucracy of *patrons,*" 145; *patrons* of non–*Research Lab souls* have their duties, 145; E is said to belong to the bureaucracy, 149; the good bureaucrat reaching *stage* nine will stay there—his *Paradise,* not the *bat-angels',* 149; M says their *densities* are in your *genes,* 196; Hans *Lodeizen* will remain in, 221; the "*rat* world," 226; for *souls* "not of a certain value," 236; 247; 253–54; M says they are *Nature's* affair, 260; 264; 309; *eternity, immortality,* and, 315; 320; and the *Five,* 340; 371; WHA says it is *Psyche's* "summer house," 413; and *number,* 423; and *Paradise,* 499; 552; see *representatives*

Burne-Jones, Sir Edward Coley, English painter and decorator (1833–98). 22.

Bynner, Witter, American poet (1881–1968). 33

Byron, Lord (George Gordon), English poet (1788–1824). 54; 61; 527

Cade, Ellen Prentiss, character in JM's lost novel. 13; modeled after Beatrice ("Betsy") Merrill *Pincus,* 13; her life with Leo *Cade* described, 47–48; tries to dismiss *Eros* as "a figment of their [her and Leo's] common fancy," 48 (see *folie à deux*)

Cade, Leo, character in JM's lost novel. 13; 34; his life with Ellen *Cade* described, 47–48; experiences in the army, 48–49; under *hypnosis* sees *Eros,* 47 (see David *Jackson*); wants a child born as *Eros's representative,* 48; briefly exchanges *souls* with a young Pueblo dead a hundred years, 49 (see Maya *Deren*); clasps a dead self dressed in his own clothes, 49; at a séance with *Joanna* and Sergei *Markovich,* 67; is healed, 71; son is born, 71

Cain, in Old Testament, eldest son of Adam, killed his brother Abel (see Genesis 4). *Joselito* raises, 12; Bat-angels claim to be the "sons of Cain," 114 (see 460); 115; and the *centaurs,* 323; *God B's* Cain-like errror, 458; and the *Monitor,* 476; see *Abel*

Caligula (Gaius Caesar), emperor of Rome (A.D. 12–41). 8, 55; Robert *Morse* on, 450–51; see *power*

Callas, Maria, American singer (1923–77). Dies, 509; on her performances, 529

Calliope, traditionally the Greek muse of epic poetry. 201; see *Muses*

Calypso, traditionally the Greek sea nymph who delayed Odysseus on her island, Ogygia, for seven years. 400–404; see *Muses*

Campbell, Joseph, American mythologist and writer (1904–87). On Maya *Deren,* 304–5

Campion, Thomas, English poet and musician (1567–1620). 262

Candide (Voltaire), 194

Capri, an island of Italy south of the Bay of Naples. Where E died, 8;

box on, which *Tiberius* wishes destroyed, 8; DJ and JM say they will visit, 9; cut from their itinerary (see *Dante* or *Paradiso*), 38; 204–5; 487

Capriccio (Strauss), 486

Caravaggio, Michelangelo Amerighi, Italian painter (1565?–1609). 291

carbon, introduced by E to distinguish different kinds of *souls,* 50; chief *salt*-oriented *elements,* 141; and the prolongation of life, 141; see *density*

Carroll, Lewis (Charles Dodgson), English author and mathematician (1832–98). The *antiworld* is described as a Lewis Carroll world, 150

Carter, James Earl "Jimmy," president of the United States (b. 1924). 188

Casals, Pablo, Spanish cellist (1876–1973). M names as one of the *Five,* 164; linked to the *element* of *water,* 164

caves, 180; *Plato's,* 263, 354, 356, 497; *Hell* is the cave of *Psyche,* 269; *Raphael's,* which is linked to *man's* cranium, 324–26, 342, 385–86 (see *scale*); identified by Gabr. with "*light*-shedding *ideas,*" 333

cells, "growth of single cells" is the third stage of *earth* as potential *Greenhouse,* 166; cell structure must be *cloned* to accept radiation, 182 (see *atomic power*); and *DNA,* 203; 206; 207; M's lessons on, 210–16; M says "the whole *Greenhouse* is but a cell" and that all *matter* is part of that cell, 210; and the *colors,* 210–19; *bat-angels* plunge deep within the *atom* of *man's* cells to implement their rules, 247; M says "you daily use and shuffle off your cells, we do not," 257; 273; "*light* stored in our cells," 274, 276; "genius of the living cell is its tie to the regenerative heat and *light* of the *sun,*" 275; *God B* is the accumulated *intelligence* in, 276; M describes from the inside, 290; M says there are "millions of differences in each category," from *plant, animal, man, soul,* and *God B,* 290; cells of the *suicide* implode, and in the red debris of ruined cells, Gabr. sees *innocence,* 333; George *Cotzias* on his research, and what DJ and JM have been learning, 375; George *Cotzias* on the cells of his own *mind,* 396; 403; 432; 455; 460; 496

censorship, when someone has "overstepped," 107–8; 128; 157; 186; 231; E "illustrates," 234–35; 237; 313

centaurs, referred to but not named ("certain ancients"), 121; early description of their death (because of the radiated stones at the *anchor sites* of the *crust world*), 125 (see *atomic power*); the sixth stage of *earth* as potential *Greenhouse:* is "organic *matter* moved off into species man has found in fossilated state but misunderstood thinking his cycle the first," 166; *electrically* powered while the *bat-angels* are *atomic,* 166, 169, 380; appearance on *Atlantis,* 167–69; *God B* gave them dominance, 167; were pastoral, 167–68; invented the *bat-angels* as messengers, 167; contest with *vegetable*

life, 167; *evolution,* 167–68; use *cloning,* 167; grave problem was their *immortality,* 167; decide to kill their primitive *immortals* ("their relics") and charge the *bat-angels* to use an *atomic* blast, 168; *bat-angels* subjugate them, and they build and maintain the *anchor sites* of the *crust world,* 168; gradually evolve into dinosaurs, 168; *God B* begins to erase all traces of *Atlantis,* 169; their fossils provide fuel and dyes, 169; "legend of the centaur is the last poetry of *Atlantis,*" 169; bred the *bat-angels* as mutant flies and fed them uranium, 169, 200 (see *atomic power*); technical skill limited only by their physical structure, 169; took pride in their speed, 169; unlike the *bat-angels* were *God B's* creatures, 169; *atomic* fusion that they used to create the *bat-angels* compared to love and *sex,* 185; their destruction and the *No Accident clause,* 200; *God B* sought to destroy them with forests, and was circumvented by the *bat-angels,* 201 (see *plant world*); taking of *atomic power* a "*Promethean* outrage," 213; *angels* created and destroyed, 294–95; Gabr. describes his *destruction* of, 316; MM on their *innocence,* 322; WHA sees *Atlantis* as *idea,* a first pasture to *innocence,* and raped by it, 322; Mich. says of them, "then *Cain* and *Abel:* is among them the perfection of *idea* gone awry," 323; *Uni* on his life in *Atlantis,* 378–80; wear the *number* of their *bat-angel* master, 379; their duty is "to be near," 379; have their "one fixed green *loss,*" 379; *Uni* describes their end, 379–80; their *electrical* current, 380; MM describes their *appearance,* 380 (see 534); *Uni* says they "resemble tales they were told," 382; *Uni* on *sex* and love, 384; WHA on, 392; *Uni's* story about love, 394–95; 460; Gabr.'s fondness for, 460; and the *white* force in the *atom,* 461 (see *scale*); 469–70; 470–71; at *Nature's* fete, 483; see *Atlantis; Uni; bat-angels*

Chaos, one of the two governing *gods* (with *God B*), 113; employs *feeling,* 113; *bat-angels* warn against the chaos they once worshiped, 113 (see 461); *bat-angels* left the work of Chaos when they shed their *feelings,* 115; biologists, physicists, and "the old contest with Chaos," 115; before *man* (and the force of *Mind*) all was "instinctive *Nature,* a chaos," 156; M says that after the *bat-angels'* world shattered, the *angels* "fixed [them] in [their] place by demonstrating that . . . the calm after [their] storm was utter chaos," 173; M says that in the race with *Mind,* if Chaos wins the race was fixed, 201; 224; if *God B's rules* are not obeyed, it is "given a wedge," 246; slips in upon the collapse of *religious* belief, 246; Mich. calls Gabr., 322; Gabr. says *God B* is the balancer of Chaos and creation, 322; Gabr. proposes, "Chaos: innocence?" 322; Gabr. says, "firstborn was Chaos," 322; DJ says, "if *idea's destructive,* then Chaos would run things, that's unthinkable," 323; JM says, "it was the original theme: Chaos, *God Biology,* those ruling opposites," 323; WHA asks if the putting down of Chaos was fratricide, 323; Mich.'s *light* said, "Back!" to Chaos, 326; twice it "rang down the curtain" on *God B's* creations, 326 (see 316); the "welter of chaotic *feeling*" at the moment of suicide, 333; Terpsichore calls

herself the "step daughter" of, 403; *Calypso* refers to "*Psyche*-Chaos, our *immortal* mother," 404; *Psyche* as, 404, 409; JM recalls that Gabr. once was called Chaos, 417 (see 322); WHA distinguishes *natural (Psychic)* from unnatural Chaos, 420; and the *Monitor,* 420 (see 453); and the *black* force in the *atom* represented by the *bat-angels,* 461 (see *scale*); as *feeling,* is present at *Nature's* fete, 488; *Nature* and Gabr.'s "liaison" with, 492, 553; 506; see *Nature,* especially the note there

Chapman, George, English poet, dramatist, and translator of Homer (1559?–1634). 345–46

Chaucer, Geoffrey, English poet (1340?–1400). 152; "twittering parliament," 299 (see his *Parliament of Fowls*)

Chester, see Chester *Kallman*

childlessness, 20; 30 (also see 38); MM is "insouciantly childless," 102, 199, 205; WHA speculates that their childlessness allows them into the seminar, 205–6; 216; of *Akhnaton* and *Nefertiti,* 225; 413; 426; the *Five* are usually childless, 468; 559; see *sex; homosexuality*

China, nuclear fire and *atomic* blast of, 56, 139, 441; with *Atlantis* first experiment on *earth,* 121; and the *Firefly woman,* 268; "adjacent experiment," 439; creature of the Chinese plain, 458–60; 469; 470; see *men before mankind; bat-angels*

Christ, effect on E's home, 8; 98; 187; 205; E on, 425; 426; 441; speaks, 443–44; 448; 449; 463; 467; was *Emmanuel,* 552; see *religion*

Christianity, M says that its *myths* are closest to "these earthy truths," 187; and fall of *Rome,* 187; see *Christ; religion*

Christo, was a "trick" according to JM. 425

Christopher, Saint, legendary Christian martyr of the third century A.D. and patron to travelers. Identified with *Emmanuel,* 343

Clarendon, A. H., his *Time Was* quoted, 58; see *time* and JM's "The Thousand and Second Night" in *Nights and Days*

Clay, John, patron of DJ. 11; 16; 19; 24; 38; quibble on his name, 59; 72; 415

Clio, traditionally the Greek muse of history. 201; 400–404; see *Muses*

Clio, Kyria, JM and DJ's cleaning lady in Athens. 53; 74; 433; see James *Merrill; time* (also see JM's "Days of 1964" in *Nights and Days* and "After the Fire" in *Braving the Elements*)

cloning, as shortcut is vital, 118; sinking into the thoughts of the *bat-angels* is a form of cloning, led to *Divine Comedies,* 121; idea of a benign *God* has lately been cloned into *man,* 137; 140; and *plant souls,* 151–52; *centaurs* used on *Atlantis,* 167; *Akhnaton* first cloned ruler, 179; and *cell* structure, 182; JM cloned with minerals that confront *fear* and despair with imagery, 183; 184; highly cloned *souls* of *atomic* researchers, 185; *bat-angels* clone the happy few, the masses they need never consider, 188; *souls*

of great *scribes* mined by the *bat-angels,* 189, 194, 217–22, 292, 497; M says *bat-angels* must clone the *scribe* to regulate *population,* 194; cloned architects on the way, 194; M on the *souls* that are not cloned, 196; heredity and environment are clonable, 198 (see *genetics*); were the *centaurs* cloned with their own destruction? 200 (see *No Accident clause*); *man* cloned to solve problems of pollution and *population,* 201; WHA on the "uncloned lives that touch our own," 205; 213; and the *V work* of *scribes* such as *Eliot, Rimbaud, Yeats, Lodeizen,* and JM, 217–22; *Homer* cloned to provide catalog and present his era with a *Pantheon,* 219; 220; may occur at any time, not just between lives, 221; 229; *man's* cloned *soul,* 239; 245; "a mere 2 million cloned *souls,*" 247; highly cloned scientist *souls,* 260; *bat-angels* and the *Firefly woman,* 268; of *Freud,* 269 (see *Hell; Psyche*); *bat-angels'* challenge is to make *man* the clone of *God B,* 269; the mining of French and German *scribes,* 292, 497; see *densities; Research Lab;* the *Five*

Clytemnestra, wife of Agamemnon in Greek mythology. WHA compares MM to, 189

Cocteau, Jean, French poet, novelist, and filmmaker (1899–1963). 291; 381

Coleridge, Samuel Taylor, English poet and critic (1772–1834). 305

Colette (Sidonie-Gabrielle Claudine), French novelist (1873–1954). 291; 378; 381; 383; 546; 557

colors (the four), and the inner workings of the *atom,* 119, 207; frantic action of the *atom black* and *white,* 120; 186; DJ's dream of, 207; square of the four colors is *infinity,* 210; 211; and *cells,* 221–22; and the house in *Stonington,* 212; 228; and sound waves, 230; ruled by *light* and the *00,* 230; 237; 239; 248; and the wings of the messenger *angel* in *M.,* 250; as DJ and JM "dress" their *minds* in preparation for Mich., 270; *angels* descend on an *arc* composed of the four colors, 293; and the *angels,* 314, 316; Gabr. is denied them, 316; 345; WHA and MM on "Mich.'s *sense* prisms," 356–57; "all the colors" at Mich.'s fete, 357; and the *number* that Gabr. adds to the *soul,* 423

"Comus" (Milton), *Blake's* sketches for, 407; see *Milton*

Congreve, William, English dramatist (1670–1729). His *The Way of the World* provides M with a name, 232; 546; his *The Way of the World,* 551

Connolly, Cyril, English critic and novelist (1903–74). 184

Cotzias, George (also Kotzias), and JM's sister Doris *Magowan,* 141, 298, 421–22, 509; discoverer of a drug to prolong life, 141–42 (see *elements; salt*); in hospital, 272; JM speculates that he is one of the "highly *cloned scientist souls*" whose work is being thwarted, 272; discusses *M.* with JM, 298–99; his dream about the *Phoenix* and about *black holes,* 299; MM did not know him well, 309; his illness, which he *resists* because he has consuming *V work,* 309; "radiations" (*X rays*) have "undone" and "il-

luminated" his *soul,* 309; in hospital, 312; addresses JM as "brother," 312; WHA says that "he is unique, a one shot *soul,* his *densities* derive from *Montezuma,*" 312; WHA says he is uncertain whether he is one of the *Five,* 313 (see 341; 375); dies, 374; will join the *elements,* 374; more on his *X ray* therapy, 374, 479; on his work with *cells* and what DJ and JM have been learning, 375; working in the *Research Lab,* 375, 377, 381; 386; 387; 390; 393; his lesson on *matter,* 395–98; believes a force "afraid of or an enemy of my *science* or your *poetry*" is dictating the poem, 398 (see 411); meets his *Phoenix,* 400 (see *Urania*); his theorem revealed by *Urania* and then lost, 403, 411–12; was *Raphael's,* is now Gabr.'s, 405; *Psyche* calls him the first *Research Lab soul* in three millenia, 410; says "we are guided by a benevolent force," after the first appearance of *Psyche,* 411; recalls a prenatal dream about *Urania,* 411; had a son, 413 (see *childlessness*); 415; says the *Muses* are "kinetics of *Mind*-perception," 416; says "aren't we being a bit oversanguine about" *Nature,* 416–17; on the possible connections among Gabr., *Nature,* and the *Monitor,* 417, 447; 420; JM reads him his sister's letter, 421–22; 423; 426; his lecture on *time* and *immortality,* 438–39 (see 452–53); Gabr. tells him he will be an *Alpha man,* 439; 441; on the *Monitor,* 447 (see 417; 453; 457); on *God A,* 447; on the *atomic black* compressed from *time's* reversibility, 452–53; 455; 457; JM had wished he was one of the *Five,* 466; 471; more on the damage to his *soul* from his *X ray* therapy, 479; his work "unfit for *man* thus far," 479; says (of the *atom*) "poso akoma" is the real motto of JM's poem, 479 (see *design*); 481; 484; 503; on *UFOs,* 507; on his next life, 507; sends his love to JM's sister, 509; lights up the Russian sky, 512; 515; 526

"Cousine Dola," 318

crust world, created by the *bat-angels,* 120; all life suspended in an ozone layer, 120; *atom* built and powered it, 120, 168; and *anchor sites,* 121, 125, 134, 168, 169; its destruction, 120, 121, 125, 133–34, 168–69; radiated stones illuminated the *anchor sites,* 125, 168 (see *atomic power*); *metaphor* for the brain's evolving cortex, 126 (see *myth; scale*); is now the *moon,* 133; composed of materials the *atom* made nongravitational, 133; flames extinguished by the servants of *God B,* 134; one landmass of *Atlantis* sank when the crust world fell, 167; *anchor sites* attacked by the *vegetable* adversary, 168; *God B* begins to erase all traces of, 169; 199; M born on, 224

culture, *density* shapes culture patterns, 144; hand in glove with *density,* 239; M's lecture on, 241–42; most rewarding of *man's V work,* 241; concepts of (survival and curiosity), 241–42; see *language; Mind; music; science*

Cupid, Roman god of love. 434; see *Eros; Venus; Aphrodite*

Curie, Marie, Polish-born French chemist and discoverer of radium (1867–1934). 55; 337 (see *Akhnaton; atomic power*)

Cynthia, JM and DJ's cleaning lady in Stonington. 190; 191

Dante Alighieri, Italian poet (1265–1321). Epigraph to *E.;* 14; *Paradiso,* III, 14 quoted, 37 (refers to the faces of souls who were inconstant to vows made on earth—see, among other entries, *Capri;* here, also, Dante regarded real spirits as reflections only), 37; Maya *Deren's* dream is a remake of the *Paradiso,* 45; how he came to write the *Paradiso,* 45; 46; E identifies *Beatrice* as a perfected *soul* who has returned from *stage* nine, 59; 69; parody of the inscription over the gateway to the Inferno, 75; three passages in terza rima, each concluding with the word *stars,* 78–82, 255–56, 502–6 (see *design*); part of the unbroken chain of *scribes,* 121; his vision was *star*-like, 132; looked into the *atom's* eye and saw the potential of *Paradise,* 132; reference to *Paradiso* XXVIII, 132; signal or song of the *universe* heard by him, 132–33, 363 (see *God B*); *Beatrice* is a kind of *music* he *personified* in female form, 132; *bat-angels* sent *80098* to him, 132, 177, 219; *bat-angels* on E's version of the *Comedy's* origin, 132; his strength and that of his time was a "fierce credulity" ("dream, *fact,* and experience were one"), 132–33 (see *belief*); vision is not of *Paradise* but the source of all *power,* 133; went down through the *stages* nine to one, from zero, 133; *angels* spoke to him, 133; 135; 136; his "luck lay in his gullible and heavenly world," 147; difference between his world and JM's, 147; M says of his superiors, "it is a *power* that stilled the tongue of Dante," 155; *Mind* is the *music* Dante heard, 161; 177; 188; 208; Robert *Morse* says, "everything in Dante knew its place," 256; heard *00,* 266; his version of *Hell* needed for dull *animalistic* lives, 269; George *Cotzias* on, 298–99; *Beatrice,* 354, 468; and *God B's* song, 363; and the *Rose (Santofior/Sandover)* tradition, 363; *Blake's* sketches for, 407; MM reveals she was *Beatrice,* 468; 479; 501; 532; 546; 557

Daphne, in Greek mythology, the personification of the laurel as a nymph choosing this metamorphosis as an escape from Apollo. And MM, 310

David, Jacques-Louis, French painter (1748–1825). The *Coronation of Napoleon,* 387

Democritus, Greek philosopher of the late fifth century B.C., he proposed a primitive atomic theory. 178; 391

density, E uses coal to distinguish different kinds of *souls,* 50; Matt *Jackson* on *souls* who are "not special," 108; "the *Jew* is chosen, the Teuton and Arab nurture brutes," 123; "are an end result of *genetic* workings," 138; the *Jew* is the density in *man* par excellence, 138, 243; and DJ and JM, 138; the subdensities, 139; Greeks next in line of density after the *Jew,* 141; maximum density in each age resides with the *Five,* 142, 230; ratio of *animal* to human densities in DJ and JM's basic formulas, 143 (see *number*); shapes *culture* patterns, 144, 239; *bat-angels* daily need five million *souls*

(density 1:20,000) in their *Research Lab,* 145; *Plato* and, 147; the dead's lack of interest in, 147; *plant soul* densities, 151–52; and *music,* 157; *vegetable* component of the *centaurs* gave them great density, 167; 182; JM and WHA's mineral densities, 183; *bat-angels* in charge of *soul* densities, 186; and *atomic power,* 186; *souls* of great *scribes* mined by the *bat-angels,* 189, 292; competitive element is an original *Jew* density, 193; M on the *souls* of those who are not *cloned,* 196; M's *00* ancestors represent the "greatest possible density" among his kind, 224; the "rat world," 226; two chief densities, physical and of the *soul,* which are linked by the *senses,* 230; *bat-angels'* work on the *soul* drew on energy sources under this "loose heading," 236; and the *elements,* 236; and *history,* 239 (see *scale*); hand in glove with *culture,* 239; 268; George *Cotzias's* derive from *Montezuma,* 312; "*salts* and *carbons,*" 315; 341; George *Cotzias* on his research into cells and what DJ and JM have been learning, 375; 396; 397; and the *black,* 451; 467; 512; WHA's *Homeric* densities, 514

Deren, Eleanora "Maya," "doyenne of our American experimental film" (1917–1961). 11; E calls her a "white witch," 22; in her first, last, and only life, 23; *patron* to her cats, 23; (also 11, 52, 63); blesses DJ and JM, 23, 25 (see *devotion*); her initial opinion of E, 23; dreams of E, 44–45 (see 27; also *appearances; personification;* her *Ritual in Transfigured Time* described, 45–46; her *Divine Horsemen* quoted, 58–59 (New York: Chelsea House, 1970, pp. 77–78 and 95–96); JM's sonnets to, 63–65; dies, 63–64; works for St. *Lucy,* 64; 72; tells DJ and JM that their talk has an end beyond itself, 73 (see *belief*); and JM's mother (Hellen Ingram *Plummer*), 84; 102; 128; her Haitian film (*Divine Horsemen*) has been edited, 304; Joseph *Campbell* on, 304–5; on *Erzulie* as "omnisex Queen of *Heaven,*" 305 (see *sex*); on her husband and his new wife, 305 (see Teiji *Ito*); and *negatives* in *C.L.S.,* 362; 371; JM and DJ see her film *Divine Horsemen* in *Venice,* 502–6; 546; 557

design (of *C.L.S.*), prose versus verse and other matters of style relating to *E.,* 3–4 (also 82); *Time* would not tell the story, 4 (also 85); design of the trilogy adumbrated in the description of the *Ouija board,* 5; E on the style of JM's lost *novel,* 13, 33, 66 (also see Merrill's "The Will"); question of revising section P, 63–65; orderings of experience, 69; note that section U (June 1974)—chronologically—precedes "M" (July 1974) and "O" (August 1974), 72; *Stevens* tells JM that a *scribe* sits by him "to interweave your lines with meanings you cannot conceive," 72; conclusion of *E.* (December 1974) established by the ultimatum of the *men before mankind* in June 1974 ("Mind your work, six moons remain"), 73; JM on the relationship between subjects and images, 76; three passages in terza rima, each concluding with the word *stars,* 78–82, 255–56, 502–6 (see *Dante*); JM on his style and his audience, 82 (also 3); on meter, rhyme, and inspiration, 85; implications of the phrase "burn the *box*" for the writing

of *E.*, 87–88 (see *memory*); in *M.* the first sound of each book echoes in one or more languages the number of that book (see 311); JM is told the material "will this time flow straight through" him, 108; JM on poems of *science* and the *language* of *science,* 109–11; JM on "subject matter," 109–11; events in *M.* take place in the summer of 1976, 112; JM is told that three more of his years are wanted, 113; *E.* is a "prologue," 113; JM on setting down the lessons in *E.* and *M.*, 114–15; *pyramid* introduced as a *metaphor* for *M.*, 127; numerals 1 through 0 will point the way, 127; *man's* measure is ten, the *bat-angels'* is fourteen, 127 (see 240); JM on his doubts about what he is hearing from the *bat-angels* ("Allegory . . . popthink"), 136; WHA calls *M.* a "play of voices," 137; M tells JM that "there is a design at work," 157; *lenses* are "central" (at 4.5) to *M.*, 174; poem needed the fierce voices of the *bat-angels,* 175; JM told that there will be one more poem, 176; *No Accident clause* and the villanelle, 179, 196; M says that the poem's bed may need to be made up with dirty sheets, 188; MM says her charade is "part of the design," 208; human characters will speak in pentameter (see *five*) whereas the *bat-angels* will speak in syllabics, 240; M tells JM, "you have set down only one of the three taps of the curtain-raising staff," 248; Robert *Morse* on the *bat-angels'* "jargon," 256 (see *language*); JM and WHA on the differences between *E.* and *M.*, 261; WHA on *fact* and fable, 262–63; JM on writing *M.*, 297–98, 311–12; WHA calls JM's poem "a *Mahler*" in reference to its many voices, 301; WHA's "MEEK" formulation sets forth the whole design "initially," 318; JM on writing *C.L.S.*, his account here mimics the history of Greek drama, 319; WHA gives JM a form for *S.*, "two golden trays of 'Yes' and 'No' with '&' as bridge or balance," 328 (see 351; 362; Gabr.'s decription of *God B.*, 322); JM on the "limpid bel canto phrases" of the *angels'* speeches, 331; JM on his "sheer walls of text," 332; the "craft" in JM's poem, that is both vehicle and guide, 336; WHA on JM's poem about the *Five,* 345; JM on catching the "full verve" of what the *angels* say by means of the "unmeasurable King James inflections," 346; JM on literary versions of *God* and "how humdrum what he says" next to his creations, 348; and the "elevator principle" in the lessons of *S.* ("to a plane of greater *power* and *light*"), 353–54; JM on *negatives* in *C.L.S.*, 362; JM says his "poem's logic calls for the shattering of a glass," 363–64, 516–17 (see epigraph to *S.* from Jean Santeuil); Plenorios's description of Artemis's temple and the writing of *S.*, 373; JM says, "enough names clog the poem," 384; WHA fears JM's poem is a "whitewash" for the *angels,* 394; JM's description of the "halfway point that tips the scale" in *S.*, 395; WHA and JM on resolving ambiguities in the poem, 399; *Psyche* outlines the remaining sessions, 410; WHA on the *language* and style of the angels, 414; JM says, "maddening the way everything merges and reflects," 415

(see *twin*); and *music,* 417–18; WHA on the teaching style of the *angels,* 420; JM on the transition to "No" in *S.,* 430; MM's role in JM's trilogy, 464–69; JM's ballade on MM, 468; JM says, "madness to imagine one could do without the apt ideogram or two," 474; *ABBA* as *God B* and as one of JM's favorite rhyme schemes, 478; thinking of the *atom,* George *Cotzias* says, "poso akoma" is the real motto of the poem, 479; Spenserian stanzas during *Nature's* fete, 483–89; *God B* asks JM to make a "*V work* giving both pause and hope," 493 (see *Yes and No*); ending of *S.* is a long sentence fragment rhymed ABBA, with the final rhyme of "*light*/night," 517 (see *black*); ending of "Coda" returns to the beginning of *E.,* 560; see *poetry*

destruction, of *God B's* works by the *black, negative, evil* forces, 293; is Gabr.'s first duty, 295; "destructive energies" and WHA's *soul,* 304; "the other side" of *God B's V work* shouldered by Gabr., 316; Gabr. describes his destruction of the *centaurs* and the *bat-angels,* 316 (see *326*); Mich.'s first text in *S.,* "the most *innocent* of *ideas* is the *idea* that *innocence* is destroyed by *ideas,*" 321; DJ says, "if *idea's* destructive, then *Chaos* would run things, that's unthinkable," 323; WHA asks Gabr., "is not destruction, much of it, for *man's* good?" 329 (see *white*); and *suicide,* 331–34; Gabr. and *Emmanuel's* pact to share the work of wiping out *God B's* errors/experiments, 334; *God B* forced to call Gabr. "to heel," apparently to keep him from destroying *man,* 335; is Gabr.'s first nature, also called "selection," 344; Gabr.'s *thought* destroys Mich.'s *ideas,* 426; Gabr. says, "of all destructive *ideas,* the most destructive is the *idea* of destruction," 438; *Psyche* says, "the most destructive of all *ideas* is that *feeling* sets it right," 438; and *time,* 440; and the *atomic black* compressed from *time's* reversibility, 453; 459; and "oblivion," 469–71; see *Gabriel*

Detre, Dr. Thomas (JM's former psychiatrist), 29–31; 87; see JM's *A Different Person*

devils, is E a devil? 9 (also see 6); DJ identifies *bat-angels* as devils, 114 (see 289); *bat-angels* say that the devil has been driven out of them into *man,* and must now be driven out again, 114; 126; 140; 169; and *atomic power,* 181; M says, "we are the force some might accuse of the devil's work," 193; JM says that M is one, "up to a point," 289; *Lucifer,* 469; see *bat-angels*

devotion, identified by E as "the main impetus," 59; (for some examples see Maya *Deren's* heart-emblem, 23, and Tania *Blixen's* actions, 52–53)

Dialogues des Carmélites (Poulenc), 312

Dickens, Charles, English novelist (1812–70). Reference to Little Nell, 70; 183; 526

Dickinson, Emily, American poet (1830–86). 526

Dinesen, Isak, see Baroness Karen *Blixen*

Disney, Walter Elias "Walt," American cartoonist, motion picture producer, and showman (1901–66). 136

Divine Horsemen [book] (Deren), 11; quoted 58–59 (New York: Chelsea House, 1970, pp. 77–78 and 95–96); see *Götterdämmerung*

Divine Horsemen [film] (Deren), 304–5; JM and DJ see in *Venice,* 502–6

DNA (deoxyribonucleic acid), 119; RNA ("remember *No Accident*"), 196; model at *Boston* Museum of Science and Sarah *Bernhardt,* 203; first DNA, 268; "lift out the fabulous necklace, in form a spiral molecule," 274; 427; 474; 495

dogs, 60; black dog in *Athens,* 107, 114, 191; and *Faust,* 114; black dog in *Stonington,* 270, 272; M says he "will be the wounded black hound of *Heaven* at your door," 271; 296

Dolly Suite (Fauré), 255

Don Giovanni (Mozart), 69

Doré, (Paul-) Gustave, French artist and illustrator (1832–83). 136

Doris, see Doris Merrill *Magowan*

doubt, see *belief*

Dryden, John, English poet, dramatist, and critic (1631–1700). 262

duality, *Psyche* introduces, 408; and *friction,* 458; see *Resistance; twin; Yes and No*

earth, in *C.L.S.* both an element and a place. WHA is linked to *element* of earth, 159, 164; M shares for the first time, 162; all *elements* of life are in the earth's crust, 163; *bat-angels* are at home in its molten heart, 163 (see *fire*); in earth's crust *time* is measured in millenia, 163; earth as one of the *Five* is a grave timekeeper, 164; as one of the *Five, Ghandi* is linked to the *element* of earth, 164; earth as potential *Greenhouse* goes through the following stages: 1) *fireball,* 2) the cooling crust, 3) steam and *water,* 4) the growth of single *cells,* 5) debut of organic life; then 6) organic *matter* moved off into a species *man* has found in a fossilized state but misunderstood (see *centaurs*), 166; reference to the "fledgling" earth, 166; *God B* governs all life on, 170; life on earth is immersed in *feeling* and manners, 172; earth is *God B,* 187; politicians are of, 188; and JM's poem (M says, "the poem's bed may need to be made up with dirty sheets"), 188; is it the single experiment or one of several? 200; *Moses* is a *myth* for, 200; (element) is ruled by *Nature,* 230; 244–45; 264; 271; Mich. on the beginning of earth life, 276; 286; *Nature* changes the costumes of, 288; 291; Mich. describes the creation of, 292–94; *Emmanuel* washes, 302 (see *Raphael*); *Raphael* is the "earth brother," 306; *Raphael* has the irradiated metals in him, 307 (see *atomic power*); WHA will "ripple" through when he joins the *elements,* 310; 315; its creation, and Mich.'s first text in

S. about *innocence* and *ideas,* 322; the *cave* dwellers, 324–26; the lake dwellers, 325–26; earth (*Raphael*) and *water* (*Emmanuel*) are innocent *Nature,* 326; 328; *Raphael's* (earth's) "shadow riches" are uranium, 343 (see *atomic power; black*); as "land" in "Samos," 369–70; MM on the seeding of, 388; MM on the *plant world* of, 388–89; WHA says we "tremble on a crust so fragile that it needs *God B's* constant vigil," 391–92; WHA on the *Monitor* within it, 392–93; was an "open book to read" for WHA and MM as they prepared the lessons in *S.*, 415 (see 414); 450; 451; is a fragile eggshell, 453 (see JM's "Transfigured Bird" in *First Poems,* and 216); 455; and the *It,* 474–76; 484; 494; 501; and the *Alpha men,* 511–12; 523; 539; the *saint* on earth brings *Heaven* to the *Mind,* the *saint* in *Heaven,* earth, 546

East German physicist, formerly *Montezuma,* 131; leads his field in the study of in-space radiant powers, 131 (see *atomic power*); see the *Five*

Eden, in the Old Testament, first home of Adam and Eve. "Eden a stage, the expulsion the drama, the mistake to believe that knowledge is *evil,*" 115; three Edens, 121, 166, 171; WHA asks, "is it not that *God B* believes in us as his third Eden?" 171; tells a parable of *atomic* fission, 192 (see *myth*); Eden 2 and the ozone belt, 199; first *Hell* was "to know that even in Eden was danger," 269 (see *fear*); see *myth*

Edward VIII, king of England (1894–1972). 467

Egypt, country of Northeastern Africa. 179

8002, *bat-angel* whom *God B* sent to *Innocent VI,* 130–31; see *Faust*

80098, sent by the *bat-angels* to *Dante,* 132; 177; 219

Einstein, Albert, German-born American theoretical physicist (1879–1955). One of the *Five,* 142; 229; joke about E and mc^2, 266; 447; 553

Eisenhower, Dwight, Thirty-fourth President of the United States (1890–1969), 40

Eleanor, see Eleanor *Perenyi*

electricity, "psychic current," 35; *power* station, 84; 141; in *Atlantis,* organic *matter* at last produced three centers of *Arcadian* culture, 166; *centaurs* are electrically powered while the *bat-angels* are *atomic,* 169 (see *Atlantis*); electrical triggers work *man's* brain, 182; *God B* returned mastery to his electronic creatures, 185; *man's* origin is electric, 199; *bat-angels* are custodians of the electrical non-angelic 12% stored in *man,* 238; 243; the *S/O/L* is of the electrical world, 252; 256; WHA speaks of "the current sweeping through us," which is identified with the *angels,* 332, 334; WHA warns JM, "beware lest *feeling's* throne prove an electric chair," 332 (see *Gabriel*); in the *centaurs* and in *man,* 380; and George *Cotzias's* theorem, 412; electric and *atomic* energies interfuse in the dinosaurs, 453; MM and "the naked current," 465; 512; see *absolute*

elements, for *E.* see *fire, power,* and *water;* 138; the *carbons* are the

chief *salt*-oriented elements, 141; *souls* correspond to different elements (WHA: platinum; JM: silver; DJ: silver and tin), 142; MM (*water*), WHA (*earth*), JM (*air*), and M (*fire*) are each linked to an element and DJ to the shaping hand of *Nature,* 159; the union of their *souls* is also a union of elements, 159; the elements are invoked, 159–61; the elements speak, 161; their *V work* is the "onward dance of things," 161; responsible for all of M but his *mind* ("your *minds* coalesce to form his"), 161; *Mind* is the energy they draw from manifest in the *five* rings around the *S/O/L/,* 161; *antimatter* was ever theirs to guard against, 161; they "keep watch" and "press back," 161 (see *Resistance*); visit of the elements frees M, 162; all elements of life are in the *earth's* crust, 163; the *Five* connect with, 164; with *Nature* come to compose a *pyramid,* 164; were once at war, but signed a truce when *God B* took control, 166; JM refers to "our elemental union," 208; ruled by *Nature,* 230, 236; and *density,* 236; the "heavy elements," 236 (see *atomic power*); 271; WHA and MM on joining, 303–4, 309–10, 315, 335, 354, 511; and the four *angels,* 347; in "Samos," 369–70; George *Cotzias* will join, 374; 441; 463; 511–12

Elias, see *Emmanuel*

Elijah, see *Raphael*

Eliot, George (Mary Ann Evans), English novelist (1819–80). *Joanna* closes *Middlemarch,* 48; 88 (see *mirrors, Middlemarch*); 313

Eliot, Thomas Stearns, American-born English poet, critic, and dramatist (1888–65). his description of Henry *James* cited, 14; 134; his *The Waste Land* ghostwritten by *Rimbaud,* 217, 219 (see *cloning*); *The Waste Land* is "the West's first (m) prewritten poem since" *Homer,* 219 (see *V work*); 547; on JM's poem and *V work,* 557–58

Elizabeth II, queen of England (b. 1926). 352; 467

Emmanuel, the Water Angel, known also as Elias. Divides the *earth* by *water,* 294; Mich. says he is as *water* sweet and fluid, 301; is "the suspension," 301; *reason* floats in, 301; balances the *moon,* 302; yields to Mich., 302; regulates the seasons, 302; born as a tear in *God B's* eye and brings balm for sorrow, 302; WHA and MM describe, 302; his *twin* is *Raphael,* 307, 315; on his names, 315; on Mich.'s first text in *S.,* including *innocence* and *idea,* 321–22; cooled the first rounded *idea* (*earth*), 322; his lake dwellers and their retreat to *innocence,* 326; 328; his pact with Gabr. to share the *destruction* of *God B's* errors/experiments, 334; says that Gabr. has changed, 335; his "two double natures" are "*reason* and pride, calm and purification," 343; his third nature brings *man* balm for sorrow, 347; is *God B's sense* of touch, 350; in "Samos," 369; *God B* has him seed the *earth,* 388 (see *plant world*); 389; 395; 406; 458; and the *It,* 474–75; and *Nature's* fete, 484; 500; 517; 535; presents Robert *Morse* with his *sense* of touch, 536; was *Christ,* 552; see *angels*

Ephesus, ancient Greek city, site of famed Temple of Artemis. 354; 370; JM and DJ visit, 372–73; MM's sermon at, 496–97

Ephraim, 4; 5; his history, 8; on *patrons, representatives,* and the nine *stages,* 8–10; *patron* to *Simpson,* 8; at *stage* six, 12, 17; on JM's lost *novel,* 13 (also 33, 66, and JM's "The Will" in *Divine Comedies*); urges DJ and JM to use their bodies and their *minds,* 15; on sensual pleasure, 15; describes his *appearance,* 16; at Versailles, 16; arranges to have Simpson reborn to Betsy *Pincus,* 19–20 (see *genetics*); JM's bad pre-E days, 21; 22; 23; Maya *Deren's* initial opinion of, 23; learns about modern history, philosophy, and music from Hans *Lodeizen,* 24; seen by DJ under *hypnosis,* 27; at his stage *souls* cannot feel, 27 (see *senses*); in trouble because of his meddling, 29 (see *genetics*); DJ and JM lose touch with him, 29; *folie à deux?* 30; contact resumes, 30–31; E and his revelations assessed, 31–32 (see *belief*); tangles with a kind of *god,* 34; enjoys their trip around the world more than DJ and JM do, 36; on Vedanta, 37 (see *religion*); in section I seen by JM as a spirit betokening forgiveness for the way he lives, 38; calls Wendell *Pincus* an angel because he has dreamed of him, 38, 81; 40; Maya *Deren's* dream of, 44–45 (see *appearances*); named *Eros* in JM's lost *novel,* 47; distinguishes different kinds of *souls,* 50 (see *carbon; density*); 51; 52; Hans *Lodeizen* has been promoted and is now above him, 54; on *Mozart,* 54; on *power,* 54–57 (see 263–65); on *Hiroshima,* 55 (see *atomic power;* 363); DJ and JM's first extended session with in two years, 54–55; JM notes how much he has come to trust him, 54, 57 (see *belief*); warns DJ and JM concerning the dependence of the *other world* on this one, 56; on the limitations of spirits who have not reached the ninth *stage,* 56; on the *men before mankind,* 56; defines *Heaven* as the surround of the living, 59; on his manner of reaching DJ and JM, 59; on *devotion,* 59; vision of the future, 59–60; "I am wisest when I look down at the precious ground I knew," 60; love of telling his life, 60; "first and last" session with DJ and JM "in ages," 72; 73; JM notes "If I fall from a high building, it's your name I'll call," 74 (see *belief*); 81–82; his absence, 85, 91; what JM has learned from him, 85; "the latest recurrent figure out of mythology," 85 (also 3); has "the affair" with E ended? 91; question of whether to burn the transcripts of his talks with DJ and JM, 91–92 (see *box*); contact is resumed after a year, 100; 101; on *appearances* in *Heaven,* 105; 106; 108; 111; says that the presence of the *bat-angels* dims the *stages,* 113; 116; 117; said to be afraid of the *bat-angels,* 118; 120; 124; 128; *bat-angels* on his version of *Dante's Comedy,* 132–33; and the limitations of *patrons,* 145; use of partial fictions to speak to DJ and JM, 145, 152, 154; said to be a member of the *bureaucracy,* 149; explains DJ's dream about his parents, 150–51; theory of the return of the *senses* discredited by M, 153; M corrects his claim that *Mozart* was a "black rock star," 164 (see *Stravinsky*); reminds DJ and JM that he is still available,

165; told *bat-angels man* was in anguish over *Hiroshima,* 183; 191; matches Chester *Kallman* and *Luca,* 197; his story about *Tiberius* and the death of *Christ,* 204–5; his own death, 205; says the *bat-angels* are of the messenger strain, 205; JM says to him, "how much you do know," 205; 212; 218; 220; M asserts that E "did not have all the facts nor does he now," 220; his story about *Luca,* 234–35; 238; 253; Robert *Morse* on, 256; WHA asks about his role in *M.,* 263; M answers, 264–66; M describes his court life, 265 (see 292); struck a bargain so that he could still be in touch with DJ and JM, 265; M speaks of the "long stylistic tradition" that includes him, 266; joke about *Einstein,* and mc², 266; is a composite voice, a formula, 266; his *number,* 266–67; says of the approach of Mich., "I dare not wonder, and may never know," 271; JM says, "poor E, we've all dropped him like a mask," 292; on the protective "human dirt," in WHA's words, 305 (see 300; 306); and the return of the *senses* in lesson 9 of "Yes" in *S.,* 354; and the *Rose,* 363 (see 55); 371; DJ suggests that he doubles as Mich., 405 (see 550); a "formula," 423 (see *number*); Robert *Morse* gives his "personality readout," 423–24 (see *number*); 424; on *Christ,* 425; on the *language* of *religion,* 425; MM on the superiority of the *angels'* knowledge to his, 425–26; 441; 454; 465; 480; gets his *senses* back at lesson 9 of the "No" section of *S.,* 487; "Mich.'s herald," 498; "much here is pure and simple mystery," 499; 516; on *Luca* and Saint *Agatha,* 525; 540; "Mr Secretary," 542, 543–44; JM's suspicions about, 543–44; 547; "Mr E," 549; reveals himself as Mich., 550; on approaching DJ and JM, 550–56; another set of *twins,* "M/E," 552; on his *earth* lives, 552–53; 558; see *Michael*

Erato/Erota, traditionally the Greek muse of lyric poetry and mime. 201; 400–404; see *Muses*

Eros, traditionally the Greek god of love, son to Aphrodite. E's name in JM's lost *novel,* 47; his history, 47; Leo *Cade* wants a child born as his *representative,* 48; Ellen *Cade* tries to dismiss him as a "figment of their [her and Leo's] common fancy," 48 (see *folie à deux*); 49; speaks to *Joanna* and Sergei *Markovich* at the *Ouija board,* 67; 70–71

Erzulie, voodoo goddess of love. 11; 23; 46; 64; 304; Maya *Deren* says she is "hermaphrodite . . . omnisex Queen of *Heaven,*" 305

eternity, *bats* symbol of, 98, 116; and *Faust,* 129–31; and the *Five,* 131; *Plato* enjoys an eternity of talk, 158; *Mind* is deathless, 161; *bat-angels* have spent their eternity damned because they offended *God B* when they destroyed the *centaurs'* primitive *immortals,* 170; the eternal *bureaucrat,* 315; MM says to Gabr. that *man* must have eternity, 330; 449; see *time; Heaven*

Eurydike, in Greek mythology, wife of Orpheus. 400–404; see *Muses*

Euterpe, traditionally the Greek muse of lyric poetry and music. 400–404; see *Muses*

Eve, in Old Testament, first woman and wife of Adam (see Genesis

3:20). 114; *Adam* and Eve are images for developments in the very nature of *matter,* 115; 121; 339; 341; 502; see *myth; power; scale*

evil, *bat-angels* are not evil but impatient, 113; *bat-angels* left the work of *Chaos* when they shed their *feelings,* 115; in *Eden,* the "mistake" was to believe that knowledge is evil, 115; "warring principles produced warring heirs so evil prevailed," 116; identified with *atomic power,* 116; *bat-angels* released but did not create an evil ("call it the void, call it in man, a will to nothingness"), 120; *Christianity* made an evil out of what had once been rites, 131 (see *religion*); and *Dante's* time ("all possible good and evil wrestling"), 132–33; is it caused by "those *black* hands" that test the *Greenhouse*? 162 (see *antimatter*); is an old, widespread legend and rooted in truth, 162 (see *myth; scale*); and the *atom,* 192 (see *scale*); Mich. says *God B* named the *black* and *negative* forces arrayed against him "evil," 293; 297; see *devil; sin*

evolution, 18–21; 50–53; 57; 59–60; ape's role in, 133; *plant* evolution, 152; of the *centaurs,* 167–68; of *man,* 179–80, 241–42, 269, 332, 344, 409; "*Mind's* ramifying tree minutely shaped through the ages," 241; 251; and *Hell,* 269; of the *Alpha men* from *man,* 308; the *cave* dwellers and the lake dwellers, 324–26; of *man's mind,* 332; *God B* entrusted *man's* evolution and *history* to Gabr., 344; *Psyche* on *man's* rise, 409; 414; see *animals; education; patrons; representatives;* the *Research Lab; souls; the nine stages*

facts, JM asks for, 120, 121, 122, 136, 137; in *Dante's* time, "dream, fact, and experience" were one, 133; JM on, 137; and "partial fictions," 145; placed in inverted commas, 166; WHA's "fact is is is fable" speech, 262–63 (see 303); and the antimasque, 263 (see *masque*); *bat-angels'* files of, 264; WHA on *poetry* and, 391; George *Cotzias* on *science* and, 397; and the *Muses,* 401–3; WHA persuades JM not to revise his fable in light of the new facts, 461–62; Gabr. says, "it seems this new breed of poets feeds on fact," 471 (see *scribes*); 499; see *belief; myth*

The Faerie Queene (Spenser), quoted, 61–62 (book 3, canto 6); see *gardens; Spenser; time*

Fall (of the bat-angels), 113; 119–20; 121; 122; 125; 133–34; 162; 168–69; 170; 171; 253; WHA on the fall of the *white angels,* 440–41; see the *bat-angels*

Fan, Empress, apparently not a historical figure. 402

Farmetton, Rufus, previous incarnation of JM (d. 1925). 11; JM relives his death, 42–43; is a "partial fiction," 145

Fauré, Gabriel-Urbain, French composer (1845–1924). 206; the *Dolly Suite,* 255

Faust, legendary magician and alchemist. WHA on, 129; M on, 130–31; Faust is *Innocent VI,* 131; 194; 196; 265

Faust (Goethe), 114; see *dogs*

Faustina, Annia Galeria, cousin and wife of Marcus Aurelius (c.125–76). 204

fear, 51; DJ and JM's fear of the *other world,* 111; fear of the *power* of the *bat-angels* stops *Paradise,* 113; DJ and JM urge not to fear the *bat-angels,* 113; MM's fear of the *bat-angels,* 123, 127–28; MM counsels DJ on fear, 128 (see 269); idea of a benign *God* has lately been *cloned* into *man* to assuage his fears, 137; *bat-angels'* fear the use of *atomic* weaponry falling into the hands of *animal souls,* 146; M had feared DJ and JM, 162; "fear and doubt put by but still kept handy," 166; DJ and JM told they may cast away their chance to meet the *angels* if they are "in doubt or fear," 171; and *virtues,* 172–73; 176–77; 183; *Hiroshima* produced two fears: of the fused *atom,* and of the fused *man* in his closely packed city (see *population*), 194; DJ and his operation, 198; of early *man,* 241–42; 269; is DJ's *Hell,* 269 (see 128); and *Hell,* 269; decline of *religious* fear, 269; repels Gabr., 314; the *cave* dwellers' "first shocking *idea:* fear of each other," 325; *Raphael* stilled *man's* fear, 343; 349; 448

feelings, *Chaos* employs, 113; feelings of *bat-angels* went up in flames when they fell, 113 (see *fire; fall*); embers of these feelings are *Mind,* 114; *bat-angels* left the work of *Chaos* when they shed their feelings, 115; 119; M says he has "come to love" DJ and JM, 155 (see 59, 88, 135, 185, 357, 384, 394–95); M says he is "filled" with *manners,* 155; M says, "your kindness keeps me in this new form," 157 (see *appearances*); M says, "now at last it is given me to share the force of *Nature,* the sweetness of *water* and *air,* the common sense of *earth,* here in your very hearth of hearts to burn," 162 (see *fire*); feelings of the *bat-angels* were formulas, 170–71 (see *number*); M says that unlike on *earth,* feeling plays no part in the *bat-angels'* existence, 172; 173; JM and WHA discuss the *bat-angels'* feelings, 186; WHA asks, "is *time* then the soil of feeling?" 209; M flees at the onset of, 209; WHA asks, "can [Gabr.] be made to feel?" 327; Mich. on "clearing our *Minds* of cloudy sentiment," 328; Gabr. says he has known feelings, all *black,* 330; WHA warns JM, "beware lest feeling's throne prove an *electric* chair," 332 (see *Gabriel*); JM's faith in, 426; MM compares hers to *black holes, 426; Psyche* says, "the most *destructive* of all *ideas* is that feeling sets it right," 438; *pain* is the only child of *time* and feeling, 455; banished to *earth,* 455; feeling is present during *Nature's* fete, where it is identified with *Chaos,* 488; 527; see *Chaos*

Fermi, Enrico, Italian-born American physicist (1901–54). Epigraph to *M.* (see note under Laura *Fermi*); and uranium fission, 116 (see *atomic power*)

Fermi, Laura, author, and wife of Enrico Fermi (1907–77). Epigraph to *M.,* 94 (Note: this arranges parts of four paragraphs from her

Atoms in the Family [Chicago: University of Chicago Press, 1954]; in order of their appearance, pp. 165, 166, and ix)

Fidelio (Beethoven), 427; see *Beethoven*

field, M describes *Ouija board* as a "field of work," 253; M's speech, "we met on this fair field," 257–58; 269; 379; *Uni* on the *mirror,* 430, 473, 483; *Mercury* on, 445; *Ouija board* again as, 478, 483

fire, "flame" paint on the walls of the dining room at *Stonington,* 5–6; the fireplace there, 5, 90–92; *Simpson's* death by fire, 6, 8; "issue hanging fire," 9; "glowing space" and "warmth" of the *Stonington* house, 22; heart emblem *Maya* burns to bless DJ and JM, 23–25; and *Joanna,* 33, 35, 67, 71; "sable bulks awince with fire," 33; firelight, 33; candles, 34; Magic Fire Music, 35; renewed the flame on the mildewed wall, 40; E's fire-clear eyes in *Maya's* dream, 44; jeans flexing white as fire, 46; "*mirror* wreath of scratches fiery-fine as hairs," 48; "automatic fire," 48; different kinds of *souls* are compared to different kinds of materials for burning, 50; (see *carbon; density*); Valhalla in flames, 56; outsoared the fire, 56; funeral pyre, 56; *nuclear* fire in *China,* 56; fire-sheer, 57; as fires within sight of each other, 59; "you communicate through my impartial fire," 59; as figures in the fire, 59; our fire, 59; firelit messages, 59; in *Issa's* haiku, 60; hangfire talks, 69; coal-fire blue scale, 70; *Joanna* jets through a sky in flames, 71; all burn to read, 72; a window fiery-mild, 77; cervello fritto spitting fire, 79; ringed round by fire, 83; firelit glances, 84; burn the *box,* 87–88; fire we huddled by, 90; question of whether to burn the *box* containing transcripts of talks with E, 91; and *Brünnhilde,* 91; *feelings* of the *bat-angels* went up in flames when they fell, 113 (see *Fall*); embers are *Mind,* 114; the physicist is drawn to, 115; MM says the *bat-angels* can use, 128; E says that DJ and JM would be protected by their dead friends if the *bat-angels* used it, 128, 190, 191, 197; after *Akhnaton's* experiment with the crystal *pyramid,* 127; fire and heat of the *bat-angels,* 128, 190, 202; *crust world* of the *bat-angels* ended by fire, 134; firefly, 139; flame of *Hiroshima* and the fire in ancient *China,* 139, 441 (see *atomic power*); "fire-flake," 141 (see *salt*); "firey, salty breakthroughs," 141; M is linked to the *element* of fire, 159; M burns in DJ and JM's "very hearth of hearts," 162; *bat-angels* at home in the *earth's* molten heart, 163; "fireball" is the first stage of *earth* as potential *Greenhouse,* 166; 183; and *atomic power,* the fuel of the *Pantheon,* 199; ruled by *Nature,* 230; 239; 241; 248; 271; 274; 290; 293; 295; 298; 299; 314; 315; Gabr.'s, 318, 325, 344, 441; 356; in "Samos," 369–70; and the last of the *centaurs,* 380; WHA on the *Monitor's* "fierce and infernal heat," 392; 417; Gabr. as, 426; 451; of *atomic* test, 456; 464; 471; and the *It* ("fire fighting itself—fire its own screen"), 475; 476; M's "nuclear fire-ache" is quenched during Mich.'s fete, 488; 553; 554; see *water*

Firefly woman, M's "escapade," 268; 514; 544

five, "the sacred quantum of five," 139; is the midway, 159; and the *elements,* 159; five rings around the *S/O/L/,* 161; "in deference to all vital groupings of five we may now insert *V* when naming work guided by higher collaboration," 162; the "transforming digit," 224; 230; and *density,* 230; human characters in *C.L.S.* will speak in pentameter, 240 (see *design*); *bat-angels* believe that the "one unspoken revelation must dwell in," 245; Mich. first speaks to DJ and JM at five o'clock, 274; 493; *S.* concludes on DJ's fifty-fifth birthday, 508; see *number; the Five; V work*

Five, the, *immortal,* 131; M names them as *Laduman, Soriva, Rachel, Torro, and Von,* 131; one was *Montezuma* and is now an *East German physicist,* 131; not in the nine *stages,* 131; return to *earth* with energy beyond the norm, 131; *bat-angels* use "extra-life" *souls* like *Montezuma* for research, 132; and *density,* 138; one is *Dag Hammarskjöld,* 142; their work must find acceptance before they can return, 142; maximum *density* in each age resides in the deathless Five, 142; compared to the 36 Just Men of the Jews, 143; *scribe's* job is to speed acceptance of the Five's work, 143; one small success of the *bat-angels* in their *Research Lab* is the Five, 145; *earth* as one of the Five is a grave timekeeper, 164; each has an affinity with the *elements,* 164; one is Galileo, 193; they loan their powers, 201; their names are "formula made word," 223 (see *number; language*); firstborn was the double-*soul Akhnaton-Nefertiti,* 223; are unique, 223; their *souls* "pass through the flames and live," 315; 335; are the *senses* of the *angels* in *Heaven,* 337–41; are visited in the *Research Lab,* 337–40; WHA says "they go straight to the head of whatever *bureaucracy,*" even the *angels'* to *God B,* 340; WHA says that "these Old Testament names ring many changes on the Five," 341 (see *Bible*); Mich. requests poems about them, 342; WHA's poem about them, 345; WHA on JM's poem, 345 (see *design*); 350; present at Mich.'s fete, 355–56; divided from DJ and JM during the fete by a "*Styx* of quicksilver," 359 (see *mirror*); 375; 446; their energies *resist* exhaustion, 447; move gladly from life to life, 447; are mediators, 447; are Gabr.'s, with *God B's* approval, 447; report on *man* to *God B,* 463; MM reveals she is *Plato,* 465–69; JM had hoped WHA and George *Cotzias* were of the Five, 466; MM says they are *gods,* 467; are largely *childless,* 468; 472; 479; parceled into more than one life at a time, 497; MM says "we of the Five are never alone," 497; and WHA, 513–14; the *angels* are the supreme moments of, 552 (see *V work*)

Flagstad, Kirsten, Norwegian singer (1895–1962). 81; 233; during Mich.'s fete, 355, 357, 358, 359; sings a "Fifth Last Song" of *Strauss,* 357; WHA on, 358, 359; 417; see *music*

flood, 56; 59–60; 119; the "legend of the flood" marks the start of the third *Eden,* 166

folie à deux, Tom *Detre's* (JM's former psychiatrist) explanation of E, etc., 30; Ellen *Cade's* effort to dismiss *Eros* as a "figment of their [her and

Leo's] common fancy," 48; "folie à deux, folie à 2,000,000, what difference?" 137; see *belief*

Ford, Kinton, patron to JM (1810–43). 12; 16; 19; 72; 145 (example of the limitations of *patrons,* and the *bat-angels'* control over non–*Research Lab souls*); 415

Forster, Edward Morgan, English novelist (1879–1970). 205; see *cloning; homosexuality; Research Lab*

4170, 378; see *Uni*

40070, one of the *bat-angels* who speaks to DJ and JM, 130 (see 125–27)

40076, one of the *bat-angels* who speaks to DJ and JM ("that martinet"), 130 (see 124); 144; 175

Francis of Assisi, Saint, Italian monk and founder of the Franciscan order (1182?–1226). 263

Franco, Francisco, chief of the Spanish state (1892–1975). 188

Frankenstein (character in novel by Mary Shelley), 118

Freud, Sigmund, Austrian physician and founder of psychoanalysis (1856–1939). 30; his *V work* "was to illumine for *science* the delicate envelope of *soul,*" 237; *bat-angels' cloning* of, and modern *Hells,* 269

friction, 458; 495; see *Resistance; matter; God B*

Frodo (from Tolkien's *The Lord of the Rings*), 218

Frost, Robert, American poet (1874–1963). 26; 547

Frye, Northrop, Canadian literary critic (1912–91). His *Anatomy of Criticism* quoted, 3 (New York: Atheneum, 1969, p. 158); see 85, and *God*

furnace, breakdown in the *Athens* house, 53; in the *Stonington* house, 90–91; *bat-angels* are called "the *Bobs,* the furnace men" by WHA, 131; 433; see *Bezelbob; Bob*

Gabriel, Angel of Fire and Death. 83; with Mich. sat on *God B's* right hand, 120; *God B* turns against him and Mich., because they saw that the *bat-angels* were *antimatter,* 120; his and Mich.'s are "children's names" for the *white* forces, 120; after the *Fall* of the *bat-angels, God B* turned to Gabr. and Mich. and said, "build me a new *Greenhouse,*" 121; trusts JM as a voice to *man,* 122; can speak in *Nature's* forces, 122; is the "shy brother," 295, 296, 310, 314, 316; his *destruction* of the *centaurs,* 295, 316; WHA describes his *music,* 296, 327; 302; WHA says, "*Elias* is the *musical angel Mozart* calls Gabr.," 303; 310; avoids *light,* 314; *fear* repels, 314; *bat-angels* belong to, 314; *00* says he is the "principal Brother," 314; is benevolent, like *God B,* but destroys "wasted talent," 314–15; shoulders the burden of the "other side" of *God B's V work,* 316; describes his destruction of the *centaurs* and the *bat-angels,* 316; is the *shadow* of his father *God B,* 316; is the "forever swinging gate between life and *Heaven,*" 316; is a "neutral *element,*" 316; denied the *colors,* 316; "tracks"

says he "intends to use his *fire* to make the great plain greater," 441 (see *China*); WHA says he "knows what he's up to and (like *time*) will tell," 442; says, "we meet in the vast fast-abandoned complex of *religion*," 443; 444; 445; says the alphabet composes "the new materials for a new faith," 446 (see *language*); the *Five* are his, with *God B's* approval, 447; defines *black* as an hourglass in which sand runs up, 448 (see *time*); 450; 451; says there is no *Hell,* 452; 454; on *sin,* 455; says that *feelings* and *time* are *black* magics, 455; his *atomic* test, 456–57; his description of the creature of the *Chinese* plain, 457–60; on *God B's Cain*-like error, 458; on *language,* 460; on *substance,* 460; fondness for the creature of *Atlantis,* 460; is nuclear commander of the *Greenhouse,* 462 (see *atomic power*); on the *shield* around *man* that shades him from the *angels* and *God B,* 463; his lecture on the *It,* 471, 473–76; on the *moon,* 477; praises JM when he asks his question about the *atom, history,* and *scale,* 478; 479; 480; and *Nature's* fete, 484; WHA praises his "4-D *imagination,*" 491; "at most inheriting his mother's [*Nature's*] one *black* or *resistant gene* as liaison with the *chaotic* forces," 492; and George *Cotzias,* 507; and the *Alpha men,* 511–512; 516; 533; presents Robert *Morse* with his *sense* of taste, 534; 553

Galadriel (from Tolkien's *The Lord of the Rings*), 218

galaxy, galactic pollen, 112 (see *Rose; atomic power*); "our sister the remotest galaxy," 161 (see *elements; Pantheon*); is *atomic power* galactic in origin? 199; *God B* came from a *Pantheon* of galaxies and *gods* as powerful as he, 330; the "pulse of the galactic radio" during *God B's* song, 360; MM refers to the galactic *Pantheon,* 388; and WHA's account of the *Monitor,* 393; *Psyche* describes her and *God B's* descent from the galaxies, 408; 417; "galactic overrun," 417; WHA on "the great fall from the galactic precipice from which *God B* signals back" to the *angels,* 441; Gabr. on *God B's* charter from the galactic councils, 458, 460; 470; 495

Galileo Galilei, Italian scientist and philosopher (1564–1642). One of the *Five,* 193; became a *saint* within his own lifetime, 193; 337 (see *Akhnaton*)

Gandalf (from Tolkien's *The Lord of the Rings*), 218

Gandhi, Indira Nehru, Prime Minister of India (1917–84). 188; 548

Gandhi, Mohandas Karamchand, Hindu nationalist and spiritual leader (1869–1948). M names as one of the *Five,* 164; linked to the *element* of *earth,* 164

Garbo, Greta, Swedish-American actress (1905–90). 69

gardens, 41; and *Spenser,* 61–62; 68; 90; and MM, 101–2, 104, 114, 117, 206, 418; 117; "*God* prefers gardens," 121; "these zodiacal gardens," 121 (see *anchor sites*); 153; 158; *man's* "garden" (*culture; evolution*), 241–42; and the *Muses,* 401, 404; Saint *Agatha's,* 404–5; after *Psyche's* first visit, 411; 455; 469; after *Nature's* fete, M will roam her gardens, 488

gene/genetics, 18–20; and *Temerlin's chimpanzees,* 18; E's paean to the great genetic *god,* 19; DJ and JM's tampering—"had left heredity, *Narcissus* bent above the gene pool," 19–20, 29–30; role of *animals* in *evolution,* 50–53; gene of a chemist added to JM in the *Research Lab,* 145; *God B* held safe in *air* the basic gene structures of *Atlantis,* 185; *Romeo and Juliet* in *Shakespeare's* genes, 191; M says *souls* of those who are not *cloned* are in your genes, 196; heredity and environment are *clonable,* 198; *V work* in *Rimbaud's* genes, 217; *bat-angels* implement *God B's rules* through, 246–47; and *twins,* 341; George *Cotzias* on his research and what JM and DJ have been hearing, 375; *man's* "*memory* tic" regarding *immortality,* 439; 455; 467; Gabr.'s inherited at most one of *Nature's black* or *resistant* genes, 492

Genesis, first book of the Old Testament. "That ancient history" told by the *bat-angels* to the *scribe,* 116; 136; JM reads, 311; see *Adam; myth; scale*

Genghis Khan, Mongol warrior and leader (1162?–1227). 55; 290; 340; see *Plato*

George, see George *Lazaretos*

Germanicus Caesar, nephew and adopted son of Tiberius (15 B.C.–A.D.19). 16

Ghédé, voodoo god of death. 64; 505

Ghirlandaio, Domenico, Florentine painter (1449–94). 305

Gibraltar, British colony on the south-central coast of Spain. 226–27

Gilchrist, Alexander, English biographer and critic (1826–61). His *Life of Blake* cited, 178

Giorgione (Giorgio Barbarelli), Venetian painter (1478?–1511). *La Tempesta,* 76; *X rays* of *La Tempesta,* 83; 468

God, incarnation and withdrawal of a god, 3, 85 (see Northrop *Frye*); E's paean to the great *genetic* god, 19; E tangles with a kind of god near *Santa Fe,* 34; linked by E to *devotion,* 59; *Stevens* on God and the *imagination,* 66; 72; *Jung* on God and the Unconscious, 74; *bat-angels* want JM to make a god of *science,* 113; two gods govern: *God B* and *Chaos,* 113; "the next race will be of gods," 117 (see *Alpha men*); M asks DJ and JM if they believe in a benign God, an idea that has been lately *cloned* into *man,* 137; WHA on the emergence of a *science* god, 137; "the *sun* god sang," 262; *God B* comes out of the *Pantheon* of *galaxies* and gods as powerful as he, 330; JM on literary versions of God, 348; and the *Alpha men,* 456; MM says the *Five* are, 467; 506; see *God Biology; God A*

God A, "the *black* God," 447; Gabr. on "antigod's *antimatter,*" 460; Mich. on "this *antimatter* and its *Monitor* God," 476; see *God Biology*

God Biology (God B), one of the two governing gods (with *Chaos*), 113; and *Mind,* 114; with *Abel* is the positive force within the

atom, 116; 117; Mich. and Gabr. sat on his right hand and held it down, the *bat-angels* waited on his left, 119; turned on Mich. and Gabr., who saw that the *bat-angels* were *antimatter,* 120; after *Fall* of the *bat-angels* he said to them, "out of my sight," and to Mich. and Gabr., "build me a new *Greenhouse,*" 121; *bat-angels* trust him to take them in again, 121; *bat-angels* fell when his handmaidens, Geology and Botany, pulled down the *anchors* of their *crust world,* 125; sent *8002* to *Innocent VI,* 130–31 (see *Faust*); his *Greenhouse* is one among others in the *universe,* 132; *Montezuma* believes that "we race for order under orders to save the *Greenhouse,*" 132; his song referred to but not named, 132, 134 (see 363); his servants put out the flames of the *bat-angels' crust world,* 134; 137; banished the anti-world, 151; WHA wonders if they are prepared for him, 159; *elements* were once at war but signed a truce when he took control, 166; in *Atlantis* gave dominance to the *centaurs,* 167; his first law, which he is revising but still finds useful, *survival* of the most agile, 168 (see 180); after *Fall* of the *crust world* he began to erase all traces of *Atlantis* and the *bat-angels,* 169; the *centaurs* were his creatures, 170; governs all life on *earth,* 170; *bat-angels* offended him when they destroyed the *centaurs'* primitive *immortals,* 170; WHA asks, "is it not that God B believes in us as his third *Eden*?" 171; three is his *number,* 171; he must be the first to understand signals from other worlds, so the *bat-angels* keep them cryptic, 172; M says, "if the place of God is indeed that whirling *light,* it is the source of an unimagined calm," 173 (see *S/O/L/*); riddle of his size, 174; his sense of *man's* limitations, 179; writes new clauses to the *survival* law (there shall be *No Accident; scribe* shall supplant *religion;* and the entire apparatus develop the way to *Paradise*), 180; limits *atomic elements* in *man's* arterial structure, 182; held safe in *air* the basic *gene* structures of *Atlantis,* 185; returned mastery to his electronic creatures, 185 (see *electricity*); 187; M says he is *history, earth,* and the *Greenhouse,* 187; nothing in *Nature* or *man* is unknown to him, 187; *scribe* stands at his elbow, 188; introduced his *religion* to *Akhnaton,* 193; imprinted the *bat-angels* with the *No Accident* formula, 194; and the *Pantheon,* 199; sought to destroy the *centaurs* with forests and was circumvented by the *bat-angels,* 201; will let *man* solve his problems of pollution *population,* 201; M says he peers through his microscope at the swimming planets, 210 (see 212; 216; and *scale*); and the *colors,* 210, 212, 213, 216; *bat-angels* are the strength of his vision, 212; his use of *atomic power,* both benevolent and chastening, 213; JM says he defines himself by "flimflam tautologies," 223; fashioned the *Five,* 223; and the formula 7154, 223; M refers to *Nature* as his favorite slave, 228; his struggle with *Nature,* 228–29; 230; "Sultan Biology," 231 (see Merrill's "The Thousand and Second Night" in *Nights and Days*); M says he is the "humblest of us all," 235; *man* chosen by, 236; *man* is his vehicle, 238; 239; *man* is his chosen ruler, 239, 241–42; his *light* floods the *scribe,* 239; directed the *bat-*

angels to guide *man's evolution,* 241–42; his command to the *bat-angels:* "make *reason,*" 242; sends *man* the idea to create a *reasoned* indirection, 242; allows *Nature* the tool of weather, 244; *bat-angels* implement his *rules,* 246–48; *man* unaware of his grand design, 247–48; Mich. is the chosen messenger of, 250; only *man* receives his main magic, *imaginative power,* 251; and the *Ouija board,* 253; holds the scales of what *man* can and cannot do, 260; M says he holds hand benevolently over *man,* 260–61; his warning to *angels* about *man* ("these are my darlings"), 261; building a *Paradise* for *man* is his work, 261; his lesson to *man* about *fear,* 269 (see *Hell*); *bat-angels'* challenge to make *man* the clone of God, 269; 272; his name is *intelligence,* 276; "is the accumulated *intelligence* in *cells,*" 276; *angels* reside in that *intelligence,* 276; Mich. says, "look into the red eye of your God," 276 (see *sun*); WHA on "the red eye of your God," 287 (see *sun*); WHA on *imagining* him, 287; "sublime structure" of his *cells,* 290; and the mystic union, 291 (see *religion*); Mich. refers to him as "our architect," 293; Mich. says he had "forever dreamed of creating a good company and a friendly place," 293; Mich. says "he had been bested before" and speaks of the "forces arrayed against him . . . the *negatives* . . . *black* suctioning, and he named them *evil,*" 293; creates the *angels,* 293; his *arc* down which the *angels* descended, 293; his "stored *intelligence*" produced the *angels* and life on *earth,* 293–94; after the *angels* fashioned *man,* he said "let him survive," and "it is my own," 294–96; his other children, 294–95; *man* is his heir, 294; *Emmanuel* born as a tear in his eye, 302; *Emmanuel* says Mich. is his most beloved, 302; *Raphael* says it is his will that *man* reduce his *population,* 307; 314; "turns away his face" from "wasted talent," which Gabr. then *destroys,* 314; 315; created Gabr. after he lost hope in his first creature, 316; Gabr. shoulders the "other side" of his *V work,* 316; his *shadow* is Gabr., 316; *Raphael* and *Emmanuel* recall their creation by him, 322; Gabr. says he is "God's scion and nature," 322; Gabr. says he is "the balancer of *Chaos* and creation," 322; his creation of Mich., 322, 326; JM says, "it was the original theme—*Chaos,* Biology, those ruling opposites," 323; *Raphael* calls *man* his darling, 324; *thought* proceeds from his "ceaselessly thinking *Mind,*" 325; told the *angels* to instruct DJ and JM, 325; twice *Chaos* rang down the curtain on his creations, 326–27; Gabr. sits on his right on a *black* throne, 329; WHA on his reaction to Gabr.'s *white* acts of *destruction,* 329; his creation of Gabr., his "darker side," whose nature is in his fist, 330; Gabr. says he comes from a *Pantheon* of *galaxies* and gods as powerful as he, 330; Gabr. and *Emmanuel's* pact to share the *destruction* of his errors/experiments, 334; forced to call Gabr. "to heel!" apparently to keep him from *destroying man,* 335; WHA believes that the *Five* report directly to him, 340; said to Mich., "divide the *time* of *man,*" 343 (see *reflection*); entrusted *man's history* and *evolution* to Gabr., 344; lifted the curse of *immortality* from *man,* 346; and *man's* sleep, 346–47; as "*light*

from elsewhere lifts the harmony to a remote, electrifying key," he speaks for the first time in *C.L.S.,* 347–48; JM on his tone, "wonder . . . distrust," 348; JM on literary versions of God and "how humdrum what he says" next to his creations, 348; WHA on the *angels'* reaction to his first words, "simply cowed," 349 (see 348); WHA and MM did not hear his voice, but saw the words JM wrote, 349; the *angels* are his *senses,* 350–51; Mich. quotes him to Gabr., "it is not done," 350; he has five additional *senses,* 351; "sings, alone, into the universe" (which the *angels* have not heard), 351; 358; 359; the "ripple within ripple on *black* water" before his song, 360; his song in decasyllabics, 360; JM on the ambiguity of his song, 360, 361–62, 362–63; only DJ and JM hear his song, 361, 363; WHA on the ambiguity of his song, 362–63, 365; his song and the *Rose* tradition (*Dante, Blake*), 363 (see 55); 364; WHA's poem about, 365; *Uni* on his law of dignity, 380; 387; Mich. sent the first signals to, 388; has *Emmanuel* seed the *Earth,* 388; WHA says *earth* needs his constant vigil to keep us afloat, 391; WHA on his two-edged gift from the *Pantheon,* the *Monitor,* 392; and the *black* and *white* forces within the *atom* and *matter,* 396–97; George *Cotzias* defines *matter* as "something from nothing," and links this to the essence of *God B,* 396; and the *Muses,* 401, 404; *Psyche* describes her descent with him from the *galaxies,* 408; *Psyche* says she and he are *twins,* 408; *Psyche* refers to him as the "creator of *matter,* the architect," 408; divides the force of *man's* nature with *Psyche,* 408; *Psyche* says he and she are "never at odds" but *man* is born to be torn between them, 409; 416; 417; WHA says they "go out laughing for God's sake," 418; and *Mozart,* 427; *Uni* says his *immortality* was a mixed gift, 429; *light* of his presence during the "No" section of *S.,* 437; George *Cotzias* says *man* is of his genius, 439; WHA on his pact with the *black* forces, 440; WHA on the great *Fall* from the *galactic* precipice from which he signals to the *angels,* 441; 444; 445; the *Five* are Gabr.'s with his approval, 447; "all consciousness was banished round" DJ and JM when they heard his song, 447; and the "*black* God" or *God A,* 447; 449; 452; George *Cotzias* on "God as *Prometheus,*" 453; 454; Gabr. says that *man's* theft of his materials is a *sin,* 455 (see *Prometheus; atom*); Gabr. on his charter from the *galactic* councils, 458, 460; and *friction,* 458; Gabr. on his *Cain*-like error, 458; and the creature of the *Chinese* plain, 458–60; Gabr. says he is of two aspects, 459; and pain, 459; 460; 462; Gabr. on the *shield* around *man* that shades him from God B, 463, 499; Gabr. on his contact with *man,* 463–64; asks for help to bury his first two experiments, 470–71; Gabr. on his commands regarding *man:* "let it *survive,* and let there be *No Accident,*" 473; and the *It,* 476; the *Monitor* trailed him from the halls of his brothers, 476; also called "*ABBA,*" 478; asks JM for a "*V work* giving both pause and hope," 493 (see *Yes and No*); traces an *X* on the board, 493–94 (see *It*); his speech in lesson 10 of "No" in *S.,* 494; 512; reprise of his song at end of

S., 517; Mars is one of his outposts, 526; and Robert *Morse's music,* 529–30

Goethe, Johann Wolfgang von, German poet and dramatist (1749–1832). 292; and the rhyming tags of the prologue to *Faust,* 344; *Faust,* 348; 547; 557

Gollum (from Tolkien's *The Lord of the Rings*), 218

Goncourt, Edmond-Louis-Antoine de and **Jules-Alfred Huot de,** French novelists and historians (respectively 1822–96 and 1830–70). 385

Gopping, see *Simpson*

Götterdämmerung (Wagner), Magic Fire Music, 35; 56; quoted, 62 (act 1, scene 3); see below

Götterdämmerung ("twilight of the *gods*"), what was only hinted in the description of a *patron's* rise through *the nine stages* (10)—the dependence of the other world upon this one—is explained in detail, 56–57; threat of the *loa* to withdraw, and their sense of their own twilight, 58–59; the final lines of *Brünnhilde's* speech on 62 might be translated as "and they shall never wrest love from me though Valhalla's sublime splendor collapse in ruins"; see *Götterdämmerung* (Wagner) above

Gounod, Charles-François, French composer (1818–93). 137

Goya, Francisco Jose de, Spanish artist (1746–1828). 215

Grace, see Grace Zaring *Stone*

Graves, Robert, English poet, novelist, and critic (1895–1985). His *The White Goddess* cited by JM, 152, 254 (see "An Urban Convalesence" in Merrill's *Water Street*); WHA calls "a useful hack," 254; see *homosexuality; sex; plant world*

Greenhouse, once wrecked by uranium fission, 116, 181 (see *atomic power*); "spare the Greenhouse . . . its precious nucleus of *Minds,*" 119; after *Fall* of the *bat-angels, God B* turned to Mich. and Gabr. and said: "build me a new Greenhouse," 121; *Montezuma* believes that "we race for order under orders to save the Greenhouse," 132; *God B's* Greenhouse is one among others in the *universe,* 132; and the *UFOs,* 133; *elements* say that *antimatter* is "magnetized by foreign beacons, *black* hands testing the Greenhouse pane by pane," 161; *antimatter* and *evil,* 162; *earth*'s stages as potential Greenhouse, 166; reference to the "fledgling" Greenhouse, 166; three dimensions of, 171; M refers to the "speed up of the Greenhouse to cover our *anchor* points," 172; MM broods over, 181; "is it *Nature's power* alone that runs it, or *powers* that frighten us in *man*?" 181; and *atomic power,* 181; is it a "sealed envelope"? 181; is everything up to the *12%* (*sun, stars, moon, Nature*), 182; *man's* turning from *Nature* and his *soul* is a threat to it, 182; is *God B,* 187; thinning in a *survival* Greenhouse, 188; confines of, 199; contains the *sun* and its whole system, 199; and the *No Accident clause,* 199; one of the *bat-angels' myths* is that from the *galactic*

Pantheon came *God B* to build his Greenhouse, 199; M says the whole Greenhouse is but a *cell* but all *matter* is part of that *cell,* 210 (see *scale*); 216; *Nature* keeps green, if untidy, 228–29; 359; George *Cotzias* on the *black* presence beyond it, 396–98; WHA on the *black* forces beyond, 440; 441; from the start an act of *Resistance,* 453; Gabr. is the nuclear commander of the Greenhouse, 462 (see *atomic power*); 493

Greuze, Jean-Baptiste, French painter (1725–1805). 305

Grieg, Edvard, Norwegian composer (1843–1907). 206

Grimm, Jakob and **Wilhelm,** German philologists and folklorists (respectively 1785–1863 and 1786–1859). 4; 340

Guelfs, Italian political family and party. 188 (see Dante's *Inferno,* X)

Guggenheim, Marguerite "Peggy," American art collector and patron (1898–1979). 75; 503

Gurdjieff, Georgie Ivanovich, Greco-American mystic and philosopher (1872?–1949). 136

Gymnopédie (Satie), 90; see "Angel" in JM's *Water Street,* and "Santorini: Stopping the Leak" in JM's *Late Settings*

Hammarskjöld, Dag, Swedish diplomat and author (1905–1961). One of the *Five,* 142; *element* is gold, 142; 228

Hans, see Hans *Lodeizen*

Hardy, Thomas, English poet and novelist (1840–1928). 262

Haydn, Franz Joseph, Austrian composer (1732–1809). 18

Heaven, defined by E as "the surround of the living," 59; preparation for a "higher more finished world or Heaven," 59–60; WHA compares to a "new machine," 87, 260; MM dsllusioned with, 101; 104; *appearances* in, 104–5, 116, 117, 118, 152–53; in Heaven, not to be used is *Hell,* 153, 198, 452; Heaven looking down on *time* passing, 164; 256; 258; M says it is "both reality and figment of *imagination,*" 260; M says it is real for each faith, 260 (see *religion*); M expands WHA's definition to "a new machine which makes the dead available to life," 260; M on the *scale* of, "could fit in this cup or be vaster than *earth* itself," 264; 266; 290; Maya *Deren* calls *Erzulie* the "omnisex queen" of, 305 (see *sex*); Gabr. is the "forever swinging gate between life and Heaven," 316; the *Five* are the *senses* of, 337–40 (see *angels*); WHA says that in Heaven "efficiency is welded . . . to beauty as the *soul* is to *survival,*" 345; and the *senses* of *God B,* 351, 353, 358, 470, 473, 489; 356; Mich. on "this Heaven it is given you to win," 358; Robert *Morse* on how *poetry* is read in Heaven, 381–82; 424; M says that it is the fourth dimension, 428; 441; 449; *feeling* and *time* banished from, 455; 465; and the *It,* 475; 490; 491; *Nature* refused to read these lines during her fete, "now let us banish gloomy dreams, for Heaven on *earth* most likely seems," 492; MM says *man* must wean himself of the fatal delusion of all-providing Heaven, 496; 502; generation gap in, 526–

27; 528; the *saint* on *earth* brings Heaven to the *mind,* the *saint* in Heaven, *earth,* 546; JM reads his poem to, 556–60

Heisenberg, Werner, German atomic physicist (1901–76). 554

Hell, in *Heaven* not to be used is Hell, 153, 198, 452; is a legend and therefore part true, 162 (see *myth*); 256; M says "it is here, is boundless," 269; versions in *Dante* and *Homer* needed by "dull *animalistic* lives," 269; enlightened are free of, 269; DJ's is *fear,* 269; JM's is doubt, 269; is the *cave* of *Psyche,* 269; and *man's evolution,* 269; first Hell was "to know that even in *Eden* was danger," 269; in *man's Mind* ("dark country" where "all the *Psyche's* woes were put"), 269; and *Freud,* 269; *bat-angels'* challenge to eliminate, 269; elided in JM's rhyme-scheme, 271; identified by JM in childhood with the German word for bright, 274 (see *light*); WHA describes Gabr.'s *appearance,* 318; 423; and *feelings,* 426; Gabr. says there is no Hell, 452

Hemingway, Ernest, American novelist (1899–1961). 79

Heraclitus, Greek philosopher of the sixth century B.C. Quoted, 60; see *Ouija board; time*

Hermes, Greek god of theft, commerce, invention, and cunning, who served as a messenger for the other gods, and as conductor of the dead to Hades; also a store in Paris and elsewhere. *Teddie's* gold compact, 58; 554; see *Mercury;* Mrs. *Smith*

Hindemith, Paul, German-born American composer (1895–1963). 206; on DJ, 418; at *stage* seven, 418

Hiroshima, city of southwestern Japan destroyed by the first atomic bomb employed in warfare. 55; 139; 183; 186; 194; see *atomic power; power; soul; fire*

history, begins with *Akhnaton,* 180; *God B* is, 187; *man's* history manifests the *bat-angels'* work on his *soul,* 239 (see *scale*); the *sun* and "physical incarnate history," 275; each history was the guidance of the accumulated *intelligence* in *cells,* 276 (see *God B*); of the *cave* dwellers and the lake dwellers, 324–26; *Emmanuel* says, "the gritty history since then (the lake dwellers) is only a wash away from *innocence,*" 326; *God B* entrusted *man's* history and *evolution* to Gabr., 344; and the *Muses,* 400–402; and the *It,* 475; JM's question about the *atom,* history, and *scale,* 478; see *scale; God B; earth*

Hitler, Adolf (Adolf Schicklgruber), Austrian-born Nazi leader (1889–1945). 55; 123; 188; 375; 451; Herr Schicklgruber, 553; see *power*

Hofmannstahl, Hugo von, Austrian poet and dramatist (1874–1929). *Strauss* on his *twin,* 355

Homer, Greek epic poet. Part of an unbroken chain of *scribes,* 121; 179; *cloned* to provide catalog and present his era with a *Pantheon,* 219; the missing name in the list of the prophets, 219; "only one great Western poem was sent intact: Homer," 242 (see *V work*); WHA on, 255; his

version of *Hell* needed by "dull *animalistic* lives," 269; 286; as one of the *Five* his *V work* is the *angels' sense* of hearing, 338; later born as *Mohammed, Mozart,* and an *East German physicist* (whom M identified as *Montezuma*), 338; listens to the *Pantheon,* 338; present at Mich.'s fete, 355; WHA's poem to, "immortal bard, you who created me," 355; 471; 497; WHA's Homeric *densities,* 514; 552

homosexuality, DJ asks, "what part . . . does *sex* play in the whole setup?" 154, 205–6; is a development of the last 4,000 years, 156; encourages such *Mind* values as produce *poetry* and *music,* 156; "is the peacock not also somewhat Athenian?" 158 (see Marius *Bewley*); MM sometimes wishes she had been "you know what," 190; 216; WHA says, "we remain . . . in a male world," 254; "the tale we're hearing is nothing if not male," 304; Marius *Bewley* says *Plato* and WHA are the chairpersons of *Heaven's* "Athenian Club," 305; MM on, 372, 468; DJ said to MM, "the Mediterranean makes such heavy prose of being male," 468; see *childlessness*

hourglass, see *time; It*

Hubbell, see Hubbell *Pierce*

Hugo, Victor-Marie, French poet, novelist, and dramatist (1802–85). 143–44 (volume 9 of the *Editions Chronologiques* contains his occult transcripts); and *sex,* 154; 178; 524; 547

hypnosis, DJ under hypnosis sees E, 26–27; Leo *Cade* under hypnosis sees *Eros,* 47

ideas, "no idea violates," 14 (see *Eliot; James);* 108; 194; and Mich.'s *appearance,* 286; 296; Mich.'s first text in *S.* is, "the most *innocent* of ideas is the idea that *innocence* is *destroyed* by ideas," 321–22; Gabr. asks, "What stands when all ideas lie ruined? Is *innocence* forming a new idea?" 321; WHA sees *Atlantis* as idea, first pasture to *innocence* and raped by it, 322; Gabr. proposes, "*Chaos: innocence*? creation: idea?" 322; Mich. asks of the *centaurs,* "is among them the perfection of idea gone awry?" 323; DJ says, "if idea's *destructive,* then *Chaos* would run things, that's unthinkable," 323; *paintings* of the *cave* dwellers ("those *innocent* images lit by an idea of *man* knowing himself"), 324 (see 385–86); *cave* dwellers received this "first shocking idea: *fear* of each other," 325; Mich. says he must bear the burden of, 326; *caves* identified with "*light*-shedding ideas," 333; Mich.'s two natures are ideas (identified with *light*) and *reflection* (identified with the "turning over" of ideas), 343; Gabr.'s *thought* is in opposition to Mich.'s ideas, 344, 347, 426; *God B* calls Gabr. "the thinker on ideas," 347 (see *thought*); Mich. says of the lessons in "Yes" of *S.,* "for will we not have *innocently* exposed ourselves to ideas?" 351; and *Strauss's* "Fifth Last Song"—"BDEA . . . I come to Be, is the idea," 357; and painting, 385; JM's "chronic shyness" vis-à-vis, 419; Gabr.'s *thought destroys* ideas, 426; WHA says, "humankind has set idea to *innocence,*" 438 (see 441, 442);

Gabr. says, "of all *destructive* ideas the most *destructive* is the idea of *destruction,*" 438; *Psyche* says, "the most *destructive* of all ideas is that *feeling* sets it right," 438; the *black* forces zero in on, 440; 442; idea of *destruction* and the *atomic black,* 452; 470; 471; and *Uni* (MM says "I now step off our second and *innocent* idea"), 486; 494

"Ignoto," meaning "unknown." 482

imagination, *Stevens* on, 66; WHA says, "if MM and I imagine you, you us, and where the powers crisscross we all imagine *741* and then transform him, when the time comes, will our knitted brows produce white wings?" 159; M is "an impulse only here at the crossroads of our four affections," 173; M says, "make of me the process somewhere operating between tree and pulp and page and poem," 173; and the *S/O/L,* 173–74, 260; and *lenses,* 174; *God B's* "main magic," 251; *fear* and the "sacred imagination," 269; when freed from *Hell,* imagination finds drugs, 269; WHA refers to Mich. as "a monument to civilized imagination" 286; WHA on imagining *God,* 287; MM defines as "that standing back at the very elbow of *intelligence,*" and it is often identified with distancing, 293 (see 287, 295, 326); 439; 447; Gabr.'s "4-D imagination," 491; see *S/O/L; appearances; belief*

immortality, and *Faust,* 130–31, 194; and the *Five* immortals, 131; *Mind* is deathless, 161; *centaurs'* first grave problem was their immortality, 167; when the *centaurs* wished to destroy their primitive immortals, they charged the *bat-angels* to use an *atomic* blast, 168; when *bat-angels* destroyed the immortals they offended *God B,* 170; is a request that all mortals make, says *oo,* 314; the "*eternal bureaucrat,*" 315; *souls* of the *Five* "pass through the flames and live," 315; *God B* lifted the "curse of immortality" from *man,* 346; *Psyche* on, 409–10; and George *Cotzias's* theorem, 411–12; *Uni* terms it a mixed gift, 429; George *Cotzias's* lecture on, 438–39; and *Atlantis,* 439 (see 429); *man's* "*memory* tic" regarding immortality, 439; and the *Alpha men,* 439; the *black* and "lost" immortality, 450; of the creature of the *Chinese* plain, 459; 511–12; see *eternity; time; Paradise*

infinity, and the *stripping* process, 209, 211; is the square of the four *colors,* 210; M says that the *12%* will take them to, 210; "ooooo," 211; *bat-angels* are the force of *oo,* 212; *Pythagoras* on, 372; has walls, 372; see *oo*

innocence, 9; 48; 54; 103; Mary *Jackson* says, "back to innocence," 106; Chester *Kallman* notes "it has a genius for getting lost," 106; "*Faust* was innocent," 131 (see *Innocent VI*); 212; Mich.'s first text in *S.,* "the most innocent of *ideas* is the *idea* that innocence is *destroyed* by *ideas,*" 321–22; MM suggests that God B has not set much store by innocence, 321; MM points to the *centaurs* as innocent, yet they were destroyed, 322; WHA sees *Atlantis* as *idea,* first pasture to innocence and raped by it, 322; Gabr. proposes, "*Chaos:* innocence? creation: *idea?*" 322; *paintings* of the *cave* dwellers ("those innocent images lit by an *idea* of *man* knowing

himself"), 324 (see 385–86); *Raphael* says the *angels* are "innocence in the face of *man's* endeavors," 325; the *cave* dwellers retreat to *water* and innocence, 326; *earth* (*Raphael*) and *water* (*Emmanuel*) are innocent *Nature,* 326; MM says to Gabr. of death, "innocence is our nature, and we innocently think it for the best," 329; Gabr. on the blankest, most utter innocence of the *suicide,* 333; WHA says to Gabr., "belief in life is purest innocence," 333; the innocence of *Emmanuel* and Gabr. just after they were created, 334; Mich. says of the lessons in "Yes" of *S.,* "for will we not have innocently exposed ourselves to *ideas*?" 351; JM says, "as with . . . innocence, do things that fade especially make sense?" 370; WHA says, "humankind has set *idea* to innocence," 438 (see 441, 442); and *Nature's* fete, 484; and *Uni* (MM says "I now step off our second and innocent *idea*"), 486; "Good Doctor, you've brought in no scents," 491; 494

Innocent VI, Pope, Etienne Aubert (b.? d. 1362). And the *Faust* legend, 130–31; 194

intelligence, 136; 179; *lights* of the *bat-angels'* intelligence plays over the *Ouija board,* 253; and *oo,* 266; and the *sun,* 275–76; accumulated energy in *cells* became an ancient and mortal intelligence, 276; each *history* was the *guidance* of, 276; formed *man,* 276; is *God B's* name, 276; *God B* is the accumulated intelligence in the cells, 276; *angels* have found DJ and JM intelligent, 276; intelligence "encompassing the energies of a *universe* of borning and exploding worlds" settled for *earth,* 292; Mich. asks, "what is this in fact?" 293; "standing back at the very elbow of intelligence" is *imagination,* 293; "stored intelligence" of *God B* produces the *angels* and life on *earth,* 294; *time* for the *angels* described as "lengths which were only the intelligence and its workings," 294; Mich. says, "how patient true intelligence," 295; Mich. says it "is the *S/O/L,*" 296; Mich. says to DJ and JM, "have no *fears* intelligent ones," 301; 512

Isabel, see Isabel *Morse*

Issa Kobayashi, Japanese poet (1763–1828). Quoted, 60 (*Zen in English Literature,* New York: E. P. Dutton, 1960, p. 390); 88; 547; see *fire*

It, 471; 472; Gabr.'s lecture on, 474–76; and *man,* 474–75; and *history,* 475, 478; and *time,* 475–76; and *atomic* waste, 475; and *antimatter,* 476; and the *Monitor* and *God B,* 476; Mich. says, "accidents have begun," 476; and the X that *God B* traces on the *Ouija board,* 493–94; and *God B's* speech in lesson 10 of "No" in *S.,* 494; see *Resistance; black; white; God B; Monitor*

Ito, Teiji, composer for the theater and dance, husband of Maya Deren (1935–82). 64; 304–5

Jackson, David, fiction writer, painter, and in *C.L.S.* the "hand." (b. 1922). 5; 6; *representative* of John *Clay,* 11; 15; confuses Jennifer *West* with Virginia *West,* 19–20; and *genetic* tampering, 20; 22; previous lives,

24; one, two, or three more lives, 24; under *hypnosis* sees E, 26–27; trust in *nature,* 26; 29; 30; 31; purchases a white sapphire for his mother, 37 (see *mirrors*); life with JM in 1957 and in 1974, 40–41; must cope with his dying parents, 41; his life with JM compared to a reflecting garden globe, 41–42 (see *mirrors*); 53; 57; 70; 72; hand pressed to the board and hurt, 73 (see *men before mankind*); 88; 91; carries the *mirror* that injures him, 98, 163; his parents' deaths, 99–100, 102–4, 105; is the psychic one, 107, 142; cannot lift his hand from the board, 108; his operation, 111, 149, 163, 176, 192, 204 (see *mirrors*); 112; is the "pen" of the *bat-angels,* 117; is *Nature,* 117, 159; reads *The Lives of the Cell,* 118; 121; MM counsels him on his *fear* of the *bat-angels,* 128; 134; 135; 137; and the *Jew,* 138; his *elements* are silver and tin, 142 (see 159); his basic formula, 143 (see *number*); guided by 741.1, 143–44, 218; will attain *stage* four, 144; dreams of his parents, 149; E explains his dream, 150–51; asks "what part . . . does *sex* play in this whole set-up?" 154; 157; senses what M means by *Athenian,* 158 (see *Bewley; homosexuality*); in the union of *elements* he is the shaping hand of *Nature,* 159; will go to *Boston* for tests, 176; 178; his first A+ from M, 185; second A+, 188; his interest in the real world, 188; *No Accident clause* and his meeting with JM, and his parents, 194–95; his dream of the *atom's* heart under anaesthesia, 198, 204, 206–7; his musical education, 206; M says his hand is a magic wand, 211; his hand again pressed flat against the board, 213; his *colors* are blue and golden brown, 216; *Yeats* moves his hand, 217–19, 424, 474, 481, 486; depressed that the lessons shut them off from living, 217; a cyst on his palm, 220; 231; 240; 243–44; 248; "looking for loopholes?" 251; his "long-standing experience with" JM, 253; 257; 260; his *Hell* is *fear,* 269; black *dog* recognizes him, 272; 285; 287; 289; 299; 300; guesses that WHA and MM will join the *elements,* 303; his tears after *Raphael's* first speech, 307; 312; 315; 317; 318; 321; says of Mich's first text in *S.,* "if *idea's destructive,* then *Chaos* would run things, that's unthinkable," 323; Mich. says he has a friend in DJ, 323; says that he "felt like a freshman in a graduate seminar," during lesson one of *S.,* 324; 326; 327; on MM's *suicide,* 335–36; questions the *language* of the elegy ("or lies"), 335 (see *poetry*); 349; 351; his and JM's twenty-fifth anniversary, 352–59; on being touched during Mich.'s fete, 358; says, "it's almost as if we were the dead and signaling to dear ones in the world," 361 (see 505); his dread of Gabr., 362; 371; 372; 373; on *Uni,* 380, 382; on describing a chair without alluding to its use, 406 (see *language*); 409; 412; 413; 415; on the "old frightfulness of Gabr.," 417; *Hindemith* on, 418; suggests that WHA is *Plato,* 420; *Yeats* and his hand, 424, 474, 481, 486; "feels dumb" during the talks, 424; 425; and life with MM, 426; 430; 441; 446; 451; 453; his pulled tooth, 457; 462; 464; 465; said to MM "the Mediterranean makes such heavy prose of being male," 468 (see *sex; homosexuality*); 467; says that furnishing the *scribe* with living

room is a thankless task, 473; 474; his question on the *UFOs,* 477; his question on the *Ouija board,* 478; his question on MM's *X ray* therapy, 479; his tears for MM, 480; 481; *Yeats* comes out of his hand during *Nature's* fete, 486; 492; on the changes in Robert *Morse,* 499; his face goes white during Maya *Deren's* film in *Venice* ("We are the ghosts, hers the ongoing party"), 505 (see 361); "happy ending?" 506; *S.* concludes on his fifty-fifth birthday, 508; 512; 514; his *Arcadian painting,* 523, 532; 524; 525; 529; 538; 539; 547; E on how he approached DJ and JM, 550–56; "brighteyed (but look how wrinkled)," 560

Jackson, George Lewis "Matt," father of DJ (1886–1976 [*sic*]). 22; visits *Stonington,* 40; life with Mary, 40, 88; comes to *Athens,* 99; his death, 99–100, 102–3; praised by JM, 105; his life with Mary, 106; "making strides," 107–8; on those *souls* who are "not special," 108; reborn in Iraq, 139; DJ dreams of, 149; E explains DJ's dream, 150–51; *No Accident clause* and, 195; 201; 335; see Matt *Prentiss*

Jackson, Mary Fogelsong, mother of DJ (1890–1976 [*sic*]). 12; *representative* of Ayako *Watanabe,* 12; model for Lucy *Prentiss* in JM's lost *novel,* 12; as a Sicilian child narrowly missed sainthood, 22; praised by her *patron,* 22; visits *Stonington,* 40; life with Matt *Jackson,* 40, 88; comes to *Athens,* 99; her death, 99–100, 102–4; DJ and JM try to "help her through customs," 100; taken up by Marius *Bewley,* 103; MM loans her voice to her, 104; praised by MM, 104; her children from past lives, 104–5; on *appearances* in *Heaven,* 105; refers to *innocence,* 106; reborn in Iceland, 107; 108; DJ dreams of, 149; E explains DJ's dream, 150–51; *No Accident clause* and, 195; 335; 353

James, Henry, American-born British novelist (1843–1916). "Past master of clauses," 14; quibble involving his surname, *Maisie,* JM's Christian name, and *What Maisie Knew,* 51; 399

Japan, ancient history of, 139; and *plant souls,* 151–52

Jean Santeuil (Proust), epigraph to *S.* (Paris: Librairie Gallimard, 1952, vol. 1, p. 315); see *Proust; mirrors*

Jerusalem, capital of ancient and modern Israel. One of the *anchor sites,* 121

Jew, the Jew is chosen, 123; *angels* spoke to the transplanted Jews, sentient life was in the seed of the Jew, and from this came all races, 133; *density* in *man* par excellence, 138; not "Jew" in any ethnic sense, 138; 139; 141; is the uranium *element* in life, 142; is a formula, 144 (see *language; number*); *bat-angels* added the "humus" of the Jew to JM in their *Research Lab,* 145; 183; competitive *element* is an original Jew *density,* 193; *number* of, 230; richest in *density,* 243; writes *Bible,* 243; *Mohammed* on, 449; see *density*

Joanna, character in JM's lost novel. 13; E's opinion of, 13; flying through a storm carrying a gift-wrapped *Ouija board,* 33–35; and smok-

ing, 33, 35, and 67 (see *fire*); and JM's stepmother, 35; relationship with *Sergei,* 35; described by reference to *Jung* on the destructive anima, 35; identified with the parched landscape of New Mexico, 35; 47–48; 66; at the *Ouija board* with *Sergei,* 67; 70; "is she the last gasp of my dragon?" 84; and JM's mother (Hellen Ingram *Plummer*), 84

Job, in Bible, upright man whose faith in God survived the test of repeated calamaties. 54

Johannesburg, city in the Republic of South Africa. 182; 197; 271–72

John Paul I, Pope, Albino Luciani (1912–78). 548

John XXIII, Pope, Angelo Giuseppe Roncalli (1881–1963). Called "apostate" on birth control, 123 (see *population*)

Joselito, representative of Hans Lodeizen. 12; 20; born to Virginia *West,* 29

Josquin des Pres, French composer (c.1440–1521). 529

Joyce, James, Irish novelist (1882–1941). *Finnegans Wake,* 83

Judas, in New Testament, one of the twelve Apostles and betrayer of Jesus. And the *It,* 476

Jung, Carl Gustav, Swiss psychologist (1875–1961). 4; *Joanna* described by reference to the destructive anima, 35; on *God* and the Unconscious, 74 (see 66); 229; see *belief*

Juno, Roman goddess, wife and sister of Jupiter, patroness of marriage and the well-being of women. hefbird (a peacock), 298 (see *Mirabell*)

Juvenal, Roman satirist (A.D. 60?–140?). 558

Kafka, Franz, Austrian writer (1883–1924). 29; identified by E as a perfected *soul* who has returned from *stage* nine, 59

Kahn, Otto, American banker and patron of the arts (1867–1934). 55

Kallman, Chester Simon, American poet (1921–75). And *The Rake's Progress,* 81, 106, 481; 128; 134; dies, 101; on his life in the other world, 106; on WHA, 106; on *innocence,* 106; and the *Jew,* 138; on *Plato,* 158; to be reborn in *Johannesburg,* 181–82; M describes his new life, 183; his "The African Ambassador" cited, 184; speaks of his new life ("fancy a nice Jewish Ms. like me . . . "), 184; on his future life, 197–98, 271–72; with *Luca,* 197, 205, 212, 235, 271–72; 240; 252; 271–72; WHA says, "we were spared our feelings" when he returned to *earth,* 289; 303; 419; WHA recalls opening night of *The Rake's Progress,* 481; 485; 507; 525

Kalstone, David, American literary critic and teacher. (1932–86). Representative of *Luca,* 124; 500; 502

Kandinsky, Wassily, Russian painter (1866–1944). 69

Keats, John, English poet (1795–1821). 61; 89; 299; 331

The King and the Corpse (Zimmer), quoted, 62 (Princeton: Bollingen Series, 1971, pp. 4–5); see *language*

"Kleo," see Kyria *Clio*

Koran, sacred text of Islam. 242–43

Kuan Yin, in Chinese Buddhism, the bodhisattva of infinite compassion and mercy. 64

Lab, see *Research Lab*

Laduman, M names as one of the *Five,* 131

La Fontaine, Jean, French poet and fabulist (1621–95). 140

Lalique, René, French jeweler (1860–1945). 203

language, *Miranda's* "happy sign," 19–20; *Ouija board* as a symbol system, 31; Heinrich *Zimmer* on evoking fresh speech from "the powers," 62; JM on "language of *science,*" 110 (see *design*); *bat-angels* on their use of, 113, 114, 117, 119, 120, 121–22, 144, 146–47, 149–50; words are one of the tools of the *bat-angels,* 114; JM is identified with, 117; is *man's pyramid* and life raft, 118–19; JM is urged to use it by the *bat-angels,* 118; words cannot describe the frantic action of the *atom,* 120; *bat-angels* are "hoping against hope *man* will love his *Mind* and language," 121; WHA praises the language of the *bat-angels,* while JM has his doubts about it, 135–36; no language in the *Research Lab,* only formulas, 140 (see *number*); *bat-angels* tap *memory* and word-banks in DJ and JM, 140, 237, 262; DJ is among the "language users," 142; *scribe's* job is to speed acceptance of the *Five's* work, 143; words like *soul, Jew, Mind,* etc. mean formulas governing human life, 144 (see *number*); *bat-angels* frequently employ "partial fictions," 145; *bat-angels'* use of *metaphor,* 146, 149–50, 173–74, 216; and *Mind,* 156; names of The *five* are "formulas made word," 223, 230 (see *number*); the *atom* and the *metaphors* of the *bat-angels,* 224; *metaphor* is the ritual of *reason,* 239; is the revealed monotheism of today, 239; early *man* develops, 241–42; needs the *scribe,* 242; WHA on language as the poet's church, 252; Robert *Morse* on the *bat-angels'* jargon, 256; WHA on *Arcadia* ("to dwell among greenwood perspectives of the mother tongue"), 262; *bat-angels'* files of, 264; *number* is M's "mother tongue," 267; JM on "the quaint idiom" that slips to his tongue, 274; WHA says describing Mich. "requires something more than language," 286; M complemented on his mastery of the "Fem Lib idiom," 288; Mich. explains what his "soft words" mean "in fact," 293 (see *myth*); JM will make the first word of each book of *M.* its number in a different language, 311; language and the elegy, 312, 335, 376; JM on the "limpid bel canto" phrases of the *angels'* speeches, 331; the contradictory names and formulas of the *Five,* 341 (see *number*); *biblical* names and the *Five,* 341; WHA on Mich.'s "wordless splendors," 345; JM on catching the "full verve" of the *angel's* talk by means of the "unmeasurable King James inflections," 346; Mich. speaks of "the *Mind* driven by word to

mine meaning," 346; JM on how "humdrum" what *God B* says next to his "word" or creations, 348; WHA on the tones of *God B's* song, 363; and the *elements* in "Samos," 370; *Pythagoras* on the *bat-angels'* reduction of formulas to words, 377 (see *number*); MM on the language of *plants,* 388–89; MM on the language of her lecture, 389–90; DJ on describing a chair without alluding to its use, 406; *angels* ask WHA and MM to prepare a human language they can use, 414; WHA on the language and style of the *angels,* 414 (see *design*); the "wholly human instrument," 414; JM says, "maddening the way everything merges and reflects," 415 (see *design*); WHA on the teaching style of the *angels,* 420; language of *religion* is "compost . . . action gone to seed, buried in idiom," 425; 437; Gabr. calls the alphabet "the new materials for a new faith," 446; JM on its misleading apparatus, 453; JM's "Bismillah" sonnet, 454; Gabr. says, "the particular fails to explain its working," 460; Gabr. on how *God B* speaks, 460; JM on the ideogram of the *It,* 474; see *poetry*

Laura, subject of Petrarch's love lyrics, traditionally Laura de Nous of Avignon (d. 1348). And MM, 354; see *Petrarch*

laws (God B's), see *rules*

Lazaretos, George, Greek friend of DJ and JM's (b. 1942). 432

lenses, the old man in Geneva's bifocals, 38; 40; syntax reversing her binoculars, 82; "no metrical lens," 85; at *Avebury,* 112; "the calm at the *S/O/L/* is (m) that slow motion which allows the dazzled onlooker his vision of the race," 173; and the *imagination,* 174; "central" to *M.,* 80; see *mirrors; negatives; X rays; design; scale*

Leo, see Leo *Cade*

Lesbia, from the poetry of Catullus. 299

Li, Po, Chinese poet (701–62). 33

Liambey, Helene ("Nelly"), Greek friend of DJ and JM's (b. 1915). His party for WHA, 134; 432

Das Lied von der Erde (Mahler), 24; see *Mahler*

light, one of the tools of the *bat-angels,* 114; *bat-angels* say they are DJ and JM's light, 127; and *Dante's* vision of the *atom,* 132; *antiworld* is without, 150; "*Mind* in its pure form is a non-*sexual* passion or a unisexual one, producing only light," 156, 215–16; M says, "we shall bathe (the lessons) in light," 157; M says, "before we board the flight to the pin of light," 159; M says, "if the place of *God (B)* is indeed that whirling light, it is the source of an unimagined calm," 173 (see *S/O/L*); calm at the *S/O/L* is "that slow motion which alone allows the dazzled onlooker his vision of the race," 173 (see *lenses*); speed of light, *time,* and radiation, 185 (see *atomic power*); and the *colors,* 215–16, 230; 227; *Nature* would fail without, 230; 234; 236; rings through *science, music, poetry,* 239; *God B's* floods the *scribe,* 239; 241; lights of the *bat-angels' intelligence* plays over the

for JM, 24; in trouble because of his meddling, 29; (see *genetics*); his silhouette, 38, 61; promoted, now above E, 54; 72; 128; 206; his unfinished *V work* given to JM, 220–21; his poem for JM in *Het Innerlijk Behang* quoted, 221; will remain in the *bureaucracy,* 221; JM wonders if he is "the key this opus began and will end in," 221; praises *M.,* 300; 371; 503; 547; 559; see *Spring Sonata; scribe; V work*

Lorenz, Konrad, Austrian psychologist (b. 1903). 51

Los Alamos, town in New Mexico where first atomic bomb was developed. Research near, 33; see JM; *atomic power*

loss, JM's chronicles of loss and love, 176; of highly *cloned souls* of *atomic* researchers, 185, 186; M says, "these unaccountable losses are somewhere a gain, but where?" 186; JM and DJ debate the *language* of elegy, 335–36 (see *poetry*); JM on "the buffeting of losses which we see . . . as gains," 376 (see *language*); *Pythagoras* on *Psyche* and, 377; of the *centaurs,* 379; JM on losing WHA, MM, and George *Cotzias,* 510; "such loss turns to profit," 534; see *stripping process*

Louis XIV, King of France (1638–1715). 292

Louis XV, King of France (1710–74). 381

Louros, Nikolas, MM's doctor, 127

love, see *feelings*

Lowell, Robert, American poet (1917–77). Dies, 508–9; 547

Luca ("La Beata Luca Spionari"), patron to David *Kalstone,* 124; cult in Milan, 124; with Chester *Kallman,* 197, 205, 212, 235, 271–72; E's story about, 234–35; and the other *saints,* 260; has his niche among the *patrons,* 260; 271–72; *Plato* said to have taken up, 291; Marius *Bewley* on, 305; 383; falls for *Nabokov,* 425; 501; 503; and Saint *Agatha,* 525; 543; 546; 549; see *saints*

Lucifer, "*thought's* pure Lucifer," 469 (see Gabr.); see *devils*

Lucy, see Lucy *Prentiss,* and then Mary *Jackson*

Lucy, Saint, Sicilian martyr (d. 304?). Maya *Deren* works for, 64; 102

Lurie, Alison, American novelist (b. 1926). 87

"Lycidas" (Milton), 472–73; see *Milton; myth*

(m), often used to signal the presence of a *metaphor;* see 173

machines, furnaces, 9, 53, 90–91, 131; WHA defines *Heaven* as "a new machine," 87; 182–183; 194; M expands WHA's definition of *Heaven* ("a new machine that makes the dead available to the living"), 260; WHA on, 345

Mademoiselle (Lilla Fanning Howard), 300; see Merrill's "Lost in Translation" in *Divine Comedies*

Maeterlinck, Maurice, Belgian poet and dramatist (1862–1949). 361

Magowan, Doris Merrill, JM's sister (b. 1914), 141; 298; 421–22; 509

Magowan, Robin, American poet and editor, JM's nephew. (b. 1936). 515

Mahler, Gustav, Bohemian-born Austrian composer (1860–1911). *Das Lied von der Erde,* 24; 301

Maisie, DJ and JM's cat. 23; 26; 40; dies in Greece, 51; quibble involving her name, Henry James's surname, *What Maisie Knew,* and JM's Christian name, 51; 196; see "Maisie" in JM's *Nights and Days*

Malin Nat-og-Dog, Miss, (from Dinesen's "The Deluge at Noderney," in *Seven Gothic Tales*), 70; see Baroness Karen *Blixen*

Mallarmé, Stéphane, French poet (1842–98). 57; 461; 547; 557; see *power*

man, emerged from the cooling sea, 116; his measure is ten, 127 (see *number*); idea of a benign *god* has lately been *cloned* into him, 137; *Mind* coeval with, 156; faith in the *number* three, 171; part *feelings* and manners play in his life, 172; M says, "to our eyes, these ethical rights and wrongs are so many blanks in (his) canvas," 173 (see *religion*); and *time,* 176; a mystery to the *bat-angels,* 177; *God B's* sense of his limitations, 179; *evolution* of, 179–80, 241–42, 269; *electrically* charged, 182, 199; *atomic* power and his arterial structure, 182; turned from *Nature* and his *soul,* 182; *atom* cannot be his *natural* friend, 182, 199; is the master of his fate, 182; plutonium is the chief link between the *bat-angels* and man, 185; nothing in him is unknown to *God B,* 187 (see *No Accident clause*); *God B's religion:* one god in man's image, 193; *God B* sees he is ripe for the *Research Lab,* 194; WHA asks if belief in a life wholly out of his hands is unnatural to him, 198; mortality allows for the divine translation, 200; forests as a metaphor for his destructive tendencies, 201 (see *plant world*); M predicts that in three decades he will solve problems of pollution and *population,* 201–2; his *power* lies in *Resistance,* 202; taking of *atomic power* a "*Promethean* outrage," 213; uses *science* to prolong *Nature's* span, 228; unknowingly savages *Nature,* 229; chosen by *God B,* 236; *bat-angels* slip first *soul* into an ape fetus, 236; his *electrical* formulas, 238; is *God B's* vehicle and chosen ruler, 238, 239; his *body* or *Psyche,* 238–39; his *history* manifests the *bat-angels' soul* work, 239 (see *scale*); *reason* will *light* his house, 239, 242; *God B* directs the *bat-angels* to guide his *evolution,* 241–42; his *Mind, culture, language, music,* 241–42; any imbalance in *population* is due to, 245; alone receives *God B's* main magic, *imaginative power,* 251; *God B* holds the scales of what he can and cannot do, 260; *God B's* warning to the *angels* about ("these are my darlings"), 261; building a *Paradise* for is *God B's* work, 261; and *Hell,* 269; "child of *Nature,*" 269; *bat-angels'* challenge is to make him the *clone* of *God B,* 269; impulses of the *universe* were as steady as his pulse, 275 (see *scale*); a species of the *sun's* making, 275–76; accumulated

intelligence in the *cells* formed him, 276 (see *light; God B*); WHA on his *imagining* of *God,* 287; *cells* of, 290; Mich. describes his creation, 294–95; is "the heir" of *God B,* 294; is the image of the *angels,* 294; *God B* said he "must struggle to gain his inheritance," 295; Mich. asks, "was *God B* putting a distance between himself and his creature?" 295 (see *imagination*); *Raphael* flings a spark of energy into his head, and *God B,* seeing a new *light* there said, "it is my own," 295–96; *Raphael* is in him, as his rib, 306; *Raphael* says that it is *God B's* will that man control his *population,* 307, 310; and the *Alpha men evolving* from, 308 (see 177); his request for *immortality,* 314–15; *history* of the *cave* dwellers and the lake dwellers, 324–26; *paintings* of the *cave* dwellers, "*innocent* images lit by an *idea* of man knowing himself," 324; *Raphael's cave* and his cranium, 325 (see *scale*); *angels* say they are *innocence* in the face of man's endeavors, 325; Mich. is man's servant, 326 (see *sun*); DJ and JM are afraid that they will hear that he is doomed, 327; WHA's "spare our world" speech, 328–29; MM says "*innocence* is our nature," 329; Gabr. says that Mich. heaps pride and ambition on man when he should "slap his cheek," 330; the *evolution* of his *mind,* 332; Gabr. learns about man from the *innocence* of the *suicide,* 333; WHA says his "belief in life is purest *innocence,*" 333; *God B* seems to prevent Gabr. from *destroying,* 335; *Plato,* as one of the *Five,* made sense of man's need for his *Mind,* 339–40; the *angels* identify the effects of their duties and natures on, 342–44, 346–47; his *history* and *evolution* was entrusted to Gabr. by *God B,* 344; WHA says that the powers of the *angels* are in man quite as much as over, 345; *God B* lifted his cures of *immortality* from, 346; Gabr. is "the restless urger-on of man's *Mind,*" 347; his *electrical* nature and the *centaurs,* 380; WHA asks Gabr., "are we yours?" 393; *black* and *white* forces in his *soul,* 396; and the *Muses,* 400–404; *Psyche* says, "we meet to study the *Mind* of man," 407; *Psyche* and *God B* divide the force of his nature between them, 408; *Psyche* takes command of his *Resistance,* 408; born to be torn between *Psyche* and *God B,* 409; *Psyche* says man "nearly rivals us," 409 (see *evolution*); *Psyche* says that she is "all for man," 409; and George *Cotzias's* theorem, 411–12; WHA says, "humankind has set *idea* to *innocence,*" 438; his *memory* tic and *immortality,* 439; George *Cotzias* says man is of *God B's* genius, 439; George *Cotzias* says *man* is in love with even his short, brutish life, 439; 441; the *idea* of *destruction* is in him, 453; Gabr. on his theft of *God B's* materials, 453, 455 (see 213); 460; Gabr. on the *shield* around man that shades him from the *angels* and *God B,* 463; *God B's* contact with, 463–64; MM says the *Five* are so often man, 467; Gabr. on man's creation, 473; and the *It,* 473–76; in man's life, the *It* is the "dull-witted, the mob, the idiot in power, the purely blank of *Mind,*" 476; at the conclusion of her fete, *Nature* says, "let me cry a last resounding *Yes* to man," 489 (see 492); *Nature's masque* focused on man, 491; in *God B's* speech in the "No" section of *S.*, 494; MM says he must

wean himself of the fatal delusion of an all-providing *Heaven,* 496; the screen between him and *God B,* 499 (see *shield;* 463); and the *Alpha men,* 511–12

man in sarong, bows to DJ and JM, 40–41; 68; see *Markovich; time*

Mann, Thomas, German novelist (1875–1955). 3; *Tadzio,* 47

manners, 19; 130; 155; 172; 224; 276; 383 (see *feelings*)

Maria, see Maria Demertzi *Mitsotáki*

Marius, see Marius *Bewley*

Markovich, Sergei, character in JM's lost novel. 34; relationship with *Joanna,* 35; 47; 49; at the *Ouija board* with *Joanna,* 67; 68; 70–71; JM imitates, 311; see JM; *man in sarong*

The Marriage of Figaro (Mozart), 301; see *Mozart*

Mars (the planet), 200

Marschallin, the (from Strauss's *Der Rosenkavalier*), 146

Marsyas, in Greek mythology, the Phrygian sailor who challenged Apollo to a musical duel. 473; 538; see "Marsyas" in JM's *The Country of a Thousand Years of Peace*

Marvell, Andrew, English poet and politician (1621–78). 152; Robert *Morse* on, 381; on empires, 381; on *poetry* and "the line," 381; 547

Mary, see Mary F. *Jackson*

Mary, the Virgin mother of Jesus, 64; 103

masque, WHA refers to DJ's dream of the four *colors* as a masque, 207; and the *stripping process,* 209, 211; 214; and "these funny verses," 248; WHA's poem opens the "minimasque," 259; *facts* and the "antimasque," 263; "another mask" says E, in reference to the approach of Mich., 271; 285; 287; "mastermasque" of *OO* and Mich., 297; and *Nature's* fete, 491; *Nature* compares life to, 512; readers of *CLS* may wish to consult Stephen Orgel's *The Jonsonian Masque*

Massenet, Jules, French composer (1842–1912). *Thaïs,* 312

Matt, see Matt *Jackson* or Matt *Prentiss*

matter, "the superfluous matter elided," 86; *Urania's* "what's matter," 111; *Adam* and *Eve* are images for developments in the very nature of matter, 115 (see *atomic power; myth; scale*); once had been a different kind of matter, which again is being tested, 115; Gabr. and Mich. had seen that the *bat-angels* were *antimatter,* 120; *atom* and *history,* 125–26 (see *myth; scale*); all matter part of the *Greenhouse,* 210; and *Mind,* 224; harnessed by *Akhnaton/Nefertiti,* 227 (see *sun*); is *Nature's* material, 288; George *Cotzias* on *Resistance* and the *black* and *white* forces in the *atom* and in matter, 396–98; George *Cotzias* defines as "something from nothing," and links this to the essence of *God B,* 396; JM on George *Cotzias's* description of, 398; *Psyche* refers to *God B* as the creator of, 408; WHA on the "*black* past matter," 440; George *Cotzias* says it "holds," 411, 453; its birth in *Resistance,* 453; and *friction,* 458; 459; "God's matter and anti-God's *anti-*

matter," 460 (see *God A; God B*); *substance* is the *Psyche* of, 460; *black* and *white* halves of, 461 (see *scale*); and the *It,* "the two *Minds* of matter," 475–76

Maya, see Maya *Deren*

Melchizedek, the king of Salem and the high priest who blessed Abraham (see Genesis 14:18). 125

memory, "deaths are traumatic; few remember them," 43; JM's lapse regarding *Wendell* and E in *Venice,* 81; "Remember?—," 87; meditation on the phrase "burn the *box*" and its implications for the writing of *E.*, 87–88; "nothing we can recollect is missing," 91; "Yet nothing's gone, or nothing we can recall," 92; *bat-angels* tap memory and word banks in DJ and JM, 140 (see *language*); before *man* (and the coeval force, *Mind*), there had been "no one to remember and mourn," 156; *Freud* and prenatal memory, 237; *bat-angels'* memory banks, 264; WHA and MM's memory of earlier selves of *Psyches* during Mich's fete, 357; and the Muses, 400–404; George *Cotzias's* prenatal memory of *Urania,* 411; man's "memory tic" regarding *immortality,* 439

men before mankind, their sounds described by E, 56; E says they may rule, 56; some have wings, 56, 73; issue their ultimatum ("Mind your work six moons remain"), press DJ's hand to the board, etc., 73 (see *design; time*); review of *E.*, section "U," 101; 116; see *bat-angels*

Mendelssohn, Felix, German composer (1809–47). 386

Mephistopheles, a devil in the Faust legend. 114; see *Faust*

Mercury, Roman messenger god, patron of commerce, travel, and thievery. 42; in *Time Was,* 58; "Mercury dropping," 90; *bat-angels* are, 246, 249; 288; 445–46; see *bat-angels,* especially reference to their work as messengers, and *Hermes*

Merrill, Charles Edward, JM's father, an investment banker, and a founder of Merrill, Lynch, Pierce, Fenner and Smith (1885–1956). 13, 22; dies, 36; contacted through the board, 36; on his *patron,* 36 (also see 13); reborn to a greengrocer in Kew, 37; 89; 195; 274

Merrill, James, the scribe (b. 1926). On his style and his audience, 3, 82 (see *design*); notes that he and E share the fact of a broken home, 8; *representative* of Kinton *Ford,* 12; "freed" by E's teaching, 15; and *genetic* tampering, 19–21, 28–31; in his last earth life, 24; does not want to be separated from DJ in any future life, 25 (see 487); loses touch with E, and visits his former psychiatrist, 29–31 (see *childlessness; folie à deux*); assesses E and his revelations, 31–32 (see *belief*); visits *Santa Fe,* 33–34; on *nuclear power,* 33, 55–56; travels with DJ around the world, 36–39; learns of his father's death, 36 (see 60); as in section I sees E as a spirit betokening forgiveness for the way he lives, 38; suggestion of his distance from this world, 36–39; compares point-by-point (presidents, food, parents, relationship with DJ) summer 1957 and summer 1974, 40–41; offers the

various qualities of a reflecting garden globe as an emblem of his life with DJ, 41–42 (see *mirrors*); relives Rufus *Farmetton's* death, 42–43; on turning to his novel, 46; recalls *Strato,* 50–51; remarks that he most loves those for whom the world is real, 51; change in his life suggested by the "Kleo"/*Clio* quibble, 53 (also see 65, 85); one extended session with E in two years, 55; notes how much he trusts E, 55, 57 (see *belief*); contemplates revising section "P," 63–65 (see *design*); sonnets to Maya *Deren,* 63–65; Leave to the sonneteer eternal youth," 65; "the good gray medium blankly uttering someone else's threat," 65 (see 3–4, 85); "only" session with E "in ages," 72; told by *Stevens* that a *scribe* sits by him, 72; told by Maya *Deren* that their talk has an end beyond itself, 73 (see *belief*); ultimatum of the *men before mankind* ("Mind your work six moons remain"), 73 (see *design; time*); tells E, "If I fall from a high building, it's your name I'll call," 74 (see *belief*); remarks that he has read *Proust* for the last time, 76; on the relationship between subjects and images, 76 (see *design*); quibble on St. James's "vision of life," 77; compares views on mankind with Wendell *Pincus,* 80; on the use of *power,* 81; on the absence of his mother (Hellen Ingram *Plummer*) from *E.*, 83–84; links her to Maya *Deren* and *Joanna,* 84; on E's absence, and life without him, 85; on what he has learned from E, 85; on meter, rhyme, and inspiration, 85 (see *design*); on the reactions of other people when he has mentioned the communications with E, 87; on memory and the writing of *E.*, 87–88 (see *design*); on being "imbued with otherness," 89; is "the affair" with E over? 91; on whether to burn the transcripts of his talks with E, 91–92; "we must improve the line in every sense, for life," 91; on *nature's* question at the conclusion of *E.,* 92; after finishing *E.*, 99, 167; resumes contact with E after a year, 100; asks about *appearances* in *Heaven,* 105; told by E that "all life and its workings" will "flow straight through" him, 108; on "poems of *science,*" 109–11 (see *design*); on "subject matter," 109 (see *design*); on the *language* of *science,* 110 (see *design*); on approaching the other world, 111 (see *Zimmer*); *bat-angels* want three more years, 113; on setting down the lessons in *E.* and in *M.*, 114–15 (see *design*); on his doubts and credulity, 115, 136, 169–70, 263, 269 (see *belief*); identified with *Mind* and words, 117 (see *language*); builds a small *pyramid,* 118; urged by the *bat-angels* to use *language,* 118, 121; his *Divine Comedies* produced through the influence of the *bat-angels,* 121 (see *cloning*); part of a chain of *scribes,* 121; his impatience with the speech of the *bat-angels,* 121–23; Gabr. and Mich. trust him as a voice to *man,* 122; MM tells him "your work is a long one and once completed must so slowly infiltrate, your nonchalance is the sleep of a vast travail and *time* runs out," 124 (see JM's "Voices from the Other World" in *The Country of a Thousand Years of Peace*); says, "no opposition graver than between credulity and doubt," 125 (see *belief*); seen by the *bat-angels* at *Avebury,* 125; on the *scale* of the

bat-angels, 125, 126; told that in *M.*, the numerals one through zero will point the way, 127 (see *design*); DJ and JM promise "to give all we can," 127 (see JM's "The Tenancy" in *Water Street*); called by the *bat-angels* 25 years ago, 127; life compared to a crystal *pyramid,* 127; 129; WHA urges him to "bear down," 131; differences between him and *Dante,* 132–33, 147; on "popthink," 136; *bat-angels* answer his doubts about the *UFOs,* 137 (see *folie à deux*); admits he resists "for form's sake . . . deep down . . . we're hooked," 138; and the *Jew,* 138; *element* is *silver,* 142; his basic formula, 143 (see *number*); guided by *741,* 143–44; will attain *stage* four, 144; and the limitations of *patrons,* 145 (see Kinton *Ford*); *bat-angels* brought his *soul* to the *Research Lab,* added the "humus of the *Jew,* the *gene* of a chemist (and failed musician)," 145 (see *music*); learns the Rufus *Farmetton* is a "partial fiction," 145; feels that the outside world grows smaller as the talks go on, 147–48; *sex* and *homosexuality,* 154–55, 205–6, 216; fondness for M, 155; told "there is a *design* at work, you are now being prepared," 157; on tears, 157; his *element* is *air,* 159, 183; M as a *mirror* of DJ and him, 162 (see *folie à deux*); his affinities with *air* are *Mind* and abstraction, 164; asks "how can a person not *personify*?" 172; M hints about his future, 176; after one more poem, he will be returned to his "chronicles of love and *loss,*" 176; on the tradition of *Milton, Blake, Hugo, Yeats,* 178–79; asks if he's *cloned* not to keep despair in mind for long, 183; his mineral *densities,* 183; when *fear* threatens his *reason,* imagery darts forth, 183, 208; on *time,* the speed of *light,* and radiation (see *atomic power*), 185; on M's *feelings,* 186; on his own *black holes,* 187; on *Carter's* convention, 188; protected and "insulated" by his dead friends, 190 (see 128; *fire*); on the *atom* as a *metaphor* for the talks with M, 191; *No Accident clause,* his meeting DJ, and his parents, 194–95; his dream of the *atom's* heart (corresponding to DJ's under anesthesia), 198, 204, 206–7; his *childlessness* and the seminar, 205, 216; his elegy for MM, 209–10; feels "whiteness" along his left side, 213–14; his *color* is lavender, 216; 220; Hans *Lodeizen's* unfinished *V work* given to him, and this *cloning* produced his *Divine Comedies,* 220–21; wonders whether Hans *Lodeizen* is "the key this opus began and will end in," 221; his defense of *Nature,* 229, 231, 232–33, 235, 289; phones his mother, 232 (see Hellen Ingram *Plummer*); names M, 232; M says he uses his word banks, 237 (see *language*); 239; 240; on how hard it is to set his poem in order, 248; 251; on how slow he and DJ are, 252; his "longstanding experience" with DJ led to the *bat-angels,* 253; his elegy for Robert *Morse,* in terza rima, 255–56 (see *Dante; design*); M on his welcoming of the dead, 257–58; *bat-angels* accumulate knowledge through, 257; on "feathers of proof," 258 (see *belief*); says to M, "how banal our lives would be, how shrunken, but for you," 258; complains about *M.* to WHA, "it's all by someone else," 261; WHA takes up his "chief and earliest anxiety, *belief,*" 263; M on why E was chosen for him

and DJ, 263–65; like E, M, and DJ, he is a formula, a "composite voice," 266; his *Hell* is doubt, 269 (see *belief*); memory of his grandmother, 269 (see *angel*); hits *dog*, 270, 272; George *Cotzias* phones, 272; his countdown to Mich., 273–75; in childhood identified *Hell* with the German word for "bright," 274 (see *light*); on the "quaint idiom" that slips to his tongue, 274 (see *language*); on the *biblical* Mich., 289; his sister, 298, 421–22 (see Doris Merrill *Magowan*); describes the writing of *M.*, 297–98, 311–12 (see *design*); discusses *M.* with George *Cotzias*, 298–99; *M.* praised by Hans *Lodeizen* and M, 300; protected by the "human dirt" of his life, 300, 305, 306; his writing of *C.L.S.* identified with Maya *Deren's Divine Horsemen* ("Such a theme . . . took all one's powers to 'document'"), 305; his elegy for WHA, 306; first exchange with the *angels*, 307; on WHA and MM joining the *elements*, 310 (see 305–6); recalls MM's visits to his house in *Athens*, 309; imitates Sergei *Markovich*, 311; visits George *Cotzias* in the hospital, 312; on *language* and the elegy, 312, 335, 376 (see *poetry*); on *immortality*, 314–15; 316; on writing *C.L.S.* ("from Romance to Ritual"), 319; on the "isolating privilege of learning," 320; he and DJ discuss whether they are about to hear that *man* is doomed, 327; WHA gives him a *design* for *S.* ("two golden trays of 'Yes' and 'No' with '&' as bridge or balance"), 328, 351, 362; WHA refers to his "utter neutrality" and says, "all too soon . . . you must begin to judge," 328; WHA urges him to "think," "ask questions," "plug away," 331–32; refers to his "sheer walls of text," 332; on MM's *suicide*, 335–36; asks if he should correct M's errors, 340; WHA on his poem about the *Five*, 345; on catching the "full verve" of the *angels'* talk by means of the "unmeasurable King James inflections," 346 (see *design*); on literary versions of *God* and "how humdrum" what he says next to his creations, 348; 349; 351; his and DJ's twenty-fifth anniversary, 352–59; and the "elevator principle" ("each lesson lifts us to a plane of greater *power* and *light*"), 353–54; on being touched during Mich.'s fete, 358; "in the *mirror*" for the first time during Mich.'s fete, 358, 359 (see 356); a "Styx of quicksilver" separated the *Five* from him and DJ during Mich.'s fete, 359 (see *mirror*); on the ambiguity of *God B's* song, 360, 361–63; on *negatives* in *C. L. S.*, 362; on the *Rose* tradition, 363; says his "poem's logic calls for the shattering of a glass," 363–64; visit to Ephesus, 369–74, 496–97; meets *Uni*, 378–80; says, "enough names clog the poem," 384 (see *design*); WHA fears his poem is a "whitewash" for the *angels*, 394 (see 398); on George *Cotzias's* description of *matter*, 398; on resolving ambiguities in the poem, 399 (see *design*); on the *Muses*, 404–5; on describing a chair without alluding to its use, 406 (see *language*); 408; *Psyche* says she will perch on his shoulder as she did on *Blake's*, 410; on the death of *Nabokov*, 412; says, "maddening the way everything merges and reflects," 415 (see *design; twin; mirror*); his prayer, 420; defends *Uni*, 421; shows his sister's letter to

George *Cotzias,* 421–22; cuts off Robert *Morse* on *number,* 424; WHA contrasts him to *Yeats,* 424; his faith in *feeling,* 426; *OO* on his *V work,* 429; on proceeding to "No" in *S.*, 430; describes his house in *Athens,* 430–34; on *Time,* 440; 441–42; 446; 447; 450; MM's "Socratic dialogue" with, about the *black,* 452 (see *Plato*); curses "*language's* misleading apparatus," 453; his "Bismillah" sonnet, 454; 455; 458; WHA persuades him not to revise the fable in light of new *facts,* 461–62; 464; on hearing that MM is *Plato* and one of the *Five,* 464–69; had hoped that WHA and George *Cotzias* were of the *Five,* 466; his ballade on MM, 468 (see *design*); on MM's tone, 472; on including the "apt ideogram or two" in *C.L.S.*, 474; his question on the *moon,* 477; *ABBA* is another name for *God B* and one of his favorite rhyme schemes, 478 (see *poetry; design*); his question about the *atom, history,* and *scale,* 478; praised by Gabr., 478; his question to MM about meeting "*Beatrice,*" 479; remembers opening night of *The Rake's Progress,* 481; 485; praised by *Yeats,* 486; E says he and DJ are "my couplet," 487; his surrender to the other world, 490–91, 492; says to *Yeats,* "you . . . have always been such a force in my life," 492; on the *X God B* traces on the board, 493–94; domesticates the *myth* in *C.L.S.*, 494–96; on MM's cassia, 501; visits *Venice,* 502–6; sees MM's film, *Divine Horsemen* in *Venice,* 502–6; sets a date with MM in Bombay, 1991, 509; on losing WHA, MM, and George *Cotzias,* 501 (see *loss*); his question about the *Alpha men* and *Resistance* in *Paradise,* 511–12; 513; his vertigo near the end of *S.*, 514–15; WHA on his *V work,* 516; 523; on writing *S.*, 524; on first meeting Robert *Morse,* 528; on "how such *loss* turns to profit," 534; his reading in *Heaven,* 540, 541, 546, 549, 556–60; *Uni* says his poem will be "a work that *whitens,*" 541; his suspicions about E, 543–44; E/Mich. on approaching him and DJ, 550–56; says "just as this life takes precedence over the next one, so does live despair over a *poem* or parlour game," 558 (see *Ouija board*); his *fear* that "written for the dead, this *poem* leave a living reader cold," 559; **Works by:** "The Broken Home," 192, 229, 495–96, 557; "Dedication," 221; "The Emerald" (from "Up and Down"), 216; *First Poems,* 216; "The Peacock," 158; *The Seraglio,* 13; "The Summer People," 68, 381; "The Tenancy," 5, 127; "Transfigured Bird," 216; "Voices from the Other World," 124, 231; "The Will," 4; "Words for Maria," 13, 465; ***The Changing Light at Sandover:*** "The Book of Ephraim," 99, 101, 115, 116, 117, 121, 212, 231, 261, 319, 362, 441, 465; *Mirabell's Book of Number,* 114–15, 127, 256, 261, 297–98, 300, 301, 303, 311–12, 319, 338, 376, 423, 441, 495, 501, 539; *Scripts for the Pageant,* 319, 328, 332, 394, 425, 430, 524

metaphor, the *atom* as, 116, 174, 191; *bat-angels* on the limitations of, 146–47 (see *negative*); *bat-angels* need to use ("how else describe"), 149–50; and M, 173–74; M signals with "a breezy parenthetic (m)," 173; and *Dante,* 177; the *atom* and the *bat-angels'* use of metaphor, 224; is the

ritual of *reason,* 239; and Robert *Morse* on the *bat-angels'* jargon, 256; 414; "metaphor shattered by *white reason,*" 477, 457 (see *black* and the "bad" *white*); see *language; myth; design*

Michael, the Angel of Light. With Gabr. sat on *God B's* right hand, 120; *God B* turns against Mich. and Gabr. who saw that the *bat-angels* were *antimatter,* 120; his and Gabr.'s are children's names for the *white* forces, 120; after *Fall* of *bat-angels God B* turned to Mich. and Gabr. and said, "build me a new *Greenhouse,*" 121; trusts JM as a voice to *man,* 122; can speak in *Nature's* forces, 122; is the chosen messenger of "our universal *God,*" 250; has had human experience, 250; JM and DJ's exercises in preparation for, 270–71; JM's countdown to, 273–75; his "look into the red eye of your *God*" speech on *sun, light, intelligence, God B, history,* 275–76; is a "guardian of the *light,*" 276; WHA and MM on his *appearance* during his first visit, 285–92; WHA terms him a "monument to civilized *imagination,*" 286; JM on his *biblical* role, 289 (see 285); WHA refers to him as "the pure photon," and to his "*white light,*" 289 (see *atomic* power); WHA refers to him as the "roi soleil," 291 (see *sun*); describes his creation by *God B,* 293; first duty is the tending of the *sun,* 293, 317; descended on an *arc,* composed of the four divine *colors,* 293; with his Brothers, fashioned the form of *God B's* creatures, including *man,* 294–95; is allowed to wonder because he is a favorite of *God B,* 295; his *light* is *man's* day, 296; 300; 301; *Emmanuel* yields to him as the most beloved of *God B,* 302, 334; his laughter, 302; and JM's writing of *M.,* 311; 314; 315; 316; has his strength in the *colors,* 316; is tracked by Gabr., 317; praises WHA's voice, 317; calls his school "*Zen* and *Plato,*" 318; a "flesh of *light,*" 321; his first text in *S.,* "the most *innocent* of *ideas* is the *idea* that *innocence* is *destroyed* by *ideas,*" 321–23; his creation as *God B* calls, "light! light!" 322, 326; on the *centaurs,* 323; says he has a friend in DJ, 323; hints at the limits of his knowledge, 323; 324; 325; is the servant of *man,* 326 (see *sun*); must bear the burden of *ideas,* 326; 327; 328; 329; Gabr. refers to him as "sly," 330; Gabr. criticizes him for heaping on *man* pride and ambition, when instead he "should slap his cheek," 330; 331; 332; Gabr. refers to *caves* as "*light*-shedding *ideas,*" 333; Mich. criticizes Gabr., "too like a rigid nature's need for formula and symmetry," 335; 336; 337; 338; 339; WHA criticizes his versification, 342, 346, 352, 390; his two natures are *ideas* (identified with *light*) and *reflection* (identified with the "turning over" of *ideas* and the effects of *light* on atmosphere), 343; 343–44; instructed by *God B* to divide *time* into day and night, 343; his *ideas* are opposed by Gabr.'s *thought,* 344, 347, 426; WHA on his "wordless splendors," 345 (see *language*); praises *man's Mind,* "driven by words to mine meaning," 346 (see *language*); his third nature is sleep, 346; *twin* to Gabr., 347; on *God B's* first words in *C. L. S.,* 348, 349; 350; is *God B's sense* of sight, 350; says of the lessons in "Yes" of *S.,* for will we not have *innocently* exposed

ourselves to ideas, 351; MM adores, 352; 353; his fete for DJ and JM's twenty-fifth anniversary, 354–59; confers "*sense* prisms" on WHA and MM, 356–57; "speaks through" *Flagstad's* singing of the "Fifth Last Song" of *Strauss* ("I com to Be, is the *idea*"), 357–58; WHA says his fete "brought us together in the *Research Lab,*" 359; he is the only brother present during the fete, 359; has made *Sandover* a "closed circuit," 371; causes *time* to run backwards at *Ephesus,* 373; his French, 387; sent for a signal to *God B,* 388; and *myth,* 388; 389; 390; 391; 392; 393; 395; refers to the *Muses* as "our daughters nine," 400; and the *Muses,* 400–404; DJ suggests that he doubles as E, 405 (see 500); introduces *Psyche,* 406–7; at midpoint of *S.* yields the chair to Gabr., 410; apparent dissention of the *angels* was his idea, 414; and the lessons in *S.*, 414–15; 416; 417; 424; MM says *religions* were his *V work,* 426; 427; his *ideas* are *destroyed* by Gabr.'s *thought,* 426; 437; 438; 443; 457; 458; 460; 461; 463; 465; 470; 471; 473; on the *It,* 476; says, "Accidents have begun," 476; and *Nature's* fete, 483, 484; Gabr./*Nature's* fete superior to his, 491; 516; 526; presents Robert *Morse* with his *sense* of sight, 532–33; 547; is technique itself, 548; is revealed to be E, 550; on his approach to DJ and JM, 550–56; see *Ephraim*

Michelangelo Buonarroti, Italian sculptor, painter, architect, and poet (1475–1564). 156; 385

Michell, John, (b. 1935). His *The View over Atlantis* quoted, 60 (New York: Ballantine Books, 1972, pp. 58–59); see 36

Middlemarch, (Eliot), 48, 88; see *mirrors;* George *Eliot*

Millay, Edna St. Vincent, American poet (1892–1950). 526

Milton, not his real name. 87

Milton, John, English poet (1608–1674). 136; 178; 219; 262; *Blake's* sketches for "Comus," 407; WHA on "Lycidas," 472–73

Mimi, see Mimi *Vassilikos*

Mind, E urges DJ and JM to use their bodies and their minds, 15; 105; real order of the *bat-angels* is "Mind and *Nature* wedded," 113, 229; and the *feelings* of the *bat-angels,* 113–14; and *God B,* 114; is the way to *Paradise,* 114; is one of the tools of the *bat-angels,* 114; JM is identified with, 117; the "precious nucleus of minds in the *Greenhouse,*" 119; and the *scribe,* 121; *bat-angels* are "hoping against hope that *man* will love his Mind and *language,*" 121; is a formula, 144 (see *number*);146; 150; Mind's eye outlasts the *body's,* 153; *homosexuality* and Mind values, 156; "*poetry, music,* song, indwell and celebrate the Mind," 156; an irresistible force coeval with *man,* 156; "Mind in its pure form is a nonsexual passion or a unisexual one," 156 (see *homosexuality; sex*); and *painting,* 156, 215–16; MM says of M, "he *appears* in us, our minds (hearts) are his *mirror,*" 157; "the life of our (DJ, JM, WHA, MM and M) minds *five* as one," 159; *elements* say they are responsible for all of M but his Mind ("your minds coalesced to form his"), 161; Mind is deathless, 161 (see *eternity; immor-*

ality); Mind is the *music Dante* heard, 161; Mind is the energy the *elements* draw from in *five* rings around the *S/O/L,* 161; JM's affinities with *air* are Mind and abstraction, 164 (see *elements*); *God B's religion* marks "a kind of pride in Mind," 193; its race with *Chaos,* 201; 222; and *matter,* 224; is the equal of *Nature,* 229; chosen by the *bat-angels* over *Nature,* 232; 238; evolution of *man's* Mind, 241–42, 251, 332; *God B* gives the *bat-angels* "pass keys to the Mind of *man,*" 241; 243; two by two the *bat-angels* enter DJ's and JM's minds, 253 (see *ark*); *bat-angels* have wrecked minds, 258; the *Hell* in *man's* Mind ("dark country" where "all *Psyche's* woes were put"), 269; "dress the Mind" in *colors* in preparation for Mich., 270; 291; and *Paradise,* 308; *thought* proceeded from *God B's* "ceaselessly thinking" Mind, 325; 331; of the *suicide,* 333; *Plato,* as one of the *Five,* made sense of *man's* need for his Mind, 340; Mich. praises *man's* Mind, "driven by words to mine meaning," 346 (see *language*); *God B* calls Gabr. the "restless urger-on" of *man's* Mind, 347 (see *thought*); 385; George *Cotzias* on the *cells* of his own mind, 396; and the *Muses,* 402–3; *Psyche* says "we meet to study the Mind of *man,*" 407; *Muses* are kinetics of Mind perception, 416; 424; 438; and the *black,* 447; 470; and the *It,* 476; JM on "how the knowing mind defeats itself," 477; the *Psyche* in *man's* Mind is "the balm," 489; 527; 530; 555

Minerva, Roman goddess of wisdom, invention, the arts, and martial prowess. 450; see *Athena*

Mirabell (741), 125; passes out punctuation marks, 129; asks about manners, 130; praised by MM, 130; on *Faust,* 130–31; on the *Five,* 131, 142–43; on the *UFOs,* 137; on the idea of a benign *god,* 137; on *science* and *religion,* 137; on *salt,* 140–42; on the *elements,* 141–42; guides JM, 143–44; on the *bureaucracy,* 145; on *time,* 146, 159, 176; on *metaphor,* 146–47 (see *language; negatives*); says he has come to love DJ and JM, 155; on his existence before DJ and JM ("I was nothing"), 155; has been granted feelings, 155; is filled with manners, 155; on *sex* and *homosexuality,* 156; changes into a peacock, 156–57; will guide DJ and JM to the *angels,* 156; MM on his *appearance,* "he appears in us, our *minds* (hearts) are his *mirror,*" 157; says, "there is a *design* at work, you are now being prepared," 157; cannot see through the *souls* of DJ and JM, 157; was soulless but now speaks "in the voice of a *soul,*" 158, 162; on *Plato,* 158; WHA speaks of him as the point where their *imaginations* crisscross, 159 (see 173; *appearances; belief; personification*); linked to the *element* of the *fire,* 159; *elements* say they are responsible for all of M but his *Mind* ("your minds coalesced to form his"), 161; "freed" by the visit of the *elements,* 162; says he has been "forgiven," 162; had *feared* DJ and JM, 162; previously has responded only to formulas, 162 (see *number*); had been forbidden knowledge of DJ and JM's files "until after that first exposure to this glass," 162; says, "now at last it is given me to share the force of *Nature,* the sweetness of *water* and

air, the common sense of *earth,* here in your very hearth of hearts to burn," 162 (see *fire*); says, "we are moving towards the great doors," 162 (see 175; 287); as a *mirror* of DJ and JM, 162 (see *belief*); JM refers to M's "lately won detachment," 166; on DJ and JM's *personification* of him and what he says, 172–73; is "an impulse only here at the crossroads of our four affections," 173 (see 159); his use of *metaphor,* 173; says "all is real, the unreal I know nothing of," 174; is late, 175 (see *time*); doubted by DJ and JM, 175–76; his trial, 177; on the *Greenhouse,* 182; on *atomic power,* 182–83; on *soul densities,* 183; on Chester *Kallman,* 183; on *losses* of highly *cloned souls* of *atomic* researchers, 185, 186; on the new *soul,* 185; compares the *atomic* fission accomplished by the *centaurs* to make them to love and *sex,* 185; JM and WHA discuss his *feelings,* 186; on *antimatter,* 187; on *religion* and *myth,* 187; on *God B,* 187; on the *scribe,* 188; on politics, 188; on *souls* of great *scribes,* 189, 217, 219; on the *No Accident clause,* 190, 194–95, 202; on the appearance of the 12%, 192; is not infallible, 192; on *religion,* 193; on *myths* of the *bat-angels,* 199–200; on the *centaurs'* hatcheries, 200; 206; WHA says he flees at the onset of *feeling,* 209; lessons on the *cell,* 210–16; on the *colors,* 212–22; has read JM's *First Poems* and "Transfigured Bird," 216; on his *OO* ancestors, 224–25; was born on the *crust world,* 224; another trial for, 231, 233, 235 (see 261); JM names, 232, 235–36; announces his "review" in ten lessons, 233; MM says, "he had not been visible, only his voice," 234 (see *appearances*); on *personification,* 235; on his name, 235–36; on *souls* in the *Research Lab,* 236–37; on *animal souls,* 237; says he uses JM's word banks, 237, 262 (see *language*); on *culture,* 241–43; on *God B's rules,* 246–48; on the *S/O/L,* 251; on the *Ouija board,* 253; the "longstanding experience" of DJ and JM formed his *field,* 253; Robert *Morse* on his jargon, 256; his speech, "we met on this fair *field,*" 257–58; JM says, "how banal our lives would be, how shrunken, but for you," 258; on the *saints,* 259–60; says he has "dissembled" when he felt the pressures on DJ and JM were too great, 261; has become a "master," 263–64; his work used to be in the womb, 264 (see *Research Lab*); chosen by his masters because he was mild and patient, 264; on why E was chosen for DJ and JM, 264–65; struck a bargain with his masters so that he could remain in touch with DJ and JM, 265; comes from a "long stylistic tradition," 266; on *OO,* 266; is, like E, DJ, and JM a formula, a "composite voice," 266; *number* is his "mother tongue," 267 (see *language*); his escapade with the *Firefly woman,* 267–68; on *Hell,* 269; his exercises to prepare DJ and JM for Mich., 270; says he "will be the wounded hound of *Heaven* at your door," 271 (see *dog*); 273; both mocked and praised after Mich.'s first visit, 287, 288; has been allowed new information, 288; his mistake about *OO's* presence during Mich.'s first visit, 288; has "changed his tune" about *Nature,* 288–89; JM and DJ discuss why he couldn't be present for Mich., 289; a *devil* "up to a point,"

says JM, 289; outranked by DJ, JM, WHA, and MM, 290; describes *plant cells* from inside, 290; his "great respect" for Mich., 291; praises JM for *M.*, 300; interrupted by *OO*, 300; 308; on George *Cotzias*, 309; on the return of WHA and MM to the *elements*, 309–10; JM on leaving him behind, 310–11; his skittishness when the *white* forces are named, 311; 312; 317; his mistakes about the *Five*, 338, 340, 341; his account of the *12%* corrected, 345; and *God B's* song, 360, 361, 363 (see 133–34); 371; 375; *Pythagoras* on the "faulty readout," of his 12:88 formula, 377; was master to *Uni* in *Atlantis*, 380; 382; 383; *Uni* quotes him on *sex*, 384; 385; 395; his account of the *Muses* criticized and corrected, 416; 419; 421; 424–25; his story of the winged horse, 427–28; on how the *mirror* works, 428; 461–62; 478; 487; his "nuclear fire-ache" is quenched during *Nature's* fete, 488; will roam *Nature's* gardens, 488; 490; MM on his errors, 495; 503; on WHA's predecessor Yan Li, 514; 535; 540; "in charge of all *souls* destined to be forced into higher cycles," 545; 549; 550; 553–54

Miranda, Temerlin's chimpanzee. 18–21; 140; see *animals; evolution; Shakespeare*

Miranda (from WHA's *The Sea and the Mirror*), 273; see *Shakespeare*

mirrors, original dust jacket for *Divine Comedies;* epigraph to *E.* (*Paradiso* XV); "spectrum-bezeled space above hot water," 4; glass room in *Stonington*, 5; mirror propped in the facing chair for the sessions with E, 6, 16, 98, 101, 353, 359, 428; reflecting water in which E sees DJ and JM, 6; mirrors at *Versailles*, 16; reflecting lake near where *Temerlin's* chimpanzees live, 18; "*Narcissus* bent above the gene pool," 20; E has Maya stand between two mirrors, 23; reflections in the glass room, 26–27; E tries to lead DJ to the mirror, 27; half mirror and half gong in which Ayako *Watanabe* sights DJ and JM, 36; in the tailor's shop at Kowloon, 36; reflecting wood, 36–37; DJ's face reflected in white sapphire, 37; reflecting ceiling at Fatehpur-Sikri, 37; reflecting panes of a steam room, 37; the Prinsengracht, 38–39; reflecting garden globe that JM offers as an emblem for his life with DJ, 41–42; mirror in which JM (as Rufus *Farmetton*) looks, 43; mirrors in Ellen and Leo *Cade's* bedroom, 48; *Leo* passes through a waterfall as through a mirror ("he finds himself on the far side of reflection"), 49: Cheval-glass, 50; in *Pope's* grotto, 61; (in JM's lost *novel*) "Landscape and figures once removed, in glass," 66; "A blue sky inverted in waterglass," 68; the figure in the mirror, 69; mirror goes black, 73 (see *men before mankind*); topmost panes catching the sunset, 74; canal in *Venice*, 75; glass that protects Giorgione's *La Tempesta*, 76; in the lies of *E.*, 85; "Fine connecting scratches on a mirror," 88 (see *Middlemarch*); transparencies of the windows and sliding doors in *Stonington*, 90; mirror taken off the wall by thieves in *Stonington*, 90; Victorian mirror carried by DJ, 98, 163; 101; 105; 120; "a mirror world," 137; for a talk WHA and MM should not hear JM and DJ are urged to find a mirrorless

room, 149; *antiworld* as a mirror image of this one, 150, 171; dead see only in DJ and JM's mirrors, 152–53 (see *appearances*); MM says of M, "he appears in us, our *minds* (hearts) are his mirror," 157; M was forbidden the files of DJ and JM "until after [his] first exposure to this glass" (not a mirror but reflecting windows), 162; M as a mirror of DJ and JM, 162 (see *belief*); 171; and *antimatter,* 187; 248; and *Mercury,* 249; and the *bat-angels'* "fair *field,*" 257–58; *bat-angels* have left many mirrors shattered, 258; E effaces himself among, 265; 273; reference to WHA's *The Sea and the Mirror,* 273; epigraph to *S.* from *Jean Santeuil,* 278; 292; 296; 297; 319; and Mich.'s *reflection,* 343–44; WHA says that for the first time DJ and JM are not reversed in the mirror, 353; and Mich.'s "*sense* prisms" for WHA and MM, 357; a "prison" and a "Styx of quicksilver" dividing the living from the dead during Mich.'s fete, 359 (see 356); the "bitter-*black*" mirror, 359 (see 361); JM says his "poem's logic calls for the breaking of a glass," 363–64, 418, 507, 516 (see Epigraph to *S.* from *Jean Santeuil*); in "Samos," 369–70; 371; 379; 381; and how new *poetry* is read in *Heaven,* 381–82; 398; 403; 412; JM says, "maddening the way everything merges and reflects," 415; 418; M on how the mirror works, 428; *Uni* describes as his *field,* 430, 473; 445; and *Mercury,* 445; 465; 473; and the *Monitor* and the *It,* 476; 483; 488; 491; 498; 500; 503; they break the glass at the end of *S.*, 516–17; 523; 535; 553; 559; see *lenses; negatives; X rays*

Mishima, Yukio, Japanese novelist (1925–70). 152

Mitsotáki, Maria Demertzi, friend of DJ and JM (1907–74). 13; 72; 99; 100; her death, 101; disillusioned with *Heaven,* 101; identified with *gardens,* 101–2, 104, 114, 117, 206; praised by Wallace *Stevens,* 101 (see *Rose; Plato;* 340); works for Saint *Agatha,* 102, 193; refuses to say whether she has a *representative,* 102; "insouciantly *childless,*" 102, 199, 205–6; said to be at *stage* four, 102 (see 209); loans her voice to the dying Mary *Jackson,* 104; her *X ray* therapy, 104, 127, 181–82, 183, 207, 208, 211, 213, 309, 324, 329, 330, 374, 422, 471, 479 (see *atomic power*); praises Mary *Jackson,* 104; children from past lives, 104; on *appearances* in *Heaven,* 105, 157; describes *bat-angels* and says she does not hear what they say to DJ and JM, 114; included in the early talks with the *bat-angels* when other dead friends are not, 117; describes the *appearance* of the *bat-angels,* 117; 120; defends *bat-angels* when JM becomes impatient with their speech, 122, 123; says *bat-angels* frighten her, 123 (see *fear*); on JM's work and *time,* 124; reiterates her *fear* of the *bat-angels* and says, "I have more to lose," 128; praises M, 130; 131; 134; JM introduces her to WHA, 134–35; JM calls her "matter-of-fact mother," 135; urges DJ and JM to hear the *bat-angels* out, 137; said to be less delighted than WHA with *Plato,* 141 (for *Plato* see 158–59, 340, 341, 419, 428, 452, 464–69, 485–86); talent rating is 5.1, 144; will shortly return to life, 149; said to be prevented from hearing an early talk with M, 149; will join the *plant world,* 153–54, 197,

303; 155; on the "miracle" of M's metamorphosis into a peacock, 156–57; on *Plato* ("déclassé"), 158–59; her *element* is *water,* 159; weeps when she hears M's account of the *bat-angels' Fall,* 169, 177; broods about *Greenhouse,* 181; proper chemical therapy would have prolonged her life five years, 182; on politics, 189; wishes she had been *homosexual,* 190; 193; on being "used," 198 (see *stripping process*); 201; WHA describes as a *Muse,* 205; *music* her first love, 206; her *soul* destroyed by her *X ray* therapy, 207–11 (see *atomic power*); *bat-angels* say she is "one of us," 208 (see 211); JM's elegy for, 209–10; M says she will *anchor* DJ and JM when they meet the *12%,* 210; 213; 214; 215; says that M "had not been visible, only his voice," 234 (see *appearances*); 237; 240; 243; 246; 252; 255; her Himmelfahrt, 256, 257; 263; 269; 271; JM on her photograph, 273; on Mich.'s first visit, 285, 286, 291; on her new status and her salon, 291; her affinities with *water,* 302; said to be joining the *elements* and the *plant world,* 303, 309–10, 315, 335; 308; JM recalls her visits to his house in *Athens,* 309; 310; 317; 318; 319; on Mich.'s first text, including *idea, innocence,* the *centaurs,* 321–33; says that she and Gabr. "fed on the same diet," 324, 329, 330; implores DJ and JM to "use your mother wit," 327; says she "vanished into that *black,*" 329; says to Gabr. on death, "*innocence* is our nature and we *innocently* think it for the best," 329; says *man* needs *eternity,* 330; says she's "semiseduced" by Gabr., 331; on her *suicide,* 334; JM and DJ on her *suicide,* 335–36; *Plato's Rose* remark echoes Wallace *Stevens's* praise of her, 340 (see 101); says that one of the *Five* has met DJ and JM, 341; 349; "adores" Mich., 352; says, "the life Maman led, she knew everyone," 352; and *Beatrice,* 354, 468; 354; Mich.'s "*sense* prisms" and her *memory* of earlier selves and *Psyches,* 356–57 (see *colors*); "thrilled by" *Nefertiti,* 358; says, "Mich. can do it all," 358; on *God B's* song, 360–61; 364; 372; on *Pythagoras,* 372 (see *homosexuality*); on visiting *Ephesus* with DJ and JM, 373–74, 496–97; meets Robert *Morse,* 376, 378; her remark that perhaps WHA has always been behind the scenes pulling strings, 378; on *Uni,* 380 (see 120); 385; 386; her lecture on the *plant world,* 387–90; speaks from within a blade of grass, 388; 394; 395; 398; on Saint *Agatha* as *Psyche-Chaos,* 404–5; 408; 411; on the increase in her humility and prestige after *Psyche's* visit, 413; behind the scenes during the lessons in *S.*, 413–15; MM and WHA camouflaged DJ and JM during the lessons in *S.* because the *angels* were "terribly strong drink," 414–15; 416; 418; on *Plato's* next life, 419; 420; JM and WHA discuss her, "one of the wonders," 422; says too many of her feelings were *black holes,* 426; once asked DJ "why were we born?" 426; WHA mentions as he speaks of *Plato,* 428; 429; 438; 442; on the *Five,* 447; 497; 448; 451; her "Socratic dialogue" with JM on the *black,* 452; speaks for *man* as his "Portia," 455; 462; reveals she is *Plato* and one of the *Five,* 464–69; her role in the trilogy, 464–69; on images as *scales,* 466; is the child of *Nature* and closest to the *angels,* 467; reveals she

was *Beatrice,* 468 (see 354); JM's ballade for, 468–69; JM on her tone, 472; 479; says she is "all nine" *Muses,* 480; has DJ and JM plan a trip to *Venice,* 481; as "*Plato* unified" enters *Nature's* fete riding *Uni,* 485–86; *Nature* calls her "dear daughter-son," 490; 491; on JM's surrender to the *other world,* 492; her sermon at *Ephesus,* 496–97; on her next life, 497; 500; JM on her cassia, 501; 507; JM sets a date with her in Bombay, 1991, 509; JM on losing her, 510 (see *loss*); *Nature* on her new life, 512; 513; 515; 523; 524; "MM alone was herself" during the lessons, 527; 528; 540; E on her life in Bombay, 542–43; her "miracles," 542–43; *Nature* on her life in Bombay, 548–49; Mich. on the approach of the other world to DJ and JM, 550, 553–54; see *Plato* and "Words for Maria" in JM's *The Fire Screen*

Mnemosnye, traditionally the Greek muse of memory and the mother of the muses. 400–404; see *Muses*

Mohammed, prophet and founder of Islam (570?–632). E as "temperamental Moslem," 37; *angels* spoke to, 133; 187; M says he was "always thrashing about, could not sit still," 242–43; 338; 441; 446; on the *black,* 448–50; WHA on, 453–54; JM's "Bismillah" sonnet, 454; 463; WHA tells JM they didn't see the real Mohammed, just a parody conceived by Gabr., 472; see *Homer; religion*

Monitor, WHA introduces in his lecture on *earth,* 392; its *fire,* "fierce and infernal heat," 392; *God B's* two-edged gift from the *Pantheon,* 392; in the *earth,* 392, 393; its "raging will," 393; and the *black,* 393; and the *black* and the *white* forces within the *atom* and *matter,* 396–98; JM asks what is Gabr.'s relation to, 399; George *Cotzias* on possible connections among Gabr., *Nature,* and the Monitor, 417, 447; WHA on *Chaos* and, 420; "past *God B* to the Monitor," 447; and the *atomic black* compressed from *time's* reversibility, 452–53; and unnatural *power,* 453; Mich. refers to "this *antimatter* and its Monitor *God,*" 476; and the *It,* 476; trailed *God B* from the halls of his Brothers, 476; is the "reflexion, the undoer to doing," 476; see *antimatter; Resistance*

Monod, Jacques, French biologist and writer (1910–76), shared 1965 Nobel prize in physiology and medicine for discoveries on genetic mechanisms inside cells. His *Chance and Necessity* cited, 179

Montezuma, last Aztec emperor in Mexico (1466–1520). 57; M names as one of the *Five,* 131; M says he lives now as an *East German physicist,* 131 (see *atomic power*); believes that "we race for order under orders to save the *Greenhouse,*" 132; 142; linked to the *element* of *air,* 164; George *Cotzias's densities* derived from, 312, 341; M mistakenly identified him as the *East German physicist,* 338, 340 (see *Homer*); as one of the *Five,* his *V work* is the *angels' sense* of touch, 338–39; also born as *Noah,* 339; present during Mich.'s fete, 356; 405; see *power*

moon, was the *crust* of the *bat-angels,* 153; made of materials the *atom* made nongravitational, 133; in the *Greenhouse,* 182; *Emmanuel* balances,

302; *Uni* and the moons of *Atlantis,* 379; 412; 420; 429; 430; 469; 474; JM's question about, 477; 490; 500; 508

Moorehead, Alan, Australian journalist and historical writer (1910–83). 52

Morse, Isabel, Stonington friend of DJ and JM, wife of Robert Morse. 255; 528

Morse, Robert, Stonington friend of DJ and JM (1906–77). JM's elegy for, 255–57 (in terza rima, see *Dante; design*); WHA included one of his poems ("Winter Eve") in *A Certain World,* 255 (see *spoonerisms*); on E, 256; on the jargon of the *bat-angels,* 256 (see *language*); WHA says "our circle charmed by our M," 157; dies, 375–76, 498–99; on his life, 376, 538; *Pythagoras* on, 378; MM on, 378; on Andrew *Marvell,* 381; on how new *poetry* is read in *Heaven,* 381–82; and Oscar *Wilde,* 382; JM on how he has been taken up by the other world, 383–84; on choosing "prenatal goodies," 385; on *painting,* 385; WHA interrupts, 386 (see *censorship*); WHA says he will return as a composer, 386; 395; announces the death of *Nabokov* to DJ and JM, 412; *Psyche* says, "why is he not among us?" 413; was a parent, 413 (see *childlessness*); his *music* lessons, 417–18; on his next life, 419, 420, 497, 524, 529–30, 531, 533, 539; his talk on *number,* 423; 425; 426; 427; 437; 441; welcomes *Wagner,* 444; 445; 446; 447; his lecture on the *black, time,* and *power,* 450–52; as *Orfeo,* 452; on the *black* and *white* forces in the *atom,* 460–61 (see *scale*); 471; 480; his "gondola serenade," 482; 484; conducts during *Nature's* fete, 485; 489; 490; 491; MM on his next life, 497; describes his death, 498–99; 503; 510; 512; 524; JM on first meeting him, 528; on his *music,* 529–30; will be crippled, 531, 533; the ceremonies preceding his birth, when he receives his *senses* from the *angels* and *Nature,* 532–41; 537; on his old self, 538; new name is *Tom,* 539 (see *The Rake's Progress*); *Uni* on his new life, 545

Moses, lawgiver who led the Israelites out of Egypt. 200; 226; 338; 405; see *Montezuma*

Mother Goose (from *The Rake's Progress*), was *Nature,* 485; see *The Rake's Progress*

Mouflouzélis, Strato, Greek friend of JM (b. 1944). Recalled by JM, 50–51; in his first man's life, 50; past *animal* life, 50–51; 74; 135; 196; WHA on the "uncloned lives that touch our own," 205 (see *cloning*); 232; see JM's *The Fire Screen* and *Braving the Elements,* and "The House Fly" in *Late Settings*

Mozart, Wolfgang Amadeus, Austrian composer (1756–91). Reborn repeatedly, 54, 164; E says that he is living now as a "black rock star," 54; *Don Giovanni,* 69; M says that he was *Stravinsky* in his last earth life and that he rang the bells JM heard in *Venice,* 164; as one of the *Five* is linked to the *element* of *Nature,* 164; 258; as *Stravinsky* proposes a new *The Rake's Progress,* 303; 403; *Beethoven* on, 427; 447; 497; 524; 540–41; see *Homer; music*

Muir, John, Scottish-born American naturalist (1838–1914). And *plant souls,* 151 (see *Rose*)

Muses, 186; 201; WHA describes MM as, 205–6; JM on MM, 210; *Urania* as, 261; *Pythagoras* on *poetry* and *number,* 371–72; Mich. refers to "our daughters nine" and introduces them, 400; each describes her functions with words like "deceptive," "enslaving," "tangled," "sorcery," 400–404; linked with *Chaos,* "our immortal mother," 403–4; WHA refers to them as the "box of horrors," 404; WHA terms them "very Kurt *Weill,*" 405; M's account of them criticized and corrected, 416; 428; 442; MM cites JM's "Words For Maria": "the Muse of your off days," 465; MM as "all nine," 480; Mich. on MM as, 554

music, Hans *Lodeizen* on "transferred experience," 24; JM is a "failed musician," 145; and *homosexuality,* 156 (see 205–6); is a *Mind* value, 156, 216; M describes his lessons in musical terms, 157; *Mind* is the music *Dante* heard, 161; unite the members of the seminar, 205–6; MM asks, "is not music like *time* retold?" 206; its vibrations light up *machines,* 215; Hans Lodeizen "is the key this opus began and will end in," 221; 228; one of the three major faiths of today, 239; and *man's evolution,* 242; of the *atom,* 243; and the hurricane sent to DJ and JM, 243–44; 272; and Mich.'s first visit, 286; and the sound of Gabr., 296; 303; and the *language* of the *angels'* speeches, 331; 347; and *God B's* first words in *C.L.S.,* 347, 349; and Mich.'s fete, 354 (see *Strauss*); the four-note theme BDEA ("I come to Be is the *idea*") during Mich.'s fete, 357; the "pulse of the *galactic* radio" during *God B's* song, 360; WHA on *God B's* song, 362–63; and the *Muses,* 403; 417–18; 427; 441; 444–45; and the *black,* 450; 481–82; *The Rake's Progress* and *Nature's* fete, 484–86; 489; 497; 513; 516; Robert *Morse's* music, 529–530; and the *atom,* 530; Gabr.'s strictures to Robert *Morse* about, 534; 537–38; 539; see *culture*

myth, *bat-angels* made myth in hard biological terms, 115; *Adam* and *Eve* are images for developments in the nature of *matter,* 115, 192; *atom* is *Adam* and life and the *universe,* 118; "is *DNA* . . . the serpent . . . in the myth?" 119; "it is sperm, egg, and cell, the *earth* and *Paradise,*" 119; 122; *atom* and history, 125–26; *crust world* is a *metaphor* for the brain's evolving cortex, 126; *bat-angels* frequently employ "partial fictions," 145; *bat-angels'* use of *metaphor,* 146–47 (see *negatives*); M says, "all legends are rooted in truth," 162; legend of the *centaur* is the last *poetry* of *Atlantis,* 169; 175; M on Buddhist, Christian, and Islamic myths, 187; JM on the *atom* as a *metaphor* for the talks with M, 191–92; *Eden* tells a parable of *atomic* fission, 192; *bat-angels'* myths about *God B* and the *Greenhouse,* 199; myth of *Prometheus* is the *bat-angels'* story, 199; *Moses* as a parable for *earth,* 200; M says that in all legend is the lava of truth, 228; "Mrs. Myth," 233 (see Mrs. *Smith*); 239; legend of *Noah,* 253; WHA's "*fact* is is is fable" speech, 262–63 (see 303, 461–62); *bat-angels'* file of, 264; Mich. explains what his

"soft words" mean in fact, 293; legend of the *Phoenix,* 299, 300; WHA says the names of the *angels* "ring through canyons of myth," 302–3; of *Cain* and *Abel* (and the *centaurs*), 323; legend of the great temple of *Artemis,* 373; MM explains her *plant world* in scientific terms, 388; 414; WHA says, "how shapely and distinct they used to seem viewed from below," 416; M says they are "more lovely than *numbers,*" 428; WHA persuades JM not to revise his fable in light of new *facts,* 461–62; WHA on *Socrates, Silenus,* and *Apollo,* 471–73; WHA on "mythic force," 473; 516; 534; see *scale*

N, see Helene ("Nelly") *Liambey*

Nabokov, Vladimir, Russian-born American novelist (1899–1977). Robert *Morse* announces his death to JM and DJ, 412–13; at the fifth *stage,* 412; *Luca* falls for, 425; 526; 543; 545–46; had a *twin,* 546; 547

Narcissus, in Greek mythology, youth who having spurned the love of Echo pined away in love with his own reflected image. 20; see *mirrors*

Nature [Note: in *E.* nature/Nature is personified as Rosamund *Smith,* also Mrs. *Smith,* later the Marchesa *Santofior;* in *M.,* as Mrs. Myth ("the resourceful Mrs. Smith . . . who with a kiss flew off to marry myth," *E.,* 67; also see 139); and appears in *S.,* as *Nature, Psyche,* and *Chaos.* Readers should consult each of these other entries.] DJ's trust in Nature, 26; her question at the conclusion of *E.,* 92, 231; still the prompter, 100; real order of the *bat-angels* is "*Mind* and Nature wedded," 113, 229; DJ is identified with, 117, 159; Mich. and Gabr. can speak in Nature's forces, 122; *bat-angels* believe that their *crust world* was beyond the reach of natural upheaval, 125, 168; *bat-angels* try to rise where Nature couldn't, 126; before *man* and the force of *Mind* all had been instinctive Nature, 156; and *Chaos,* 156, 420; in the union of *elements* DJ is the shaping hand of Nature, 159; 160; M shares for the first time, 162; as one of the *Five, Mozart* is linked to, 164; the *elements* "with Nature as the hidden fifth face" come to compose a *pyramid,* 164, 270–71; and the *Greenhouse,* 181, 182, 228–29; *man* turned from, 182; *atom* cannot be *man's* natural friend, 183; nothing in Nature is unknown to *God B,* 187; after *Galileo* the priesthood began its reluctant reappraisal of Nature and her laws, 193; M says it knows no limits, 196; "little lustful tricks" of, 202; M describes as a favorite slave of *God B,* 228; struggle with *God B,* 228–29; profusion of, 228–29, 245, 247–48 (see *population*); savaged by *man,* 229; JM's defense of, 229, 231, 232–33, 234–35, 289; her physical *densities,* 230; rules the *elements,* 230, 236; measured on the fair scales of *light* is of an inferior rank, 230; would fail without *light,* 230; female reigns in, 230; *bat-angels* are her friendly rivals, 231; *bat-angels* chose *Mind* over Nature, 232; and JM's mother (Hellen Ingram *Plummer*), 232–33; and "Mrs. Myth," 232–33 (see Mrs. *Smith*); 234; M says she is famous for her pride, 235; not the *bat-angels'* to use, 236; *bat-angels* send a hurricane to DJ

and JM, 243–45; is allowed the tool of weather by *God B,* 244, 246; balances the *population* in her lab, 245; her physical *rules* of thumb, 245; *bat-angels* are also her messengers, 245; and *God B's rules,* 246–48; and *atomic* power, 247; impatient with over-*population,* 247–48; her "other signal: reproduce," 248; non–*Research Lab souls* are her affair, 260; *man* as the child of, 269; and the *elements,* 270–71; M has "changed his tune" about, 288–89; M says *matter* is her material, the costumes of *earth,* and *man's* flesh, 288; M says supernatural does not exist and she is number two person, 288; 291; Gertrude *Stein* calls her "the mother of us all," 313; *earth (Raphael)* and *water (Emmanuel)* are *innocent* Nature, 326; the "wronged and wilful queen" of WHA's poem, 365; Robert *Morse* on Nature and *painting,* 385; and the *Muses,* 401, 404; *Psyche* is "the third and fairest face of," 407; *Psyche* on her aspect of Nature, 409; and George *Cotzias's* theorem, 412; 413; George *Cotzias* on possible connection among the *Monitor,* Gabr., and Nature, 416–17; WHA distinguishes natural (*Psychic*) from unnatural (*Chaos*), 420; MM describes her hectic pace when she cleans house, 426; 440; 447; 448; presses *Mohammed* to tell about the *black,* 449–50; natural and unnatural *power,* 453; 454; 455; MM calls her "Mother," 455–56, 472; 457; 462; MM is the child of, 467; her grief over *God B's* first two experiments, 470–71; 473; 476; says she is "fond of tides," 477; 480; her fete, 483–90; "Mother Goose" in *The Rake's Progress,* 485; says Nature is the balm, 489; her "last resounding *Yes* to *man,*" 489 (see 492); and the *masque,* 491; "misread" the text at her fete, 491; Gabr. has inherited at most one of her *black* or *resistant genes,* 492; refused to read these lines at her fête, "now let us banish gloomy dreams, for *Heaven* on *earth* most likely seems," 492; 506–7; 508; on the new lives of MM, WHA, and George *Cotzias,* 511–12; answers JM's question about the *Alpha men* and *Resistance* in *Paradise,* 512; her final speech in *S.,* 516–17; on Robert *Morse's music,* 530–31; 540; as Robert *Morse* is born, 541; *Psyche* rests on, is her shadow, 545; on MM's life in Bombay, 548–49; 550; 553; 554; 558; 559; see *Rose; Santofior; Time*

Nebuchadnezzar, king of Babylon (630?–562 B.C.). 70

Nefertiti, queen of Egypt in the early fourteenth century B.C. and wife of Akhnaton. *Akhnaton's* crystal *pyramid,* 126–27, 225; her death, 127, 228; with her *twin Akhnaton* firstborn of the *Five,* 223, 337; her *childlessness,* 225; and *Thebes,* and the *sun,* 225, 227; and the *Moses* legend, 226 (see *myth*); patron of the *bat-angels,* 228; drew up the first *V work* schedules and set order in the *Research Lab,* 228; and *00,* 228; her role in *evolution,* 242; as one of the *Five,* her *V work* is to serve as the *angels' sense* of taste, 339; also born as *Rachel* and *Shiva,* 339; "the dual nature of taste: bittersweet Nefertiti," 339; later *Plato's twin,* 339, 341; 345; present during Mich.'s fete, 356; on the *mirror* that divides the living from the dead during Mich.'s fete, 356 (see 359); MM "thrilled by," 358

mean formulas governing human life, 144; by nine, the *bat-angels* mean that knowledge whereby *souls* from the *Research Lab* will build *Arcadia,* 149 (see *Paradise*); and *metaphor,* 149–50; M took the formula called "peacock" from the file, 158; and the *five elements,* 159; and *V work,* 161, 162; *five* rings around the *S/O/L,* 161; M had previously responded only to formulas, 162; on the significance of fourteen to the *bat-angels,* 170; *feelings* of the *bat-angels* were formulas, 170–71; WHA on *man's* faith in the number three, 171; three is the number of *God B,* 171; the *five* are formula made word, 223 (see *language*); *five* is the transforming digit, 223; vibrations of number, 230; and the *Jew,* 230; and the *language* of the *bat-angels,* 230; formula is the revealed monotheism of *science,* 239; *bat-angels* believe that the "one unspoken revelation must dwell in the number *five,*" 245; 252; "formulas" and the *arcs/arks* of *Noah* and the *Ouija board,* 253; 263; E, like DJ, JM, and M, is a formula, a "composite voice," 266; number is M's "mother tongue," 267; the names and formulas of the *Five,* 341; 345; *Pythagoras* on *poetry* and number, 371–72; *Pythagoras* on the *bat-angels'* reduction of formulas to words, 377 (see *language*); M is quoted by *Uni* as preferring number to *sex,* 384; Robert *Morse* on, 423–24; Gabr. adds to the *soul's color* mix, 423; JM's impatience with, 424; *Yeats* devoured by, 424; M says *myths* are more beautiful than number, 428; WHA on the number nine, 509–10; see *design*

Oberon (from Shakespeare's *A Midsummer Night's Dream*), 263; see *Shakespeare*

"Ode: Intimations of Immortality from Recollections of Early Childhood" (Wordsworth), read by Marius *Bewley* to Mary *Jackson,* 103

Odette (from Proust's *A la recherche du temps perdu*), 70; see *Proust*

Offenbach, Jacques, German-born French composer (1819–80). His *La Perichole* quoted, 331

O'Keefe, Georgia, American painter (1887–1986). 215

Orfeo, legendary Thracian poet and musician. Robert *Morse* as, 452; see *Orfeo ed Euridice,* act 2, by Gluck

other world (its dependence on this one), if only as a hint, this idea is present in the description of a *patron's* rise through the nine *stages,* 10; explained in detail, 56–57; M on, 257–58; see *Götterdämmerung.* [Note: the attributes of the other world are otherwise too various and extensive to be brought together in a single entry: see *Heaven; patrons; representatives; stages; time; appearance; Research Lab.*]

Ouija board, the board, the pointer, and the manner of address and dictation, 5–7; *design* of the trilogy adumbrated in the description of the board, 5; an *arc,* 5, 253; Ouija board as a symbol system, 31 (see *language*); *Joanna* carries a ouija board, 33–35; "board game" in the quotation from *Heraclitus,* 60; *Joanna* and Sergei *Markovich* at the board, 67; 98; 137; 147;

252; and *arc/ark,* 253; a "*field* of work," 253; *lights* of the *bat-angels' intelligence* play over it, 253; 285; 299; 301; 307; 354; and the *black* setting of *God B's* song, 361; MM on "our connection," 371; 385; 459; Mich. describes as *Sandover,* 478; *God B* traces an *X* on, 493–94 (see *It*); reproduced in text, 493; 515; 536; "just as this life takes precedence over the next, so does live despair over a *poem* or a parlor game," 558

paintings, and *Mind,* 156, 215–16; 242; in *Raphael's cave,* 324, 385–86, 424; Robert *Morse* on, 385; "at best interpretive, at worst a botch," 385; and *Nature,* 385; 424; DJ's *Arcadian* painting, 523, 532; see *sex*

Pandora, in Greek mythology, the first woman, bestowed upon mankind as punishment for Prometheus's theft of fire; entrusted with a box containing all the ills of the world, she opened it. 304

Pantheon, other systems and the *sun* and *gods* of each, 199; *God B* selected from, 199, 388, 476; and the *Greenhouse,* 199; *atomic power* is the fuel of, 199; *Homer's,* 219, 338; *God B* comes out of the Pantheon of *galaxies* and *gods* as powerful as he, 330; *Homer,* in the guise of an *East German physicist,* listens to, 338; and *God B's* song, 362; *God B* in, 388; *God B's* two-edged gift from (the *Monitor*), 392; 417; *Monitor* trailed *God B* from the halls of his brothers, 476; 477; 494

Paradise, E on, 60 (see 426); *man's fear* of the *power* of the *bat-angels* stops Paradise, 113; and *Mind,* 114; no figure of speech, 114; "earthly eternity," 116; the next race will be of *gods,* 117 (see *Alpha men*); 119; *Dante* looked into the *atom's* eye and saw the potential of Paradise, 132; *Dante's* vision is not of Paradise but the source of all *power,* 133; Paradise of the *bureaucracy* and the nine *stages,* 149; Paradise of *Research Lab souls* will be *earth,* 149; antiworld may be a *black twin* Paradise, 150; after the visit of the *elements,* "we had a taste of Paradise today," 162; will come through the *Five,* 165; distinguished from *Arcadia,* 165; 180; M says to be used here is the true Paradise, 198 (see 59, 153, 452); M describes three decades ahead, 201; and the four *colors,* 207; 229; *atom* must be returned to, 247; building a Paradise for *man* is *God B's* work, 261; JM says, "every grain of dust, each waterdrop . . . suffused with our *minds* . . . will be Paradise," 308; WHA on the *Alpha man* of, 308 (see 117); 426; in George *Cotzias's* lecture on *time* and *immortality,* 439; MM on its race of *gods,* 455–56 (see *Alpha men*); and *Venice,* 481, 502, 506; in *God B's* speech in the "No" section of *S.,* 494; and the *bureaucracy,* 499; JM's question about *Resistance* in Paradise, and *Nature's* answer, 511–12; DJ's *Arcadian painting,* 523, 532; 524; see *heaven*

Paradiso (Dante), epigraph to *E.* (XV, 61–63); quoted, 37 (III, 14—alludes to the faces of souls who were inconstant to vows made on earth—among other entries, see *Capri*); Maya *Deren's* dream is a "low-budget remake" of the *Paradiso,* 45; how *Dante* came to write it, 45; in

Dante the vision is *star*-like, 132; as *Dante* looked into the *atom's* eye, he saw the potential of *Paradise,* 132; *bat-angels* on E's version of its origin, 132–33; *Dante's* vision is not of Paradise but of the source of all *power,* 133; 219; 241

Parigory, Tony, Greek friend of DJ and JM (b. 1925). MM on, 158; 240; 335; see JM's "Words for Maria" in *The Fire Screen*

Parsifal (Wagner), 210; 328; see *Wagner*

pastoral poetry, and *plant souls,* 151–52

patrons, relationship with their *representatives,* 8–10; forbidden to intervene for their *representatives* except between lives, 9–10, 24; "peace from representation," 10; role between lives, 10, 11–17, 19; relations of the patron-spirits with the *men before mankind,* 56; efforts to communicate with their *representatives,* 59; often weaker than their *representatives,* 59; "no punishment like that of being given a gross or sluggish *representative,*" 66; could forget the horror of the first moments after death, 100–101; E says that the world is with them through their *representatives* and their past lives, 105; and the *density* of their *representatives,* 138; *metaphor* of the blacksmith and the shoe of gold, 144–45, 149; *bat-angels* leave to the patrons their 3.5 billion *souls,* 145; their limitations, 145; patrons of non–*Research Lab souls* have their duties, 145; *bat-angels* comb the *bureaucracy* for pairs of compatible patrons, 254; see *bureaucracy; the nine stages*

Patton, George, American general in World War II (1885–1945). 214

Paul VI, Pope, Giovanni Battista Montini (1897–1978). On birth control, 123 (see *population*); 543; 548

Pavlova, Anna, Russian ballerina (1881–1931). 54

Pegasus, in Greek mythology, winged steed who caused Hippocrene, the fountain of the muses on Helicon, to well forth with a stroke of his hoof. And *Uni,* 426–27; legend of, 427–28, 517; 549

Peking (Beijing), capital of China, in the northeastern part of the country. One of the *anchor sites,* 121

Perenyi, Eleanor Spencer Stone, American journalist and novelist (b. 1918). 255

Pergolesi, Giovanni Battista, Italian composer (1710–36). 516

Perón, Juan Domingo, president of Argentina (1895–1974). 188

personification (of the other world), DJ and JM attempt to visualize the other world, 16–17; DJ under *hypnosis* sees E, 27; Maya *Deren* in a dream sees E, 44; E's light reveals the *souls* who gather around DJ and JM to each other, 59; countless faces of the Queen of Heaven, 64; *Beatrice* is a kind of *music Dante* personified in female form, 132 (see *universe*); M says that DJ and JM have "peopled not ideated what has been and is"—to which JM replies, "how can a person not personify?" 172; 173; 235; WHA refers to the *angels* as these "asexual *imagined* powers we have

personifed," 327; *Psyche* is "a force more often felt than personified," says WHA, 413; see *appearances; imagination*

Peter Pan (Barrie), 234

Petrarch, Francesco, Italian poet (1304–74). *Laura,* 354

Phidias, Athenian sculptor of the fifth century B.C., 296

Philemon and Baucis, in Greek mythology, elderly Bithynian couple who, after kindly entertaining Zeus and Hermes, were granted a wish such that they became a pair of trees growing side by side. Matt and Lucy *Prentiss* are compared to, 47

Phoenix, in Egyptian mythology, bird that consumed itself by fire after five thousand years, and rose renewed from its ashes. Legend of, 299, 300; 375; and *Urania,* 400; see *myth*

Pierce, Hubbell, friend of DJ and JM (1926–80). Designs *wallpaper* for DJ and JM, 99, 111, 116

Piero della Francesca, Italian painter (1420?–92?). 215

Pincus, Beatrice "Betsy" Merrill, JM's "niece." 13; model for Ellen Prentiss *Cade* in JM's lost *novel,* 13; pregnant with *Simpson,* 19–20; gives birth to Wendell *Pincus,* 29; 78

Pincus, Wendell, born as JM's "nephew." 29; dreams of E, 38, 81; in *Venice* with JM, 78–82; views on mankind, 79; seen by E, 105; 503

plant world, plant *souls,* 151–52; plant *souls* are tapped by the *bat-angels,* 151; plant *souls* and the *carbons,* 151; examples of plant *souls* are *Muir* and *Burbank,* 151; plant *soul densities* produce a lack of destructive rivalry, 151, 152; and *pastoral poetry,* 151–52; and plant *evolution,* 152; *bat-angels clone* the plant world, 151–52; M says that MM will join the world of plant life, 153–54, 208, 303, 309–10, 315; fertility in the vegetable world, 163, 167, 168 (see *population*); after vegetable life emerges, the *centaurs* create the *bat-angels* as messengers to carry their word above the trees, 167; vegetable adversary attacks the *anchor sites* of the *crust world,* which leads to its destruction, 168–69; and *atomic power,* 181; 193; *God B* sought to destroy the *centaurs* with forests, 201; as a metaphor for tendencies in *man,* 242; 254; and the *soul* of the *Firefly woman,* 268; M describes its *cells* from the inside, 290 (see 388); 294; MM's lecture on, 387–90; MM speaks from within a blade of grass, 388; the *language* of plants, 388–89; plants are the resting place of *soul,* 389; its rhythms and the human pulse, 389 (see *scale*); 397; and Saint *Agatha's garden,* 404–5; 415; 455; 494; MM's cassia, 501; 544; see *Research Lab*

Plato, Greek philosopher (427?–347 B.C.). Intervened for Wallace *Stevens,* 24; WHA is seeing much of, 141; MM said to be "less delighted" with, 141 (for MM see 158–59, 189, 340, 341, 419, 428, 452, 464–69, 485–86); not interested in *density,* says WHA, 147; squints through keyholes "at some lithe young bod," 147; Marius *Bewley* on: "tattletale gray nightgown off one shoulder," 158 (see 305); MM terms him "déclassé,"

158; Chester *Kallman* calls him "a gas," 158; M says, "he has reached *stage* nine and enjoys an *eternity* of talk, he clung to an ideal both lofty and sterile," 158; 163; 184; his *soul* mined by the *bat-angels,* 189 (see *cloning*); as one of the *Five,* his powers are on loan, 201; his *cave,* 263, 354, 356; 273; said to have taken up *Luca,* 291; 292; Marius *Bewley* says he is cochairperson of *Heaven's* "Athenian club," 305 (see *homosexuality*); Mich. calls his school "*Zen* and Plato," 318; his *twin* is *Nefertiti,* 339, 341; as one of the *Five* his *V work* is the *angels' sense* of smell, 339–40; made sense of *man's* need for his *mind,* 340; later born as *Khan* and *Muir,* 340; his *Rose* remark echoes Wallace *Stevens's* praise of MM, 340 (see 101); said to be between lives, 341; 345; present during Mich.'s fete, 356; says "never disapprove, it warps the *soul,*" 356; MM says he is in the *Research Lab* with WHA, 378, 381; 415; 418; MM on his next life, 419; WHA on his *V work* as a biochemist, 419; DJ suggests WHA is Plato, 420, 422; WHA mentions MM in the middle of his discussion of Plato's next life, 428; will be born in Bombay, his father a mathematician and banker, his mother a doctor, 428; WHA describes his intervention for Wallace *Stevens,* 429; 441; MM's "Socratic dialogue" with JM on the *black,* 452; 453; MM revealed as, 464–69; is the child of *Nature* and closest to the *angels,* 467; WHA on *Socrates,* 472–73; MM appears as "Plato unified" during *Nature's* fete, 486; 491; and MM's next life, 497; JM on the changes in his appearance from *M.* to *S.,* 501; 525; 540; 543; 558; see Maria *Mitsotáki*

Plenorios, architect of *Artemis's* temple at *Ephesus,* 373 (see *design*)

Plitsetskaya, Maiia Mikhailouna, Russian ballerina (b. 1925). 143

Plummer, Hellen Ingram, JM's mother (b. 1898). 83–84; 195; JM phones her, 232–33; and *Nature,* 232–33

Poe, Edgar Allan, American author (1809–49). 299

poetry, *pastoral* poetry, 151–52; and *homosexuality,* 156; is a *Mind* value, 156; legend of the *centaur* is the last poetry of *Atlantis,* 169; and *earth* ("the sand grain that made *Dante's* pearl . . . the poem's bed may need to be made up with dirty sheets"), 188; one of the three major faiths of today, 239; in *man's evolution,* 242; WHA says, "diffy to write a poem about a poem," 252–53; WHA on the minor part the self plays in a work of art, 262; WHA on poetic tradition, 262; WHA criticizes Mich.'s versification, 342, 345–46, 352, 390; WHA on Mich.'s "wordless splendors," 345; JM on literary versions of *God* and "how humdrum" what he says next to his creations, 348; *Pythagoras* on poetry and *number,* 371–72; Andrew *Marvell* on, 381; Robert *Morse* on how new poetry is read in *Heaven,* 381–82; MM on the *language* of her lecture, 389–90; WHA on poetry and *fact,* 391 (see 401, 471); and the *Muses,* 400–404; Gabr. says the alphabet contains "the new materials for a new faith," 446; JM's "Bismillah" sonnet, 454; JM's trilogy as "cooked poetry," 466; MM's role in JM's trilogy, 464–69; Gabr. says "this new breed of poets . . . feeds on

facts," 471; JM's ballade on MM, 468–69; JM on the "apt ideogram or two" in *C.L.S.,* 474; "just as this world takes precedence over the next one, so does live despair over a poem or parlor game," 558 (see *Ouija board*); JM's fear that "written for the dead, this poem leaves a living reader cold," 559; see *design; scribe*

Pope, Alexander, English poet (1688–1744). 12; his grotto, 61; on *E.,* 72; 99; 547; 557

population, population explosion in *Venice,* 75; the need for limiting, 118–19; birth control and Popes *John* and *Paul,* 123; death is productive, 130, 145; overpopulation in *Japan,* 139; plagues, wars, and *suicides* to diffuse the population explosion, 145; *bat-angels* on birth control and *science,* 163; profusion of *Nature* and fertility in the *plant world* means a constant struggle for space, 163, 166–77, 168, 186–88, 228–29, 247, 248, 389, 390; after *Hiroshima fear* of the fused *man* in his closely packed city, 194; M says that in three decades *man* will solve this problem, 201; *bat-angels* come in to thin, 229; *Nature* balances in her lab, 245; any imbalance of population is *man's* work, 245; *God B's rule,* "two children per couple," 247; *Nature* impatient with overpopulation, 247; *Nature's* other signal: "reproduce," 248; unisex fashions and, 248 (see *sex*); *Raphael* says it is *God's* will that *man* reduce his numbers, 307; 310; and Gabr.'s two natures, *destruction* and *selection,* 344; 350; and the *plant world,*389, 390; and the *Muses,* 403–4; *Psyche* on, 409–11; 412; and the *angels'* thinning process, 449–50, 451, 476; *Nature* on thinning, 506, 507, 508; 530–31; 535; 548

Portia (from Shakespeare's *The Merchant of Venice*), MM as, 455; see *Shakespeare*

Poulenc, Francis, French composer (1899–1963). *Dialogues des Carmelites,* 312

Pound, Ezra, American poet, critic, and translator (1885–1972). 79; and T. S. *Eliot's The Waste Land,* 219; 453

power, *atomic* research at *Los Alamos,* 33; power plants by the Nile, 52; 54–57; kicks upstairs those who possess it, 54 (see 263–65); how power's worst abusers are handled in the other world, 55; power of *Mallarmé* and of *Montezuma,* 57; "as to the composition few had found a cleaner use for power," 81 (see *Stravinsky*); power station in the lost *novel,* 84; "the *absolute,*" 84–85; *bat-angels* say JM must tell of power, and that *man's fear* of the power they are stops *Paradise,* 113; MM says that the "game" of the *bat-angels* is power, 123; all energy sources must be covered, 126 (see *shield*); nuclear energy is the destruction of the *atom's shield,* 126; *East German physicist's* study of in-space radiant powers, 131 (see *atomic power; the Five; Montezuma*); *Dante's* vision not of *Paradise* but of the source of all power, 133; *salt* is the switch of *man's* sleeping power, radium of the *bat-angels',* 140 (see *elements; atom*); salt is "raw power and

its insulation," 141 (see *shield*); M says of his superiors, "it is a power that stilled the tongue of *Dante,*" 155; *souls* of DJ, JM, MM, WHA, and M "must begin to be a single power," 159 (see *elements*); M says, "all power attracts and must be denied" the *bat-angels,* 162; inside *souls,* 180; *man's* power lies in his *Resistance,* 202; resides in the *color* red, 212; and the *S/O/L,* 251; *God B's* "main magic, *imaginative* power," 251; M on E's dictum that "power kicks upstairs those who possess it," 263 (see 54); JM asks, "will *light* learn to modify its power?" 274; MM and WHA will become "power stations," 310; WHA on the *angels* as "asexual *imagined* powers we have *personified,*" 327; 331; *Akhnaton* in his present incarnation researches thermal energies, "powers clean and abundant," 337; WHA says the powers of the *angels* are "in us quite as much as over," 345; and the "elevator" principle in *S.,* 353–54; Robert *Morse's* lecture on, 450–51; *natural* and unnatural power, 453 (see *Monitor;* 498)

Prentiss, Lucy, character in JM's lost novel. 13; 35; 47; 84; see Mary *Jackson*

Prentiss, Matt, character in JM's lost novel. 35; 47; 84; see Matt *Jackson*

Prometheus, in Greek mythology, the Titan who stole fire from Olympus and gave it to man. His *myth* is the *bat-angels'* story, 199; and *atomic power,* 213; Gabr. on, *man's* theft of *God B's* materials, 455, 456; 543

Prospero (from Shakespeare's *The Tempest*), 364; see *Shakespeare*

Proust, Marcel, French novelist (1871–1922). His *A la recherche du temps perdu* quoted, 61 (Paris: Bibliotheque de la Pleiade, 1954, vol. 3, p. 86; London: Chatto and Windus, 1967, vol. 9, p. 108); allusions to *Swann* and to *Odette,* 70; "foreshortening in Proust," 70–71 (see *time*); line that opens section V is not to be found in the work of this author, 75; "above E, throned on high," 76; JM says he has read for the last time, 76; part of the unbroken chain of *scribes,* 121; 146; M says he is at *stage* eight and is a 5.1, 189 (see *density*); his *soul* mined by the *bat-angels,* 189 (see *cloning*); epigraph to *S.* from *Jean Santeuil* (Paris: Librairie Gallimard, 1952, vol. 1, p. 315), 278 (see *mirror*); 381; 383; *Albertine,* 403; 547; 557

Psyche, "psychic *atom,*" 191; *Freud's V work* is to illumine, 237, 269; the delicate envelope of *soul,* 237; the breath of *soul,* 237; 88% environment, 238; the dwelling place of *soul* is "the house called *man,* Psyche, or simply *body,*" 238; the *12%* lodged in *Psyche's* forehead, 239; M says, "the *body* and its Psyche are your auditorium, JM," 239; and *reason,* 239; *bat-angels* implement *God B's rules* through, 246; M asks, "is not the *soul* in its transit and change like the Psyche in daily life?" 252; *Hell* is the *cave* of, 269; *Hell* is where all its woes were put, 269; and the *bat-angels' cloning* of *Freud,* 269; "psychic dents," 349; Mich.'s "*sense* prisms" which prompt WHA and MM to peel away *memories* of earlier selves or psyches, 357;

Pythagoras on the *bat-angels'* "faulty read-out" of "that vague increment of Psyche," 377; *Calypso* refers to "Psyche/*Chaos,* our immortal Mother," 404; JM on Psyche as *Chaos,* 404; WHA refers to the *Muses* as her "box of horrors," 404; and Saint *Agatha,* 404–5; Mich. introduces as the "*twin* sister to *God B,*" 407 (see 408–9); "the third and fairest face of *Nature,*" 407; says, "we meet to study the *Mind* of *man,*" 407; on her descent from the *galaxies* with *God B,* 408; *God B* divides the force of *man's* nature with, 408; takes command of *man's Resistance,* 408; says she and *God B* were never at odds, 409; says *man* is born to be torn between her and *God B,* 409; on her aspect of *Chaos,* 409; on her aspect of *Nature,* 409; says she is "all for *man,*" 409; on *immortality,* 409–10; says death is the *Resistant* force defining the forward movement of life, 410; says George *Cotzias* is the first *Research Lab soul* in three millennia, 410; kissed WHA when he wrote down the title to the *Age of Anxiety,* 410–11; says she will perch on JM's shoulder as she did on *Blake's,* 410 (see 408); MM says Gabr. is hers, 411; asks of Robert *Morse,* "why is he not among us?" 413; WHA says she is a force more often felt than *personified,* 413; the *bureaucracy* is her "summer house," says WHA, 413; "a liberated Psyche?" 413; 416–17; JM's prayer to, 420; WHA distinguishes *natural* (Psychic) from unnatural (*Chaos*), 420; kissed Wallace *Stevens's* cheek, 429; present during the "No" section of *S.,* 437; says, "the most *destructive* of all *ideas* is that *feeling* sets it right," 438; 440; 441; *substance* is the Psyche of *matter,* 460; Psyche in *man's Mind* is "the balm," 489; 506–7; 508; and the *UFO's,* 507; rests on *Nature* and is her shadow, 545; see *Nature,* especially the note there

Ptolemy, Greek astronomer, mathematician, and geographer of the second century A.D. In JM's lost *novel, Eros* is his household slave, 47; see *Tiberius*

Pueblo man, exchanges *souls* with Leo *Cade,* 49

punctuation, the ellipsis, 86 (see *black*); tools passed out by M, 129

Purcell, Henry, English composer (1659?–95). 530; see JM's "Verse for Urania" in *Divine Comedies*

pyramids, *Teddie* at the Pyramid Club, 58; that JM builds, 118, 274; *man's* pyramid is *language,* 118; *Akhnaton's* crystal pyramid, 126–27, 146, 225, 227 (see *atomic power*); *metaphor* for *M.* and the lives of DJ and JM, 127; negative forcefield of *Akhnaton's* pyramid still exerts an influence in the Caribbean (the Bermuda Triangle), 146; the *elements* with *Nature* come to compose a pyramid, 164; and *Paradise,* 165; and the *number* three, 171; 226; the prism, 227; JM's cracks, 274; JM says that *M.* is "now more tower of Babel than pyramid," 311; 555

Pythagoras, Greek philosopher of the sixth century B.C., 370; his lecture on *number,* 371–72; MM on, 372; on the *bat-angels'* "faulty read-

out" of the 12:88 ratio and other *numbers* and formulas, 377; on Robert *Morse,* 378; 423; 503; 556

Quennell, Peter, English biographer, poet, and critic (b. 1905). His *Alexander Pope* quoted, 61 (New York: Stein and Day, pp. 185–86); see *Pope*

Rachel, M names as one of the *Five,* 131; a "formula made word," 223 (see *language; number*); 339; 341; see *Nefertiti*

The Rake's Progress (Auden, Kallman, Stravinsky), 81; 106; a "new" one proposed by *Mozart/Stravinsky,* 303; quoted, 370 (act 1, scene 2); the brothel scene is quoted, 481; WHA and JM remember its opening night, 481; a recording of it plays during *Nature's* fete, 484–86; *Nature* was "Mother Goose," "Tom" our "threatened *atom,*" "Shadow" the "*black* of *time* reversed," 485; 508; 538; Robert *Morse's* new name is *Tom,* 539

Rakewell, Tom (from *The Rake's Progress*), 484; is "our threatened *atom,*" 485

Raphael, the Earth Angel, also known as Elijah. Mich. terms him "our true inventor," 295; flings a spark of energy into the head of *man,* and *God B,* seeing "a new *light* there," says, "it is mine," 295; *Emmanuel* washes him, 302; is the "*earth* brother," 306; his *wit,* 306–7; in *man* is the rib, 306; named Cosmos by many, 306; as *earth,* he has the irradiated metals in him, 307 (see *atomic power*); *twin* of *Emmanuel,* 307; described by MM and WHA, 307; 309; his "game" before Gabr.'s first visit, 315; linked to WHA, 317; his "contest," 317–18; recalls his creation by *God B,* 322; his *cave* and the *cave* dwellers, 324–26; his *cave* parallels *man's* cranium, 325 (see *evolution; scale*); 326; his two natures are protection and supply, 342–43; his (*earth's*) "shadow riches" are uranium, 343 (see *atomic power; black*); his third nature involves the "sleep" of living tissue and materials stored in *man,* 347; is *God B's sense* of hearing, 350; in "Samos," 369; his *cave* and *ideas,* 385–86; 395; George *Cotzias* was his but is now Gabr.'s, 405; 406; 407; 424; 458; and the *It,* 474; and *Nature's* fete, 484; 508; 517; 526; presents Robert *Morse* with his *sense* of hearing, 539; 552

rats, rat *souls* in the *Research Lab,* 52; in *Venice,* 80; "rat world," 226; 303; see *animals; evolution*

reason, one of the tools of the *bat-angels,* 114; Pope *John* turned from reason as does *Paul,* 123 (see *population*); when *fear* threatens JM's reason, imagery darts forth, 183; the blue *cell* of, 212 (see *colors*); "the new house godlet: pure reason," 239; not "knowledge merely, but reason run through the *fires* of *man's cloned soul,*" 239; *metaphor* is the ritual of, 239; *God B* sends the idea of, 241–42; and *God B's rules,* 247; 250; "floats" in *Emmanuel,* 301; WHA says to Gabr., "oh let reason speak," 329; *Emmanuel's* two double natures are "reason and pride, calm and purifica-

tion," 343; *Urania's* sphere is "icy rationality," 403; "*metaphor* shattered by *white* reason," 447; and the *It,* 474; 488; and Gabr.'s gift of the *sense* of taste to Robert *Morse,* 534–35

Rebekah, in Bible, the wife of Issac and mother of Jacob and Esau. 192; see *twin*

A la recherche du temps perdu (Proust), quoted, 61; (Paris: Bibliothèque de la Pleiade, 1954, vol. 3, p. 86; London: Chatto and Windus, 1967, vol. 9, p. 108); see *Proust*

Redon, Odilon, French painter and lithographer (1840–1916). 265

reflection, Mich.'s second nature, identified with the division of *time* into night and day, and with the effect of *ideas* upon atmosphere, 343–44; in "Samos," 369–70; see *mirrors;* Mich.

reincarnation, see note at *other world*

religion, Baptist church in *Stonington,* 5; effect of *Christ* on E's home, 8; abortion talks in Rome, 20; "Its missionary rancor and red tape," 20; E on Vedanta, 37; value of "plain old virtue," 54; JM quotes a Church of Rome friend on E, 111; Popes *John* and *Paul* on birth control, 123 (see *population*); WHA could "curse my high Anglican principles," 128; WHA on the "dreary, deadbang wrong church," 128; the curse of *Faust/Innocent VI* ended in a thriving paganism in Europe, 131; Christianity made an *evil* of what had not been bargains, but rites, 131; idea of a benign *God* has lately been *cloned* into *man,* 137; *science* more and more forced to share the religious field, 137, 193; emergence of a *science god,* 137; morality and *God B's* first law, 168; *fear* and virtue, 172; M says, "to our eyes, these ethical rights and wrongs are so many blanks in [*man's*] canvas," 173; the *scribe* must supplant religion, 178–80; M on Christian, Buddhist, and Islamic *myths,* 187; "outstripped faiths," 188; M says that the last use of religion is to keep at swordpoint the great factions of East and West, 193; *God B* introduces his religion to *Akhnaton,* 193; Roman Catholic censorship and *Dante,* 219; the *scribe* issues from the burnt pages of theology, 239; *bat-angels* say that they have torn down the "superannuated church," 239; *Chaos* slips in upon the collapse of religious *belief,* 246; M on the *saints,* 259–60; M says that *Heaven* is real for each faith, 260; *Hell* and, 269; decline of religious *fear,* 269; JM on the *biblical* Mich., 289; WHA refers to the "mystic union," 291; Mich. calls his school "*Zen* and *Plato,*" 318; its *language* is "compost . . . action gone to seed," 425; religions were Mich.'s *V work,* 426; as "destroyed energies," 426; 440; 441; 442–43; Gabr. on "the vast, fast-abandoned complex of religion," 443; *Mohammed* on, 448–50; 463; and the *It,* 476; 543; and the *angels,* 550–51; see individual religious figures such as *Buddha, Christ, Mohammed*

Renard, Jules, French writer (1864–1910). His description of Sarah *Bernhardt,* 203 (cf. *Journal,* 1887–1910, Pleiade, Paris: 1966, p. 361)

representatives, relationship with their *patrons,* 8–10; *patrons* forbidden to intervene for their representatives except between lives, 9–10, 24; the *patron's* "peace from representation," 10; the *patron's* role between the lives of his representative, 10, 16–17, 19; efforts of *patrons* to communicate with their representatives, 59; often stronger than their *patrons,* 59; "no punishment worse than being given a gross or sluggish representative," 66; horror of the first moments after death, 100–101; E says that the world is with the dead through their representatives and their past lives, 105; and *density,* 138; *metaphor* of the blacksmith and the shoe of gold, 144–45, 149; the *bat-angels* leave to the *patrons* their 3.5 billion *souls,* 145; the limitations of *patrons,* 145; *patrons* of non–*Research Lab souls* have their duties, 145; see the nine *stages, bureaucracy*

Research Lab, E introduces without naming, 52; use of *animal souls* in, 52; could again be wrecked, 115; nine *stages* are the Lab of the *bat-angels,* 116; use of *animal souls* in, 117, 140, 145–46, 196; death is productive, 131, 145; where *densities* are added to *souls,* 140, 145–46; directed by the *bat-angels,* 140, 144; raw material is all kind of *souls* (from the *Five* to *animals*), 140; no *language* there but formulas, 140 (see *number*); *metaphor* of the blacksmith and the shoe of gold, 144–45, 149 (see *patron; representatives; souls*); one small success so far is the *Five,* 145; daily needs five million *souls* (*density* 1:20,000) and has not half that number, 145; *bat-angels* have before them all events concerned with the Research Lab for the next three decades, 146; by nine the *bat-angels* mean that knowledge whereby *souls* from the Research Lab will build *Arcadia,* 149 (see *Paradise;* the nine *stages*); use of *plant souls* in, 151–52; 180; *bat-angels* spot-check for the unusual or totally human *soul,* 185; in great mass deaths a *soul* of great value has been known to slip through, 185; *losses* of highly *cloned souls* of *atomic* researchers, 185; new *soul* must be fashioned *resistant* to the *atomic* acid and to the abrasions of human *thought,* 185; is a fairly late addition to world three, 187; and *cloning,* 188; six Lab-*souls* at *Carter's* convention, 188; *souls* of great *scribes* mined by the *bat-angels,* 189, 194, 217–22, 292, 497; *God B* sees that *man* is ripe for, 194; and the *bureaucracy,* 196; WHA on the "uncloned lives that touch our own," 205 (see *cloning*); JM addresses about MM, 209–10; 213; 220; *bat-angels* pour *souls* into as good *bodies* as they can get, 220; and the fashioning of the *Five,* 223; *five* is the transforming digit of, 224 (see *number*); *Akhnaton/Nefertiti* together were the first Research Lab *soul,* 225; with the creation of the Research Lab work becomes *V work,* 225; *Nefertiti* drew up the first *V work* schedules and set order in the lab, 228; 229; *bat-angels* create first *soul* in, 236; 239; "a mere 2 million *cloned souls,*" 247; M defines *Heaven* for lab-*souls,* 260; and the manufacture of the *Firefly woman,* 268; *bat-angels* oversee "*soul* intensities" between lives ("constant rough stuff"), 290; 335; Gabr. leads a visit to, where the *Five* are unveiled, 336–40; WHA

says Mich.'s fete "brought us together in the Research Lab," 359; George *Cotzias* describes his research into the *cell* and its relation to what DJ and JM have been learning, 375; George *Cotzias* in, 377, 381; *Pythagoras* on the *bat-angels'* "faulty read-out" of the 12:88 ratio and other Research Lab *numbers* and formulas, 377; 395; in George *Cotzias's* lecture on *matter,* 396–97; 409; *Psyche* says that George *Cotzias* is the first Lab *soul* in three millennia, 410; 412; 416; 439; and the *Five,* 447; and the *monitor,* 447; 467; and *Nature's* fete, 483; 511; 524; 535

Resistance, JM's "resistance" of the *bat-angels,* 138; *elements* say they "press back" against *antimatter,* 161; new *soul* must be more resistant to the *atomic* acid and the abrasions of human *thought,* 185; power of *man* resides in, 202; 253; *light* unobserved until resisted, 285, 437; WHA says that *oo* is the silhouette of, 297; 315; in *God B's* song, 360; and WHA's account of the *Monitor,* 393; George *Cotzias* on the *black* and *white* forces within the *atom* and *matter*—"*white* (good) resists *black* (bad)," 396–97; and the mandala, 398; JM on George *Cotzias's* description, 398; *Psyche* on, 408–10; *Psyche* takes command of *man's* resistance, 408; identified with the "dark," 408 (see *black*); *Psyche* says that death is the resistant force that defines the forward motion of life, 410; Mich. says "all good discourse must . . . know resistance," 414; 437; 441; 447; and the birth of *matter,* 453; *Greenhouse* was an act of resistance from the start, 453; and *substance,* 460; and the *It,* 474–76; 477; Gabr. has inherited no more than one of *Nature's black* or resistant *genes,* 492; in *God B's* speech in the "No" section of *S.,* 493–94; JM's question about resistance in *Paradise,* and *Nature's* response, 511–12; the *angels* are the "resisters," 551; 555

Rilke, Rainer Maria, Austrian poet (1875–1926). 110; 292; 547; 557

Rimbaud, Arthur, French poet (1854–91). his *V work* spoke too soon, 217; ghostwrote *The Waste Land,* 217, 219 (see *Eliot*); 557

Ring [Der Ring des Nibelungen] (Wagner), Magic Fire Music, 35; quotation from *Götterdämmerung,* 62 (act 1, scene 3); *Brünnhilde,* 81, 91; *Siegfried,* 83; see *Wagner*

Ritual in Transfigured Time (Deren), 45–46; see Maya *Deren; negatives; time*

R/Lab, see *Research Lab*

Robin, see Robin *Magowan*

Robin, character created by Bob Kane. 288

Le Roman de la Rose (Guillaume de Lorris and Jean de Meun), 404

Rome, fell when Christianity was needed, 187 (see *No Accident clause; religion*)

Romeo and Juliet (Shakespeare), 191

Roosevelt, Eleanor, American diplomat and writer, wife of FDR. (1884–1962). 143

Roosevelt, Franklin Delano, president of the United States (1882–1945). epigraph to *M.*

Rose, "*Time,* the very attar of the Rose," 3; rosy-lit interior, 26; roses hung on every wall, 26; dessicated rose light, 33; pale blue wax roses, 34; "the doomsday clock—its hands our own: the same rose ruts, the red-as-thorn crosshatchings," 55 (see *atomic power; time*); JM's lost *novel* "nipped in the bud" by E, 66; and the characters in JM's lost *novel* ("Each the abraded, vast baked-rose detail of a primeval circulatory system"), 66; my red flower, 68; young man in dark rose, 83; the rosy dregs, 88; white roses climb, 99; Wallace *Stevens* on MM: "she belongs to that select few who prefer to sniff the rose, not be it," 101; *galactic* pollen, 112; "through eyelids, a veined rose," 119; the *Marschallin* (*Der Rosenkavalier*), 146; and John *Muir,* 151, 340; MM joining the *plant world* ("centripetally into a white rose"), 153; "very pollen of the *power* plant," 251; and MM's clothes, 252; "the rosebrick manor" of *Sandover,* 262, 319–20; 340; *Der Rosenkavalier* is played during Mich.'s fete, 354–55; and Mich.'s fete, 354, 358; JM on the rose tradition, *Dante, Blake,* 363 (see 55); 398; 404; after *Psyche's* final visit, 411; 423; 468–69; see *Sandover; education; nature;* Rosamund *Smith*

Der Rosenkavalier (Strauss and Hoffmanstahl), the bestial *Marschallin,* 146; 292; played during Mich.'s fete, 354–55; Tanya *Blixen* as Robert *Morse's Marschallin,* 383; see *Rose; Strauss*

Rossini, Gioacchino Antonio, Italian composer (1792–1868). 243; 405

Rubinstein, Artur, Polish-born American pianist (1886–1982). 143

rules, *God B's* first law: survival of the most agile, 168; "there shall be *No Accident,* the *scribe* shall supplant *religion,* and the entire apparatus develop the way to *Paradise,*" 180; *Nature's* physical "rules of thumb," 245; the *bat-angels* implement *God B's* rules, 246–48; *God B's* rule: two children per couple, 247 (see *population*); "the rule of the rulers," 247; *God B's* law of dignity, 380

Saint-Simon, Duc de (Louis de Rouvroy), French writer (1675–1755). 291

saints, M on, 259–60; and the *S/O/L,* 260; 263; 291; "saintly elevations" such as MM and WHA's return to the *elements,* 309; 546; see *religion*

salt, switch that turns on *man's* "sleeping power," 140; is "food for thought," 141; "fuel and stabilizer . . . raw *power* and its insulation," 141 (see *shield*); and the *carbons,* 141; and *fire,* 141; and the prolonging of life, 141–42 (see George *Cotzias*); 160; 182; *bat-angels* use in the *Research Lab*

to create the first *soul,* 236; 270; 273; 315; 353; 356; 468; Gabr. on, as he presents his *sense* of taste to Robert *Morse,* 534–35

Sam (from Tolkien's *The Lord of the Rings*), 218

Samos, Greek island. 354; 364; JM's canzone, 369–70; 374

Sandover, "the rosebrick manor," 262; JM describes the manor, 319–20; has become a "closed circuit," 371; *Psyche* is "the chatelaine" of, 407; implicit in the *It* ideogram, 474–75; Mich. calls the *Ouija board* "Sandover," 478; JM says, "the manor is condemned," 482; 510; 513; 523; the ballroom, 549, 556–60; 559; see *Dante; Rose; Santofior;* Rosamund *Smith; time*

Santa Fe (New Mexico), *atomic* research near, 33; landscape, 35 (see *Joanna*)

Santofior, the Marchesa, character in JM's lost novel. 13, 75; the Palazzo, 68; see *Sandover;* Rosamund *Smith; Rose; Nature*

Sappho, Greek poet of the seventh century B.C., 178

Satie, Erik, French composer (1866–1925). *Gymnopédie,* 90; 206

scale, "small town" is largely a state of mind, 97 (see 273–75); at *Avebury,* 112 (see *lenses*); "if *Adam* was a fish he swam, if *Eve* was land she bred," 114; parable and *myth* in hard biological terms, 115; *Adam* and *Eve* are images for developments in the very nature of *matter,* 115, 192; the "real order" of the *bat-angels* ("*Mind* and *Nature* wedded") is echoed in their descriptions of DJ ("*Nature*") and JM ("*Mind*"), 117; *atom* is *Adam,* and life and the *universe,* 118; "is *DNA* . . . the serpent . . . in the *myth*?" 119; *atom* is "it is sperm, egg, and *cell* and the *earth* and *Paradise,*" 119; JM questions the scale of the *bat-angels,* 122, 125; *atom* and *history,* 125–26; *crust world* is a *metaphor* for the brain's evolving cortex, 126; *bat-angels* frequently employ "partial fictions," 145; *bat-angels'* use of *metaphor,* 146–47 (see *negative*); M says "all legends are rooted in truth," 162 (see *myth*); M helps explain the scale of "the *atom* is the key," 173–74 (see 22); and *lenses,* 174; riddle of the scale of *God B's* size, 174; the *Bible* is a code of blurred but oddly accurate biohistorical data, 187; *God B* is *history, earth,* and the *Greenhouse,* 187; JM on the *atom* as a *metaphor* for the talks with M, 191–92; *Eden* as a parable of fission, 192 (see *atom; myth*); *Moses myth* as a parable for *earth,* 200; scale of the lives of DJ and JM and *God B,* 210, 212, 217; *man's history* manifests the *soul* work of the *bat-angels,* 239; the scale of *Heaven* ("could fit in this cup or be vaster than *earth* itself"), 264; impulses of the *universe* were as steady as *man's* pulse, 275; *Raphael's cave* and *man's* cranium, 325; the rhythms of the *plant world* and the human pulse, 389; George *Cotzias* on *Resistance* and the *black* and *white* forces within the *atom, matter* and *man's soul,* 396; the *black* and *white* forces in the *atom* and the *bat-angels* and the *centaurs,* 460–62; JM's question on the *atom, history,* and scale, 478

Schicklgruber, Adolf, see Adolf *Hitler*

Schönberg, Arnold, Austrian composer (1874–1951). 206; 418; 529

science, JM on *poems* of science, 109, 113; JM on *language* of science, 110 (see *design*); *bat-angels* want JM to make a *god* of science, 113; 122; *East German physicist's* study of in-space radiant powers, 131 (see *atomic* power); and the *UFOs,* 136–37; science forced more and more to share the *religious* field, 137; WHA on the emergence of a science *god,* 137; *bat-angels* praise: "bravo science," soon "*man's* only ungovernable pangs will be hunger," 163; sciences were late in flowering, 179; 183; 193; used by man to prolong *Nature's* span in her struggle with *God B,* 228; and *Freud's* illumination of the *soul,* 237; one of the three major faiths of today, 239; in *man's evolution,* 242; highly *cloned* scientist *souls,* 260, 272; George *Cotzias* says it is interested in M, 298; 300; George *Cotzias* on science and *facts;* 397; George *Cotzias* fears that "a force afraid of or an enemy of my science and your *poetry* is dictating" *C.L.S.,* 398; and the *Muses,* 401–4; 408; 411; 439; 512; Robert *Morse* on "proud science," 526

scribes, *Stevens* tells JM that a scribe sits by him, 72; *bat-angels* have always spoken through poets, 114; invented by the *bat-angels,* who told "that ancient history" (*Genesis*), 116; names of the *bat-angels* are the invention of the scribe, 120; unbroken chain of scribes, 121; role of the poet as a "*science god*" emerges, 137; scribe's job is to speed acceptance of the *Five's* work, 143; he must supplant *religion,* 178–80; each prophesies his next life, or his use in *Heaven,* or use of his *soul* in *cloning,* 184; his day is at hand, 188; at *God B's* right hand and charged with the *V work,* 188; their *souls* mined and *cloned* by the *bat-angels,* 189, 194, 217–22, 292, 497; M says he must be *cloned* to regulate *population,* 194; adore the color yellow, 213–14; great scribes exist out of *time* in radiance, 217; *God B's* need for in his struggle with *Nature,* 228–29; issues from the burnt pages of theology, 239 (see *religion*); and the rites of *language,* 239; *God B's light* floods, 239; *music* stands near, 242; *culture* and *language* need the scribe, 242; 274; mining of French and German scribes, 292 (see *cloning; density*); 342; 371; *Uni* says to DJ and JM, "we call you the scribes and the namegivers," 382; temple scribes in Delos, 427–28; 461; Gabr. says "this new breed of poet feeds on *fact,*" 471; Gabr. on the scribes' *V work,* 473; WHA says, "we scribes will write it as it is," 495; 497; 510; see *belief; poetry*

senses, return *stage* by *stage,* 12; at E's *stage souls* cannot feel, 27; do they indeed return *stage* by *stage*? 57; 149; E's theory of their return discredited by M, 153; M says that E "lacks in every sense an ear," 164; 259; the *Five* are the senses of the *angels* and *Heaven,* 337–39, 463; *angels* are the senses of *God B,* 350–51, 473; E's dream of the return of the senses at *stage* nine and lesson 9 of "Yes" in *S.,* 354; during Mich.'s fete, 354–59; Mich.'s "sense prisms," which prompt WHA and MM to peel away

memories of earlier selves and *Psyches,* 356; in "Samos," 369–70; 414; E gets his back during *Nature's* fete (lesson 9 of "No" in *S.*), 487; Robert *Morse's* pun on, 491; the *angels* and *Nature* present Robert *Morse* with his senses, 532–41; see *appearances; personification*

The Seraglio (Merrill), 13 (Readers might wish to consult pp. 237–48 of this novel for an earlier version of events that are treated in *E.*)

Sergei, see Sergei *Markovich*

Seurat, Georges, French painter (1859–91). 244

741, see *Mirabell*

741.1, bat-angel. Guides DJ, 144

7154, 371

77036, 291

Seven Gothic Tales (Dinesen), 52–53; *Miss Malin Nat-og-Dag* (character in "The Deluge at Noderney"), 70; see *Blixen*

Sévigné, Marquise de (Marie de Rabutin-Chantal), French writer (1626–96). 381

sex, DJ asks, "what part . . . does sex play in this whole set-up?" 154, 205–6; 156; *homosexuality,* 156, 158, 205–6; "*Mind* in its pure form is a nonsexual passion or a unisexual one," 156; *atomic* fusion used by the *centaurs* to create the *bat-angels* compared to love and sex, 185; sex of the *bat-angels,* 200; 241; 248; asexual messenger angel in *M.,* 250; Robert *Graves's The White Goddess* cited, 254; WHA says, "we remain in a male world," 254; 304; "the tale we're hearing is nothing if not male," 304; the "Ewig-Weibliche," 305; *Erzulie* is "omnisex Queen of *Heaven,*" 305; Gertrude *Stein* on gender, 313; WHA on the *angels* as "asexual *imagined* powers we have *personified,*" 327; *Uni* quotes M as preferring *number* to sex, 384; and *time,* 384; 419; DJ said to MM, "the Mediterranean makes such heavy prose out of being male," 468; *Plato* and, 501; see *childlessness*

shadow, see *black, twin,* or *It*

Shadow, Nick (*The Rake's Progress*), is the *black* of *time* reversed, 485; see *black, twin, or It*

Shakespeare, William, English poet and dramatist (1564–1616). *Romeo and Juliet* in his *genes,* 191; *Merchant of Venice,* 219; *Oberon,* 263; *Bassanio,* 304; *Prospero,* 364; 420; MM as *Portia,* 455; *Bottom* and *Titania,* 480, 549

Shaun (from Joyce's *Finnegans Wake*), 192; see *twin*

Shaw, George Bernard, English dramatist and critic (1856–1950). 16–17

Shelley, Percy Bysshe, English poet (1792–1822). "Adonais," 310; 527; 558

Shem (from Joyce's *Finnegans Wake*), 192; see *twin*

shield of the atom, *atom* glimpsed is a nearly fatal consummation,

119; all energy sources must be kept covered, 126; nuclear energy is the destruction of the *atomic* shield, 126; *salt* is "fuel and stabilizer . . . raw *power* and its insulation," 141; that surrounds *man* and shades him from *God B* and the *angels,* 463, 499

Shiva, Hindu god of destruction and reproduction. 339; 443; see *Nefertiti*

Sidney, Philip, English poet (1554–86). 152

Siegfried (from Wagner's *Der Ring des Nibelungen),* 83; 299; see *Wagner*

Silenus, in Greek mythology, a woodland spirit and companion to Dionysius. 473

Simpson, Ephraim's representative. 6; 8–9; reborn at Gopping, 16; drowns at Gopping, 19; E arranges to have him reborn to Betsy *Pincus,* 19–20; reborn as Wendell *Pincus,* 29; 212; 554; see Wendell *Pincus*

sin, and *Hell,* 269; WHA introduces during Mich.'s first lesson in *S.,* 322–23; Gabr. on, 452, 454–55; as *pain,* 455; the unwritten sin is *man's* theft of *God B's* materials, 455, 456 (see *atomic power; Prometheus*); *Nature* made of *feeling* a sevenfold sin, 488

Skinner, Burrhus Frederic, American psychologist (1904–). 118

Smith, Rosamund, character in JM's lost novel. 13; later, the Marchesa *Santofior,* 13; in the lost *novel* she would have been "out of sight until the close," 13 (see *Nature's* question on 92); 34; *Teddie* at the *Pyramid* Club ("My name . . . is Mrs. *Smith.*"), 58; flew off to marry *myth,* 67 (see Mrs. *Myth,* 233); at the Palazzo *Santofior,* 68, 75; *Nature* and "Mrs *Myth,*" 232–33; 554; see *Nature,* especially the note there; *Rose; Sandover*

Socrates, Greek philosopher and teacher (470?–399 B.C.). 471; WHA on, 472–73; see *Plato; myth*

S/O/L (source of light), the *elements* say, "*Mind* is the energy we draw from, manifest in the *five* rings around the S/O/L," 161; M says, "if the place of *God B* is indeed that whirling *light,* it is the source of an unimagined calm," 173; the calm at the S/O/L is "that slow motion which alone allows the dazzled onlooker his vision of the race," 173 (see *lenses*); "the very pollen of the *power* plant," 251; messenger *angel* belongs to, 251; is imaginable only to human minds, 251; rooted in the lived life, 251; full mystery kept from the *bat-angels,* 251; of the *electrical* and ruling world, 252; and the *saints,* 260; is "our own *imagination* working in the world," 260; is none of the *bat-angels'* business, 260; Mich. says it is *intelligence,* 296; and Gabr.'s avoidance of *light,* 314; see JM's "The Tenancy" in *Water Street*

Soriva, M names as one of the *Five,* 131

souls, question of when they enter a fetus, 20; souls dead for at least one hundred years locate and enter a sleeping form their own age and sex—Maya *Deren* and a woman at stage one (44–45), a Sioux bear and a

hibernating bear (45), Leo *Cade* and a young Pueblo, 49; E distinguishes different kinds of souls, 50 (see *carbon; density*); *animal* souls, 52, 237, 268; and the word "animus," 53; destructive effect of *atomic* power on the soul, 55, 181–82, 183, 185–86, 207–8, 210, 303–4, 309, 330, 374, 422, 479; E describes the souls of the *men before mankind,* 56; E refers to perfected souls who have returned from *stage* nine, 59; Matt *Jackson* on those who are not special, 108; some will miss the earthly eternity when it comes, 116; some will be used to endow beings they cannot be, 116–17; *bat-angels* use "extra-life" souls like *Montezuma* for research, 132 (see the *Five*); and *density,* 138; 88% is chemistry, environment, etc., *12%* a "dry euphemism for those realms sky shrouds" from the *bat-angels,* 139; two categories of soul, "run-of-the-mill" and "at the most 2 million fleet achievers" to whom *densities* are added between lives, 139–40, 145, 149, 196, 247; souls are the raw material of the *Research Lab,* 140; *bat-angels'* direction of soul taken from them when they lost theirs, 140; correspond to different *elements,* 142; soul is a formula, 143–44 (see *language; number*); *metaphor* of the blacksmith and the shoe of gold, 144–45, 149 (see *patrons; representatives*); *bat-angels* leave to *patrons* their 3.5 billion lives, 145; *patrons* of non–*Research Lab* souls have their duties, 145; *bat-angels* daily need five million souls, *density* 1:20,000 and have not half that number, 145; *bat-angels fear* the use of *atomic* weaponry falling into the hands of *animal* souls, 146; and the *bureaucracy,* 145, 149, 196, 226, 236, 315; *Paradise* of the *bureaucracy* and the nine *stages,* 149; *Paradise* of *Research Lab* souls and the *bat-angels,* 149, 260; *plant* souls, 151–52; and *music,* 157; M cannot see through DJ and JM's souls, 157; souls of DJ, JM, MM, WHA, and M "must begin to be a single *power,*" and the union of their souls is also a union of the *elements,* 159; M says "like all soul, or shall we say, ex–life force, we are inextinguishable," 169 (see *immortality*); and *cloning,* 179, 185, 189, 194, 217–22, 247, 292, 497; 180; *man* turned from his, 182; M on soul *densities,* 183; destroyed by *atomic power,* 183, 208; highly *cloned* souls of *atomic* researchers and *losses* to the *Research Lab,* 185, 186; the "totally human soul," 185; in great mass deaths a soul of rare value has been known to slip through, 185; new soul must be fashioned more *resistant* to the *atomic* acid and the abrasions of human *thought,* 185; and the *Bible,* 187; souls of great *scribes* mined by the *bat-angels,* 189, 194, 217–22, 292, 497 (see *cloning*); the fate of useless lives, 196 (see *bureaucracy*); MM's soul destroyed by her *X ray* therapy, 208–11; and the *stripping process,* 211; *bat-angels* pour souls into as good *bodies* as they can get, 220; of the *Five,* 223, 315, 447 (also see 132); *Akhnaton/Nefertiti* together were the first *Research Lab* soul, 225; the rat world, 226; 229; one of the two chief *densities,* with those of physical *Nature,* 230; M on *Research Lab* and *bureaucracy* souls, 236; soul needs a *body* to be useful, 236; is an invention of world three, 236; created in the *Research Lab* by the *bat-angels,* 236; and the *elements,* 236; *bat-angels* slip first

soul into an ape fetus, 236; *oo* and, 236; *bat-angels* use *12%* of *animal* souls, 237; and prenatal *memory,* 237; soul is the chromosome lacking in the mongoloid, 237; *Psyche* is the breath of, 237; its dwelling place is "the house called *man/Psyche* or simply *body,*" 238; M says it is the key, 239; *bat-angels* transport and deliver, 246; "a mere 2 million *cloned* souls," 247; M asks, "is not the soul in its transit and change like the *Psyche* in daily life," 252; of the *saints,* 260; M defines the *Heaven* of *Research Lab* souls, 260; 266; of the *Firefly woman,* 268; "soul intensities" overseen by the *bat-angels,* 290; constant rough stuff for *Research Lab* souls between lives, 290; the "structureless structure" of the soul *cell,* 290; WHA on the *destruction* of his, 303–4 (see *atomic power*); *X rays* have "undone" and "illuminated" MM and George *Cotzias's* souls, 309 (see *atomic power*); and *immortality,* 314–15; souls of the *Five* "pass through the flames and live," 315; of the *suicide,* 333; and *survival,* 345; 356; *X rays* have left George *Cotzias's* soul "like a Swiss cheese," 374; George *Cotzias* on the *Research Lab's* "non-*genetic* stuff of the soul," 375; *Pythagoras* on "the faulty read-out" of the *bat-angels' numbers* and formulas for the soul, 377; 388; *plants* are the resting place of, 389; 395; *Resistance* and the *black* and *white* forces within *man's* soul, 396–98; *Psyche* says that George *Cotzias* is the first *Research Lab* soul in three millennia, 410; 417; Gabr. adds *number* to, 423; and *power,* 450–51; 452; WHA on MM's soul, 472; George *Cotzias* on the damage that the *X ray* therapy did to his soul, 479; JM on "the pilgrim soul," 501; 524; 527; and M's "reform school," 545

source of light, see *S/O/L*

Spenser, Edmund, English poet (1552–99). His *Faerie Queene* quoted, 61–62 (book 3, canto 6; see 384; *time*); 135; Spenserian stanzas during *Nature's* fete, 483–99

spoonerisms, and *time,* 69–70; and Robert *Morse,* 255

Spring Sonata (Beethoven), 12; also see "a vernal music," 24; and "that Spring night," 54; see *Beethoven;* Hans *Lodeizen*

stages, the nine, advancement to and along, 10, 54; and the *senses,* 12, 57, 354, 487; limitations of spirits who have not reached the ninth stage, 56; E refers to perfected *souls* who have returned from stage nine, 59; 101; E says presence of the *bat-angels* "dims our stages," 113; *bat-angels* are *oo* beyond the nine stages, 116; stages are the lab of the *bat-angels,* 116; the *Five* are not in the scheme of, 131; *Dante* went down through the stages nine to one from zero, while JM ascends them, 133; DJ and JM will attain stage four, 144; and the *bureaucracy,* 145, 149–50; the good *bureaucrat* reaching nine will stay there, his *Paradise,* not the *bat-angels',* 149; *bat-angels* have a very different sense of nine ("by nine we mean that knowledge whereby *souls* from the *Research Lab* will build *Arcadia*"), 149 (see *Paradise*); E's theory of the return of the *senses* discredited by M, 153; *Plato* said to be at stage nine, 158; 309; E's dream of the return of the *senses*

on what they are losing, 237–38, 239–40, 248, 252, 255; JM and DJ on what they are losing, 240; culminates in MM and WHA joining the *elements,* 309–10; and Mich.'s "*sense* prisms" that prompt MM and WHA to peel away *memories* of earlier selves and *Psyches,* 357; and Robert *Morse,* 499; see *loss*

substance, "no 'quarrel' between *light* and shadow, so long as *matter* stands between them," 460, 461; see *Resistance*

suicide, *Mishima's,* 152; 182; 202; of *Akhnaton/Nefertiti,* 228; 229; Gabr. and WHA on, 332–33; MM's, 334–36

sun, 167; in the *Greenhouse,* 182, 199; *bat-angels* feel for gamma rays what *man* feels for sunlight, 185 (see *atomic power*); and the *colors,* 212–13, 216; an example of *God B's* benevolent use of *atomic power,* 213; and *Akhnaton/Nefertiti,* 225, 227–28; *Akhnaton/Nefertiti* harness *matter* with, 227; 230; 259; "the sun *god* sang," 262; 270; 273; genius of living *cell* is its tie to the regenerative heat and *light* of, 275; ancestor of *man,* 275; *man* is a species of its making, 275–76; and *God B,* 275–76; and the accumulated *intelligence* in *cells,* 276; Mich. says, "look in the red eye of your *god,*" 276, 287; 285; 286; WHA on "the red eye of your *God,*" 287; 290; WHA on Mich. as "le roi soleil," 291; Mich.'s first duty is the tending of, 293 (see *light*); 294; 311; and Gabr.'s avoidance of *light,* 314; 317; 318; and the creation of Mich., 322, 326; as sun, Mich. is *man's* servant, 326; 342; and Mich.'s division of *time* into day and night, 343; 353; in "Samos," 369–70; in MM's lecture on the *plant world,* 388; 412; 438; 440; 443; 452; 472; 477; 516; 517; 552; see *Michael*

Sunday, William Ashley "Billy," American evangelist (1862–1935). 54

survival, *God B's* law of, 168; 180; 242; 246–48; and the *soul,* 345; 351; a theme of *God B's* song, 360, 517; and WHA's account of the *Monitor,* 393; *God B's* command, 473; and the *It,* 473–76; and *God B's* speech in the "No" section of *S.,* 517; 555; see *Resistance*

sutras, Buddhist scriptural narratives. "Sent intact," 242 (see *V work*)

Swann (from Proust's *A la recherche du temps perdu*), 70

Tadzio (from Mann's *Death in Venice*), 47.

Tania, see Baroness Karen *Blixen*

Teddie, apppears in section Q of *E.* His newly won *wings,* 58; compact (from *Hermes*), 58; "My name . . . is Mrs. *Smith,*" 58; see Saint *Theodore;* and A. H. *Clarendon* [Readers of *C.L.S.* may also wish to consult Martin Green's *Children of the Sun* (New York: Basic Books, 1976, p. 316) for the anecdote about Brian Howard.]

Teiji, see Teiji *Ito*

Tel-el-Amarna, village in central Egypt, site of the ancient city of Akhnaton. 226

stood still it took a little nap," 112; JM is told that three more years are wanted, 113; MM tells JM, "your nonchalance is the sleep of a vast travail, and time runs out," 124; is a regressive *animal* trait, 146; *bat-angels* say they have no sense of it, 146, 290; M says, "it is time you knew," 149; before meeting DJ and JM, M did not experience time, 155; M says, "you are early," 159; in the *earth's* crust, time is measured in millennia, 163; *Heaven* looking down at time passing, 164; *earth* as one of the *Five* is a grave timekeeper, 164; M is late, 175, 215; *man*-made element, 176; JM on time, the speed of *light,* and *atomic* radiation, 185; M's description of three decades hence, 201; M says his grasp isn't perfect, 202; M asks, "is *music* not like time retold?" 206; WHA asks, "is time the soil of *feeling*?" 209; great *scribes* exist out of time, in radiance, 217; JM and DJ are early, says E, 218; the *bat-angels* and the future, 222; 265; 269; does not exist for the *angels,* 294; JM on the *bat-angel's* "immunity to time" proving contagious, 312; 325; 326; Mich. instructed by *God B* to divide time into day and night, 343 (see *reflection*); 346; Mich. causes to run backwards at *Ephesus,* 373; and *sex,* 384; 428; is the name of Gabr.'s "magic," 438; is Gabr.'s "theme," 438; and *destruction,* 438–40; and *immortality,* 439–40; and the *black* forces, 439, 440; JM on, 440; WHA on "time without *God* or *Nature* running wild," 440; is Gabr.'s, 440; 442; 445; *black* is the hourglass in which sand runs up, 448; *Mohammed* on time made *black,* 449–50; Robert *Morse's* lecture on, 451–52; the *black* beyond *black* is of time running back, 451; MM's "Socratic dialogue" on time and the *black,* 452; the "*atomic black* compressed from time's reversibility," 452–53; 454; *pain* is the child of time and *feeling,* 455 (see *sin*); Gabr. says it is banished from *Heaven* to *earth,* 455; 457; and the *immortality* of the creature of the *Chinese* plain, 459; 462; and the *It,* 474–76; Gabr. compares spent time to *atomic* waste, 475; Nick *Shadow* turns back the clock in *The Rake's Progress,* 485; *shadow* is the *black* of time reversed, 485; in *God B's* speech in the "No" section of *S.,* 494; 506; 507; 508; 509–10; and the *angels'* approach to DJ and JM, 555; also see *Santofior; Resistance*

Time Was (Clarendon), quoted 58; see JM's "The Thousand and Second Night" in *Nights and Days*

Tinker Bell (from Barrie's *Peter Pan*), 234

Titania (from Shakespeare's *A Midsummer Night's Dream*), 480; 549; see *Shakespeare*

Titian (Tiziano Vecellio), Italian painter (1488?–1576). 257

Toklas, Alice B., American author, companion of Gertrude Stein (1877–1967). 72; 313; 500; 547

Tolkien, John Ronald Reuel, English author and philologist (1892–1973). 218; 364

Tom (JM's former psychiatrist), see Dr. Thomas *Detre*

Tom (from *The Rake's Progress*), see Tom *Rakewell*

Tom, is Robert *Morse's* new name, 539; see *The Rake's Progress*

Tony, see Tony *Parigory*

Torro, M names as one of the *Five,* 131; 136; a "formula made word," 223 (see *language; number*)

Tosca (Puccini), 31; 529

Tristan und Isolde (Wagner), 355; 365; see *Wagner*

Les Troyens (Berlioz), 365

Truelove, Anne (from *The Rake's Progress*), 484

Tsu Wung, apparently not a historical figure. 402

Tullia, apparently not a historical figure. 45

12%, the, is "a dry euphemism for those realms which sky shrouds" from the *bat-angels,* 139; M says, "*earth, moon,* and *sun* are a question for the 12%," 171; the *bat-angels* will stand between JM and DJ and the power of the 12%, 171; *Greenhouse* is everything up to the 12% (*sun, stars, moon,* all *Nature*), 182; and elitism, 186; M on the approach of, 192, 198; M says they are "the heart of good," 192; 193; 200; M says the 12% will take them to *infinity,* 210; 216; 225; 12% of *soul* entrusted to the *angels,* 236; *bat-angels* use 12% of *animal souls,* 237; could not operate without prenatal *memory,* 237; the 12% lodged in *Psyche's* forehead, 239; 260; *matter* follows the 12:88 ratio also, 288; JM asks, "will the twelve *personified* emerge as Mich.?" 289; the 12% is the four *angels* multiplied by their three natures or powers, 345, 347; *God B* tells Mich. "you have told them the twelfth of it," 348; "12 figures reproduced to 12 x 12" during Mich.'s fete, 356; *Pythagoras* on the "faulty read-out" of the *bat-angels'* 12:88 ratio and other formulas, 377; 438

twin(ning), 150; *Shem* and *Shaun,* 192; 223; 228; 229; 236; 242; 246; *Emmanuel* and *Raphael,* 307, 315, 316, 322, 330, 369; the "twinned emblem" that is both guide and craft, 336 (see *design*); *Akhnaton* and *Nefertiti,* 337; *Nefertiti* and *Plato,* 339, 341; WHA on the genealogy of twins, 341; *Emmanuel's* "two double natures," 343; Mich. and Gabr., 347; the *12%,* the twelve natures of the *angels,* "six pairs of twins," 347; Gabr.'s "twin *senses,*" 350; *Strauss* and *Hofmannsthal,* 355; and the *Muses,* 400–404 (see 416–17); *Psyche* and *God B,* 407, 408, 417; doubles, 415–16; JM says, "maddening the way everything merges and reflects," 415; the *Muses* as "side-splitting, dead-accurate symbols of the process," 416–17; MM says "stop seeing double," 418; 438–40; 442; 454; 457; 471; 533; 534; 546; E and Mich., 551

UFOs, 132; scout the *Greenhouse,* 133; attracted to forests and jungles, 133; *bat-angels* believe that they are charged "with the transfertilization of sense-data," 133; 136; *bat-angels* have verified them, 136–37; foreign to the density of world *science,* 136–37; 146; 477; 507

is to serve as the *senses* of the *angels* and *Heaven,* 337–40; *Akhnaton's,* 337; *Homer's,* 338; *Montezuma's,* 338–39; *Nefertiti's,* 339; *Plato's,* 339–40; "V" is Roman "five" and "life" in French, 340; Mich. gives an outline of "our V work ahead," 351 (see *design*); and *God B's* song, 363; pun in "eau de V work," 364; *Plato's* next life as a biochemist, 419; *oo* on JM's, 429; 455; MM's role in JM's trilogy, 464–69; Gabr. compares *God B's* to the *scribes',* 473; George *Cotzias* on what the *X rays* have done to his, 479 (see *atomic power*); *God B* asks JM for a "V work giving both pause and hope" to *man,* 493–94; WHA on JM's, 516; Jane *Austen's,* 524; Eliot on, 557–58 (see 217, 219); Vasili *Vassilikos's,* 559; see *soul; cloning*

Valéry, Paul, French poet (1871–1945). 547

Van Allen belt, either of the two zones of high-intensity particulate radiation trapped in the earth's magnetic field and surrounding the planet. Is the ozone layer that the *bat-angels* broke with a last thrust of *atomic* fission, 121; the ozone belt, 199

Vassilikos, Dimitra Atsides "Mimi," wife of Vasili Vassilikos (1934–78). 432; 524–25; dies, 544; and the *Firefly woman,* 544; 545; 547; 557; 558; 559

Vassilikos, Vasili, Greek novelist (b. 1933). 524; phones about Mimi's death, 544; 549; 558–59; 560

Vaughn, Henry, English poet (1622–95). His "they are all gone into a world of *light*" quoted, 274

vegetable world, see *plant world*

Venice, Italy, port city at the head of the Adriatic, located on 118 islands. *Proust* on, 61; winged Lion in, 74; JM in, 75–76; line that opens section V is not to be found in the work of the author of *A la recherche du temps perdu,* 75; storm in, 76–77, 83; M says that the bells that JM heard in Venice were rung by *Mozart/Stravinsky,* 164; 257; Venetian glass in the epigraph to *S.* from *Jean Santeuil,* 278; MM proposes a visit to, 481; and opening night of *The Rake's Progress,* 481; as a *Paradise,* 481, 500, 502, 506; JM and DJ visit, 502–6

Venizélos, Eleuthérios, Prime Minister of Greece (1864–1936). MM on, 286

Venus, Roman goddess of love and beauty. 434; see *Aphrodite; Cupid; Eros*

Verdi, Giuseppe, Italian composer (1813–1901). 4; 497

Verdurin, Madame (from Proust's *A la recherche du temps perdu*), 147

Vermeer, Jan, Dutch painter (1632–75). 258; 437

Versailles, France, site of the palace of Louis XIV. 16, 238

A View over Atlantis (Michell), quoted, 60; (New York: Ballantine Books, 1972, pp. 58–59); see 36

virtue, value of, 54; see *religion*

A Vision (Yeats), 13–14; see *Yeats*

Vivaldi, Antonio, Italian composer (1680?–1741). *The Four Seasons,* 347, 349

Voltaire (François-Marie Arouet), French poet, dramatist, and satirist (1694–1778). *Candide,* 194

Von, M names as one of the *Five,* 131; 136; a "formula made word," 223 (see *language; number*)

Vuillard, Jean-Edouard, French painter (1868–1940). 215

Wagner, Richard, German composer (1813–83). Magic Fire Music, 35; 56; *Götterdämmerung* quoted, 62 (act 1, scene 3); house in *Venice,* 81; *Der Ring des Nibelungen,* 81; *Brünnhilde,* 81, 91; *Siegfried,* 83, 299; "the doomed Dutchman," 112; *Parsifal,* 210, 328; Siegfried, 299; *Tristan und Isolde,* 355, 365; 364; 417; 441; speaks, 444–45; 451; Valhalla, 489

Waller, Thomas "Fats," American musician (1904–43). 206

The Waste Land (T. S. Eliot), ghostwritten by *Rimbaud,* 217, 219 (see 557–58); is the West's first prewritten poem since *Homer,* 219; see *cloning*

Watanabe, Ayako, patron to Mary F. Jackson. 12; 22; sights DJ and JM in a half *mirror* and half gong at Kamakura, 36; 103

water, and *time,* 4; diningroom in Stonington, "now watermelon, now sunburn," 5; water reflecting naked DJ and JM, 6; lakeflesh, 6; E's stream of consciousness, 9; each "new wave" of dead, 17; Miranda's lake, 18–19; "*Narcissus* bent above the *gene* pool," 20; *Joanna* flies through a storm, 33; 34; psychic current's flow, 35; the Prinsengracht, 38–39; "spring, or source" that E leads Maya to in her dream, 44; "the spry nuances of a Bach courante or brook," 49; the waterfall Leo steps through, 49; the flooded Rhine, 56; and devotion, 59; the flood, 60; current that sweeps away the pieces of the dragon before it can reassemble itself, 60; *Pope's* grotto, 61; current events no sooner sped than din, 69; 70–71; when the urge comes to make water, 71; the lapse that tides us over, 74; canal in *Venice,* 75; storm in *Venice,* 76–78; and *La Tempesta,* 83; 85; taps glumly trickling, 90; the flood, the arc, and the life raft, *language,* 119; and the *atom,* 119; boiling water ended the plague in Europe, 130, 194 (see *Faust; Innocent VI*); MM is linked to the *element* of water, 159, 302; M shares for the first time, 162; *Casals* as one of the *Five* is linked to, 164; 166; 182; waterfall, 192; 225; is ruled by *Nature,* 230; role in *man's evolution,* 242; 271; 275; *Emmanuel* divides *earth* by water, 294; *Emmanuel* is the "water Brother," 301–2; MM's affinity with, 302; 315; 317; 322; 332; 340; 347; the "ripple within ripple on *black*" water before *God B's* song, 360; and the breaking of a glass at the poem's end ("eau de *V work*"), 364, 517 (see *mirror*); in "Samos," 369–70; 387–88; 406; 437; 471; 472; 481; 501; 503; 505; 515; 516; 536; see *fire; mirrors*

Weill, Kurt, German-born American composer (1900–1950). 405

Wells, Herbert George, English author (1866–1946). 511

Wendell, see Wendell *Pincus*

West, Jennifer, friend of DJ, mistakenly identified as Virginia West. 20, 29

West, Virginia, confused with Jennifer West. 20, 29; gives birth to *Joselito* in a state asylum, 29

white (the white forces), Mich. terms *God B* "that whitesmith," 293; M's skittishness as they are named, 311; WHA on Gabr.'s kindly, white acts of *destruction,* 329; Mich.'s blinding white *light,* 330; WHA fears that JM's poem is a "whitewash for the Brothers," 394 (see 398); George *Cotzias* on *Resistance* and the *black* and *white* forces within the *atom* and *matter,* 396–98; their *Fall,* 440–41; "*metaphor* shattered by white *reason,*" 447, 457 (see *black; negative*); *black* and white forces in the *atom* and the *bat-angels* and the *Centaurs,* 461–62 (see *scale*); and the *It,* 476; MM wears white during *Nature's* fete, 486; 492; in Maya *Deren's* film, *Divine Horsemen,* 504–5; 515; final rhyme in *S.* is "*Light*/Night," 517 (see *black; design*); *Uni* says that JM's poem will be a "work that whitens," 541; see *angels*

Whitman, Walt, American poet (1819–92). 141; 527

Wilde, Oscar, Irish poet, novelist, and dramatist (1854–1900). 30; 382; 383

Williams, William Carlos, American poet (1883–1963). 461

Wittgenstein, Ludwig, Austrian-born English philosopher (1889–1951). His *Tractatus* quoted, 223, 274

Woolf, Virginia, English novelist and essayist (1882–1941). 3

Wordsworth, William, English poet (1770–1850). Marius *Bewley* reads "Ode: Intimations of Immortality from Recollections of Early Childhood" to Mary *Jackson,* 103

Wotan, chief Teutonic god. 445

Xanthos, in Asia Minor, where E was born, 8; see *Ephraim*

X rays, of *La Tempesta* (Giorgione), 83, 468; MM's ray therapy, 104, 127, 181–82, 183, 207, 208, 213, 309, 324, 329, 330, 422, 479 (see *black*); Hans *Lodeizen* was spared, 221; 303; ray therapy has "undone" and "illuminated" MM and George *Cotzias's souls,* 309; and *"negatives,"* 362; 374; 420; WHA on their effects on MM, 422; 466; 468; George *Cotzias* on what they have done to his *V work* and his *soul,* 479; see Maria *Mitsotáki; atomic power; lenses; mirrors*

Yan Li, WHA's predecessor (1855–1906). 514

Yeats, William Butler, Irish poet and dramatist (1865–1939). 13–14; his "Dialogue of Self and Soul" quoted, 65; and *sex,* 154; 178; moves DJ's hand, 217, 218–19, 220, 424, 474, 481, 486; 220; his "Sailing to

Byzantium" quoted, 232, 474, 481, 486; WHA on, 424; "devoured by the chimera" of *number,* 424; *00* also spoke to, 424; a "wordless presence" during the talks, 424; speaks a poem from DJ's hand, 474; Mich. refers to him and DJ as "two old *Zen* monks," 478; Gabr. refers to him as "the one that got away," 478; says he will speak during *Nature's* fete, 480–81; does not answer JM's question, "was our instruction of a piece with yours?" 481; shakes DJ's hand, 481; emerges from DJ's hand during *Nature's* fete and speaks, 486; praises JM, 486; 491; JM says, "you . . . have always been a force in my life," 492; 527; 532; 547; 555

Yes and No, JM is "of two minds" when he hears that this is his last earth life, 24; "Reality, Projection," 46; "I'm divided. Wrong things seen in the right light are fair," 63; 119; 137; to the question of whether he is a *mirror* of DJ and JM, M replies, "Yes, no, perhaps," 162; JM, like any *atom,* is two-minded, 232; WHA gives JM a *design* for *S.,* "two golden trays of 'Yes' & 'No' with '&' as bridge or balance," 328; MM of two minds about her *suicide,* "one more yes/no for JM," 336; MM's teasing response to the question of which of the *Five* has seen DJ and JM, 341; WHA's answer to JM's question about his and DJ's presence in the *mirror,* 358; WHA says to JM, "one's not my boy brushed by such wings to be still to be of two minds," 399; 441; 452; Gabr. "of two minds," 457; *God B* "of two aspects," 459; the *It* and the two *minds* of *matter,* 475; and *Nature's* mood during her fete, 484; *Nature's* "last resounding Yes" to *man,* 489 (see 492); *God B* asks JM for a "*V work* giving both pause and hope," 493; final rhyme of *S.* is "*Light*/Night," 517 (see 420); see *black; Resistance; design; duality; belief; lenses*

Zen Buddhism, 318; 478; see *religion*

00, the *bat-angels* are the force of 00, 212; M on his 00 ancestors, 224; 00 speaks to DJ and JM, 224–25; taught M as well as *Akhnaton/Nefertiti,* 225, 266; *Akhnaton/Nefertiti's* formula includes a partial 00, 228; rules the *colors,* 230; 231; 235; present in the eyes of the first ape fetus to receive a *soul,* 236; *Dante* heard, 266; M calls "our most glowing *intelligence,*" 266; and the *angels,* 266; present during Mich.'s first visit, 288–89; "Batman to M's Robin," says DJ, 288; WHA describes his *appearance,* 297; interrupts DJ and JM's talk with M, 300; speaks, 308; M says, "or so they think at 00," 309; JM terms him "punctilious," 313; prepares DJ and JM for Gabr., 314; on *immortality,* 314; refers to the *angels* as his masters, 317; and *God B's* song, 361 (see 363; 134); gives Robert *Morse* clearance to review the "Mirabell files," 383; taught *Uni* to speak to DJ and JM, 384; and *Uni,* 421, 422; also dictated to *Yeats,* 424; 429; on JM's *V work,* 429; and *Nature's* fete, 483; 510; see *bat-angels; infinity*

00470, 211–14; see *bat-angels*

Zimmer, Heinrich, German-born authority on the art and religious philosophy of India (1890–1943). His *The King and the Corpse* quoted, 62 (Princeton: Princeton University Press, 1971, pp. 4–5); see 111; *language*

Zola, Emile, French novelist (1840–1902). 183

Responses

Divine Comedies (1976)

Harold Bloom
From "*The Year's Books*"

James Merrill, now fifty, had convinced many discerning readers of a greatness, or something like it, in his first six volumes of verse, but until this year I remained a stubborn holdout. The publication of *Divine Comedies* (Atheneum; $8.95) converts me, absolutely if belatedly, to Merrill. Technically, Merrill began as a master, but even *Braving the Elements* (1972) seemed to stay within a too-conscious control, as though Merrill were too fine an artist to accept ultimate risks. *Divine Comedies* is an astonishing return-of-the-repressed, an American book that dares everything in order to achieve what Emerson called the essential American trope of power: *surprise.* The book's eight shorter poems surpass nearly all the earlier Merrill, but its apocalypse (a lesser word won't do) is a 100-page verse-tale, *The Book of Ephraim,* an occult splendor in which Merrill rivals Yeats's *A Vision,* Stevens's ghostly *The Owl in the Sarcophagus,* and even some aspects of Proust. I don't know that *The Book of Ephraim,* at least after some dozen readings, can be overpraised, as nothing since the greatest writers of our century equals it in daemonic force. Merrill has written an uncanny romance of dallying with the spirit-world that moves with the dangerous persuasiveness of an excessive fiction, yet nevertheless interprets itself as though it had, for its author, proper as well as figurative meaning. Directly autobiographical, the poem creates an obsessive cosmos of mediums, singular reincarnations, and preternatural voices which uncomfortably have a social plausibility that is quite overwhelming. The penultimate section ends with a quietly sinister epiphany: "Young chameleon, I used to / Ask how on earth one got sufficiently / Imbued with otherness. And now I see." Otherness, or the overcoming of solipsism, henceforth for Merrill will be an occult journey, and the poetic results, should they equal or go beyond *The Book of Ephraim,* will make him the strangest, the most unnerving of all his country's great poets.

HELEN VENDLER
Divine Comedies

Since he published his *First Poems,* James Merrill's energies have been divided between successive books of increasingly brilliant lyric poems (the most recent, *Braving the Elements,* in 1972) and attempts in larger fictional forms—two plays (1955 and 1960) and two novels (1957 and 1965). The flashes and glimpses of "plot" in some of the lyrics—especially the longer poems—reminded Merrill's readers that he wanted more than the usual proportion of dailiness and detail in his lyrics, while preserving a language far from the plainness of journalistic poetry, a language full of arabesques, fancifulness, play of wit, and oblique metaphor. And yet the novels were not the solution, as Merrill himself apparently sensed.

In his new collection, where most of the poems have a narrative emphasis, Merrill succeeds in expressing his sensibility in a style deliberately invoking Scheherazade's tireless skein of talk: the long poem, "The Book of Ephraim," which takes up two-thirds of this volume, is described as "The Book of a Thousand and One Evenings." In explaining how he came to write this novelistic poem, Merrill recapitulates his struggle with fiction:

> I yearned for the kind of unseasoned telling found
> In legends, fairy tales, a tone licked clean
> Over the centuries by mild old tongues,
> Grandam to cub, serene, anonymous.
> Lacking that voice, the in its fashion brilliant
> Nouveau roman (including one I wrote)
> Struck me as an orphaned form.

He once more tried his hand at writing a novel, but it lost itself in "word-painting":

> The more I struggled to be plain, the more
> Mannerism hobbled me. What for?

From *New York Review of Books,* March 18, 1976. Also published in *Part of Nature, Part of Us* (Cambridge: Harvard University Press, 1980). Reprinted by permission of Helen Vendler and Harvard University Press.

Since it had never truly fit, why wear
The shoe of prose?

His narrative forms in verse allow Merrill the waywardness, the distractions, the eddies of thought impossible in legends or in the spare *nouveau roman,* and enable the creation of both the long tale and of a new sort of lyric, triumphantly present here in two faultless poems, sure to be anthologized, "Lost in Translation" and "Yannina."

Divine Comedies marks a departure in Merrill's work. He has always been a poet of Eros, but in an unwritten novel, about "the incarnation and withdrawal of / A god," "the forces joined / By Eros" come briefly together and then disperse:

Exeunt severally the forces joined
By Eros—Eros in whose mouth the least
Dull fact had shone of old, a wetted pebble.

And Merrill's servant in Greece, whose name (Kleo) he had never seen written, turns out to be named not Cleopatra, as he had thought, but Clio; she is not the presiding surrogate for Eros but the incarnation of the Muse of history, Merrill's new patroness:

"Kleo" we still assume is the royal feline
Who seduced Caesar, not the drab old muse
Who did. Yet in the end it's Clio I compose
A face to kiss, who clings to me in tears.
What she has thought about us all God knows.

If the divinity of youth was Eros, the divinity of middle age is Clio; if the metaphor for being thirty was embrace, the metaphor for being fifty is companionship; and if the presence in the mind was once love, it is now death.

Quickened by the thought of death, which so resists the rational intelligence, the imaginations of poets react and react and react, pressing back (to use Stevens's phrase) with all the inventions, illusions, conjectures, wiles, seductions, and protests of which they are capable. Nothing so compels poets to complication: and if what they conjure up to talk to them from the dark is a voice recognizably their own but bearing a different name, they (and their readers) are peculiarly consoled by the reflected Word. So Milton found his own best voice speaking back at him under the names of Phoebus Apollo and

St. Peter; so Dante fell into colloquy with his elder self, Vergil; so Yeats invented his "mysterious instructors" who dictated to him and his wife his elaborate system of history and the afterlife; and so James Merrill, in his divine comedies, communicates with an affable familiar ghost named Ephraim, first evoked at the Ouija board in Stonington twenty years ago, and a frequent visitor since.

In his 1970 volume, *The Country of a Thousand Years of Peace* (literally Switzerland, but since Merrill's friend Hans Lodeizen had died there, also metaphorically the country of the dead), Merrill published his first Ouija poem, in which a candid, if ineptly expressed, stanza offers the motive for listening to "voices from the other world":

> Once looked at lit
> By the cold reflections of the dead
> Risen extinct but irresistible,
> Our lives have never seemed more full, more real,
> Nor the full moon more quick to chill.

These lines give at least some notion of the origins of "The Book of Ephraim." It is a poem in twenty-six sections, each beginning with a different letter of the alphabet, from A to Z, exhausting the twenty-six capital letters of the Ouija board. And yet, for all its ninety pages, the Book is not finished, scarcely even begun, its dramatic personae—living, dead, and invented—hardly glimpsed, and only partially listed, its tale of an unfinished novel still untold, its gaily inventive theology linking this world to the otherworld barely delineated.

Merrill casually and mockingly praises his own "net of loose talk tightening to verse" through his surrogates among the dead. Ephraim ("A Greek Jew / Born AD 8 at XANTHOS"), who communicates of course in the caps of the Ouija board, tells Merrill,

> . . . POPE SAYS THAT WHILE BITS
> STILL WANT POLISHING THE WHOLES A RITZ
> BIG AS A DIAMOND.

Instead of Vergilian solemnity, this guide to the otherworld uses social chitchat:

U ARE SO QUICK MES CHERS I FEEL WE HAVE
SKIPPING THE DULL CLASSROOM DONE IT ALL
AT THE SALON LEVEL.

For rationalists reading the poem, Merrill includes a good deal of self-protective irony, even incorporating in the tale a visit to his ex-shrink, who proclaims the evocation of Ephraim and the other Ouija "guests" from the other world a *folie à deux* between Merrill and his friend David Jackson. But once the "machinery"—not here the sylphs and nymphs of *The Rape of the Lock,* but the ghosts of dead friends and other revenants—is accepted as a mode of imagination, what then can be said of the import of this strange poem?

It is centrally a hymn to history and a meditation on memory—personal history and personal memory, which are, for this poet at least, the muse's materials. The host receives his visible and invisible guests, convinced that Heaven—the invisible sphere—is "the surround of the living," that the poet's paradise is nothing other than all those beings whom he has known and has imagined. Through Ephraim,

We, all we knew, dreamed, felt and had forgotten,
Flesh made word, became . . . a set of
Quasi-grammatical constructions . . .
   Hadn't—from books, from living—
The profusion dawned on us, of "languages"
Any one of which, to who could read it,
Lit up the system it conceived?—bird-flight,
Hallucinogen, chorale and horoscope:
Each its own world, hypnotic, many-sided
Facet of the universal gem.

These "facets of the universal gem" shine throughout "The Book of Ephraim," which aims at being a poem of a thousand and one reflecting surfaces. The irregularities and accidents of life are summed up in the fiction of reincarnation which animates the book's theology: people pass in and out of life as the bodies in which their spirits are incarnated die of heart attacks, in fires, or by less violent means; spirits get placed in unsuitable bodies; and in the crowded world of the afterlife a constant influx of souls makes for an agitated scene. Merrill's father, dead and between lives, gets through on the board:

Then CEM gets through,
High-spirited, incredulous—he'd tried
The Board without success when Nana died.
Are we in India? Some goddam fool
Hindoo is sending him to Sunday School.
He loved his wives, his other children, me;
Looks forward to his next life.

The next life of Charles Merrill, announces Ephraim, is in Kew:

YR FATHER JM he goes on (we're back
In the hotel room) WAS BORN YESTERDAY
To a greengrocer: name, address in Kew
Spelt out.

This social comedy between otherworld and this world is one tone of "The Book of Ephraim": another is reminiscence of a simpler ego:

Götterdämmerung. From a long ago
Matinee—the flooded Rhine, Valhalla
In flames, my thirteenth birthday—one spark floating
Through the darkened house had come to rest
Upon a mind so pitifully green
As only now, years later, to ignite . . .
The heartstrings' leitmotif outsoared the fire.

Still another tone juxtaposes the eternal confrontation of youth and age, Eros and entropy, Prometheus and the eroding Parthenon:

Leave to the sonneteer eternal youth.
His views revised, an older man would say
He was "content to live it all again."
Let this year's girl meanwhile resume her pose,

The failing sun its hellbent azimuth.
Let stolen thunder dwindle out to sea.
Dusk eat into the marble-pleated gown.

Merrill's company of the dead comes in late exchange for the abandoned dream of the immortal couple, echoed through the book in Wagnerian terms, in Tristan's "*höchste Lust,*" and in Brünnhilde's choice of love over Valhalla: "*Nie Liebe liesse ich nie, mir nähmen nie sie die Liebe.*" These sublimities remain, icons unattainable but not disallowed, at the edges of this deliberately social and tempered poetry. Wanting consuming passions, Merrill says, he has found only refining ones.

Merrill's lines, in their exquisite tones, are often painful to read. Though they keep their beautiful poise on the brink of sense and feeling, and aim here at the autumnal, or the ironic, they keep echoes, undimmed, of the past: Merrill is not yet, and I think will never be, a poet free of sensuality, love, and youth, actual or remembered. Enshrined with Brünnhilde in the section (Q, of course) of Quotations in "The Book of Ephraim" is Spenser's transcendent dream of the Garden of Adonis, where in "immortal blis . . . Franckly each paramour his leman knowes," in an equable and unfallen counterpart of Wagner's doomed couples.

"The Book of Ephraim," for the most part, refuses the postures thought appropriate to age—stoicism, resignation, disbelief, patience, or cynicism. The mild conviviality of Merrill's unearthly symposium is boyish in its welcome to comedy, sympathy, and nostalgia at once; and the poet's naive enthusiasm for "learning" from Ephraim the ins and outs of behavior and fate in the otherworld is so different from Dante's and Yeats's gloomy reverence for their guides that we are moved to delight by the refraction of these "divine comedies" from their more religious antecedents.

On the other hand, "The Book of Ephraim" is not really a comic poem. When Merrill and Jackson protest Ephraim's offhand tone about death, and say "Must *everything* be witty?" Ephraim answers, in a phrase that could be applied to the whole poem,

AH MY DEARS
I AM NOT LAUGHING   I WILL SIMPLY NOT SHED TEARS.

If life is "a death's head to be faced," it is also, in this poem, the repository of counterpointed treasures.

The claim of this long poem to moral significance rests in the way it balances two entirely opposite truths about middle age. One is the truth of perceived fate, as it declares itself in the simplest of sentences: *This is who I am; This is where I live; This is the person I live with; My father is dead; I will not fall in love again.* The other is the truth of received experience, as it glitters in a cloud of witnesses—all the things seen, the people met, the places traveled to, the books read, the faces loved, the lines written, the events lived through, the events imagined, the past absorbed—the past not only of personal life but of cultural history as well. The glowing dialectic of restriction of present life and expansion of experienced soul animates these pages into a visionary balancing of scales, now one pan up, now the other. Merrill's imagination has always been mercurial, airy, and darting, but here the counterweight of death adds a constant pull toward grief.

"The Book of Ephraim" might seem to risk the accusation of triviality, in its apparent refusal to take large issues seriously:

> Life like the periodical not yet
> Defunct kept hitting the stands. We seldom failed
> To leaf through each new issue—war, election,
> Starlet; write, scratch out; eat steak au poivre,
> Chat with Ephraim.

But under this briskness lies a wasting ennui:

> The whole house needs repairs. Neither can bring
> Himself to say so. Hardly lingering,
> We've reached the point, where the tired Sound just washes
> Up to, then avoids our feet.

In this repetitive routine, Merrill is free to admit all the flotsam and jetsam floating in his mind, and to let us judge that mind as we will.

Because Merrill is a poet whose devotion goes to the Absolute under the form of the Beautiful, his range, like that of the Beautiful itself, is diverse: the Good and the True do not really participate in a spectrum of more and less in quite the same way. From bibelots to Beatrice, from embroidery to altarpiece, goes the scale, and Merrill's tone modulates along with its object. Like Proust and Nabokov, two other sensibilities more attached to the Beautiful than to the Scientific, the Philosophical, the Ethical, or the Ideological, Merrill avoids being polemical or committed, in the ordinary sense of those words. By taking conversation—from lovers' exchange of vows to friends' sentences in intimacy—as the highest form of human expression (in contrast to the rhapsode's hymns, the orator's harangues, or the initiate's hermetic colloquies with the divine) Merrill becomes susceptible to charges of frivolity, at least from readers with a taste only for the solemn. But this espousal of the conversational as the ultimate in linguistic achievement is a moral choice, one which locates value in the human and everyday rather than in the transcendent.

It is no accident that Merrill appropriates for himself Keats's image of the chameleon poet, as delighted by an Iago as by an Imogen; he draws out a constantly changing veil of language like the endless scarves of silk from the illusionist's hands, now one color, now another, scattering light in rainbow transparency over and under his subject. And yet the severity of death fixes a new, unwavering color on the apparently boundless earlier sympathy with the attractions of experience:

> Already I take up
> Less emotional space than a snowdrop.
> . . . Young chameleon, I used to
> Ask how on earth one got sufficiently
> Imbued with otherness. And now I see.

Though the other poems in this collection share the conversational immediacy of "The Book of Ephraim," they also, in their persistent elegiac tone, seem to be fragments from a modern version of *The Prelude.* "Lost in Translation," of which the putative subject is Merrill's putting together, as a child, a complicated jigsaw puzzle with the aid of his governess, is really a gorgeous combination of Popean diversity of surface talk and Wordsworthian rumination on the past, and on the powers and lapses of memory. It is an easier poem than "Yannina," an elegy for Merrill's father set in the Turkish town of Yannina, once ruled by Ali Pasha, who becomes in the poem the surrogate for Charles Merrill. We see Ali flanked by "two loves, two versions of the Feminine": one the "pious matron" Frossíni, drowned at Ali's order for having refused compliance; the other Vassilikí, pictured with Ali sleeping in her lap. Byron (whose ottava rima Merrill here borrows and rings changes on) visited Ali, and found him "Very kind . . . indeed, a father." Merrill continues,

> Funny, that is how I think of Ali.
> On the one hand, the power and the gory
> Details, pigeon-blood rages and retali-
> Ations, gouts of fate that crust his story;
> And on the other, charm, the whimsically
> Meek brow, its motives all ab ulteriori,
> The flower-blue gaze twining to choke proportion,
> Having made one more pretty face's fortune . . .
>
> Ali, my father—both are dead.

Around this center vacillate feelings about the Oriental multiplicity of Yannina—its provincial promenade cluttered with sellers' booths, a magician's tent, loudspeaker music—and feelings about the two women, the wronged matron and the complaisant concubine. The scene on the promenade resembles the London Fair in *The Prelude,* but the human jumble of sight and sound, so inimical to the recoiling Wordsworthian sensibility which required solitude and massive forms, is the food of life to Merrill, who needs movement, color, the vulgar and the passionate together. As for the two women, one, the wronged Frossíni, has become a secular saint:

And in the dark gray water sleeps
One who said no to Ali. Kiosks all over town
Sell that postcard, "Kyra Frossíni's Drown,"
Showing her, eyeballs white as mothballs, trussed
Beneath the bulging moon of Ali's lust.
A devil (turban and moustache and sword)
Chucks the pious matron overboard.

Frossíni's fate is half farce, half martyrdom; and "her story's aftertaste / Varies according to the listener," especially when her garish memorial postcard is placed against the skillful, still preserved, painting of Ali and Vassilikí—"almost a love-death, höchste Lust!" In the end, though, both versions of the feminine—"one virginal and tense, brief as a bubble, / One flesh and bone"—go up in smoke, and the poem dips momentarily into ghoulish images of death:

Where giant spits revolving try their rusty treble,
Sheep's eyes pop, and death-wish ravens croak
. . . At the island monastery, eyes
Gouged long since to the gesso sockets will outstare
This or that old timer on his knees.

The empty sockets would seem to betoken the end of Ali and his women, and of the blushing girls and radiant young men courting on the promenade as well:

Where did it lead,
The race, the radiance? To oblivion
Dissembled by a sac of sparse black seed.

This is Merrill's most complicated retelling of his family history. But since living, of itself, perpetuates nothing, he turns, almost reluctantly, to his pain and his pen at home, far from Yannina, and invites us to enter with him, in fantasy, the magician's tent on the promenade where a woman can be sawed into two, then miraculously healed, a reassuring myth to set over against Frossíni's fate:

A glittering death
Is hefted, swung. The victim smiles consent.
To a sharp intake of breath she comes apart . . .
Then to a general exhalation heals

Like anybody's life, bubble and smoke
In afterthought.

Afterthought may, in comparison to life, be only "bubble and smoke," but afterthought is also the domain of art, where a dreamy eternity envelops Ali. In afterthought, the "elements converge":

Glory of windless mornings that the barge
(Two barges, one reflected, a quicksilver joke)
Kept scissoring and mending as it steered
The old man outward and away,
Amber mouthpiece of a narghilé
Buried in his by then snow white beard.

In this universe, the poet's reflective mind meets and internalizes all the Oriental opulence of Ali and his town, the prudishness and pathos of Frossíni, the luxuriousness of Vassilikí, and the recurrent chorus of the courting couples on the promenade: "What shall the heart learn, that already knows / Its place by water, and its time by sun?" It also accepts the ghastly permanence of the deal bodies visible in the monastery underground burial-place, and the dying animals turning on spits. But it believes that in writing it can make "some inmost face to shine / Maned with light, ember and anodyne, / Deep in a desktop burnished to its grain." The lights have vanished along the lake in Yannina, but

Weeks later, in this study gone opaque,
They are relit. See through me. See me through.

The pun, like most of Merrill's plays on words, is serious, and the elegy has gone as far as a poem can go in attempting to take into its stylized world of "bubble and smoke" the fleshly lusts of Ali and the theatrical immolation of Frossíni, the Vanity Fair of the world and the gruesome end of the sexual impulse. It is an odd, crowded, and baroque elegy, with a remarkable joining of filial and paternal spheres.

It remains to be seen how Merrill, whose inventiveness is to be trusted, will continue with such narrative poems and, perhaps, with more installments of "The Book of Ephraim." Mozart, according to Ephraim, has been currently reincarnated as a black rock star: it makes one want more news from that source.

Mirabell: Books of Number (1978)

STEPHEN YENSER

Dantean Andante

The dust jacket refers to James Merrill's *Mirabell: Books of Number* as the sequel to *The Book of Ephraim* (in *Divine Comedies*), but the poem implies several times that it would be more accurately described as the second part of a trilogy in progress. The difference signifies, for just as *Mirabell* throws new light on *Ephraim*, so perhaps the third volume will put the extraordinary elements of *Mirabell* in a different perspective. Not that the third part figures to be more ordinary than the first two. By now it is clear that Merrill has committed himself to a singularly demanding and rewarding venture. Having undergone something similar to what Yeats had to call in his case, in the introduction to *A Vision*, "an incredible experience," he is making of it a poetry of epic sweep that is utterly distinctive, sometimes deliciously comic, often uncannily beautiful, and deeply moving.

Those who have not yet read *Ephraim* must be told that Merrill and his friend David Jackson have been in touch for over twenty years, by means of a Ouija board and a teacup they use as a pointer, with the other world. During most of this period their familiar spirit has been Ephraim, an urbane, convivial sort who in his last life was a Greek Jew born in 8 A.D. In the earlier book we learned how he had put JM and DJ, as they are known in these poems, in contact with departed friends and other souls and had briefed them on what he knew of the *au-delà*. They discovered that the other world has a hierarchical arrangement of nine stages; that each of us is the "representative" of an otherworldly "patron"; that the quality of our lives determines whether we will escape reincarnation and become patrons ourselves. They also be-

---

came aware of certain ominous presences on Ephraim's end of the line—presences Ephraim described, in the board's caps and the shorthand used by all of the spirits, as "MEN B4 MANKIND," some of whom "HAVE WINGS TO WHICH / THE TRAILING SLEEVES OF PALACE ROBES ALLUDE"—but these superior beings remained aloof.

They, and one of them in particular, dominate the new volume, which consequently differs strikingly from its predecessor. In contrast to Ephraim, a kindred spirit more likely to chat than to lecture, they come to JM and DJ to teach them about the nature of the universe, so that JM can write "POEMS OF SCIENCE" that will advance their own project: the creation of "PARADISE" on earth. Two of the mediums' dead friends, Maria Mitsotáki and W. H. Auden (MM and WHA), sit in on the seminars. Since the instructors have a good deal to impart, this poem is much longer than *Ephraim:* almost 6,500 lines as compared to about 2,500. Like *Ephraim, Mirabell* is divided into sections, but whereas Merrill's former organization alluded to the board's letters, his arrangement here draws upon its numbers. Apparently out of half-ironic deference to his mentors' penchant for mathematical formula, he subdivides each of ten main sections, 0 through 9, into ten and designates each of these subdivisions after the first by a decimal figure.

The figures behind these figures challenge the imagination. Unlike Ephraim, who is far below them in the scheme of things, they were never human. They go by numbers rather than names. "THINK IN FLASHING TRIGONOMETRIES," and represent a force that is at once physical and moral: they "SPEAK FROM WITHIN THE ATOM" and claim to be its "NEGATIVE" potential. Asked to describe themselves, they disconcertingly refer JM and DJ to the bats in their Chinese carpet and wallpaper, and MM confirms that they are "HUGE SQUEAKING" creatures "WITH LITTLE HOT RED EYES." (The characters usually speak as though the dead have physical forms, but we understand that they might be just keeping up appearances.) We learn that they lived on earth when it was ruled by a race of centaurs, whom they served first as messengers and later as architects and physicists charged with devising atomic weapons, until finally they overthrew the centaurs and created their own civilization—a shimmering network of "SMOOTH PLAINS & LATTICE CITIES" suspended above the earth and anchored to it at fourteen points. (That number is sacred to them, so JM arranges the transcriptions of their messages in lines of fourteen syllables.) Encroaching vegetation eventually weakened the moorings, and because they were too proud to repair them, the bats perished with their antigravitational world.

So 741—or Mirabell, as JM names him for the Congreve character, after he changes one day from a bat into a peacock—tells his little class. Not the first of the bats to speak, he becomes their spokesman after he proves the most sympatico. Only the salient points of his lectures—as startling a mélange of information as anything since alchemy—can be given here. Black holes, soul densities, clones, angels, DNA, and salt all come into them. Far from being the hub of the universe as Ephraim imagined, the nine-stage hierarchy is a virtual backwater. The presiding power in our sector is God Biology, at whose right hand are forces of whiteness as the bats are forces of blackness. Also known as "THE 12 PER CENT," the former are led by Michael the archangel and make only a few impressive appearances. "EVERYTHING UP TO THE 12: / STARS MOON ALL NATURE" is "GOD B'S GREENHOUSE," where experiments go on continuously. The crucial work is carried out in "the *Research Lab*," where Mirabell and his peers assist their even more intimidating ancestors in refining "R/LAB" souls, an elite group of two million "MOVERS AND DOERS," especially writers, musicians, and scientists, whose avatars labor toward the earthly paradise. The R/lab is "AN EMPTINESS PACKED FULL. No language here / But formulas unspeakably complex / Which change like weather. No raw material / Other than souls." Those in the nine stages pass the time fretting over the lives of the 3.5 billion non-lab souls whose effect on history is negligible.

Much goes on outside Mirabell's ken. He knows little of certain "OTHER SYSTEMS / & THE SUNS & THE GODS OF EACH THESE ARE THE PANTHEON." He cannot tell us whether antimatter is a malevolent power or "A BENIGN POLICE FORCE KEEPING WATCH ON US,"and he does not know much about the white angels, except that they come from "THE SOURCE OF LIGHT" (the origin, by the way, of poetic inspiration in Merrill's "A Tenancy," in *Water Street*). It dawns on us that his view is what he calls Ephraim's, a "SATELLITE TRUTH THAT ORBITS THE ESSENTIAL."

What are we to make of all this? More to the point, what does Merrill make of it? For one thing, he makes of it what only a man who combines a rare receptivity with a skeptical intelligence can. Especially toward the beginning, he entertains "grave doubts" about his teachers. In one session, prompted by JM's scornful reaction to the news that flying saucers are scouts for obscure alien powers, Mirabell insists that they have verified the saucers on their "SCREENS."

Dear 741,
That's excellent. But *your* verification,
While you yourselves remain unverified?
You can't expect us—well, thanks anyhow.
CURIOUS THAT YOU ACCEPT THE CUP & NOT THE SAUCER

But the cup—this—is happening to *us*!
This by definition's half-subjective.

And indeed throughout the poem we are reminded that Mirabell and the others might well be the product of a folie à deux. In punning response to Mirabell's excitement at being freed at last, after his metamorphosis, "TO SPECULATE," JM muses *sotto voce:* "If only we were less free to reflect; / If diametrics of the mirror didn't / Confirm the antiface there as one's own. . . ." Mirabell likes his new name because it "HAS SOMETHING / OF THE MIRACLE? THE MIRAGE? & SURELY OF THE PLUM!"—but Merrill sees as clearly as we do that it has something of his own as well.

But whether Mirabell and the others are projections or not, in order to have such an experience one must submit to it. As MM says, "SARCASM MON ENFANT WILL GET U NOWHERE." His "SYMPATHY," on the other hand, gets him Mirabell, and in case we are therefore tempted to take too seriously his comparison of DJ and himself with the audience of *Peter Pan* we should recall both that his credulity *is* laced with suspicion and that Mirabell is a far cry from Tinkerbell. It is DJ who is said to be fearful, but no one could think that JM remained undaunted himself—just as no one could imagine that Mirabell and his lessons were coldly invented. As JM complains, surely not altogether disingenuously, it is precisely the foreignness of the material that he finds "maddening—it's all by someone else! / In your voice, Wystan, or in Mirabell's." WHA rejoins with a magnificent defense of self-effacement:

THINK WHAT A MINOR
PART THE SELF PLAYS IN A WORK OF ART
COMPARED TO THOSE GREAT GIVENS THE ROSEBRICK
MANOR
ALL TOPIARY FORMS & METRICAL
MOAT ARIPPLE! FROM ANTHOLOGIZED
PERENNIALS TO HERB GARDEN OF CLICHES
FROM LATIN-LABELED HYBRIDS TO THE FAWN
4 LETTER FUNGI THAT ENRICH THE LAWN,
IS NOT ARCADIA TO DWELL AMONG
GREENWOOD PERSPECTIVES OF THE MOTHER TONGUE
ROOTSYSTEMS UNDERFOOT WHILE OVERHEAD
THE SUN GOD SANG & SHADES OF MEANING SPREAD
& FAR SNOWCAPPED ABSTRACTIONS GLITTERED NEAR
OR FAIRLY MELTED INTO ATMOSPHERE?

In *Mirabell,* of course, humility leads not just to such bravura performances as that breathtakingly reflexive passage (WHA would be the first to point out that it necessitated some self-effacement) but also to a jumble of "MYTH & LEGEND, FACT & LANGUAGE." WHA, more tolerant by nature than JM, attributes this gallimaufry to "URANIA," epic muse of astronomy, "BABBLING ON THE THRESHOLD OF / OUR NEW ATOMIC AGE," and from the beginning he finds it "VERY BEAUTIFUL." At first JM won't have any of it, and he responds with brilliant indignation:

> Dear Wystan, VERY BEAUTIFUL all this
> Warmed-up Milton, Dante, Genesis?
> This great tradition that has come to grief
> In volumes by Blavatsky and Gurdjieff?
> Von and Torro in their Star Trek capes,
> Atlantis, UFOs, God's chosen apes—?
> Nobody can transfigure junk like that
> Without first turning down the rheostat
> To Allegory, in whose gloom the whole
> Horror of Popthink fastens on the soul,
> Harder to scrape off than bubblegum.

Understandably, he mistrusts the poetic result, and Mirabell himself acknowledges the difficulty: "OUR GREAT ORNAMENTAL & BIZARRE OBJECT HARDLY / ABLE TO BE GOT THRU THE DOOR IS IF NOT LAUGHABLE / AT THE LEAST ODD TO THE HOUSE."

And yet, to the extent that the proof of the worth of a framework is the quality of the detail that it elicits, Merrill's is invaluable. WHA's apology and JM's diatribe (I have quoted only part of each) are two of a host of splendid instances—which only the scope and richness of the poem permit us to think of as details. *Mirabell* confirms what *Ephraim* suggested, that Merrill has made himself the most versatile of American poets. . . . Of course he has the benefit of all those voices speaking through him. Here he and Chester Kallman, the latter in a state of manic disgust at the news that he will be reborn as a black, heterosexual, unpoetic South African, join in a very funny duet:

> FANCY A NICE JEWISH MS LIKE ME
> (Chester after dinner) GETTING T H E
> ULTIMATE REJECTION SLIP IS GOD
> CYRIL CONNOLLY? . . .
> You shock us, Chester. After months of idle,
> Useless isolation—ALL I HEAR

ARE THESE B MINOR HYMNS TO USEFULNESS:
LITTLE MISS BONAMI OOH SO GLAD
TO FIND ARCADIA IN A BRILLO PAD!
LAUGH CLONE LAUGH   AH LIFE   I FEEL THE LASH
OF THE NEW MASTER   NOTHING NOW BUT CRASH
COURSES   What does Wystan say?   TO PLATO?
HAVING DROPPED ME LIKE A HOT   O SHIT
WHAT GOOD IS RHYME NOW   Come, think back, admit
That best of all was to be flesh and blood,
Young, eager, ear cocked for your new name—MUD

Confront your writing student who complains about the *constriction* of rhyme and meter with that passage and you will change his life.

The same matrix brings forth passages of great mystical beauty, as when the pooled creative energies of Mirabell and his four students produce a vision of the union of the four elements and nature. It begins with Mirabell using the pointer to establish the ground bass:

Our peacock marks time back and forth from One
   To Zero: a pavane
Andante in an alley of green oaks;
The ostinato ground we each in turn
Strum a division soundlessly upon;
   A prayer-wheel whose four spokes
   Flow and crumble, breathe and burn.

Even this septet form (which Merrill invented in "The Black Swan" in his first book over thirty years ago) proves admirably various. When WHA takes over the cup he has his own silver manner and tone, and the elements speak with a thrilling resonance when they warn of a possible enemy: "THE MATTER WHICH IS NOT WAS EVER OURS / TO GUARD AGAINST. ITS POWERS / ARE MAGNETIZED BY FOREIGN BEACONS, BLACK / HANDS TESTING THE GREENHOUSE PANE BY PANE."

Limited as it would seem to be by the paucity of action and a cast that is mostly invisible, Merrill's poem is dramatic through and through. It justifies time and again his metaphorical transformation of the twenty-six letters on the board into footlights and the bats' red eyes into exit lights. Often using the fewest words, those in the other world convey gestures, facial expressions, poses, and strike whole chords of emotion. Late in the poem Mirabell (who proudly signals his metaphors with an "(M)" must look forward to the day when he will no longer be JM's and DJ's chief contact: "WHO KNOWS, I MAY DO / SOME USEFUL WORK IN THE (M) FUTURE? & AT NIGHT COME HOME / SLIP INTO MY MIRABELL ROBES AND DREAM OF THESE OLD TIMES." And there are moments of greater drama, as vivid as they are inventive, in which Merrill turns the limitations of set and props to his advantage—as when Mirabell and his cohorts react to an unintentionally devastating remark:

> For the cup goes reeling to the Board's brink—
> AH MES ENFANTS HE FELL BACK AS IF STRUCK
> Had you been listening? NO AN EVER LOUDER
> RUSTLING OF THEIR 28 WINGS DROWNED OUT
>
> Wystan (as if deafened): WHAT WHAT WHAT

In section 9 the group even manages a picnic at the beach. Here WHA's forced economy works the magic, as he converts the light from the xerox machine that has copied the first pages of this poem into the "MILD SUMMER LIGHTNING" of a storm that threatens to wash out the fete. Waste not, want not.

In spite of JM's early worries on this score, science inspires some of the poem's finest lyrical moments. Mirabell's dismaying determinism provokes a chilling villanelle on the theme of "*No accident,*" and the rigorous, predestining form suits the proposition perfectly. "DNA, that sinuous molecule, / The serpent in [the bats'] version of the myth," shapes one passage in which both the undulating margin and the interweaving of two voices suggest the double helix. JM's meditation on the possibility of poems of science produces this subatomic pastoral:

> The day will come . . .
> The day has never gone. Proton and Neutron
> Under a plane tree by the stream repeat
> Their eclogue, orbited by twinkling flocks.
> And on the dimmest shore of consciousness
> Polypeptides—in primeval thrall
> To what new moon I wonder—rise and fall.

He ingeniously affirms the possible union of these two universal languages at the outset of each section, where the first sound repeats, in one language or another, that section's number. Thus section 0 begins "Oh very well then," and section 1 echoes its number in both French and English: "UNHEEDFUL ONE." 3's "Trials and tremors" make use of Greek and the reader's choice of several other languages, 4's "Fear" of German, 5's "Go" of Japanese, 6's "She stood" of Russian, 7's "CHILDREN" of Chinese, 9's "NO VEIL" of Italian and Portuguese. 2 and 8 ring changes on the device, the one beginning with the second letter of the Hebrew alphabet (sometimes used in place of the number) in "Bethinking," the other with "8."

Now fused, now confused, Merrill's facts and fictions seem more and more inextricable—which should not surprise us, since history shows us that the one may change into the other, rather as 741 changes into Mirabell the peacock. As WHA has it: "THE ELDER FACTS IN LIVERY OF FABLE / HAVE JOINED THE DANCE FOR FACT IS IS IS FABLE: / THIS IS OUR GIFT FROM MIRABELL MY DEARS." Perhaps fable is the afterlife any good fact can look forward to. Or perhaps, as the peacock was there within the bat all along just wanting some sympathetic attention to free him, so the fable waits inside the fact. In any case, the truth that both fact and fable point to, this poem implies, is a fundamental unity. If at times Merrill's conjunction of science and poetry resembles a double helix less than a centaur, he has no honest alternative. *Mirabell* intimates a unity that of course it cannot define once and for all. As Randall Jarrell put the dilemma in another context, "as everyone must realize, it is possible to tell the truth about the world in terms that are false, limited, and fantastic—else how should we have told it?"

The relationship between science and poetry is just one aspect of a radical paradox, the intuition of which unifies this volume. If *Mirabell* in itself lacks a certain architectural elegance, as one of JM's friends hints in 8.8, it nonetheless has a center everywhere evident, a sense of "One nature dual to the end." "Good? Evil? is it all the same?" JM wonders in a characteristic passage. The universe and God are perhaps also one. If Mirabell sometimes speaks of God B as though he were transcendent, he interprets things in Hegelian and pantheistic terms as well ("GOD B IS NOT / ONLY HISTORY BUT EARTH ITSELF HE IS THE GREENHOUSE"), and Michael, in the superb conclusion, also tells us that he is immanent and evolving: "GOD IS THE ACCUMULATED INTELLIGENCE IN CELLS SINCE THE DEATH OF THE FIRST DISTANT CELL."

One crucial set of terms here is "mind" and "nature." The first of the bats to contact JM and DJ implores them to "RAISE A SONG TO OUR REAL ORDER MYND AND NATURE WEDDED"; and later JM counters some teasing by MM and WHA by arguing that Nature is "Mind's equal. Not a slave / But mother, sister, bride. I think we're meant / To save that marriage." The poem's dramatic structure embodies the marriage, for the individuals in each pair of speakers complement one another much as the pairs themselves do. Borrowing part of his phrase from Spenser, Merrill describes WHA and MM as "Father of forms and matter of fact mother," and just as WHA is always off to see Plato, MM devotes herself to gardening. Correspondingly, while JM's work with "numbers" associates him with mind and form, DJ is "THE SHAPING HAND OF NATURE." At the same time, the other world is related most closely to mind (the bats, destroyed because they separated themselves from Nature, are still her "FRIENDLY RIVALS") and this one, inevitably, to nature—though nature, personified as one Mrs. Smith in *Ephraim,* appears at one point here as Mrs. Myth. As the dualisms proliferate and overlap one comes to feel that they might be only provisional, that mind and nature might be different words for the same whole, as Adam and atom (a recurrent pun) are for the same microcosm of it. The "lenses, the twin zeros" that are "Central to this bOOk," and its literal point of departure ("O Oh"), begin as binocular in a sonnet in 4.5 and end as a "spyglass," either end of which can be looked through. These are *Books of Number,* and the basic numbers are 2 and 1, which keep turning into one another.

It might be, as Stevens dryly suggests toward the end of his own *Notes toward a Supreme Fiction,* that "They will get it straight one day at the Sorbonne," that we will return at twilight from a lecture pleased to find that the rational and the irrational are one. But between now and then there will not be many poetic projects as daring, absorbing, ambitious, and richly varied as the one Merrill is now at work on.

Thom Gunn

A Heroic Enterprise

I feel rather as if I were setting out to review *Ulysses* in 1922. "The Book of Ephraim" is a ninety-page poem from the volume *Divine Comedies* (1976), and *Mirabell* is its book-length sequel, published in 1978. It is not that they are so difficult to understand as that they are so unprecedented, their ambitions are so high, the relationships both to each other and to the rest of Merrill's work are so complex.

James Merrill is one of the few members of that generation of poets from the 1950s who still writes in rhyme and meter. Most of the rest converted to free verse once and for all in the early 1960s, and inveighed against their previous metrical misdeeds with the uncompromising energy of old sinners who have seen the light in the barracks of the Salvation Army. Out of such testimony arose the curious phrase "naked poetry." Of course, Merrill, like any good poet, had never used meter and rhyme as if they were clothes that could be put on or off the naked body of his meaning. They were part of that body.

His poetry was as personal, in its way, as Ginsberg's—it too was about travels, family, male lovers, friends. And while the impulsive life of Ginsberg has been exposed to us through an impulsive style, improvisatory and unrevised, the elegant life of Merrill was presented in an elegant style, witty and punning, in rhymed stanzas or grouped sonnets. It was elegant, again, not like clothing, but like the behavior—the manner and movement and gesture—of the body itself.

If style is an instrument of exploration, Merrill's developed into a most precise instrument. He explored certain aspects of his childhood through seven run-together sonnets in his well-known poem "The Broken Home" of 1967. It is an honest but disturbing poem: it answers all the questions it can about the past and candidly leaves open those it can't. One of the questions left open is that of the distance between "I" in the present and "I" in the past. There is an odd reserve in the portrayal of his adult self: we are told more

From *San Francisco Review of Books,* August 1979.

about what he does not do and what he is not than about what he does and is: and dealing with the adult first person was to be a recurring problem, I think a conscious one, for Merrill in his poetry of the 1960s and early 1970s. His poetry has been, typically, personal and anecdotal, but the narrator was most comfortable as an almost anonymous observer (as in the very funny "Charles on Fire"), least comfortable at the center of the poem, where on occasion (as in "Days of 1964") the treatment becomes positively rhetorical. The rhetoric amounts to a kind of withholding, but I am not sure of what.

A writer goes from good to better by acquiring a grasp over new kinds of material. The material may well have been there, in the writer's life, for a long time, but the grasp is a matter of being able to accommodate it in the imaginative life of his writing. The advance in "Ephraim" is striking. The shorter poems had dealt with marvelous fragments of a sociable life—a rather grand one, as sociable lives go. The two parts of the trilogy present a "world" as complete, as foreign, as inclusive, and as detailed as those of Mann in the Joseph books and of Tolkien.

It turns out that Merrill and David Jackson, the man he lives with, had for twenty years been communicating with spirits on a Ouija board, and with one especially, an affable familiar called Ephraim, who had been a courtier on Tiberius's Capri, where he was strangled at the Emperor's order for having had sex with the young Caligula.

Much of the conversation is about the transmigration of souls, which pass through many bodies, and Merrill and Jackson speak with other spirits (the dead between bodies) including those of two recently dead friends, one famous and one not: W. H. Auden and Maria Mitsotáki (who was the subject of an earlier short poem).

The sessions at the board are set against the domestic and social life of the two men over a period of twenty years. Not only against this, though. During these years Merrill was attempting to transform the accumulating mass of fascinating material into a novel. Ephraim disapproves of the novel, as involving too great a transformation of the facts, amounting to a falsification; Merrill describes it amusingly and perhaps unfairly as weighed down with crude symbolic meanings; eventually his subconscious enables him to lose the troublesome manuscripts in a taxi.

In his novel of 1965, *The (Diblos) Notebook,* Merrill had tried to discuss the process of writing a work of fiction while actually writing it, but "Ephraim" is even more complicated: not only does he discuss the poem while writing the poem, he also discusses the lost novel. And so we have fictional characters, living and dead, rubbing shoulders with real characters, living and dead. Extremely complex relationships, need I say, are built up.

The poem is discontinuous, in a sense. It is divided into twenty-six parts, arranged in chronological order, but each a separate poem with its own thematic organization. The style varies in pace and density. Merrill has never before been so eloquent and so lucid: he speaks, for example, of how "power's worst abusers" (Hitler or Caligula) are held "incommunicado" after death, their souls not for re-use, "cysts in the tissue of eternity." At another point he refers to a spirit "in whose mouth the least / Dull fact had shone of old, a wetted pebble." The succinct but almost laconic force of such metaphor is the fruit of some twenty-five years or more of writing.

Merrill's attitude to his "sources," the voices from the other world, is disarmingly open-minded. He is aware of the possibility of self-deception. Are the spirits real or are they a projection of the people who evoke them? He doesn't profess to know. In future years there are bound to be arguments about the legitimacy of the sources of this poetry, but for me, simply, it all works—as mythology, as history, as a possible interpretation of existence. It works for me as say Dante almost always does and as Blake in the Prophetic Books rather seldom does: the terms are plausible, humane, never arbitrary, and always interesting.

There is indeed a continual consciousness of Dante throughout these works, though wisely no real attempt to imitate him. (It would be an act of desperation to compare them to the *Inferno* and the *Purgatorio*. But many scholars are desperate men and women, and no doubt such detailed comparisons will be made.) But there *is* a great resemblance to Dante, not so much in the fact that the poetry constitutes an ambitious work of otherworldly instruction as in the easy mingling of all the poet's kinds of experience—in particular of personal friends with the famous and historical.

Of otherworldly instruction, there is considerably more in *Mirabell* than there was in "Ephraim," which in retrospect takes on some of the characteristics of a prologue. Much of *Mirabell* consists of the story of the Fallen Angels, of whom Mirabell is one. They are a race of enormous bats who by their science once raised a "crust world" into the stratosphere, anchored to the earth at fourteen points by radiated signals. Their sin, the reason that their world breaks apart, was—in both literal and metaphorical terms—that of abandoning earth.

> THE 14 POINTS OF CONTACT HELD OUR SKIN IN PLACE THEY STRAIND
> & BROKE & OUR VAST SKEIN OF SMOOTH PLAINS & LATTICE CITIES
> (TO OUR EYES FAIR & NATURAL) SHIVERD BROKE INTO FLAME

(I should point out that spirits speak in upper case.) Much later, in the era of man, the angels are set to work by "God Biology" to improve and refine souls as they go from body to body, the ultimate aim being to bring about an earthly paradise. The discussion of all this is carried on in a "seminar" consisting of Merrill, David Jackson, the dead Auden, the dead Maria, and Mirabell.

This book is much more of a straightforward and connected *story* than "Ephraim." Merrill feels time pressing in on him, he

cannot spare those twenty
Years in a cool dark place that *Ephraim* took
In order to be palatable wine.

It is plainer, but it is also easier and racier. The exposition of idea, fact, and myth is given narrative pace by a growing "worldliness" and humanity that Mirabell assumes in contact with the living and dead humans. His style becomes more circumstantial and more metaphorical as the book progresses.

I do not mean to imply that *Mirabell* is all written in one measure or that it is all narrative without variation. The bat-angels speak in prose-like syllabics, the others in meter. Lyrics are embodied in the story. There is also room for flashbacks, asides from the dead Auden on the art of poetry, and incidents that have only indirect bearing on the incidents at the Ouija board. The style varies from the simplicity of a phrase like "the cool, smalltown dawn" to the complexity of this reference to Noah (Mirabell has explained that the Ark carried the dust saved from the Fall—"its particles were / formulas, atomic structures, communicants of life"):

THAT WAS GOD B'S METHOD & WE, APPROACHING U HANDS CUPPD
WITH LESSONS, HELPD U TO CONSTRUCT A METHOD OF YR OWN.
2 BY 2 WE HAVE ENTERD YR MINDS & NOW YEARS LATER
THE COMMUNICATION IS AFLOAT OVER A DROWND WORLD.

The density of metaphorical life in such a passage gives some indication of the scope, the inclusiveness, the richness of Merrill's heroic enterprise. Fact is seen as metaphor, metaphor as fact; there is a constant movement between the two, making of *Mirabell* a myth even more complex and exciting than "Ephraim." Keats spoke of the long poem (as opposed to the short) as somewhere he "could turn round in," and in *Mirabell* Merrill does indeed turn round and stretch and show us his powers—at their full, I think, for the first time. Elegance has become an extended and graceful strength, and dramatic talent is displayed that never had such a chance before in shorter forms. There are certainly criticisms that can be made—some of them are made by a friend and neighbor, Robert Morse, *in* the poem—but they seem to me small compared with the size of the achievement.

The first person is at last dealt with adequately. It is never suppressed into anonymity, it is never falsified by rhetoric. One of the triumphs, and it is no minor one, of these two long poems, is in Merrill's portrayal of the domestic situation in the middle of which it all takes place. It is also, not incidentally, the most convincing description I know of a gay marriage. Much of what makes any marriage successful is the ability to take the importance of one's partner for granted, to *depend* on the other's love without being in a state of continuous erotic or passional tension. Merrill's indication of these abilities is the firmer for being indirect. The men's life together is presented to us in detail which is almost casual: we see them choosing wallpaper, keeping house, traveling, entertaining, and above all sitting at the Ouija board. It is not a minor triumph and it is not an incidental one because, after all, it is the two of them in their closeness who have evoked the whole spirit world of "Ephraim" and *Mirabell,* or perhaps even created it.

PHOEBE PETTINGELL

Voices from the Atom

"Poems of *Science*? Ugh. / The very thought. To squint through those steel-rimmed / Glasses of the congenitally slug- / Pale boy at school, with his precipitates, / his fruitflies and his slide-rule? Science meant / Obfuscation, boredom." So James Merrill describes his first reaction in *Mirabell: Books of Number* when the spirits who speak through his Ouija board announce that he has been chosen to reveal the ways of "God Biology" to man.

Ouija? Heavenly messengers? Their appearance will not surprise readers of Merrill's *Divine Comedies* (1976). In that work, the poet told of bizarre communications that he and his companion, David Jackson, had received over a twenty-year period from "Ephraim"—a first-century Hellenistic Jew who claimed to have been a slave at the court of Tiberius. This singular informant gossiped about his past and present, and instructed his listeners on the heavenly hierarchy—seemingly as bound by red tape and bureaucratic mismanagement as any on earth. Through him, though, JM and DJ were able to contact dead friends, in particular two quasi-parental figures: W. H. Auden, Merrill's poetic mentor, and Maria Mitsotáki, whom Merrill once addressed as "the Muse of my off-days" (*The Firescreen,* 1969). Such a high comic romp was rather startling after the previous "chronicles of love and loss." Still, it was undeniable that in shaking the burdens of nostalgia and regret, the poet's voice deepened with impressive authority.

Now it turns out that "The Book of Ephraim" was merely a curtain-raiser for *Mirabell's* more solemn masque. Mysterious powers who "SPEAK FROM WITHIN THE ATOM" (readers must get used to the Ouija board's uppercase letters) have come to tell of the dangers of atomic energy. "Maria and Wystan," who also communicate through the board, describe them as enormous black bats with gargoyle faces and red eyes. The voices identify themselves as "bad angels," the negative charge of energy, creators of the black holes in space, and pure reason without matter. Their fall was a nuclear explosion brought about when they tried to wrest power from the positive

From the *New Leader,* December 4, 1978. Reprinted with permission of *The New Leader,* granted September 3, 1992.

forces. They founded, then destroyed Arcadia on Atlantis; later they instructed the heretic pharaoh Akhnaton to build a crystal pyramid that, had it not been slightly flawed, would have immolated the earth. Since 1938, when Enrico Fermi first split the atom, mankind has teetered on the brink of a similar cataclysm, but God Biology does not want his supreme creation destroyed. Therefore these messengers, repentant of their former mischief, have arrived to warn against the evil of energy that does not come from the sun. "THE DEVIL HAS BEEN DRIVEN FROM US INTO MAN WE NOW / MUST DRIVE IT OUT OF HIM OUR TOOLS ARE MIND WORDS REASON LIGHT."

Although intrigued, the poet and his friend are understandably nervous. "I really only like Ephraim and his crowd," complains DJ. It is one thing to enjoy gossip from the beyond, quite another to accept an atomic bat as one's preceptor. As for JM, who had planned to compose austere odes to DNA, he indignantly protests this farrago:

> Atlantis, UFOs, God's chosen apes—?
> Nobody can transfigure junk like that
> Without first turning down the rheostat
> To Allegory, in whose gloom the whole
> Horror of Popthink fastens on the soul,
> Harder to scrape off than bubblegum.

Despite this initial bleak view, the general movement of *Mirabell* manages to metamorphosize the ordinary, the trivial, the ridiculous into the sublime. Enter 741, a gentle bat, who conducts a seminar on the new religion of symbolic language. In the process, his four pupils—JM, DJ, Maria, and Wystan—teach him about human manners, which elevate us above the animal world, and he is transformed into a peacock. JM names him "Mirabell," after the romantic hero of Congreve's *The Way of the World*. To celebrate the newfound faith, there is a picnic of words—a love feast or agape, introduced by Auden, whose much-missed voice Merrill resurrects with uncanny fidelity.

But even these affirmations of the triumph of Love over time and place give way to a deeper revelation. "From the winedark sea of space," the guardian of light, Archangel Michael, brings a divine message: Man is "A SPECIES OF THE SUN'S MAKING," and the accumulated energy of the cell is "AN ANCIENT AND IMMORTAL INTELLIGENCE," which is God. On this awesome note, the poem abruptly ends.

Lest readers get the impression that *Mirabell* is chiefly devoted to the exposition of dubious metaphysics, I hasten to note that no summary can convey the variety or cohesion of its dramatic changes. A matter as frivolous as redecorating a room turns out to have cosmic significance. There are numberless subplots, each more delightful than the last. One involves the horrifying discovery by the late poet, Chester Kallman, that he is to be reborn as an African political leader; another relates how the spirit of Rimbaud ghostwrote *The Waste Land.* Akhnaton and his Queen Nefertiti, doomed by love and pride, provide what Merrill mockingly styles "*Nuits de Cleopatrè.*" Instruction in science, history and theology, Arabian Nights stories, arguments and debates are all interwoven with "set pieces"—lyrical poems of exquisite musicality, reminiscent of the songs in Goethe's *Faust.* There is something for everyone, yet it all forms a unity, bonded like those atoms the poem celebrates.

Perhaps the most powerful enchantment of the book is the vividness and charm of its characters. The angels are radiantly otherworldly; the bats frighteningly so, except for the human Mirabell. One easily learns to distinguish different speech mannerisms for the various humans, who use "rough pentameter, our natural birthright" (the immortals speak in syllabics). Emotions are rife. "Maman" Maria furiously attacks the bats for bullying, mothers everybody, and preens in her new clothes. Wystan and JM are the seminar's intellectuals, indulging in introspection about their own poetic gifts, and a certain semirepressed rivalry. DJ, the most intuitive of the group, is also the most fearful and inclined to suspect Gothic horrors. The details of these lives (and afterlives) make as beguiling a story as any pastoral novel of manners from Jane Austen's *Emma* to E. F. Benson's *Make Way for Lucia.* When JM asks Wystan if he believes what the powers have been saying, he replies: "Let me say my dear / I think the four of us are touchingly believable."

What, then, of the "poems of science"? When his voices tell Merrill that "MAN'S TERMITE PALACE BEEHIVE ANTHILL PYRAMID JM IS LANGUAGE," they assume our ability to accept a metaphor that compares structures collectively built by social insects to human culture. While our ancestors tended to describe ants and bees in anthropomorphic terms as provident, industrious, or dutiful, today the comparisons have been reversed and we easily identify our regimentation and genetic impulses as akin to the insects'. To insist that science and art are diametrically opposed is to ignore how much our thinking has been shaped by the "imaginative" tropes of scientists from Darwin and Freud to Leakey and Skinner. Unpleasant as the thought may be, we cannot help suspecting that the mysterious motivation of cells controls our actions—that we have no more free will than the animals.

Nevertheless, the Muses of most poets today parade like the Madwoman of Chaillot, dressed in outmoded fashions of thought, ready to do single-handed battle against modernism. *Mirabell,* by contrast, is not afraid to tackle the problem head-on. Suppose that the cell *is* the source of our behavior, Merrill asks, how can we adjust our thinking without losing our sense of worth and purpose? When theology, with its system of ethics, was paramount, God was "WRATHFUL IF IF IF JUST." But "NOW SCIENCE, FORCED MORE AND MORE TO SHARE THE RELIGIOUS FIELD OF CONSCIOUSNESS, MUST TRY TO REASSURE," since it cannot offer "justice"; morality is not part of its terminology. God Biology is no *deus absconditus,* however, but an intensely personal deity. If He is in the "accumulated intelligence" of DNA, then the impulses transmitted must be His.

Ultimately, Merrill's celestial circus is a brilliant philosophy of metaphor—that "ritual of the new religion." At all times it is affirmed that there *are* no bats—spirits have no form. Maria explains that they are products of "the mind's eye," the imagination that must see an idea to conceive it. The poet's function is to translate the abstract into the vividly concrete. No reader of *Mirabell* will ever think of atoms quite the way he did before encountering the personifications of their forces. Yet after all the grotesques, arabesques, human interest, we become more sophisticated, and are prepared for the unadorned revelation of the angels.

James Merrill has created a poem as central to our generation as *The Waste Land* was to the one before us. *Mirabell* holds a mirror up to our deepest fears: that our actions are impelled, not chosen; that we cannot assimilate the increasingly complex way in which our world must be viewed; that we have lost religion and morality; that our race is doomed to extinction. But at the same time it acknowledges this state of affairs, the poem offers numinous reassurance that we can be saved by "the life raft of language"—that beyond our myopic vision gleams a profounder understanding of life than we have yet conceived.

Helen Vendler

Mirabell: Books of Number

James Merrill's *Mirabell: Books of Number,* which won the National Book Award for 1978, is the middle volume of a trilogy composed with the aid of a Ouija board. The Ouija board is a symbol system that offers potentially unlimited combinations of letters and numbers, affirmations and denials; it can stand, we might say, for language itself. The first installment of Merrill's trilogy, "The Book of Ephraim" (printed in *Divine Comedies,* in 1976), exhausted the letters of the board; it was composed in twenty-six sections labels "A" through "Z." The current volume uses up the numbers of the board in ten books going from zero to nine. The final volume, to be called *Scripts for the Pageant,* is left with "Yes" and "No." The Ouija board is a shared system, used by the dead and the living, in which tradition, in the person of the dead, meets an individual talent—or, in this case, the joint talents of the poet and his friend David Jackson. Together, as JM and DJ, in their house at Stonington, where the action of *Mirabell* occurs, they transcribe the rapid gestures of a blue-willow cup that they use instead of a planchette. The messages from "the other side," all in the uppercase of the board, are edited by Merrill—compressed, made intelligible, made into poetry. The books of the trilogy consist of board messages interspersed with commentary and colloquy by the poet.

The pages of the books are typographically unnerving, as blocks of otherworldly uppercase—looking, as a friend remarked, like a computer printout—alternate with blocks of mortal lowercase. The uppercase, in the board's peculiar spelling—"before" becomes "B4,"you" becomes "U"—is sometimes a ten-syllable line (when dead people talk), sometimes a fourteen-syllable line (when the spirits, who enact "a fall from metrical grace," take over). Human talk is always decasyllabic, in "this rough pentameter, our virtual birthright." From time to time, a lyric form, like a strain of music, appears. The talk of the dead and of the living alike tends to rhyme in

---

From *New Yorker,* September 3, 1979. Also published in *Part of Nature, Part of Us* (Cambridge: Harvard University Press, 1980). Reprinted by permission of Helen Vendler and Harvard University Press.

couplets and quatrains, but that of the spirits does not rhyme. The spirits, who are here represented chiefly by one among them bearing the number 741, seem to be in part what Milton would have called the fallen angels, and are first conceived of as black batlike creatures. At the center of the third book, 741 metamorphoses into a peacock, and he is later given the name Mirabell, supposedly after the "strut and plumage" of Congreve's hero, but also after "Merrill." Mirabell, "a paragon of courtly gentleness," here replaces the earlier Ephraim as familiar spirit. Ephraim was chatty, conversational; he was comfortable in iambic pentameter, since he was human ("A Greek Jew / Born AD 8 at XANTHOS . . . / a favorite of TIBERIUS . . . Died / AD 36 on CAPRI throttled / By the imperial guard for having LOVED / THE MONSTER'S NEPHEW (sic) CALIGULA"). However, Ephraim spoke rather rarely, and his book is narrated mostly by Merrill. Mirabell, on the other hand, speaks in ungainly syllabics, and the poet's interpolated lines serve as connective tissue between Mirabell's speeches and the speeches of the dead. The dead, principally, are Wystan Auden and Maria Mitsotáki, a childless Greek friend of Merrill's, whom he celebrated in a lyric, "Words for Maria" (1969), and who died of cancer.

Mirabell is a poem about the dead in part because it is a poem of the single life and childlessness; since there is no question of posterity, life is composed of oneself and one's friends, the dead as much as the living. The four bound together round the Ouija board—JM, DJ, Wystan, Maria—are chosen for their lessons because of their childlessness. To Auden's question "Why the four of us?" Mirabell answers, "KEEP IN MIND THE CHILDLESSNESS WE SHARE THIS TURNS US / OUTWARD TO THE LESSONS & THE MYSTERIES." The scale of the poem is both domestic and cosmic. The domestic life includes day-by-day details of life in Greece and in Stonington, the visits of friends, the deaths of parents, an operation. The cosmic life, presided over in Manichean fashion by two gods—Chaos, the god of feeling, and an inexorable "God B" (for "biology")—is evolutionary, hierarchical, mythological, and intermittently purposive. God B's successive projects have included Atlantis, the centaurs, and Eden; he "is not only history but earth itself." The literary tradition in which the poem falls includes all works written by men to whom the angels speak outright: Dante, the four Apostles, Buddha, Mohammed, and, in later days, Milton, Blake, Victor Hugo, and Yeats. Merrill himself diffidently admits to doubts about "all this / warmed up Milton, Dante, Genesis," fearing "Allegory in whose gloom the whole / Horror of Popthink fastens on the soul"; he worries about being "cast / Into this paper Hell out of Doré / or Disney." On the other hand, the quintet of Merrill, Jackson, Auden, Maria Mitsotáki, and Mirabell is said to be an example of the "vital groupings of five," who do "V work"—the work of mind and heart (primarily poetry and music)—encouraged, according to Mirabell, by loves that do not envisage the production of bodies:

> LOVE OF ONE MAN FOR ANOTHER OR LOVE BETWEEN WOMEN
> IS A NEW DEVELOPMENT OF THE PAST 4000 YEARS
> ENCOURAGING SUCH MIND VALUES AS PRODUCE THE BLOSSOMS
> OF POETRY & MUSIC, THOSE 2 PRINCIPAL LIGHTS OF
> GOD BIOLOGY. LESSER ARTS NEEDED NO EXEGETES:
> ARCHITECTURE SCULPTURE THE MOSAICS & PAINTINGS THAT
> FLOWERD IN GREECE & PERSIA CELEBRATED THE BODY.
> POETRY MUSIC SONG INDWELL & CELEBRATE THE MIND . . .
> HEART IF U WILL.

Few painters or sculptors enter this life of the mind, Mirabell adds, since they, "LIKE ALL SO-CALLED NORMAL LOVERS," exist for no purpose other than to produce bodies. This Platonic myth is mocked by Mirabell's listeners: "Come now, admit that certain very great / Poets and musicians have been straight." But the claim, however whimsical, has been made, and the whole of Merrill's trilogy can be seen as a substitution of the virtues of mind and heart—culminating in music and poetry—for the civic and familial and martial virtues usually espoused by the epic.

We might hesitate to think of *Mirabell* in epic terms, since it learns at least as much from Pope and Byron as from Dante. But in its encylopedic instructions about the history of the cosmos and its cast of characters from Olympus (if we may so locate the spirits) and from Hades as well as from earth, its traits are epic ones. For all its rueful tone as it fears and doubts its own matter and method, it goes irrepressibly along, piecing together shards of myth from all cultures—Akhnaton rubs shoulders with Mohammed and centaurs, while Mother Nature, in conjunction with the Sultan God B, presides overall. The hymn to nature in the seventh book articulates the ebb and flow of loyalty—now to mind, now to nature—implicit in the whole poem. Fearful of the power of the senses, Merrill, like some modern metaphysical, asks what rational instruments they have robbed him of—"What have you done with / My books, my watch and compass, my slide-rule?"—but nature answers with her own fascination of texture, whether in constellations or in bodies, "those infinite / Spangled thinnesses whose weave gosling and cygnet / Have learned already in the shell."

When Merrill contemplates what he has done in writing this book, he complains to Auden that the result is maddening:

it's all by someone else!
In your voice, Wystan, or in Mirabell's.
I want it mine, but cannot spare those twenty
Years in a cool dark place that *Ephraim* took
In order to be palatable wine.
This book by contrast, immature, supine,
Still kicks against its archetypal cradle.
. . . I'd set
My whole heart, after *Ephraim,* on returning
To private life, to my own words. Instead,
Here I go again, a vehicle
In this cosmic carpool. Mirabell once said
He taps my word banks. I'd be happier
If *I* were tapping them. Or thought I were.

Auden replies in a magisterial defense of convention, tradition, and fable. On convention:

THINK WHAT A MINOR
PART THE SELF PLAYS IN A WORK OF ART
COMPARED TO THOSE GREAT GIVENS THE ROSEBRICK MANOR
ALL TOPIARY FORMS & METRICAL
MOAT ARIPPLE!

On tradition:

AS FOR THE FAMILY ITSELF MY DEAR
JUST GAPE UP AT THAT CORONETED FRIEZE:
SWEET WILLIAMS & FATE-FLAVORED EMILIES
THE DOUBTING THOMAS & THE DULCET ONE
(HARDY MY BOY WHO ELSE? & CAMPION).

On the superiority of fable to facts:

FACTS JM WERE ALL U KNEW TO WANT,
WRETCHED RICKETY RECALCITRANT
URCHINS THE FEW WHO LIVE GROW UP TO BE
IMPS OF THE ANTIMASQUE.

In fable, "A TABLE / IS SET & LAMPS LIT FOR THE FEASTING GODS." Auden concludes that, given time, facts themselves take on the livery of fable, and become material for art. The poem ends as Mirabell withdraws in favor of a stern-voiced angel Michael, speaking in long, irregular lines: he will be the next instructor, an unfallen rather than a fallen one, as Merrill proceeds into the *Paradiso* of his "Divine Comedies."

"Ephraim" is, on the whole, a cheerful book, constructed around a mythology of reincarnation: most people live on, over and over, even if in someone elses's body. In *Mirabell,* Merrill and Jackson discover that their dead companions Auden and Maria will not be reincarnated, but will dissolve into their elements, having first been stripped of their earthly connections. The end of the book celebrates "Maria's Himmelfahrt" and Auden's. Goodbyes are said, of a careful lightness:

How
We'll miss you! We'd imagined—I know CIAO

JM had imagined a thousand and one nights of conversation with these indispensable voices. But the Ouija board meets the law of dissolution, and in the last episode Auden and Maria seem to have disappeared, leaving behind only a snapshot—"Young, windblown / Maria with dark glasses and Gitane"—and a book "by Wystan / Face up . . . all week / Open to Miranda's villanelle." *Mirabell* is a book of long farewell to the parental figures of Auden and Maria, a book that holds on to the dead as long as possible. They are the people who call JM and DJ "MES ENFANTS" (Maria, known as "Maman") or "MY BOYS" (Auden). When these voices fall silent, there will be no one to whom the poet is a child. Though Merrill's mother is alive, she is deliberately left out of the trilogy, as "Ephraim" explains:

All of which lights up, as scholarship
Now and then does, a matter hitherto
Overpainted—the absence from these pages
Of my own mother. Because of course she's here
Throughout, the breath drawn after every line,
Essential to its making as to mine.

The deaths of David Jackson's parents preface the appearance of Mirabell. In the usual biological cycle, parents die after their children have become parents; the internalizing of the parental role, it is believed, enables the parents to be absorbed into the filial psyche. In the childless world of *Mirabell,* the disappearance of parents, or parental friends, is the disappearance of the parental and therefore of the filial; JM and DJ can no longer be "boys," but must put on the mortality of the survivor. However, much the sweetness of posthumous conversation with Auden and Maria may be prolonged—with analyses of their character, examples of their wit, descriptions of their lives—

the end of the exchange is envisaged from Maria's first warning, at the end of Book 1: "I HAVE MORE TO LOSE." In Merrill's myth, Maria will become a plant, not a human being; the radiation she endured as a treatment for cancer reduced her human soul to the vegetative level. Auden will be "stripped, reduced to essences, joined to infinity," like one of his beloved minerals:

> What must at length be borne
> Is that the sacred bonds are chemical.

The "seminar" of the participants round the Ouija board is itself such a "stripping process," since Mirabell, Wystan, and Maria will gradually fade away. Merrill's work in creating the trilogy is a comparable "stripping":

> Art—
> The tale that all but shapes itself—survives
> By feeding on its personages' lives,
> The stripping process, sort of. What to say?
> Our lives led *to* this. It's the price we pay.

If the artist needs new resources in middle age, it is not because the old ones are exhausted. On the contrary, the old ones, accumulating exponentially, seem to forbid the acquisition of the new. At some point the writer begins his replay in slow motion of all the eclectic litter and learning that crowds his mind: unburdening himself, he discharges, in an art relatively random by contrast to that of his earlier years, portions of everything he knows. So the board throws up bits and pieces of Merrill's reading (as *A Vision* threw up Yeats's, as *History* threw up Lowell's), and one of the difficulties with the trilogy is that no one of us duplicates Merrill's reading bank, any more than we duplicate Blake's or Milton's. The jumble that is any fifty-year-old memory poses for a reader the problem of other minds; the encyclopedic modern poem, from the *Cantos* on, presses the question almost intolerably.

Though the allusive density of *Mirabell* makes the poem at first difficult, the test of such a poem is not in the first reading (though if there is not enough pleasure in that, the reader is lost for good), but in the reading that takes place once the scheme, the family relations, and the life histories in question have become natural and familiar. In this poem Merrill is enterprisingly (with some incidental wreckage) enlarging his theater of operations. He avoids for lines on end the effortless jeweled effects for which has has been known, and he has turned aside from lyrics of the personal life to narrative, to mythological and metaphysical "explanations" of a discursive order ruled not by "feeling" or by "beauty" but by "truth." He is writing in voices other than his own. These undertakings are not wholly new: Merrill said as far back as 1962: "If I am host at last / It is of little more than my own past. / May others be at home in it." But the past of the earlier volumes was on the whole a selective one, careful of its references, arranged in exquisite forms, and restricted to crises of feeling. Two poems in *Nights and Days,* of 1966, appear to anticipate the trilogy. In a sequence of reflections on love called "The Thousand and Second Night," "the rough pentameter / Quatrains give way, you will observe, to three / Interpolations, prose as well as verse," reflecting on "mind, body, and soul (or memory)." The second instance is the inquiry into the nature of Eros in a long sequence called "From the Cupola." The poet adapts the myth of Eros and Psyche, and is himself both Psyche's poet (like Keats) and Psyche herself, receiving letters from the unknown Eros. Two caricatured evil sisters mock Psyche's claim to an invisible lover, but Psyche's real anxiety derives not from their realist cynicism but, rather, from her own distrust of love's distorting idealism. She is consoled by her poet in Audenesque cadences:

> Psyche, hush. This is me, James
> Writing lest he think
> Of the reasons why he writes—
> Boredom, fear, mixed vanities and shames;
> Also love.
> From my phosphorescent ink
> Trickle faint unworldly lights.

By the end of *Mirabell* the faint unworldly lights have brightened into the radiance of enlightenment. But in his pursuit of truth Merrill has by no means forgotten his earlier homage to the senses. The daily life described in *Mirabell,* which offers itself as one realized version of human existence, is attentive to the senses, to friendship, to domesticity, to art—all the elements found in Merrill's lyrics—as well as to the dead, for whom the poet has had to invent his trilogy. "The dead," "Ephraim" tells us, "are the surround of the living."

Merrill's argument for the senses denies the old propriety that would distinguish the aesthetic from the sensual. (In this, he resembles Keats rather than his other master, Auden.) A continuity between the aesthetic and the sensual is at the heart of Merrill's work, from the earliest lyrics on—as if it were inconceivable that a love of textures, shapes, lines, light, and color should not also be a love of faces and bodies, even if "one falls back, soiled, blurred." Merrill's primary intuition is that of the absolute ravishment of the senses. As they combine and mingle, the senses create, in the order of flesh, interrelations and reinforcings that are like the elements of an artwork. Yet Merrill's interest in the translation of the data of the senses into the nonpictorial forms of verse and music poses difficulties. Language cannot imitate reality in any easily describable way; and the well-known pitfalls of testifying in verse to the more sensuous of the world's pleasures—pitfalls that are clearest in early Keats and Hopkins—argue against a too literal rendering of sensuality. Language, an abstract medium, is always in allegorical relation to perception and sensation.

In arguing that the sensual and the spiritual are indivisible, Merrill places his trust in the affections as a middle term. Faithlessness and infidelities are acts not of the flesh but of the spirit, and they occur when affection doubts or betrays its own powers. The certain loss of all "sacred bonds" underlies Merrill's verse. But as disbelief and death depopulate his real and imagined worlds, Merrill compensates by a poetry of exuberant mythology and a symposium of incarnate and discarnate voices. The eclectic banquet of youth is replaced in middle age by a Proustian feast of memory. In the fiction of *Mirabell,* the blessings of conversation replace the blessings of sensuality. The audible conversation of tongues—life's addendum to the sensual conversation of bodies—gives way to the inaudible ghostly converse of the dead and the disembodied, as language, letter by letter, assembles itself through the Ouija board. As narrator of, and Prospero to, the whole pageant, Merrill, though fictionally the child of the "father of forms and matter of fact mother" on "the other side," is the adult progenitor of all that happens. The providential and parental figures of Mirabell, Auden, and Maria are only the creatures of his creation.

We might ask whether Merrill's case, at least in the trilogy, is too special to be susceptible of translation into our own terms. Does this flood of transcriptions from another world, this massive treatise on "science" and "history," imply anything for us? Merrill's implicit protest against the censorship of feeling by our relentless ironic intellectualizing of life (he speaks here for all reflective people) takes the form of a defiant mythology—though, in a charming revenge exacted by the time we live in, the mythology must couch itself in "scientific" terms. The mysterious instructors told Merrill to write "Poems of Science." He went home and waited, but nothing happened, since his "word bank" was unfurnished with material. He resorted to potted science (Isaac Asimov, Lewis Thomas) and to remembered childhood myths, inventing macrocosmic and subatomic perspectives from which nothing can be hidden to the enlightened eye. Merrill's mythology attempts to ask what work we can find for that part of the mind hitherto occupied in inventing religious systems. Unlike Robert Lowell, who considered the really interesting people in history to be the emperors, the kings, and the politicians, Merrill thinks that the most attractive souls are those who thought up Edens and afterlifes, saints and satyrs.

It is surprising that Merrill, a poet of infinite finish, should come down so decisively in favor of large mythological outlines and of expository theology. Or perhaps it is not so surprising. The epic poetic of the trilogy demands the large, and even the prosaic. Whereas the lyric is discontinuous, and rejects the narrativity that (however much it may be submerged) links the successive events of drama and fiction, the epic goes beyond narrativity to an encyclopedic account of all things in heaven and earth. The instructors promise to return Merrill to his "chronicles of love and loss" after the trilogy is done, but he will not be the same poet who set down the first lines of "The Book of Ephraim"—the stretching and straining of this large effort cannot be forgotten in a contraction to lyric shapes.

The lessons of *Mirabell* are the unpopular ones of middle age. Most people, the poem tells us, are unevolved, and remain in an animal unawareness, in which they grow, couple, reproduce themselves, and die. Some souls evolve beyond this—into thought, vision, and art. (They are the souls "cloned" in the "Research Lab" of the spirits and sent into the world to do the "V work" of civilization—creating religions, symphonies, temples, cultures, poems.) There is no permanent culture; ours is one of successive attempts by God B to order chaos. The achievements of mind always seem to excel their material origins: hence the myth of inspiring Muses, mysterious instructors, visions, and oracles. The honey of generation is an opiate; the childless have freer access to the spiritual life. Everyone dies. The conversation of friends is precious. As parents and friends die, we dwell more and more on the dead. Our minds become a repository of all we have read, learned, been brought up on. We begin to think in larger terms—about history, about the survival of the planet, about genius.

But it is not for these or other worthy observations in their bald sense that we prize *Mirabell*. It is, rather, for the intimate and solid circumstantiality in which those truths are based. We know the death of parents not propositionally but circumstantially, in the long, particular narration of the death of David Jackson's parents, in "stupor, fear, incontinence," and their burial in a "raw trench." We know the loss of friends as Merrill accustoms us, through a hundred and seventy-eight pages, to the tender and solicitous raillery of Auden and Maria, and then, once we look forward to hearing them indefinitely, strikes the knell of their disappearance. We come to prize even the most frail creations of culture as Merrill's myths link the oldest constructions, like Atlantis and Eden, named rather than evoked, to the creation, metamorphosis, and humanizing of the bat-peacock Mirabell. First an inhuman other, Mirabell becomes, through "this world of courtesy"—the board of communication—someone who can love ("I HAVE COME TO LOVE U"), someone self-conscious and aesthetically reflective. In his becoming we see the coming-to-be of every conscious creature, through language and love:

> B4 OUR MEETINGS I WAS NOTHING NO TIME PASSED BUT NOW
> YR TOUCH LIKE A LAMP HAS SHOWN ME TO MYSELF & I AM
> ME: 741! I HAVE ENTERED A GREAT WORLD I AM FILLED
> WITH IS IT MANNERS?

There are stretches of flats in the exposition of the mythology, yet its density shares with all systems—from Leviticus to *The Book of Mormon* and Melville's cetology—a sheer willingness to bore. The visionary mind has its own pedantries. Just as complicated poets, like Milton, have to learn to be simple, so Merrill, natively compact, has here decided to learn a discursive plainness.

Before the concluding speech of the archangel Michael, who announces the next act of the comedy, Merrill speaks in his own voice of the world's diversity, as he glances out to numberless brilliances of light over the water:

> The message hardly needs decoding, so
> Sheer the text, so innocent and fleet
> These overlapping pandemonia:
> Birdlife, leafplay, rockface, waterglow
> Lending us their being, till the given
> Moment comes to render what we owe.

Merrill has offered a self-definition through metaphor in the course of the poem: his metal is silver (Auden's is platinum), his element air, his mineral crystal, his color "cold lavender." In themselves, these specifications are definitive. By middle age, one knows what one is. If Merrill reminds us sometimes of Ariel, he is yet an Ariel making a deliberate gesture toward an enlarging of style in his refusal to be exclusively beautiful. By its admission of the learning, conversation, and random use of language that underlie the crystallizations of lyric, Merrill's poem pays homage to the riches of unordered literary experience:

> MANS TERMITE PALACE BEEHIVE ANTHILL PYRAMID JM
> IS LANGUAGE USE IT STIR THE THINKERS & DETER THE REST.

Language "of such a depth, shimmer, and force" is the "life raft" that carries the poet over the flood of sensation. *Mirabell* is more a diary, in fact, than a planned "system": each section encompasses whatever rises to the surface at a given moment of composition. The mind whose word banks and image banks are here tapped is not in any way a typical one. It is preternaturally knowing, and eclectically read; it strikes attitudes; it is fond but acutely critical; it likes puns perhaps more than it should; its relativism is both despairing and elated. It never lacks fit language—silky and astringent by turns, lustrous and decorative one moment, attenuated and scholastically drab the next, candid or esoteric as its author decides.

What is in the American mind these days—the detritus of past belief, a hodgepodge of Western science and culture, a firm belief in the worth of the private self and in the holiness of the heart's affections, a sense of time and space beyond the immediate—is here displayed for judgment. Somewhat less general in reference, perhaps, is Merrill's examination of what, as a personal aim, can replace self-reproduction in childbearing. Once the biological purpose of life is even theoretically put aside as a justification of living, we must (theological justification having been abandoned long since) advocate something like Merrill's civilizing "V work." The Arnoldian doctrine of the saving remnant seems in this poem to have a new defender; but Merrill dwells, as Arnold does not, on the parallel necessity of private affection. Love and civilization here go hand in hand, the work of art and science refining life in public as the bonds of affection refine life in private. *Mirabell* is Merrill's hymn to the spiritual evolution that seems possible, if precarious, now that biological evolution has invented man; its dark undersong is Hiroshima in the realm of science, and subhuman stupidity in the realm of the private life.

What Merrill once said of Eugenio Montale—that his emotional refinement is "surprisingly permeable by quite ordinary objects: ladles, hens, pianos, half-read letters"—is true of Merrill himself. The claim of ordinary objects and ordinary events on lyric is a mark of the democratic sense in every modern poet of quality—from the priestlike Eliot down through the alchemizing Merrill—that the things of the world can lend a myth (as Crane said of the Brooklyn Bridge) to God. The tendency of modern American lyric poets to reclaim whole tracts of language and experience ceded in the nineteenth century to novels or nonfictional prose continues in Merrill. It is this tendency that has caused us to outstrip our parent stock in England. If to play so free with tradition one poet needs the Ouija board, and another, like Ginsberg, needs visions, and another, like Eliot, needs Buddhism, those who are not poets can only conclude that the work of creation proceeds by its own means.

Scripts for the Pageant (1980)

CHARLES MOLESWORTH
Scripts for the Pageant

James Merrill brings his epic poem to a conclusion with *Scripts for the Pageant,* the clearest and best of the three parts of his cosmological probe. So now is the time to ask the large question: why should anyone begin an epic poem in the last quarter of the twentieth century? Many people readily admit that the age is not ripe for major works; a *fin de siècle* compromise with finials and graceful flourishes seems more the order of the day. One partial answer might be that the epic is an attempt to avoid the burdens of the self. A cosmology, or even a national epic, Whitman notwithstanding, would give the poet a chance to escape the ephemeral losses and misgivings of the "confessional" self. But for Merrill, or JM as he calls himself in his epic role, this is only part of it, for he has chosen to people his afterworld with his departed friends such as W. H. Auden, Maria Mitsotáki, a woman he knew from his summers in Greece, and now, in the final book, George Cotzias, another Greek friend, and Robert Morse, an American. In fact, many of the most moving passages from the epic concern JM's circle of living friends, especially David Jackson, known as DJ, whose twenty-fifth anniversary with Merrill is celebrated in *Scripts.*

Another partial answer: the epic is often conceived of as a compendium of other, "lesser," poetic forms. So writing an epic is the logical next step for Merrill, since his poetic skill always has been protean, sophisticated, ambitious, and often baroque. *Scripts* includes a wide range of smaller genres and forms, including the sonnet, heroic couplets, terza rima, a ballade, and, most important, the masque. Also the didactic function of the epic is here both completed and parodied (a typical Merrill strategy), as *Scripts* presents us with a series of twenty-five "lessons," complete with classroom setting. The drama of this final book becomes in some senses that of drawing-room

---

From *New Republic,* July 26, 1980.

comedy, as gossip and ritualized initiation form much of the poem's surface. But drama in a higher sense also occurs when the four angels, the chief protagonists, instruct JM in the secrets of creation, the structure of the universe, metempsychosis, and the final end of things. JM has written a poem that includes everything, everything he feels and has felt, but also everything he's dreamed and feared. He has made *his* world, a way out of himself, but also the grandest act of self-assertion.

But why use the Ouija board as the organizing conceit of the epic, especially when this instrument is often associated with the parlor games of a bored leisure class? Like the Rosicrucian spirits in Pope's *Rape of the Lock,* the Ouija board seems designed to render the cosmic in terms of the cosmetic, turning the largest questions into problems of anxious vanity. However, the board does have the basics: the alphabet, which formed the organization for "The Book of Ephraim"; the ten numbers of the decimal system, used in *Mirabell: Books of Number;* and "Yes and No," which now serve to mark off the tripartite structure of *Scripts.* Merrill, despite his sophisticated tastes, his hedonism, his anxiety, longs for some set of irreducible principles. He reminds us, for example, that his summer home in Greece is "three flights above the whitewashed waterfront where Pythagoras was born." Even in the most elliptical and complex narrative poems of his earlier books, Merrill pursued basic questions, such as the irreversibility of time, the onward push of mortal things, and the destiny of personality. In *Scripts* he again makes clear one of his aesthetic principles, that the self is a story, that in the simple unfolding of time the complexities of character are manifest. The narrative frame of "First, then, and finally" claims the same structural clarity (or the illusion, the hope of clarity) as does "1,2,3" or "A,B,C" or "Yes and No." One of the spirits in *Scripts* tells JM, "WELL I & MINE / RATHER RESEMBLE TALES WE WERE TOLD," and JM responds, "So do we. Tales shape us, of all kind." JM, as scribe and namegiver, involves himself in deep taxonomic mysteries, and in the confounding clarity of narrative as well.

"Yes & No": taken serially these three words form irreducible language acts, namely assertion, qualification, and denial. Taken all together they form the essence of equivocation, which can be seen as either the fullest sort of language act or the very subversion of language. Merrill, by using this expression as the framework of the final book of his epic, also points toward the question-and-answer format of *Scripts,* the stichomythia between the secular world and the afterlife. But actually there are three levels of discourse involved: JM and DJ, then Auden and Maria, and then the four angels. While Merrill confronts the essential questions of structure, function, and purpose in the cosmos, he also shows that all the questions must be answered equivocally, with yes and no. As scribe he rewrites all the messages that come through the Ouija board; but Auden and Maria guide much of the dialogue; and of course the angels themselves correct and interpret some, but no all, of their own answers. Is it, then, Merrill's poem? Yes and no. Is the poem a projection of interior meanings, the self writ large, or the discovery of exterior "reality," the world measuring itself? Yes and no. Is the message of the poem affirmative or cautionary or doomladen? Is the poem a domestic game, a highly displaced paean to Merrill's circle, or a grand literary structure for all to see and admire? Yes and no.

For several reasons, the masque is the most appropriate form to serve as the center of the epic's final book, and JM includes three in *Scripts.* Renaissance masques are both playful and serious, infatuated with stagecraft and spectacle, yet capable of presenting serious philosophical subjects, though often in mythological or allegorical disguise. They also rest on a cultural compact which is essentially elitist, so Merrill's political and cultural values, adumbrated throughout the poem, here find full expression. And JM's sensibility, often neoclassical in his earlier work, indulges in other Renaissance structures as well, especially of a numerological and hierarchical kind. The four angels, for example, each have three manifestations (Emmanuel is the Water Angel, but is also reason and pride, for example), and five immortals (among these are Homer and Plato) also serve as the five senses. The nine muses appear, as do four famous "prophets" (Gautama, Jesus, Mercury, and Mohammed), and the interlocutors from the two previous books, Ephraim and Mirabell, return, often to be thanked for their earlier efforts, but also to be corrected. The discussions and pageants are concerned with such questions as God B's (God Biology) two previous races of creatures who were destroyed (a survivor from the second, a unicorn-like creature called "Uni," acts as a "turnkey" for the classroom where the lessons are held), the problem of population control, the technical details of the poem's verse forms, the arrival of Nabokov (whom JM relegates to silence, claiming the cast is already too crowded), and dozens of other matters great and small. Throughout, JM is the willing and often awestruck student, while DJ, with William Butler Yeats residing in a lump in his hand, acts as fellow scribe and initiate. Much of the delight of reading the poem comes from watching the tension between JM as student and JM as maker of the poem, as amanuensis and "onlie begetter," and the many ingenious ways he does and doesn't resolve this tension. At one point he even advances a set of parallels between the account of the two earlier lost races and his own childhood, as he was preceded by two siblings and his parents divorced while he was still a child. Autobiography and creation myth: by hinting they're the same Merrill deals with a key modernist, and a key American, theme.

Without offering a complete interpretation, of either this book or the whole epic, I think JM is chiefly concerned with the question of what the poem calls "resistance." It is both an idea and a natural force, a form of "innocence." *Scripts* opens with a long discussion of the relation between idea and innocence, borrowing from Blake and others. But "resistance" comes to dominate the second half of the book, as its main idea, its central unanswered question. Very briefly, "resistance" keeps time from flowing backward, from sinking into the blank beyond the black of chaos. In the future transumption of the race into "heaven" (there is no hell in JM's world), there will be no "resistance." JM is told by Nature (God B's twin) how man

> WILL YES, SWIM & GLIDE,
> A SIMPLER, LESS WILFUL, BEING. DULLER TOO?
> IF SO, IS THAT SHARP EDGE NOT WELL LOST
> WHICH HAS SO VARIOUSLY CUT AND COST?
> WE WILL WALK AMONG HIS KIND MADE NEW
> (THE MASQUE CONCLUDED, WE & OURS
> STEPPING FROM STAGE TO MIX WITH MORTAL POWERS)

By his own admission, JM has always been uneasy with "ideas" as such, and one of his greatest surprises is that his friend Maria had earlier been Plato, and often was partially revealing secrets to JM during their long talks in Greece. JM, in other words, is more a poet of character and personality than a poet of ideas and final answers. But the epic, after all, is also definable as the genre that blends the dramatic, the narrative, and the philosophical modes. And so this poem offers us a loving portrait of JM's special friends and a searching but tentative anatomy of the universe. Merrill knows how problematic is the question of the "self-born mockers of man's enterprise," but he has decided to be fully enterprising nonetheless.

Unlike many other long poems, Merrill's improves as it progresses. The egregious punning, the fussiness about detail, and the convoluted bureaucracy that made the afterlife sound like a bad version of corporate personnel policies, the overly elliptical syntax (as if Merrill impatiently resented the necessity of providing expository clarity for the reader): if these faults don't disappear in *Scripts* they present much less of a problem than they did earlier, especially in *Mirabell,* for me the weakest of the three books. The creation hymn in *Scripts,* for example, is a triumph of an elevated style free of strain. Merrill always has been willing to borrow styles, to use his eclecticism hungrily, both as a tribute to, and a transgression of, earlier poets. But to write a long poem one has to put aside many scruples. The distinctive thing about JM is that he never lets the reader forget that the question of signature, of uniqueness, is one that can be (and in this latter age, perhaps it must be) approached with a sense of play. Five years ago, Merrill hoped to be measured by Auden and Stevens; now his work asks comparison with that of Yeats and Blake, if not Milton and Dante. But the clearest analogue may be that of Byron, who, desiring a scale both intimate and grand, yet wanting a hero, decided to fill the role himself.

Denis Donoghue

What the Ouija Board Said

"Scripts for the Pageant" is the third and final volume of an enormous poem, about five hundred pages long, which James Merrill has been writing for the past five years. The first part "The Book of Ephraim," was published in 1976 as a section in Mr. Merrill's "Divine Comedies." The second, *Mirabell: Books of Number,* was published in 1978. The entire poem is the record of many evenings spent by the poet and his companion David Jackson attending upon the Ouija board. "The Book of Ephraim" was composed of twenty-six separate but consecutive poems, corresponding to the board's alphabet from A to Z. *Mirabell: Books of Number* was divided into ten sections, corresponding to the board's numbers from zero to nine. *Scripts for the Pageant* consists of three sections, corresponding to the board's Yes and No.

Mr. Merrill and David Jackson, or JM and DJ as they appear in the poem, have evidently been dealing with the Ouija board for at least twenty years. The first report of their transactions, so far as I know, was a poem, "Voices from the Other World," first published in the *New Yorker* and later in *The Country of a Thousand Years of Peace* (1959). On that occasion the conjunction of board and teacup produced the voice of a German engineer who died young but lived long enough to receive hard advice from Goethe. The next report was made in a poem, "The Will," included in *Divine Comedies:* "It's June, we're at the Ouija board / David the True and I and our familiar spirit"—the spirit being one Ephraim, a fellow with some ambition to play the sage, despite gentle mockery administered by JM. Indeed, two pages later, with only enough intermission for an epigraph from Dante's "Paradiso," Ephraim has been given his own show.

The plot of "The Book of Ephraim" was to disclose "the incarnation and withdrawal of a god," and its style

> the kind of unseasoned telling found
> In legends, fairy tales, a tone licked clean

> Over the centuries by mild old tongues,
> Grandam to cub, serene, anonymous.

As for characters: The chief spirits were W. H. Auden and Maya Deren, but there were also JM and DJ, DJ's parents and Ephraim, who presides over the narrative. The scene was changed from Stonington, Conn., to Greece and then to Venice; distance was never a problem. If you add the usual domestic routines, illnesses, visits, weather, a problem with wallpaper, a failure of the telephone, you have enough, given Mr. Merrill's inventiveness, to make a poem of eighty or ninety pages.

"The Book of Ephraim" turned out to be a remarkable poem. Mr. Merrill has always been sensitive to "the golden things that go without saying," and the things, equally golden, that have gone without saying until he has said them. His common style is a net of loose talk tightening to verse, a mode in which nearly anything can be said with grace. Auden is his chosen master, a familiar spirit more important to him than Ephraim ever was. "The Book of Ephraim" was not Ephraim's but JM's. Ephraim provided the chances, but JM seized them and made wonderful music of them, especially near the end. These poems are continuous with Merrill's justly famous poems, such as "From the Cupola," "Time," "Days of 1935," "The Broken Home," and a dozen more, mainly from *Nights and Days* (1966), *The Country of a Thousand Years of Peace,* and the superb *Braving the Elements* (1972), Mr. Merrill's well-earned triumph.

It was appropriate that "The Book of Ephraim" appeared in *Divine Comedies* beside a group of shorter poems, chronicles of love and loss. In the form of Ephraim's table-talk, the poet was able to establish communication not only with dead friends but with his own past, recalled but not necessarily recuperated by memory. He was also able to introduce chance to a poetic talent more famous for choice—as in Mr. Merrill's *The (Diblos) Notebook,* which retains its false starts, inadequate phrases, and erased possibilities as evidence of the interrogation that constitutes the novel. "The Book of Ephraim" gave inspiration a new life by providing lines not only ghost-ridden but, at least in some measure, ghost-written.

With *Mirabell,* something went wrong. There was nothing wrong with the ghosts; mainly Auden again, now enjoying a love affair with Plato, but also a lively friend named Maria Mitsotáki and Auden's companion Chester Kallman, whose next incarnation turns him into a heterosexual black man. The chief messenger has not a name but the number 741. He is responsible for several improbable epiphanies. But the real misfortune is that JM is instructed to write a poetry of Science and that he accepts the wretched assignment and turns in a report that sounds like a rejected script for "Star Trek" or the notes one might take in a course called "Astrophysics for You." At one point the messenger reports that Rimbaud wrote *The Waste Land:* "we fed into the like-cloned Eliot," he tells the unquestioning JM. Unfortunately, 741 does not warn JM of the risks attendant upon trying to out-Auden Auden. It is reasonable to admire Auden's long poems, especially "New Year Letter," "For the Time Being" and Auden's supreme performance in this genre, "The Sea and the Mirror." I am sure Mr. Merrill likes Auden's style in these poems for the same reason that Auden liked Byron's, because the poetic voice "does not make me jump." But you can't rival Auden by turning popular science into verse.

One of the minor characters in *Mirabell,* Robert Morse, should have been taken more seriously when he told JM what was wrong with "Mirabell":

> Everything in Dante knew its place.
> In this guidebook of yours, how do you tell
> Up from down? Is Heaven's interface
>
> What your new friends tactfully don't call Hell?
> Splendid as metaphor. The real no-no
> Is jargon, falling back on terms that smell
>
> Just a touch fishy when the tide is low:
> 'Molecular structures'—cup and hand—obey
> 'Electric waves'? Don't *dream* of saying so!

I agree with Morse, and with DJ, who had severe misgivings about resorting to the other world again after "The Book of Ephraim," one such book being enough.

And now we have *Scripts for the Pageant,* the same form but with a larger cast. Auden still queens the show, but he has to make room for Maya Deren and George Cotzias, not to speak of the interminable speaking parts given to Michael, Raphael, Emmanuel, and Gabriel. The pageant is from time to time a Platonic symposium, a Miltonic masque, a Lucretian essay on the nature of things, a tale told by Boccaccio "amid time's howl." There are brief messages about Homer, Plato, W. B. Yeats, Richard Strauss, Andrew Marvell, Pythagoras, and Kirsten Flagstad. Auden has much to say on the subject of atoms, and Morse on the subject of Time. DJ is curious about UFOs. The scenes are Athens, Samos, Venice, and Athens again. Michael tells DJ that the Ouija board was necessary because the messengers had already tried giving JM dreams, and even "inspiration," so the board was a last resort. At this stage JM seems too weary to care, but he stirs himself to ask a cogent question:

". . . Resistance—Nature's gift to man—/ What form will it assume in Paradise?" No reply for a page or two: The answer then comes as "none." The poem ends on DJ's birthday, September 16, 1977.

I am afraid *Scripts for the Pageant* persists in the portentousness and vanity of *Mirabell.* Its subject is nothing less than the meaning of life, but the poem degrades the theme and makes a poor show of itself with camp silliness and giggling. When Auden, Mitsotáki, Cotzias (or GK), and Morse (or RM), newly gone over, have an evening in Paradise, the poem reports the event as follows:

> Now Maria
> Interrupts: ENFANTS THESE DAYS WE 4
> GATHER AT MEALS (GK SPATTERED WITH HORRORS.
> WYSTAN ALL GRITTY. MAMAN GRASS-STAINED) & IN
> GLIDES DEWYFACED RM NEAT AS A PIN.
> CHOCKFULL OF STARRY GOSSIP & WE ROAR!
> Isn't it tomorrow we begin
> Our lessons? Are your papers ready? YIPES
> MAMAN GOES FIRST CAN'T DAWDLE WITH U TYPES
> AU RESERVOIR
> 2 DAYS FROM NOW MY DEARS:
> USUAL TIME B4, COLD SHOWER & STRONG
> COFFEE DRESS OPTIONAL NO CIGS SO LONG

Too much *son et lumière,* not enough light and dark. Or, to use a metaphor culled from the poem, *Scripts for the Pageant* hasn't enough wind in its sails, chiefly because it relies upon the ripples of demeanor in the appalling absence of conviction. JM and his friends disport themselves on deck, throwing languid remarks to the waves: Meanwhile the poem has nowhere to go. "The Book of Ephraim" was apparently undaunted by the epigraph from Dante with which it began. Now, five hundred pages later, the work has dwindled so far into mannerism that I would choose for a motto Mademoiselle de Nazianzi's swoon in Ronald Firbank's *The Flower beneath the Foot:* "Help me, heaven, to be decorative and to do right!" (I take the quotation from Auden, who found it in Firbank.)

True, there are good things in the poem, a few jewels available for the labor of sifting the rubble. The opening of the "Samos" section is beautiful, its splendor the direct consequence of the fact that the poet is speaking in his own voice. And again, seventy pages later, he writes wonderfully of the house in Athens. These passages are heart-breaking, as compelling as anything James Merrill has written since "Up and Down" in "Braving the Elements." But it is wretched to have to cross such a dismal terrain to reach them.

Clara Claiborne Park

Where *The Waste Land* Ends

First, in 1976, *Divine Comedies,* containing *The Book of Ephraim.* In strong pentameter, James Merrill at once made clear what it was: not at all the usual thing in form or content, but the "Book of a Thousand and One Evenings Spent With David Jackson at the Ouija Board / In Touch with Ephraim Our Familiar Spirit." The poem's material would be the carton of messages spelled out over twenty years to Merrill and his friend at their house in Stonington, Connecticut, by the dime-store cup which pointed to the board's twenty-six letters. Spelled out to them or by them? Do they follow the cup or guide it? Questions of which Merrill is never unaware, and to which he himself can give no final answer. Imperceptibly, however, they recede in importance as the poetry takes over; by the end of *Ephraim* disbelief has long been suspended.

Ephraim was followed two years later by *Mirabell: Books of Number.* JM and DJ (as the board's capitals identify them) were still at it. The letters now spelled out, instead of messages from departed friends and the gay revelations of Ephraim, giddy Greek, more difficult lessons, imparted by a crew of red-eyed, red-hot bats who identified themselves by number. They "describe themselves now as fallen angels, now as volatile subatomic particles; the scale, accordingly, wobbles throughout, from vast to microscopic." (The authoritative explanatory prose quoted is Merrill's own, not part of the poem, but prefaced to an excerpt published in last summer's *Kenyon Review*). The new familiar is 741; he and JM and DJ become as fond of each other (and he of them) as they did of Ephraim, so that everyone is delighted when he metamorphoses into a peacock and changes his numerical designation for the name they give him, Mirabell—M's having, for Merrill, multiple mana. Mirabell's realm is the complex of mathematical formulas that frame? support? explain? express? the macro- and microcosm of physical and human nature. He speaks often of God B—Biology.

Mirabell's "main fields," writes Merrill, "are History and Science, often much mythologized."

> Thus we are told of an Arcadian Atlantis whose immortal denizens resembled centaurs and themselves created the bat-angels to serve them. It didn't work. Two rival worlds—one electrically, one atomically powered—ended in mutual destruction. It would be for Man to reconcile those opposites. . . . [Mirabell's] visits prepare us for a seminar with the Angels—whose 25 lessons are in fact the marrow of the third volume.

Merrill lets the Ouija board itself set the poems' structure. *Ephraim*'s reveals itself gradually: twenty-six sections, beginning with successive letters of the alphabet. *Mirabell*'s is immediately apparent, as befits what the bat-angels asked Merrill to provide, POEMS OF SCIENCE: ten parts, each subdivided in ten, and numbered from 0 to 9.9. After letters and numbers, there remained on the board YES, NO, and the ampersand—the manifest of the reconciliation of opposites assigned to Man.

Man, God, and the cosmos. High talk. How softly and seductively *Ephraim* began, then, we only now realize. That was the kindergarten, Merrill tells us, for the school of *Mirabell,* and for the Angel's seminar of these final *Scripts for the Pageant,* YES & NO. White and Black, Matter and Antimatter, Life and Death, two scripts for a future performance. Between them we, as readers and as human beings, are left to choose. JM wants that perfectly clear; he asks, and is answered in capitals. "We do the judging? Everyone? INDEED."

Tentative in title, cannily ambiguous in structure and content, these *Scripts* are no more ambiguous in spirit, no less committedly affirmative, than the *Paradiso* to which they are already being compared. How otherwise, when the first of the trilogy appeared initially in a book called *Divine Comedies*? And as the reviews appear, the comparisons accumulate: *Ulysses, The Waste Land,* Proust. Sober critics, some themselves poets, reach for the sky: Blake's Prophetic Books, *Paradise Lost* and *Regained,* the *Comedy* itself. Recalling these in scope, however, the trilogy is like none of them in manner. And the manner is the matter, Merrill being a supreme mannerist.

Yet the matter is no less substantial for that. To have the poem now completed is like the reception of an immense, unhoped-for present: the long poem that it's been proved a hundred times over we can't expect in this age of anxiety, privatism, fragmentation, and the loss of the confidence and will to speak any public language. In *Ephraim* Merrill had already brought off something miraculous enough—eighty-nine pages of solid poetry. So we thought, not yet able to glimpse the grand design (though it was there). *Mirabell,* transitional, was longer still (182 pages); the bard suspended our hopes but did not disappoint them. Now *Scripts* is nearly half as long again. At its completion Merrill, like Prospero, breaks the mirror that has been since *Ephraim* the symbol of his poetic field, as well as what it was in actuality, the central focus of the room where his spirits gathered. He does not drown his book, however, but leaves it for us to read and live with.

"James Merrill has created a poem as central to our generation as *The Waste Land* was to the one before us." So Phoebe Pettingell in *The New Leader.* If so, our generation is in luck. Might Eliot's long legacy at last be spent? The trilogy is sufficiently unlike the literature of the last sixty years, the best and the worst, that we need have no trouble recognizing its differences. In the midst of fragmentation, it unifies—science and poetry, past and present, public and private, cosmic and domestic, the dead and the living—as epic used to, as no short poem can. In the midst of literature (and lives) made out of heartsick discontinuities, it is continuous, with the continuity not only of reason—purposeful narrative, tightly connected event—but of the heart—of loyalty, friendship, of love that so yearns for continuity that it seeks it beyond even that black discontinuity that JM and DJ refuse to take as final. In the midst of personal and linguistic privatism, it manifests for the reader an affectionate concern that we'd forgotten could exist in serious literature, and a shining faith in the power of language to render shareable our grandest imaginations and our most personal experience, to make the private public.

Public, not popular. These Divine Comedies (as must not the final, three-part assemblage eventually be called?) will not be that. But they will reach that same enduring public that learned its way to sharing Dante's experience—not the credulous, the Castaneda-freaks and horoscope-watchers to whom its apparatus initially might seem to appeal but all those who care enough about the pleasures and responsibilities of life and language to do the work (and play) of reading a poem extraordinary enough that its author well might think—as Dante and Milton thought—that in some decisive way it came from Somewhere Else. And if it didn't, Merrill's flipped coin still comes up heads. What a piece of work is man, out of whose hot and busy brain heaven, purgatory, and paradise can spin themselves?

YES & NO. This is the final message. *Scripts* is both the gayest and the darkest of the three volumes. SUDDEN FIREWORKS OF PLEASURE, spells one of the calm Angels, thinking about man's life and not quite understanding it. He might have been talking about the experience of reading these poems.

Certainly the language here dazzles against the dark. It also, as appropriate, glitters, glistens, glimmers, glints, or glows, as well as bringing off a great many other special effects I lack alliterative verbs for. The lines are crammed with jokes and puns, Olympian *jeux d'esprit* in several foreign tongues plus dialects of English. Examples? Hopeless to quote; it is in context that the words light up. Perhaps these lines (from *Mirabell,* 9.9) on Hell? Hell is

> (a syllable identified
> In childhood as the German word for *bright*
> —So that my father's cheerful "Go to Hell",
> Long unheard, and Vaughan's unbeatable
> They are all gone into a world of light
> Come, even now at times, to the same thing.)

Certainly the gleam is gone. Yet this casual parenthesis, thrown into the midst of a sentence on its way to somewhere else, which I picked out merely because it was self-contained and illustrated a pun, demonstrates how inseparable Merrill's wordplay is from his highest seriousness; only as I write do I perceive that it manages to embody what the whole poem is about: brightness and death, the loved human being, and the flashing revelations of language.

And the verse! "Make it new!" Merrill can do anything with these old forms we've been told so often are outworn. This poem should reinstate the study of prosody in the English curriculum. Sonnets crystallize so effortlessly out of his narrative pentameter that we often don't realize we're reading them. Like *Ephraim* and *Mirabell, Scripts* has its terza rima canto, ending, for a flourish, with Dante's key word, "stars." Each order of creature speaks in his appropriate meter. Throughout *Mirabell,* the bat-angels manifest their numerical nature in the tuneless syllabic fourteeners they speak in. But when Mirabell himself sweeps into the splendid farewell fete of *Scripts* in full peacock fig, transfigured into "blue, green, gold, a comet-streak," his fourteen syllables have been transfigured too; now divided into eight and six, his lines are rhyming tetrameter and trimeter. Mortals, dead and living, speak in pentameter. The Angels' verse is free and ample. The unicorn from Atlantis, four-footed, speaks in the four-beat alliterative line of *Beowulf,* as befits an early creature, but rhymed and speeded up to match his light canter.

Like the peacock, the unicorn is enchanting—one of the many delights and surprises of this last book. But the magician, the poet-Prospero, controls all meanings; the flying bats, the pterodactyls of the early world, it turns out, are a metaphor for THE BLACK VOLATILE HALF of the atom, followed, MINUTES ONLY AFTER THE BIG BANG by THE FIRST NUCLEI OF HELIUM, which are stable, DEPENDABLE. . . . FOURFOOTED—like the unicorn creature of Atlantis. The enchanting creatures have been transformed—into the irrefutability of metaphor.

"But," JM asks, "if it's all a fable,

Involving, oh, the stable and unstable
Particles, mustn't we at last wipe clean
The blackboard of these creatures and their talk,
To render in a hieroglyph of chalk
The formulas they stood for?

The answer comes from W. H. Auden in the spirit world. He speaks for all poets:

WHY MAKE A JOYLESS THING
OF IT THROUGH SUCH
REDUCTIVE REASONING?

Merrill has not done so. The celestial elevator swoops up and down through all the levels of meaning. But Merrill knows the trick—or truth—of Dante's allegory: that all the levels must be founded on the literal, in which we live. The poem's ultimate gaiety is the most serious of all—the daily life and affection of DJ and JM over twenty-five years, celebrated in this volume with a silver anniversary party, and of their families and friends, beloved beyond death.

YES & NO. The text of YES is naturally affirmative, propounded by God's favorite, Michael, Angel of Light and the Air which makes light visible: THE MOST INNOCENT OF IDEAS IS THE IDEA THAT INNOCENCE IS DESTROYED BY IDEAS. Paradise is gained, not lost, by the work of intelligence. Yet in the last of these ten lessons of light a new, strange voice is heard. God's voice is lost in darkness. The mirror-field is "bitter-black and vast." The god who set life's cosmic enterprise going is signaling to unknown brother gods in the galactic emptiness a song even the angels cannot hear. But humans can; its lonely, persistent permutations are the song of life.

I AND MINE HOLD IT BACK BROTHERS I AND
MINE SURVIVE BROTHERS HEAR ME SIGNAL ME . . .
ALONE IN MY NIGHT BROTHERS I AND MINE
SURVIVE BROTHERS DO YOU WELL I ALONE
IN MY NIGHT I HOLD IT BACK I AND MINE
SURVIVE BROTHERS SIGNAL ME IN MY NIGHT
I AND MINE HOLD IT BACK AND WE SURVIVE

"Song of the blue whale," asks JM, "alone in space?" Or (in an exquisite lyric moment) God seen in all the vulnerability of the human. From *Tristan,* Act I,

> ONE SAILOR'S CLEAR
> YOUNG TENOR FILLS THE HOUSE, HOMESICK, HEARTSICK

God himself in need of comfort.

After that, the five lessons of &, the central section, connect (of course) and relax. A dazzling sestina is at once a hymn to the four elements of the four Archangels—Earth, Air, Water, Fire—and the Chronicle of DJ's and JM's perfectly real trip from Athens to Samos. It introduces the arrival in the beyond of dear friends whose death the poem has already prepared for. George Cotzias, doctor and scientist, is a specialist in cell biology; Robert Morse is a gifted amateur from Stonington, from whose wrists (*Mirabell,* 8.8) "fugue by fugue Bach's honeycomb / Drips . . . then whoops! the Dolly Suite." Fire is GK's element; it is he who explains about helium and stable and unstable particles. Light-minded TINY BOB, his element Air, slips disconcertingly in and out of E.F. Benson baby-talk, but he is one of those whose joking, like JM's own, is a way to cope with the dark without denying it. "Barbarity," JM will say later, "To serve uncooked one's bloody tranche de vie." Grownups do not ask for sympathy. Grace under pressure, if you like, though that's the phrase of a shade Merrill does *not* call up. "Style" is Merrill's word for it, which can turn, "in mid-sentence . . . iron to sunlight."

Now Merrill's four main human contacts with the universe are in place, one for each element; RM and GK have joined Auden and Maria Mitsotáki (Earth and Water), known already from *Ephraim* and *Mirabell.* It is they who, with JM, junior poet, and DJ, the faithful Hand on the cup, hear what's inaudible even to angels. And WHA voices the message of these middle lessons: EQUIVOCAL NEWS of mankind trembling ON A CRUST SO FRAGILE / IT NEEDS GOD'S CONSTANT VIGIL TO KEEP US AFLOAT. It is a measure of the power of Merrill's elegantly established light-mindedness that he can make WHA ask the big, simple question straight out, rendered no whit less serious by a poet's pun:

> THEREFORE I SAY OF THIS OUR FRAGILE EARTH:
> IS IT DOOMED? IF SO, WILL OUR LINEAGE, OUR LINES
> MEAN MUCH, LOST IN A POLLIWOG SEA OF ATOMS?

But as the lessons of YES contained NO, so NO makes room for YES. The negative text to Michael's affirmative is proposed by Gabriel, Angel of Death, his element Fire and the atom's own dark power, if not black antimatter itself. This text too is equivocal: OF ALL DESTRUCTIVE IDEAS THE MOST DESTRUCTIVE IS THE IDEA OF DESTRUCTION. Do we ignore death and destruction their constructive function? Ideas indeed destroyed the Garden, but were we meant to stay there? Maria, plant-lover, water-nature, nurturant Muse and Mother, pleads eloquently for Man. WE COME, WE MORTALS, FROM AN AVID WEED / CALLED CURIOSITY. God and Nature in all they do have shown that they WANT THESE SECRETS OUT, so that WE, MANKIND, may DO IMMORTAL WORK, to save the future and perfect it. And if EARTH BECOMES PARADISE, greedy mankind, OUR RACE OF THIEVES, will be justified, like Prometheus, who stole heaven's fire for man's good.

So the poem proceeds, a succession of songs of creation and destruction—individuals and species and civilizations destroyed, buried, but over them (and this in the lessons of NO) A WREATH OF GREEN STRONGER THAN ANY BLACK. God B sings all alone, and his words close the poem:

> . . . I ALONE IN MY NIGHT
> HOLD IT BACK HEAR ME BROTHERS I AND MINE

But the permutations are new, and they take on new meaning in this final context. God's eerie decasyllabics subside to mortal pentameter; we realize that the lonely song of survival is our own. It is MAN who MUST PROVIDE and, in the poem's recurring phrase, MAKE SENSE OF IT.

And the sense we make is anchored in the personal life that takes place daily on this fragile earth on which past all believing the cosmic mystery has placed us. Jimmy and Dave and their manifold affections—their friends, their cat, their wallpaper, their carpet, their mirror, have sustained the whole cosmic pageant, as if (strike that; why hedge?) to affirm the truth: that the cosmic imperatives, LOVE, SURVIVE, rise out of our own "undestroyed heart-scape," and that if they have no roots in our personal experience they have no roots at all. YES or NO? When JM, at sunset in the house in Athens, the spirits dispersed, the whole incredible enterprise over, leans over the balustrade to look down at the three-story drop and feel the urge that is so simply gratified, we know what must HOLD BACK the night if anything can, when DJ comes wordlessly to take his place beside him.

Enough. Too much, in fact. This is too rich a poem for review; commentators will be at work for years to come, MAKING SENSE OF IT. But we are in at the beginning. So forget all this, get the books, and make your own discoveries. Readers these days have a hard enough time guarding the virginity of their responses from the aggravated assaults of critics. All too soon the snow will be trampled under our heavy boots. Get to the poem before it's taught in the academy, as in five years' time it surely will be. Start with *Ephraim,* of course, and move to *Mirabell;* this one can't make its sense unprepared for. But buy these *Scripts* now. It can't hurt to salt away a first edition.

The Changing Light at Sandover (1982)

David Lehman
Merrill's Celestial Comedy

"I feel rather as if I were setting out to review 'Ulysses' in 1922," wrote poet Thom Gunn when James Merrill began publishing, in book-length installments, the masterpiece in progress that would grow into *The Changing Light at Sandover.* Many years in the making, the now complete edition shows just how well Merrill has earned the compliment. Inspired by more than a thousand and one storytelling nights at the Ouija board, in turns comic, elegiac, and darkly prophetic, *Sandover* is as ambitious in scope as it is audacious in concept. Something of a James Joyce in verse, Merrill manipulates styles and modes with magisterial ease. He modulates from one intricate formal arrangement to another, combining an epic intent with dramatic and lyric meanings and means. The result may well be the greatest long poem—and, at 560 pages, it is undoubtedly the longest great poem—an American has yet produced.

In August 1955, Merrill and David Jackson, his lifelong companion, contrived the parlor game that engendered this cosmic comedy. Using a willowware teacup as a pointer on their homemade Ouija board, "The Rover Boys at Thirty" spelled out messages transmitted by a host of otherworldly guests—the "ghostwriters" from whom Merrill, at his seat in "the angelic secretariat," has taken dictation ever since. His celestial informants, for all their sometimes disquieting subject matter, speak with the insouciance of revelers at a mad tea party. Plato drops in for a casually instructive chat or two. So does Yeats. So, shortly after their deaths, do Robert Lowell, Maria Callas, and Vladimir Nabokov, all restored to poetic life in this most affirmative of elegies.

From *Newsweek,* February 28, 1983.

Merrill relies on his formidable resources of wit, irony, and charm to overcome the reader's resistance to such sublime goings on. We learn about the place black holes, the Bermuda triangle, and other odd phenomena have in the grand scheme of things; there is, apparently, a "no accident" clause in all our contracts with destiny. Heaven exists as a divine metaphor, "THE SURROUND OF THE LIVING," but also as a place where "TH 19TH CENTURY ENGLISH, ALL BUT BYRON," are reportedly "VEXED TO HAVE FOUND NO HARPS." Language, meanwhile, is "THE REVEALD MONOTHEISM OF TO-DAY," capable of redeeming Hell ("a syllable identified / In childhood as the German word for *bright*") through a merrily made pun. In their upper-case, telegraphic style, Merrill's familiar spirits are not above contradicting one another on points of information or gossip. According to Ephraim, a first-century Hellenic Jew who himself awaits reincarnation, Mozart is now "A BLACK ROCK STAR / WHATEVER THAT IS." Rubbish, declares the late W. H. Auden, who plays Virgil to Merrill's Dante. "M'S LAST LIFE WAS STRAVINSKY."

Like its famous predecessor, Merrill's divine comedy comes in three parts. On its way to the climactic "Coda," in which the poet reads his completed work to an audience of assembled immortals, the poem constantly changes its shape before our astonished eyes. It works as an apocalyptic epic, an autobiographical memoir, a fantasia on the themes of time, origins, and endings. ("Time," Merrill quotes Heraclitus, "is a child, playing a board game.") A verse opera punctuated by dozens of show-stopping arias—a canzone here, a villanelle there, plus sonnets and sonnet sequences galore—the poem warns of nuclear *Götterdämmerung:* "While heavy-water nymphs, fettered in chain / Reaction, sang their soft refrain *Refrain.*" Yet the dominant chord is a jubilant optimism singularly rare in modern poetry. Converting science fiction into poetic truth, *The Changing Light at Sandover* holds out a vision of paradise heroic in its dimensions and too beautifully inventive to be false.

From the First Nine: Poems 1946–1976, an indispensable companion volume, offers ample selections from the poet's previous collections (though any omission is a loss). The book adds one delightful new work. "Clearing the Title" sounds a poignant farewell to the changing light of three decades, "because I guess / My poem (what to call it though?) is finished." Merrill has also touched up some of his earliest poems for the occasion. Here, for example, is both "The Cosmological Eye" and its revised version, "The Blue Eye." The revisions give dramatic evidence of Merrill's development—from a precocious master of nuance to a poet of enduring power.

R. W. Flint

Metamorphic Magician

If ever two books came up to the starting line in the guise of hare and tortoise, they are James Merrill's *From the First Nine* and *The Changing Light at Sandover.* The first is an ample, mostly unrevised collection of 139 poems from his previous books except for the "divine comedies" proper; the second is a 560-page collection, under a new general title, of all three "divine comedies" unabridged, plus a new, 37-page coda, "The Higher Keys."

From the First Nine is relatively slim and sleek, an Olympic contender of well-tested powers. Including as it does the memorable poems in the 1976 volume called *Divine Comedies* before "The Book of Ephraim," it asks of reviewers only the complacent murmur of approval that greets a sure-fire winner. The Merrill who wrote these has long since taken his place as one of the most accomplished satirists, wits, and lyricists of the age.

But this other prodigy, bedizened with capital letters, swinging its huge cerebellum and its new long tail, carrying its swarming offspring on its back like an exotic Asiatic toad, what can it be doing among the sprinters? There are almost as many plausible, semiplausible, and purely fanciful answers to the question—not a few supplied by the author himself—as there are pages in the book. Although it embodies the work of some twenty-five years in partnership with David Jackson, his nonwriting but hardly silent fellow medium, in converse with other worlds through the agency of a Ouija board, its mere existence seems to have surprised its authors more than anyone else; in the course of gestation it became a kaleidoscope of provisional self-definitions, misgivings, jokes, and conjectures surely unique in modern American poetry. In contrast, say, to Pound's *Cantos,* Williams's *Patterson,* or Charles Olson's *Maximus Poems*—works not famous for their shrinking modesty—*The Changing Light at Sandover* has a healthy enough ego and definite designs on the reader, but both are so well sequestered within its virtuosity as to be almost invisible to the suspicious or the initially ill-disposed.

In *The Changing Light* Mr. Merrill has carried the problem of formal definition a step or two beyond the point reached by any ambitious, moderately coherent long poem outside the surrealist or purely aleatory orbits. It's an essentially conservative, elitist poem that stretches its own conventions to their outer limits and beyond. Is it all a game? Yes, if one is guided by his use of the elements of the standard Ouija board as organizing principles—twenty-six sections in "The Book of Ephraim" correspond to the alphabet; ten sections in *Mirabell's Books of Number* express the ten digits; and in *Scripts for the Pageant* two long sections reflect the "YES" and "NO of the board, separated by fourteen short sections under the symbol "&." Each book has much to say about its governing signs, "Ephraim" being concerned with story, speech, and chants and a passage "from romance to ritual"; *Mirabell* with a domestication of the evil presumed to lie in numbers and a conversion of number to poetic language; and *Scripts* with a balancing up of the positive and negative forces in life and the universe at large.

But that is only the beginning. Once one has agreed on its playful genesis, is it perhaps an epic, because of its length, its large cast of characters, and its increasingly weighty concern with matters of general interest? Lacking any "myth of assured growth," in David Kalsone's words—beyond, that is, the growth of trust and affection among friends—it must be the most sprawlingly inconclusive epic ever conceived. Is it perhaps what Richard Sáez calls a theodicy masquerading as "a sustained camp pageant?" *Paradise Lost* in ruffles and spangles? Blake's prophetic books in drag? Yes again if one lets oneself be mesmerized by its mere exoterica, its conundrum glitter of coincidence and correspondence.

To allow oneself to be so distracted, however, would be a crippling mistake. In the surprise and confusion of first readings, several sensible critics were scared off this poem, which is more considerably affecting than its purposefully frivolous outer machinery might lead one to suppose. One can hardly persevere beyond "The Book of Ephraim" in the conviction that Mr. Merrill is heartless, as some critics have claimed, or incapable of a strong, oblique humanity. The poem entire is a rigorous read, not to be taken at a gulp. But Mr. Merrill's often genial, often anguished, plaintive or saturnine, detachment from his own ingenuity proves in the long run—and what a long run it is!—to be a winning trait. Frequent undermining of one's apparent intentions is a regular feature of the mock-heroic. Mr. Merrill is never heroic, but serious he certainly is, sometimes hyperbolically so. It's a gauge of his confidence that in the act of working out his grand design he should lay so many lurid smoke screens, indulge in so much twittering or cackling jollification. Very Byronic, to be sure, though the model was most likely

Alexander Pope. As a sympathetic critic has justly written, "Merrill's version of the sublime is immensely sociable. Insight is celebrated communally and conversationally, culminating in grand choral fetes."

Das Rheingold in the Boulez/Chéreau production seen recently on television reminds one how easy it is for this kind of metamorphic magician to turn himself, like Alberich in the opera, into a toad, the better to be pinned down and trussed—if that is indeed the critic's only task. Toad and dragon, sibyl and sybarite, angel, god, and clown, all are at home in Mr. Merrill's inspired phantasmagoria. According to one's momentary disposition, it is possible to accept any one of the above for the oracle in chief. Mr. Merrill often alludes to his immersion in Wagner during the great era of Kirsten Flagstad and Lauritz Melchior at the Metropolitan Opera; he prepared himself in good time to spring on the public a big, heterogeneous, cyclical work like the Ring Cycle in which "music," meaning poetry as such, is far and away the prime shaping force. With something like the Bayreuth master's mixture of innocence and guile, he may have hoped to invent a Science Poetry of the Future, as Wagner was said, mostly by disciples, to have composed a Music of the Future.

But let us not drown in antecedents before reaching the real one. His eleven professorial advocates in the new book *James Merrill: Essays in Criticism,* rightly insist on his debt to Dante all along the line. The *Changing Light*'s tripartite organization, with a coda, has obvious affinities with *The Divine Comedy.* "The Book of Ephraim" is the most anecdotal part, entertaining and suffused with what in simpler times would have been called sins of the flesh and spirit.

Mirabell's Books of Number, featuring a brainy celestial bat that turns into a peacock and assumes the name of the hero of Congreve's *Way of the World,* is purgatorial in too many ways to recount. Painful deaths, dramatized with great dignity and tact, and an operation on David Jackson are counterpointed by speculation on such things as black holes—Dante's hell-pit being the poetic original—divisions within the atom itself and a volatile recalcitrance in otherworldly affairs all too familiar to earthlings. But despite menace and confusion, communication is established (always through the Ouija board in its habitual uppercase and its boyish telegraphic tricks—U for "you," "4 for "for" and so on) with the "research lab" where newly deceased souls are rated and reassigned to earth.

Mr. Merrill's fairly democratic, un-Dantean hierarchy is set up, at least among the Powers and those lucky "cloned" souls, about 12 percent of the total, worthy enough to engage in "V work" after rebirth. Its name derived from the French "*vie,*" from the five human senses and from the five supreme avatars of concentrated vitality—Akhnaton, Homer, Montezuma, Nefertiti, and Plato—V work sounds oddly like any high-minded cultural calling, except for a certain accent on Jewish, homosexual, or bisexual qualifications. Mr. Merrill seems to think that though heterosexuals may abound in lesser arts like painting or sculpture and can even be discovered in higher pursuits like poetry, music, or science, the balance of achievement may be shifting the other way. Tactfully, he doesn't labor the point but allows the poem's numerous felicities to speak for themselves. And felicities there surely are in *Mirabell:* the lyric on his mother, for instance, in section 7.6 and a storm at Stonington, Conn., where much of the poem was written, in section 8.1.

Before going on to *Scripts for the Pageant,* we must look again at Dante. The *Paradiso* which Mr. Merrill sees as both prophetic and scientific, means more to him than the *Inferno,* with its strictness about transgression and retribution. Pre-eminently there among the classics he finds "the still point of the turning world," a point immeasurably small, sure and bright from which true contentment emanates. He was told by his spirit friends to write "poems of science." With the aid of the medical biologist Lewis Thomas—God B, Sandover's supreme divinity, is biology personified—and other unspecified authorities he swotted up on during long winter days at Stonington, he dutifully went ahead. But many of the age's pressing enigmas, like gravity or Einstein's unified field theory, interest him scarcely at all. It's not surprising that Mr. Merrill's is a peculiarly literary science, descending from Darwin, the Huxleys, Bergson, and Whitehead. No one should read the poem in search of sugar-coated capsules of the hottest news from the scientific front. But neither is it by any means all pseudo or pop.

His aim is to extract from schoolboy commonplaces the most beguiling imaginative expansions and analogies, as when the DNA spiral is likened to the serpent of Eden and to Sarah Bernhardt descending a circular staircase. Stern ukases from the heavenly angels who dominate *Scripts for the Pageant*—Michael, Gabriel, Raphael, and Emmanuel, speaking respectively for light, fire and death, earth, and water—ascend to rhetorical heights that can only be called Drydenesque. But even these characters turn out to be abstracted renderings of qualities salient in his former old friends on earth: W. H. Auden; Maria Mitsotáki, an avid gardener in life; Robert Morse, a witty old Stonington crony; and a gifted biologist, George Cotzias, a victim like Maria of cancer. Up there in the hereafter, besieged by angels, demons, and assorted semidivinities, all four have grown more mercurial than ever, less prudent or shy.

Many others have parts to play: the poet Hans Lodeizen, Mr. Merrill's long-dead Dutch friend; Maya Deren, the avant-garde filmmaker who has a substantial role in the first book and the coda; and Mimi Vassilikos, the wife of a Greek novelist whose grief at her early death almost brings the poem to an abrupt halt before its relatively serene ending in Athens. Some others, in no particular order, are the Muses, Jesus, Gautama, Mercury, Mohammed, Pythagoras, Maria Callas, Kirsten Flagstad, Wallace Stevens, W. B. Yeats, and Richard Wagner. Except for Judaism, the old religions are rather rudely dismissed after a pat on the back for their often betrayed founders. The gradual narrowing of the inner circle to Auden and Maria Mitsotáki does after all follow naturally from the intimacy that Mr. Merrill and Mr. Jackson shared either with their persons or their spirits as manifested in their works. To them only Plato seems in the end to measure up.

Thus even in the rather austere *Scripts for the Pageant,* swung like a hammock between "YES" and "NO," every utterance is alembicated in a growing understanding of and affection for the high qualities of his departed friends. This means rough times for the living, skeptical David Jackson and even for some of the more difficult departed, like Chester Kallman. But Mr. Merrill's portrait of Auden steadily gains in stature and sweetness until it debouches in handsome lines like the following:

> Wystan. Can we bear to part with him,
> Our mine of good sense? Ah, he'll doff his dim
> Red shift (the mufti of a star's retreat)
> To vanish into quarry and tarpit,
> Sandgrain and stylus, thorn the raw March wind
> Piping through despondent makes a wand
> In bloom. He'll draw the desert round his knees.
> Brows knitted where the thinking icecaps freeze.
> He'll be the nurse whose charges "for their own
> Good" go without tea—and herself lies
> Till morning haunted by reproachful eyes.
> He'll be the glinting, faithful heart of stone.

Contrary to one's first impressions, *The Changing Light*'s strength lies less in the growth of the author's mind, at the top of its form before he began publishing the poem, than in the growth of his humanity. The latter generates an attractive willingness to look a bit foolish. In episodes dealing with the visit of his cousin Wendell to Venice, Auden's visit to the house Mr. Merrill and Mr. Jackson shared in Athens, the roadside death of a black dog, the decoration and furnishing of houses, the sponsoring of a young Greek family in Stonington, various jaunts and abrupt displacements, Mr. Merrill wistfully depicts himself as one of Henry James's or Edith Wharton's sensitive gentleman bachelors, caught in a tangle of self-begotten travesties, parodies, and sudden embarrassments (as when his Stonington apartment is broken into but mysteriously left untouched, so decorous are even the criminals in that "Enchanted Village"). Near the beginning of "Ephraim" he confides:

> We'd long since slept through our last talk on Thomist
> Structures in Dante. Causes
> Were always lost—on us. We shared the traits
> Of both the dumbest
>
> Boy in school and that past master of clauses
> Whose finespun mind "no idea violates."

One comes eventually to believe that. It's not the complexity of his "revelations" that dazzles or confounds, or even the very subtle play of correspondences and metric proportions, but the speed and vivacity of a mind that submits every cliché of daily intercourse or popular wisdom to penetrating second thoughts, to highlighting, backlighting, poetic heightening. The whole grand *garbuglio* of pop, sci-fi, and genuine science fantasy, of lessons and lectures and transcendental chatter, can easily be read as the pretext for an extended sequence of personal lyrics hinging on the execution of a slightly mad project that holds certain people together.

One doubts that the elaborate efforts of Mr. Kalstone, Mr. Sáez, Rachel Jacoff, J. D. McClatchy, Peter Sacks, or Stephen Yenser in the Festschrift for Mr. Merrill will result in *The Changing Light*'s full admission into the academic canon. Nor, one surmises, in his heart of hearts does Mr. Merrill expect them to. The poem is too much like Poe's *Eureka* or E. A. Robinson's "Man against the Sky" for easy acceptance in the commonality of American edification. It's a very private work. Its extreme conviviality is a lonely man's tribute to a bygone era and an always immanent hope. The gifts that presented us with such a copious parade of first-rate lyrics and amusing *nugae*—devastating couplets, single and double sonnets adroit enough to be overlooked as such, intricate canzoni (the "Samos" interlude in *Scripts for the Pageant*), supple terza rima, opulent masques and some of the best ordinary quatrains to show up in modern verse—are now a public trust to be honestly weighed and above all to be enjoyed.

MICHAEL HARRINGTON

Paradise or Disintegration

It is possible that James Merrill's *The Changing Light at Sandover* is one of the significant works of the second half of this century.

It would, of course, be foolish to try to be more precise. It is simply too early even to hazard the semblance of a definitive judgment. Time must participate in a decision which can only be made looking backward at a distance; the book, like the shades of the dead whom Merrill summons back to life, must be seen in a rear-view mirror. But to say that the future might well regard *The Changing Light* as major is to make a very large present claim for a powerful and unique poem.

Before supporting that claim, however, I should admit to at least three reasons why I might be overly enthusiastic. First, Merrill is culturally (and chronologically) of my generation. His points of reference—Blake, Eliot, Auden, Stevens—are my own and there is even a passing reference to the Village bar in which I gloriously misspent most of my twenties and early thirties. Secondly, I read, and re-read, *The Changing Light* during a five-month stay in Europe, i.e., in a time when I was deprived of the boring reassurance of everyday life and perhaps became hypersensitive as a result. Not so incidentally, I visited two cities—Athens and Venice—which figure in the poem and even went sightseeing with its images in my mind. And thirdly, I came upon the book shortly after finishing my own analysis of what is one of Merrill's central themes, the effective decline of religious belief in Western society. The poem therefore had—has—a relevance for me which could be personal and exceptional.

Even so, I am convinced that *The Changing Light at Sandover* is an event of importance in our culture and not just in my own life. Why?

The book is "about" a series of revelations from heaven and the dead, communicated to a Ouija board whose "Hand" is "DJ" and whose interpreter is "JM" (David Jackson and James Merrill, but both are characters in a fiction and I will call them DJ and JM when they appear in that guise). The setting is the religious social crisis of the contemporary world which, with its menaces of atomic and population explosions, must face the question of whether reality is ultimately benign or whether it is tending back toward the chaos from which it emerged. These issues are posed in terms of new myths—the old faiths, Merrill thinks, are unbelievable. Will God B (for biology) and Mother Nature triumph over anti-matter and disintegration? Will the spiritual forces accumulated over the generations produce "a great glory or a great puddle"?

More simply put: modern men and women have lost that basic, essentially religious, trust in the ultimate goodness of existence at the very moment at which they themselves have acquired the power to destroy, if not the cosmos, then a good part of our small corner of it. Two previous worlds, we are told, did self-destruct, either through a nuclear blast or by a Malthusian conflict between a race of centaurs and their batlike helpers. Ours is the third and last world.

My summary and prose brutalization of the poem should not be taken to suggest that it is a compound of cobwebs and Weltschmerz. On the contrary, *The Changing Light* is intricately architectonic and intellectually serious. Like *Finnegans Wake* it comes full circle: it concludes as JM begins reading all that has gone before to a heavenly audience and intones its first word as its last word. This preposterous notion, and many others, is so totally and convincingly imagined that, when JM and DJ finally break off contact with three of the dead, there is a poignant sense of present loss. Indeed, if all of its parts failed, which is in no way the case, *The Changing Light* would still be a triumph as an incredibly realized whole.

The poem is divided into three main sections and a brief coda. The first book, *Ephraim,* consists of twenty-six separate poems beginning with the successive letters of the alphabet. It establishes the basic dramatic premise about the Ouija board and introduces some of the central themes: the decline of the old myths, presented in a lovely elegy telling how "Venice, her least stone / Pure menace at the start, at length became / A window fiery-mild, whose walked-through frame / Everything else, at sunset, hinged upon—"; a debate between JM and his artist nephew over realism (science, facts, this world) and faith-art (the otherworldly); the fearfulness of power as JM learns that the bomb at Hiroshima destroyed souls as well as bodies; and, with an allusion to Wallace Stevens, the idea of God as that which (who) conserves an unstable universe whose black holes are scientific intuitions of an unthinkable and metaphysical possibility.

Ephraim also contains a poetic fragment of a lost novel which is confusing and wisely forgotten, and many more personal references than the rest of *The*

Changing Light, references which are sometimes excessive and obscure. The whole project, one suspects, did not become clear to Merrill until he began to work on the next book, *Mirabell;* and thus *Ephraim* is marred by some loose threads. It is in *Mirabell* (twice as long as *Ephraim,* followed by *Scripts for the Pageant,* which is even longer) that the dramatic fascination of a marvelously articulated fictional (symbolic of the real) world becomes quite dominant.

"Mirabell" is a batlike creature, the survivor of one of those self-destructed worlds, who becomes a peacock as he talks to JM and DJ. Indeed he turns a scientific account of the genesis of reality into a poetic myth so that his own transformation from bat to peacock is a refraction of his subject matter. This section is divided into ten sections, numbered from zero through nine, which, not so incidentally, is the number of heavens in Dante's *Paradiso,* one of the many ghosts which haunt this poem. In *Mirabell* the shades of three dead people—W. H. Auden; Maria Demertzi Mitsotáki, an Athenian friend of JM and DJ and the daughter of a former Greek prime minister; and Robert Morse, a neighbor and friend from Stonington, Connecticut—become central. And a basic theme is fully defined: that there must be "POEMS OF SCIENCE" (the supernatural characters speak upper case, a convention which, strange to say, is not at all bothersome). At first, JM is appalled at the notion ("To squint through those steel-rimmed / Glasses of the congenitally slug- / Pale boy at school, with his precipitates, / His fruit flies and his slide rule?").

> Not for nothing had the Impressionists
> Put subject-matter in its place, a mere
> Pretext for iridescent atmosphere.
> Why couldn't Science, in the long run, serve
> As well as one's uncleared lunch-table or
> *Mme X en Culotte de Matador?*

Mirabell ends with a serene meditation by JM, to which I will return, and the appearance of the Archangel Michael, one of the key figures of the next book, *Scripts for the Pageant. Scripts* is divided, typically, into three subsections, "Yes," "&," "No." In this poem everything is dialectical, from matter (which is white and black, order and chaos), through images (which, like photographs, are positives of a negative and vice versa), to Michael (who is good, but perhaps a sentimental liberal) and his sometimes antagonist, the angel Gabriel (who destroys, but perhaps as a necessary work for the sustaining of life).

In *Scripts,* another shade joins the group: George Cotzias, Greek scientist. Buddha, Ahknaton, Jesus, Homer, Montezuma, Plato, and a false

Mohammed also put in significant appearances. (Plato is, for reasons which will not be explained here, major.) This is the book in which the chaos-order antagonism is explored and it ends as JM and DJ break a mirror—and thereby their relationship with Auden, Maria, and George. The coda (*The Higher Keys*) ties up various loose ends but also focuses upon the rebirth of Robert Morse who, in his new guise (which includes a clubfoot, one more sign of the unity of this imperfect world and its ethereal interpretation), will be a great composer. As JM prepares to read *The Changing Light* to twenty-six spirits, including Dante, Jane Austen, and Proust ". . . a star trembles in the full carafe / As the desk light comes on, illuminating / The page I open to." The lectern lamp—the ordinary—becomes a star. As bats turn into peacocks and science into poetry, the poet goes back to the beginning and ends with the first word, "Admittedly. . . ."

Before moving to some of the most important particulars within this extraordinary structure, I should acknowledge some problems. Merrill is possessed, he himself understands, of an "unrelenting fluency," a talent to turn everything into "slant, weightless gold." But does one, then, confuse a craftsman's formal genius with deep meanings, knowing with Merrill that "affection's / Poorest object, set in perfect light / By happenstance, grows irreplaceable"? Bob Adelman, a photographer friend and collaborator, once said to me that you should not cover a war with color film since the carnage will come out vividly beautiful.

That is a problem with Merrill; it is also a glory. For instance, in *Scripts* he describes a changing of the light in a supernatural schoolroom: "not / The lights we've seen according to thus far /—Spectral gems, first waters of a star—/ But Light like bread, quotidian, severe, / Wiped of the sugar sprinkles of Vermeer; . . . " And there is ubiquitous wit in this poem, sometimes as frivolous as a pun, sometimes more ingenious as when Jane Austen addresses the newly dead Robert Morse "As *Mr. Robert*—a shrewd estimate. / He's after all not Heir to the Estate. / Its goods and duties, but a Younger Son / Free to be ornamental and have fun." My greatest difficulty is not, however, aesthetic but political. *The Changing Light* has, as we will see, a very explicit political content: anti-nuclear, environmental, and sometimes a kind of upper-class, elitist Malthusianism. It is that last attitude, I will suggest, that creates problems.

With these qualifications, let me return to the poem and a very basic question: what is it "about"? One answer is, the changing light at Sandover. The name, Sandover, we are told, is a corruption of the French, Saintefleur, or the Italian Santofior, "An English branch of that distinguished tree / Through whose high leaves light pulses and whose roots / Rove beyond memory." It is, as "WHA" (the shade of Auden) suggests, the community of art and spirit which lies beyond doing your own thing, the "ROSEBRICK MANOR" of language and culture whose family includes Shakespeare and Emily Dickinson. "IT WAS," WHA says, "THE GREATEST PRIVILEGE TO HAVE HAD / A BARE LOWCEILINGED MAID'S ROOM AT THE TOP." "Sandover" is also the Ouija board and, I suspect, the heavenly flower at the end of the *Paradiso.* But, for my present purpose, its most significant meaning is the heritage of culture, and that relates to one of the central myths of *Mirabell* and to one of the basic theories of the age.

It was, Mirabell tells JM and DJ, language, culture, which marked the beginning of the transition "OF THE TWO BASIC APECHILDREN" toward humanity. Emile Durkheim, and Friederich Nietzsche, both of whom thought grammar a key to God, would agree; so would Wittgenstein and, in our day, Jurgen Habermas. So signal gave way to sign and then sign became symbol and symbol music and the "REASONED INDIRECTION" of the garden of human culture was on the way. But now, the old symbols lose their power and we move from symbols back toward signs: the clock face, Henri Lefebvre remarks, at least imitated the revolutions of the day; the digital watch is pure information. But if, to go back to Merrill, "IN THE BEGINNING WAS THE WORD" and now the word is no longer what is was, how are we to face our crises as the light changes in our culture?

Without the sustaining myths, Mirabell tells JM, "MAN IS AMOK & CHAOS SLIPS IN (UPON / COLLAPSE, IN INTELLIGENT MEN, OF RELIGIOUS BELIEF)." That is hardly an original thought, and a theologian like Bultmann is more radical than Merrill in his demythologizing. But what Merrill makes of this commonplace—both as poetry and poetic meaning—is anything but a cliché. The past two or three hundred years, JM comments, "have seen a superhuman / All-shaping Father dwindle (as in Newman) / To ghostly, disputable Essence or / Some shaggy-browed, morality play bore / (As in the Prologue to Faust)." And then there comes a key intuition (it is, I will suggest later, central to the entire poem):

> Why should God speak? How humdrum what he says
> Next to His word: out of a black sleeve, lo!
> Sun, Earth and Stars in eloquent dumb show.
> Our human words are weakest, I would urge,
> When He resorts to them.

But if God is in crisis, so is literature. The old vocabulary becomes stale, "translucent, half-effaced," but science creates a new language: ". . . through

Wave, Ring, Bond, through Spectral Lines / And Resonances blows a breath of life, / Lifting the pleated garment." Since JM, openly acknowledging his debt to Matthew Arnold, thinks the scribe must replace the priest, it is therefore incumbent on the poet to marry science and poetry (and music), matter and man, nature and spirit, to reconcile all the dialectical contraries. It is necessary, WHA argues, to bring "WM CARLOS WM'S THOUGHTFUL THINGS / & THE COLD VIRGIN VERB OF MALLARME / TOGETHER. . . ." One must, JM puts it, "tell round what brass tacks the old silk frays."

In confronting this challenge, JM presents three new God(s). First there is the God who holds back the chaos: a distant figure, not at all as human and compelling as Mother Nature in her best mood (Nature, for JM as for the Greeks, is a trinity). The second God reminds me of the divinity defined by Hegel in the *Phenomenology:* an imminent transcendence which develops historically, not simply in nature (which would be a rather simple pantheism) but in the evolution of nature and man. As WHA puts it ". . . GOD B IS NOT / ONLY HISTORY BUT EARTH ITSELF. HE IS THE GREENHOUSE." JM is, I think, even more daring: God B is one

(Who, lacking human volubility,
Has no word for His own power and grace;
Who, left alone, just falls back on flimflam
Tautologies like *I am that I am*
Or *The world is everything that is the case);*

That is remarkable: to equate the God of Abraham and the empirical reality of Wittgenstein. But then I suspect Wittgenstein might have agreed even though he insisted that this was a matter upon which one must keep silent.

This second, "Hegelian" God is described more prosaically—more scientifically—by the Archangel Michael at the close of *Mirabell.* The genius of life is, he says, its responsiveness to the sun "AND SO AS YOU FACE THE SETTING SUN YOU FACE YOUR ANCESTOR." Cells accumulated energy through the suncycles and "THIS ACCUMULATED ENERGY BECOMES THROUGH EONS AN ANCIENT AND IMMORTAL INTELLIGENCE . . . AND AT LAST AFTER EXPERIMENT THIS INTELLIGENCE FORMED MAN. / THIS IS GOD'S NAME." And yet, for all of the demythologizing, *The Changing Light* is a religious poem. In a commentary on Michael's cosmology, Maria says:

FOR MICHAEL/SUN
READ GENERATIVE FORCE FOR GENERATIVE FORCE
READ: RADIATION TO THE BILLIONTH POWER
OF EXPLODING ATOMS. FOR EMMANUEL,

H_2O. FOR SEEDS, THAT COSMIC DUST
LADEN WITH PARTICLES OF INERT MATTER
FOR GOD READ: GOD.

Ultimately, all the scientific myths—and for that matter, the scientific non-myths—encounter the mystery of the beginning. Kant was, and is, right (and on this count, Hegel agreed with him): you cannot deduce the infinite from the finite. But JM—and Wittgenstein—are right, too: one can imagine in silence or in poetry, a godly source of that beginning. *The Changing Light* does more than that. It projects a supernatural effort to help humans toward an earthly paradise, in part through biology—the "no accident clause" of DNA, time standing still in the clockwork of genes—and in part through an otherworldly research lab, making use of the reborn, reapportioned souls of the great dead.

There was, I thought, more than a little poetic license in all of this. Wasn't the transmigration of souls merely a way of saying that Shakespeare and Buddha still live in us? But then I happened to read the comments of a French scientist, Claude Allegre, in an article in *Le Monde:* "To know that the stars are immense nuclear laboratories whose activities continually change the chemical composition of our galaxy . . . to discover that the physical laws which rule liquid crystals, a plate of spaghetti, a pile of sand are finally the same . . . these are some of the elements which today infuse the most profound human thought."

Science, then, is becoming science fiction and *The Changing Light* with its "R" (for Research) Lab where new types are cloned is not so otherworldly. But is is here, in the domain of the science God, that the elitist neo-Malthusianism emerges. Of course, the bomb and nuclear power are a threat to human existence; of course, the sense of the holiness of the environment is perhaps the most genuine and spontaneous religious emotion of these times; and of course there must be a limit to population. But to blame and despise the mass of the "breeders" is another thing. Mirabell makes the essentially aristocratic point: "A MERE TWO MILLION CLONED SOULS LISTEN TO EACH OTHER WHILE / OUTSIDE THEY HOWL AND PRANCE SO RECENTLY OUT OF THE TREES." At the time when Malthus wrote, attacking decency toward the poor as an incentive to excess population, most enlightened Britons thought my Irish forebears—and James Joyce's, more to the point—a race of savages.

There were even those—Nassau Senior, for instance—who thought that the Irish did not die in sufficient numbers during the Potato Famine to restore the proper economic equilibrium between food supply and the "demand" for life. WHA, in welcoming the coming of the "alphas" (from *Brave New World*) asks, "WHAT OF THE OMEGAS? / 3 BILLION OF EM UP IN SMOKE POOR BEGGARS?" And JM interjects: "Wystan, how *can* you?" The reply comes: "COURAGE: GABRIEL / KNOWS WHAT HE'S UP TO & (LIKE TIME) WILL TELL." When humans thus play God they take on too great a responsibility, to put it mildly. In fairness, JM has his doubts—and I presume James Merrill does, too—and the worst statements are made by assorted angels and shades.

I don't want to be priggish. Some of the poem's perceptions of the problems of mass society are insightful enough. Finishing this essay in Venice, tramping as a member of the democratic mass through the aristocratic precincts of the Doge's Palace, I would be a hypocrite to deny that an occasional snobbish thought occurred to me. But then the thought was dismissed as both unworthy and untrue, for the point is to expand the human potential of the billions—just as we have already in fact expanded the potential of the millions, including me.

All of this raises the truly vexed question of the relation between art and politics. How does one deal with Ezra Pound's beautiful evocation of the corruption of art by money in the *Cantos* when one knows that it is quite likely inspired by fascist nonsense about the Jewish bankers? Or with the poignance in Brecht's Stalinist play—an agitprop play at that—on the Chinese Revolution? I do not want to equate Merrill's ambivalent and liberal elitism with fascism or Stalinism, yet the problem it poses is similar to the one raised by Pound and Brecht.

Of course one doesn't judge a work of art by political standards. Marx well understood that Balzac, the reactionary, was a greater novelist than Zola, the socialist. And there can be a sort of "willing suspension of disbelief"—I think. But then Balzac's monarchism does not threaten me while neo-Malthusianism does. Whatever the high theoretical solution to the problem, I must confess that I was aesthetically put off by the suggestion—and it is not made by JM himself—that a famine in Africa may be part of a benign plan for the future.

I regret the criticism for the objectionable material arises precisely because Merrill is becoming more socially concerned. The transition from *Ephraim* to *Mirabell* is, in part, a shift from the more personal to the more public and it marks a gain in power—it is one of the reasons why this strange poem may be truly great. If in one aspect of that excellent transition Merrill nods as politician and utopian more than as poet, that is to be noted and regretted; it should not be a reason for turning against *The Changing Light*.

In this spirit, I conclude, then, with one of the finest passages in the poem, a key to Merrill's third God and his basic meaning. I cite but a few lines of this magnificent meditation, first about DNA:

> The world was everything that was the case?
> Open the case. Lift out the fabulous
> Necklace, in form a spiral molecule
> Whose sparklings outmaneuver time, space, us.

Then JM explains that Hell in German means bright

> —So that my father's cheerful, "Go to Hell,"
> Long unheard, and Vaughan's unbeatable
> "They are all gone into a world of light"
> Come, even now at times, to the same thing—

But how will Hell—in that double meaning—render what it owes? That is, JM thinks, a "quaint idiom," perhaps "from the parchment of some old scribe of the apocalypse." So then one must

> . . . render *it* as the long rendering to
> Light of this very light stored by our cells
> These past five million years, these past five minutes
> Here by the window, taking in through panes
> Still bleary from the hurricane a gull's
> Ascending aureole of decibels,
> As numberless four-pointed brilliancies
> Upon the Sound's mild silver grid come, go?
> The message hardly needs decoding, so
> Sheer the text, so innocent and fleet
> These overlapping pandemonia:
> Birdlife, leafplay, rockface, waterglow
> Lending us their being, till the given
> Moment comes to render what we owe.

In Paris at the Beaubourg earlier in the summer, I saw a series of Kandinsky paintings assembled to show his progression (which I am not sure was a progression in this case) from representational to non-representational art. The first painting was of a woods, and the light makes a marvelous pattern upon the dark ground. That, it struck me, was what all Kandinsky's work was about: the light in the woods was the *donnée,* all else was implicit in it. So with Merrill. His third God is reality, the world that is the case, but enchanted, sheer, innocent, and fleet with its overlapping pandemonia. A page earlier, the same insight in different language:

> Things look out at us from a spell
> They themselves have woven.

That is, I think Merrill's perception of God, and it pervades—it illuminates—every page of one of the most extraordinary poems of our times, a theology for the godless and godly.

ROBERT MAZZOCCO

The Right Stuff

With the publication now of *From the First Nine* and *The Changing Light at Sandover,* one can better trace James Merrill's development over the last thirty years, from the voyages and tours of the "international theme" in his earlier poems through the supernatural forays of the trilogy—always bearing in mind that in the dandified body of this poet's works there lurks a giant's strength, a giant, of course, with consummate tact and balance.

Merrill comes from a world of wealth and culture, *le gratin;* "exquisite" is the adjective most frequently applied to him—until recently, anyway. So the jolt of experience that could really hit another life, another milieu was, I think, a necessity. Privilege cushions the blows, limits the appetite, or refines it, often beyond all recognition. Being an American, Merrill was also a Puritan; by temperament he was an aesthete, perhaps a hedonist. Greece, then, with its countryside of "old ideas," its "salt, wine, olive," "Graces, Furies, Fates," became the ideal place, beginning in the middle of the uptight Fifties, for the "young chameleon" to set the contrary forces in motion. There what he'd later call the "dumbest"—that is, the earthy, the primitive—rose to the surface, while always being counseled (or opposed) by the "cleverest"—his Jamesian finesse, the "visiting mind" of the detached traveler. ("Prism" and "numbskull": two of his favorite words.)

For Merrill the "realm of hazard" is the realm of art, but the creative juices always flow from an exotic "elsewhere." The elongated syntax and filigree style, the deft modulations (Merrill's vocal range, though obviously more studied than spontaneous, is remarkably varied, like the range of those singers who can be tenor or bass, employ light or dark inflections at will)—this idiom (at its strongest the most accomplished rhetoric, I believe, of any American poet since Crane) could only have worked once he'd broken past his upbringing and made a strategic use of the senses in a foreign country.

The best of the dramatic or comedic sketches in *From the First Nine* are

---

not of chatty dowagers, whom he could just as easily have met back home, but of elegant roughnecks ("Kostas Tympakianákis," "Manos Karastefanis," "Strato in Plaster")—the proverbial *bel indifférent:* "I knew the type: / Superb, male, raucous, unclean, Orthodox / Ikon of appetite feathered to the eyes / With the electric blue of days that will / Not come again"—a vitality and high-handedness, the allure of the lawless available to him only as an expatriate. And if a dowager makes an appearance, as in "Words for Maria," there the decorative impulse achieves an appropriate resonance, with even the dancing-master's wit learning to suggest something of the reek of the human. And of course this particular dowager, Maria Mitsotáki, will later become one of the most memorable of the spectral figures inhabiting the trilogy.

Much of *From the First Nine* is autobiographical or quasi-autobiographical, but the hard data behind it are characteristically slight: the fantasying boy and the divorced parents; the Oedipal triangulation of the "merger of Heart and Hurt / that made me"; stockbroker's son and opera buff; the long and sustaining union with David Jackson, his *pièce rose;* the two troubled affairs, one with Hans Lodeizen, a Dutch poet dead at twenty-six, the other the person varyingly called "Strato" or "S," his *pièce noire.* Around such data, the poems—embedded miniatures, hermetic cameos—are constructed, subtracted from, poems full of definitions and redefinitions, the interweaving of themes and frames periodically connecting one collection to the next. "Scenes of Childhood" and "Five Old Favorites," for instance, are clearly trial runs for the dolors of "The Broken Home" (echoes of which filter through the interpretation of a Giorgione painting—son, mother, dragon—in *The Book of Ephraim,* the first Book of the trilogy).

The introspective tonalities of "An Urban Convalescence," a turning point in Merrill's career, gain full weight, intricacy, and exuberance in "The Thousand and Second Night." The satirical "Charles" poems have linkages with a later bit of salon portraiture, "The Friend of the Fourth Decade"; Charles being also the first name of Merrill's father, who appears in a provocative coupling with Ali Pasha in the historical reverie "Yánnina," where the young Byron (perhaps the young Merrill), a guest in Ali's kingdom, "likes / The luxe, and overlooks the heads on pikes." While the hysterical complaint of "Childlessness," written in his thirties, is eventually redeemed in the unexpected openness, ease, and poignance of "Up and Down," particularly the last stanzas in which the poet's mother gives her son an emerald ring, "a den of greenest light," that "grows, shrinks, glows." It had been given her by the poet's father in honor of Merrill's birth. "Here, take it for—/ For when you marry," she stammers; "For your bride. It's yours."

> *I did not tell her, it would sound theatrical,*
> Indeed this green room's mine, my very life.
> We are each other's; there will be no wife;
> The little feet that patter here are metrical.
> *But onto her worn knuckle slip the ring.*
> *Wear it for me, I silently entreat,*
> *Until—until the time comes. Our eyes meet.*
> *The world beneath the world is brightening.*

Poetry like Merrill's in *From the First Nine,* that depends so much on settings, on objects, touches, at times, animism (the small-town iconography of one poem has a postmaster, Mr. Bird, and two neighbors, Old Miss Tree and Mrs. Stone, "mute on her dazzling lawn"), delights as much in spoonerisms as in Freudian *lapsus linguae* or James's "torment of taste." It relishes images of tenancy ("mornings in a new house," "closets full of clues"), of the Apollonian *flâneur* and the Dionysian *voyou,* or the banquet of Auden's "precious five," what the tongue savors and the eye catches ("lemon trees," their gusts of sharp cologne, "bearing and in bloom at once"). Cosmopolitan attitudes are continually being struck or struck down, masks both decried and accepted, especially "the erotic mask / Worn the world over by illusion / To weddings of itself and simple need."

Memory is the magical vehicle through which the problem of age is best understood, most readily absorbed—evenings becoming grayer, daylight colder, the poet resembling a "smiling ghost / Neither harmed nor warmed, now, by the fire." Fire, or alternatively, water or mirror, are the most recurring symbols, and each is redeemed by time, changed by time. Topical allusions, generally rare, have the effect of a grenade lobbed onto a garden party ("Yesterday also Robert Kennedy's / Train of refrigerated dignitaries / Last seen on TV burying Dr. King / Wormed its way to Arlington Cemetery").

In such a poetry, then, it's hardly surprising that a character will come "to his senses through a work of art," or surprising to find long lines, full of hyphens, parentheses, semicolons, followed by abrupt inversion ("Backbreaking it was to haul them home"), or that the diction, always melodious, often dense, as related to Proust as to Campion, is not exempt from occasional affectation: "Great drifts of damask cleaned our lips of grease" is not altogether apt, I should think, as a description of two people wiping their mouths during dinner.

Nor is it surprising that Merrill bears little relation either to what a member of his class would be doing in the era of the jet set or to the lives of most of his colleagues, academic or bohemian, in the parochial world of American poetry—too rigorous for the one, he's too *raffiné* for the other. He's not acquired a school of epigones like John Ashbery or emerged as a representative figure like Robert Lowell, though in stature he's easily the equal of both. He remains singularly himself, uniquely set apart.

Cavafy said of his flat at 10 rue Lepsius: "Where else could I be better situated than here amid these three centers of existence; a brothel, a church which forgives, and a hospital where you die"—the irony reminds us of Heine, the conceit behind it of Baudelaire, and these echoes are meant to reverberate in the cultivated reader's mind. This is a mandarin sensibility, as learned as it is casual, one ill at ease in the amnesiacal modern world, and with little chance of continuation in the future. Such a sensibility Merrill of course shares. Unlike Cavafy, however, Merrill can often seem more sensibility than personality, the "marked if undecipherable feeling," the perfect cadences ("Life-sentenced to the honey-cell of song, / Harsh melisma, torturous diphthong") appearing now and again to be made out of the sheerest ephemera. So one always has to read a lot of Merrill before his chimerical features or fictions, psychologically speaking, come clear.

Aside from a certain aura of youthfulness, the indelible signature of his entire career (the trilogy even has a scientist friend at work on a wonder drug to prevent aging), the catalyst energizing most of *From the First Nine* is, I feel, the isolating of an individual trait, a "flaw" in the prevailing equanimity, the grain of sand in the shell of the oyster that creates the pearl. Usually that takes the form of *amour propre,* either in a bittersweet, universal sense, as in Merrill's rendering of what he dubs "Proust's Law": "Whatever least thing our self-love longs for most / Others instinctively withhold," or it becomes mysteriously heartless, as in the emblematic Jack Frost, "years older / Than his twenty-year-old face," the oblique playboy and hero of "The Summer People," one of Merrill's most piquant and accessible ballads—the "famous host," with his ritual of bridge, gossip, croquet, ultimately strangled in "pride and regret."

But Merrill's *amour propre,* beneath the convoluted wryness, has deeper entanglements: sexual or filial guilt, the dual knot of family romance and romantic agony, the tyrannical beloveds who betray or enslave, the authority figures who condemn (or the reverse: note Merrill's rich boy in "Days of 1935" ratting on his once glamorous thug and moll: "You I adored I now accuse . . ."). With these obsessional properties come the sadistic or masochistic intruders on his Parnassian surfaces ("We love the good, said Plato? He was wrong. / We love as well the wicked and the weak"), who serve less for emotional fulfillment, I think, than, paradoxically, for escape from emotional bondage. How can one be set free *of* love *through* love? How can the lover sacrifice his possessive need of the beloved, or vice versa, in order that the beloved go about his or her own adventure, which may include another and different love, another and better "elsewhere"? The poet or persona in his relation to the look, the feel, the mirroring presence of the other ("Father Time and Mother Earth," Eros and Thanatos) wishes to be either free of the need to be possessive or free of the one who needs to possess him.

Because in Merrill's work dreams and dream narratives are so often paramount, along with the antiphonal use of questions and answers (a device expanded to encyclopedic density in the trilogy), the more a tale is retold, the more truth, presumably, it will reveal. But there's a danger. The more a tale is retold, the more it loses its original intensity (or indeed the emotional indignity that had most likely inspired it), and hence the basis of its emotional power. Also the more attention one pays to the various possibilities of translating a tale from one poem to the next—the pyrotechnical "Lost in Translation" is itself a kind of palimpsest: a memoir of Mademoiselle, Merrill's childhood governess, who speaks French with an *accent allemand,* and an evocation of a Rilke paraphrase of Valéry's "Palme"—the more nuances the poet accumulates, yet at the same time the more distance he places between himself and the original text. As in Karl Kraus, "The closer the look one takes at a word, the greater the distance from which it looks back."

This is one reason, no doubt, why in the Merrill of *From the First Nine,* despite the irresistible verve, there is, normally, so little of the rawly honest, still less of brute force. (One cannot get "close" to Merrill: the perennial complaint of his critics.) A reason why, too, the fateful figures one thinks of in connection with him are never the canonical ones of anomie, no Sisyphus or Tithonus laboring under a harsh existential curse, and no *voix de la foule;* rather one thinks of Marsyas, say, challenging Apollo, human virtuosity as against the superhuman, Penelope each night unraveling what she's woven by day, or Scheherazade continually postponing her death through the thousand and one ruses of art. One thinks, that is, of figures of fancy, exilic or triumphant; with the drama lying primarily in states of estrangement (libidinal, geographical, familial), the anxiety over fortune or misfortune (not knowing how long one's good luck will last, how much worse one's bad luck may become).

"The Thousand and Second Night," practically a treasury of much of the above, is an *éducation sentimentale,* a poet's travel journal set against the decaying cities of Athens or Istanbul, the splendors of "frantic West," "passive Orient"; a comedy of manners (including glimpses of a family scandal) with a tag from Hofmannsthal: "All manners are symbolic," and intimations of Mauberley or Prufrock in contemporary dress. Here once again the "dumbest" and "cleverest" emerge, the aesthete gently mocking his own fastidiousness, his "precious sensibility," the adventurer slyly ironic about the risks involved. The poem is orchestrated in suitably diverse keys and combinations, brisk and Byronic in one of the earlier sections, courtly and ornamental in the last, the concluding quatrains emphasizing Merrill's favorite *abba* rhyme scheme, as the previous meditations on illness and health, soul and body, art and disease effortlessly rise now to a sovereign, mythic grace:

> And when the long adventure reached its end,
> I saw the Sultan in a glass, grown old,
> While she, his fair wife still, her tales all told,
> Smiled at him fondly, "O my dearest friend,"
>
> Said she, "and lord and master from the first,
> Release me now. Your servant would refresh
> Her soul in that cold fountain which the flesh
> Knows not. Grant this, for I am faint with thirst."
>
> And he: "But it is I who am your slave.
> Free me, I pray, to go in search of joys
> Unembroidered by your high, soft voice,
> Along that stony path the senses pave."
>
> They wept, then tenderly embraced and went
> Their ways. She and her fictions soon were one.
> He slept through moonset, woke in blinding sun,
> Too late to question what the tale had meant.

By the time of the trilogy, though, Merrill is in his fifties; neuroses lessen, horizons widen, another threshold is at hand—indeed a stratospheric one. Merrill's abiding wish to "act the part," write it, and witness the performance at one and the same time is here granted, with all its problems. The overall question of love, of dependency and independence, metamorphoses into the greater question of human destiny. How free is man in his existence? How controlled? The phantasmagorical, always a factor in Merrill, is in the trilogy the guiding principle; the precedent for such ontological investigations, even if unacknowledged, is to be found, not so much in Dante, as has been claimed, but rather, I believe, in Carlyle, Borges, Mallarmé. The possibility being explored is that reality is a "universal book," that all artists write one "common book," that we do not live so much as we are lived; or one can think of a precedent in Schopenhauer's "multiplicity of phenomena," his idea of time and space as a "vast dream, dreamed by a single being, in such a way that all the dream characters dream too, so that everything interlocks and harmonizes with everything else." (In Merrill's gloss: "everything merges and reflects.")

These ideas as ideas, not new, certainly, almost primitive, are "new," however, in the startling use that Merrill has made of them, in an audacious, and audaciously amusing, conjunction with the arcana of contemporary culture, the post-Einsteinian, postmodern, information society of today. (Also, equally unacknowledged, is the use he has made, or the use they've made of him, of both our most private and our most public languages, dream and wit, the one to defeat the "reality principle," the other to augment the "pleasure principle.") Thus Merrill's earlier motif, the world as a bazaar selling innumerable cosmopolitan illusions, now is becoming the cosmological bazaar of the trilogy, of innumerable myths along with innumerable universes, with Greece, Merrill's earlier, liberating "elsewhere," becoming in turn the even more liberating heaven that surrounds us, or the "heaven" that is "the surround of the living."

All such *fabulae* are to be had for the price, as it were, of a Ouija board—the most audacious act of all. As Merrill (JM) and Jackson (DJ) sit together at their house in Stonington—the contrary aspects of Merrill's temperament once more at play: the "dumbest" fostering credulity, the "cleverest" his skepticism—they commune with their "familiars," Ephraim or Mirabell, an assortment of recently dead friends (Auden, Maria Mitsotáki, Chester Kallman, *et al.*), august spooks (mostly poets, musicians, philosophers), and the tutelary angels, archangels, and gods representing the bureaucracy of outer space and also monitoring (none too well it would appear) the little planet Earth. So in the trilogy we find a red room to receive the messages, a blue room to transcribe them, and a printout typography to differentiate from among the assemblage—lower-case lettering for the auditors, upper-case for the spirits and their astral mysteries: nine stages in *Mirabell's Books of Number,* twenty-five or so lessons in *Scripts for the Pageant,* and five ceremonies in the coda.

While obviously more ludic than tragic, and more epiphanic than epic, the trilogy is epic for all that. It is a colloquy with the immortals and a commentary, with many pointedly cryptic asides, on the nature of immortality, or the "mortality" that "allows for the divine translation." It is also a retrospective cataloguing of Merrill's past *oeuvre,* past themes (including a farewell to the romantic agony) and an augury of events to come (we learn how much longer DJ has to live, that JM will not repeat his karma, this life is to be his last). Allegory mixes with tomfoolery, Dantean spirals with Proustian *longueurs,* game theory and catastrophe theory nuzzle heavenly ascents (egalitarianism and elitism, war and peace are debated vis-à-vis the gods in their cloning shops and "R Labs" promoting or demoting the primates they keep manufacturing from one age to the next).

As mercurial in doctrine as in its rhetorical flourishes or sibylline *mise en scène, The Changing Light at Sandover* has, also, a musical structure (roughly a trio of key voices in the kaleidoscopic first book, a quintet in the second, a grand ensemble in the last) with JM, the maestro of the spheres, learning to "let the silence after each / Note sing." There is an element of suspense: can we outwit chaos (currently the burden of Hiroshima) and bring paradise earthward, so that we can achieve the "heaven" that has been given us, time after botched time, "to win"? This is an uplifting quest: works of the arts and sciences. "V WORKS," which once enlarged our world, now must be enlisted in order to save it, the trilogy being itself an example of one such possible endeavor (Merrill is asked by his "voices" to write "poems about science").

And the poem has a utopian hope: waiting on the next rung of the evolutionary ladder, immune to our muddled battles and disasters, are the Alpha Men, not Nietzsche's "dragon slayers," but those who will, if all goes well, be saner, happier, but also duller than our current lot (the ultimate apotheosis, I guess, of dumbest and cleverest). And throughout the common center remains, of course, the magical dexterity of the poet himself. For as MM (Maria Mitsotáki) neatly puts it: "ALL THINGS ARE DONE HERE IF U HAVE TECHNIQUE."

Now in this all-night talk show of the dead, this "spyhole on the Infinite," some of the otherworldly one-liners are certainly funny (Callas, fretting in heaven: "THEY CALL THIS THE STAR'S DRESSING ROOM THIS HOLE?"), and many of the extraterrestial disquisitions are arresting, to say the least; yet it's precisely because of all the wit and wisdom that it's a little hard for me to believe in the *basis* of Merrill's "vision"—that is, his "stray souls maneuvering / Round the tea cup." At times they seem all too like a distillation—the mandarin's own—of previous seances, divinatory or childhood texts, classic poems, dramas, fictions resting on library shelves here on earth. On and off while reading the trilogy, I thought of *Orphée, The Fall of Hyperion, La Jeune Parque, Magister Ludi, Finnegans Wake,* both the Ring cycles (Tolkein and Wagner are mentioned), *An Experiment with Time* (the theme of infinite regression), *Back to Methuselah* (orations on the life force), *Cities of the Red Night* (the notion that a nuclear apocalypse had occurred eons ago somewhere in the Gobi), *The Psychopathology of Everyday Life* (see Freud's negative remarks on "Determinism, Chance, and Superstitious Belief"), Blake's Los,

Carroll's Alice, much of Firbank (isn't the elfin and avuncular Ephraim—" MY DEARS I AM BEST SUITED WHEN U STRIP"—quite as good as any character in Firbank?), as well as those once popular gurus of the Sixties' flower kids, particularly Edgar Cayce (his messages from Atlantis burbling at the bottom of the Bermuda Triangle).

In addition, MM has, I think, a touch of Auntie Mame, and not a few of the gibes of WHA (Auden), wonderful though they are, reminded me of the kind I'd heard more than once at St. Mark's Place in the Village. (Evidently the experiences of the hereafter do not radically alter personality. A pity. One looks for novelty—in this life or out of it. True, Auden does regret his past Anglicanism—not up to sci-fi standards—but isn't that also like those unexpected bolts of disclosure he dropped from time to time in his essays?) While the most unusual, or upsetting, insights have really less to do with science (all the "biophysichemical" graffiti) than with, significantly enough, literature. Rimbaud, for instance, "ghostwrote 'The Waste Land'" because, we learn, "R SPOKE TOO SOON," and did not accomplish his own "V WORK." Actually this seems to me very flattering to Eliot, but that does not prevent him from politely chastising Merrill in a fleeting appearance near the end of the trilogy's coda: "ONE THING YOU SHOULD KNOW / THESE WORKS YOU UNDERSTAND? THAT OTHERS 'WRITE' / . . . ARE YET ONE'S OWN." A good way, also, of summing up Merrill's own powers of transmogrification, which in any case had earlier, playfully as usual, garnered Yeats's stamp of approval. Speaking of *A Vision:* "MR. M., / I MADE A HASH. YOU'VE MADE IT CLEAR. THANK YOU. . . ."

The trilogy, as everyone must have gathered, is an arduous poem, steep and lofty, more than a little difficult to climb, explore, and comprehend, its intricate faceting of the serious and unserious, sacred and profane, vexing to many a reader; but is has, I believe, one controlling stratagem, Merrill's persistent use of doubling or "entwining"—the "sparkling" that "comes easy to the Gemini," as announced previously in "In Nine Sleep Valley." It is a stratagem that can serve as a guide to all the *bizarrerie,* a diversity ultimately embracing a unity, and also, if one has a taste for litany, as a kind of "plot."

To cite but a few pertinent examples: JM and DJ, representing the Dioscuri themselves; God Biology (God B) and Psyche, his female "double," akin to our "twin parents," or "brother sun and sister moon," with MM and WHA now and then moonlighting, in a counterpoint of unusual delicacy, as JM's surrogate mum and dad. Then there is the epigraph from Dante, introduced at the beginning of the trilogy, exemplifying the doubling motif of mirroring, *lo speglio* and its thoughtful gaze embodying all, *minori e' grandi* (the Dante who also said, "For if we have no knowledge of half we can never understand double, and so of the rest"), or the mirror at the house in Stonington both summoning and releasing the spirits of the dead.

Reincarnation is seen both as a parable of the artist (the many styles, roles, voices, the creative temperament is heir to) and as an analogue of historical *ricorso* (man and his many cycles). The "twin forces" of "history's great worm" are likened to those "within / any least atom"; the celebration of the five senses is presented against the invocation of the trilogy's five regnant avatars (Akhnaton, Homer, Montezuma, Nefertiti, Plato). MM, it turns out, is, or has been, all the nine Muses, as well as Plato; Ephraim is also Michael the Archangel, or vice versa. There is a Mozartian lightness in the causerie of the mortals, a Wagnerian texture in the declamations of the gods (this justaposition is a bit of a strain; a little Puccini would have helped, befitting JM and DJ's *vissi d'arte*). If DJ, "the True," "the Wise," has a patron in the beyond who's a clergyman, JM has one who's edited Pope's work, plus his old love Hans, the dead poet, his unused artistry now energizing JM's poem.

If "duality"—"FOR IN DUALITY IS DIMENSION, / TENSION, ALL THE TRUE GRANDEUR WANTING IN A PERFECT THING"—is meant by Merrill to stand as a definition of mankind, it can also accommodate the labors of the higher powers, who occasionally, or so we're told, bravely "double" as human beings (as with MM). And if we have myths about the gods, the gods have myths about themselves, "myths that antecede myths." And if the gods are monitoring us, they too are being monitored by mysterious forces outside their ken (indeed we never do discover just who is the Lord High Everything Else). Finally, the trilogy itself appears as the ultimate act of doubling: opening with the word "admittedly," it closes with the word "admittedly," with Merrill beginning to recite, for most of those who've already appeared in it, and to others of the illustrious dead gathering to hear it, in the celestial bailiwick at Sandover, which is also "the old ballroom of the Broken Home," the long poem (560 pages) we've just read. ("*Our* poem, now," as Merrill remarks to DJ, in the recent and separate "Clearing the Title," the postscript to *From the First Nine.* "It's signed JM, but grew / From life together, grain by coral grain.")

Though I've obviously been emphasizing the trilogy as a brilliant *jeu d'esprit,* which it mischievously is, Merrill and Jackson as the eternal students in an extravaganza of instruction and illumination, the poem's real power, and not the least of its charms, lies, I think, elsewhere. It is eclectic, eccentric, wildly ethereal or abstruse. The theology is basically a crossweaving of Manichaeism and Zen Buddhism, with Christianity as mostly another variant of literary mysticism, as in, say, Novalis: "To the truly religious man, nothing is sin." Merrill admirably forbids all fanaticism, particularly Jehovah and his tribal lore (and this despite the many compliments paid to "Jew density" or the Kaballah).

But the trilogy is also, oddly enough, the closest that Merrill has yet come to showing life in flesh and blood. Detail after mosaic detail—antics of Ephraim, arabesques of MM and WHA, fete at Venice, storm in Stonington, masque at Sandover, interrelated snapshots of JM and DJ's life on earth, elegiac strains or consolatory ones—all have the quiver and shimmer, ripple-within-ripple texture of a kind of impressionist commedia dell'arte, and with a good amount of unblinking empathy besides. Merrill's old penchant for tidying up the universe is still around, as are touches of the old preciosity or the old "heartlessness" ("heredity" is characteristically described as "Narcissus bent / Above the gene pool"). But a sensibility once overrich in secondary sources and seemingly bankrupt of primary ones has been happily, if no less ruefully, adjusted—experience now truly haunts, for the most part, the lightest of his lines.

Indeed the trilogy is best read, I suspect, as Merrill's own highly idiosyncratic way of making peace with a number of former battlegrounds. Posterity, for instance: the children one will never have, the child ("*enfant*") one has always been, the family romance suffered, sustained, never mastered; a many-tracked theme (is it significant that JM and God B are both the youngest scions of their respective houses?) which includes not only the childless homosexual union of JM and DJ (at the trilogy's conclusion these "Rover Boys" celebrate twenty-five years of "marriage," DJ obligingly taking his place "beyond words" at JM's side), but also the childless heterosexual union of Vasíli and Mimí, two of their close friends.

The trilogy provides a way, as well, of including the gods in one's own mortal predicament: the cry in the wilderness, the song of God B, signaling to one of his brothers in the outermost reaches of the empyrean, attempting to hold back the annihilating presence of universal night, like a prisoner tapping on the walls of his cell to another prisoner trapped on the other side. A way, also, of comprehending art's own terrible entrapment: "Art—/ The tale that all but shapes itself—survives / By feeding on its personages' lives. / The stripping process, sort of. What to say?" "Our lives led *to* this. It's the price we pay" (one recalls here Beatrice's humiliation of Dante the better to redeem him). This is JM's answer to DJ's repeated questioning of art's sacrificial nature or his wish to break free of the Ouija board's thralldom ("Isn't it like a door shutting us off from living?").

Above all, the poem provides a way for the mandarin's "overfurnished mind" to reconcile itself with civilization's supersaturated complexity, or a way of making sense of anxiety by way of making sense of fragmentation, so that all the elements of a particular life, "love and loss," drawing room and *basfond,* "the wicked and the weak," even the ancient business of the "flaw"—RM (Robert Morse), charming wastrel in his previous Stonington incarnation, is to be reborn as a musical genius, but with a club foot: "BEFORE YOU LIMPED, NOW HOBBLED YOU WILL LEAP!"—at last cohere into the transfiguration of a grand design, which is both a culmination and something continually subject to further depletion and repletion, part of the enigmatic rhythms of " REVELATION'S CONSTANT PROCESS"; a thesis expounded in its simplest, most abbreviated guise in the lovely villanelle, with its faintly Tennysonian hum, located in the middle of *Mirabell,* but capable, for all its fragility, of encompassing the trilogy as a whole (Maisie, another beloved, is the poet's dead cat):

> It sinks in gradually, all that's meant
> By this wry motto governing things here
> Below and there above: *No Accident.*
>
> Patrons? Parents? Healthy achievers, bent
> On moving up, not liable to queer
> The Lab work. It sinks in, what had been meant
>
> By the adorable dumb omen sent
> TO TEST EXALT & HUMBLE U MY DEAR
> Strato? ET AL Maisie? NO ACCIDENT
>
> Gunman high-strung and Archduke negligent,
> Warnings garbled in the dreamer's ear?
> All, all, it sinks in gradually, was meant
>
> To happen, and not just the gross event
> But its minutest repercussion. We're
> Awed? Unconvinced? That too's no accident.
>
> The clause is self-enacting; the intent,
> Like air, inscrutable if crystal-clear.
> Keep breathing it. One dark day, what it meant
> Will have sunk in past words. *No Accident.*

But the trilogy goes wrong for me in one significant respect: Merrill's underlying assumption, however qualified or jollied along, that science, the great demythologizer of the world, is somehow confirming all the rigamarole of a grand design. Or, even worse, that it's sanctioning the stuttering belief (unwisely put in the mouth of Auden) that "FACT IS IS IS FABLE." Perhaps so, *sub specie aeternitalis.* But such a belief has surely been disastrous in our history, and in science's as well, from the first tyrant to the last demagogue. In the realm of morals nothing's "new"; what changes are one's attitudes—social, political, sexual—toward the moral life; and hence the possible basis of a grand design. In the realm of science the dictum does not hold; science being perpetually concerned with discovering the hidden, exploding the old, establishing the new. So to be told, as one of Merrill's "scientific" explanations of "evil," that the perfidious pride of the "BLACKS" or "MONITORS" (similar to Yeats's "Frustrators" in *A Vision*), in yielding, at creation's dawn, to the temptation of power and of splitting the original atom, had thus brought about all our earthly woe, is merely to reenter, with yet another fable, the illustrated Bible of childhood, complete now with a *nota bene* a bit more *au courant:* "THE ATOM CANNOT BE MAN'S FRIEND."

Further, the professed inability of the trilogy's celestial orders to set things right after "980,000,000 sun years" (to use just one of the awesome measurements of time here) hardly bodes well, I should think, for the fate of the earth, or its eventually turning into utopia, and indeed brings into question the entire cosmic enterprise, to say nothing of the dubious talents of the deities themselves. The point being that once teleological or eschatological concerns are presented in the alien terms of physical, geological, or chemical laws, in which vitalist or finalist theories do not apply, they tend, alas, to become farcical. And while that may well be the truth of the matter (the only poets I know actually related to science—Omar Khayyam because he was an astronomer and Lucretius because he wrote *De Rerum Natura*—were both, more or less, nihlilists), I doubt that was Merrill's intention in the trilogy.

Still, what is the point of complaining? As Homer once sang of arms and the man and in praise of the Olympians for creating his panoply of earthly contention, as the Venetian painters of the Renaissance often subverted Biblical subject matter with a gorgeous paganism, so Merrill, throughout the trilogy, is continually aestheticizing the claims of science just as he is aestheticizing those of religion (or even the Ouija board). And with the same end in view, since, of course, his only real god, here and elsewhere, is the god of the imagination, "a way of telling that inspires belief," whatever else he might fancy he's intimating to the contrary. (The coupling, at one point, of Mallarmé and Montezuma—"Powers of lightness, darkness, powers that be," the coupling, that is, of artistic genius and worldly might—says as much.) Indefatigable in its verbal ingenuities, its fierce and amiable wit, polysemous in all the thematic machinery, exemplary in prosody (sonnets, ballades, villanelles, sestinas, blank verse, terza rima, ottava rima, a style at once colloquial and exalted, and with a warmth and conviviality new to Merrill), the trilogy (though it goes on far too long, gets periodically dizzy, has too much *felix culpa* and not enough *mea culpa*) is, surely, an astonishing performance, not a masterpiece, but as near to one, I think, as anything else that American poetry has produced in the last two or three decades, and the capstone—for now, anyway—of an extraordinary career.

When one compares Merrill's career, early and late, or the methods behind it, with that of Lowell or Ashbery; Merrill's sexual disclosures with those of Cavafy or Cernuda, George or Thom Gunn; his general reflections on the times with the works of Brodsky or Milosz; the domestic details with Montale's "Xenia" poems; his use of mythology with the procedures of Geoffrey Hill in England; or even the campiness, Merrill's "high camp," with the more demotic sort found in O'Hara and Schuyler, one sees immediately how singular, how polished, how untouchable, in every sense of that word, a creator he is.

One also realizes his limitations. Wholly a poet, Merrill is not, obviously, a poet given to exploring the worst as well as the best. (His "both ways" philosophy, as I've already suggested, is not that ecumenical.) In real life, MM had cancer and committed suicide—a subject, typically, only tentatively or ambiguously remarked upon, as are Merrill's own teasing admissions of "waste, self-hatred, boredom." And the complaint of his nephew heard in the marvelous terza rima of *The Book of Ephraim* (Merrill's version of Dante's encounter with his ancestor in the fifteenth canto of the *Paradiso*), that mankind is "Doomed, sick, selfish, dumb as shit. . . . They talk about how decent, how refined— / All it means is, they can afford somehow / To watch what's happening, and not to mind"—that complaint, though crude, is also just, including its implied rebuke of the nephew's uncle or the uncle's sensibility. And those Alpha Men—don't they, after all, really presuppose the final eclipse of that sensibility and the culture it so insouciantly represents?

Merrill is a happy elegist in an equivocal time, with an unspoilable delight in art and beauty, in his hymn to the recuperative powers of "love and loss." "Childless," and so outside the mainstream, yet "scissoring and mending," he's a maker nonetheless; "shy" with "ideas," but protean in inventiveness, against the evanescent, the "changing lights," he pits himself and sees in language the mastery of the word in a disordered world, "the life raft of language," his own best hope, and ours, discovering himself, again and again, as other poets have done, "more truly and more strange."

Geoffrey Stokes

The Red Eye of God: James Merrill's Reasons to Believe

We forgive poets their craziness. Indeed, whether in the mundane sottishness of Berryman and Lowell or the cosmic weirdness of Blake and Kit Smart, we half expect them to be moonstruck. Yet nothing in the glamorous, witty, gay-in-all-senses career of James Merrill—nothing in the last hundred-odd years of our language's literature—quite prepares us for the full-bore strangeness of *The Changing Light at Sandover.*

And I do not mean merely the oddness of the enterprise, though it rather passeth understanding that someone in the last quarter of the twentieth century should choose to publish a 560-page narrative poem ("Admittedly I err by undertaking / This in its present form," Merrill blandly begins). No, the poem as artifact is ordinary compared to its content, for we are asked to believe that *The Changing Light at Sandover* is in some decisive way the word of God. Who presents Himself, I am obliged to report, through a Ouija board.

I know, I know, "Man here says he's seen God," happens all the time. Messages coming through the teeth of midtown placard-carriers; a small eddy in the crowd, and things go on much as before: theater curtains rise at their appointed hours, afterward there is a struggle to find a cab, the sign-bearer is by now asleep in some doorway. But Merrill is different. To persevere through *Sandover*—to work and play at the poem with its earthly author—is to risk the permanent suspension of disbelief.

The story begins in the summer of 1955, early in the long and loving relationship between Merrill and David Jackson. At their Stonington home, they idly amuse themselves with a Ouija board:

> Was anybody there? As when a pike
> Strikes, and the line signing writes in lakeflesh

From *Village Voice, Voice Literary Supplement,* March 1983. Reprinted by permission of Geoffrey Stokes and *The Village Voice.*

Highstrung runes, and reel spins and mind reels
YES a new and urgent power YES
Seized the cup. It swerved, clung, hesitated,
Darted off, a devil's darning needle
Gyroscope our fingers rode bareback . . .

The visitor announced himself as EPHRAIM (Merrill's all-caps convention for reporting what is spelled on the Ouija board's plane turns out to be only momentarily off-putting); a Greek Jew born in 8 A.D. In the twenty-six alphabetical sections of "The Book of Ephraim" (first published in 1976 as part of Merrill's Pulitzer-winning *Divine Comedies*), DJ and JM, as the board styles them, are gradually introduced to the notion that life is never-ending, that although souls—except for some special few—forget their past existences, they are steadily recycled until they earn a permanent place in Heaven. While souls await reentry, as it were, they too can be reached through the board. In a series of literally death-defying conversations, Ephraim's lessons are glossed by (among others) Maya Deren and W. H. Auden.

Not surprisingly, Merrill begins to fear that he is mad and consults his "ex-shrink."

"Quite," the doctor said

Exuding insight, "There's a phrase
You may have heard—what you and David do
We call folie à deux
Harmless; but can you find no simpler ways

To sound each other's depths of spirit
Than taking literally that epigram
Of Wilde's I'm getting damn
Tired of hearing my best patients parrot?"

"Given a mask, you mean, we'll tell—?"
Tom nodded, "So the truth was what we heard?"
"*A* truth," he shrugged. "It's hard
To speak of *the* truth. Now suppose *you* spell

It out. What underlies these odd
Inseminations by psycho-roulette?"
I stared, then saw the light:
"Somewhere a Father Figure shakes his rod

At sons who have not sired a child
Through our own spirit we can both proclaim
And shuffle off the blame

For how we live—that good enough?" Tom smiled
And rose. "I've heard worse . . ."

But Ephraim ("FREUD / We learned that evening DESPAIRS / OF HIS DISCIPLES") is unruffled by their doubts. "He didn't cavil. *He* was the revelation / (Or if we had created him, then we were)."

These passages demonstrate the easy virtuosity with which Merrill shapes conversational language into complex verse forms (one may sometimes realize only after the fact that a batch of almost random-seeming lines lead through a sonnet sequence). They also dramatize that while *Sandover* is drenched in belief, it is hardly credulous. For each celestial thrust, Merrill offers us an earthly parry. Thus, when "Ephraim" was first published, critics could praise—be awed by—the poem without confronting its content.

But compared to the rest of *Sandover,* "Ephraim" is a kindergarten, its reassuring sun-dappled surface cracked only once:

DAVID PUT OUT YR CIGARETTE NOW PLACE
YR FREE HAND PALMDOWN YES ON THE BOARDS EDGE
—That very palm, in no time, creased, red, sore
As if it had been trod on for attention—

By What? or Whom? Our cup,
Our chinablue-and-white tearoom

Shanghaied. A scroll wiped blank. A bone
Well of cold blood where the wits had been.

If *this* is a projection, it's hardly of the carefree Epicureanism long associated with Merrill. Indeed, the voices, which dominate *Mirabell's Books of Number,* the trilogy's next section, demand something one would have thought Merrill unprepared to give:

UNHEEDFULL ONE 3 OF YOUR YEARES MORE WE WANT WE MUST HAVE
POEMS OF SCIENCE THE WEORK FINISHT IS BUT A PROLOGUE
ABSOLUTES ARE NOW NEEDED YOU MUST MAKE A GOD OF SCIENCE

"Poems of *Science*? Ugh," is Merrill's first response, but he reads texts in biology and physics, tries somehow to make sense of the information given him by these fallen angels who are (as his recently dead friend Maria Mitsotáki describes them) QUITE LIKE BATS / HUGE SQUEAKING ONES WITH LITTLE HOT RED EYES, and who have, in Ephraim's words, THE AIR / OF CERTAIN BLACKBOARD SOLDIERS OF TIBERIUS / WHEN WE SAW THEM ON THE TERRACES / A SHRIEK & A SPLASH SOON FOLLOWED.

But these creatures are also subatomic particles whose interactive dance informs both matter and antimatter, and even the most attentive reader is likely to echo Merrill's "Stop trying to have everything both ways. / It's too much to be batwing angels *and* / Inside the atom, don't you understand?" It *is* too much (as Merrill admitted in a brief *Kenyon Review* introduction to a portion of *Mirabell,* "the scale . . . wobbles throughout, from vast to microscopic"), but the outlines of their story gradually become clear. Before "Eden," God B (biology, the force entwined with chaos) created—and destroyed—two other worlds. The first, which these creatures peopled, was more or less in China and was ended—Gabriel and Michael triumphant over their siblings—by an atomic blast; the second was Atlantis. Eventually, God B gazed into the eyes of an ape, and the resulting third creation, Man, is 88 percent chemistry, 12 percent forces beyond science. Merrill, "talking" to Auden, is in despair:

> Dear Wystan, VERY BEAUTIFUL all this
> Warmed-up Milton, Dante, Genesis?
> This great tradition that has come to grief
> In volumes by Blavatsky and Gurdjieff?
> Von and Torro in their Star Trek capes,
> Atlantis, UFOs, God's chosen apes—?
> Nobody can transfigure junk like that
> Without first turning down the rheostat
> To Allegory, in whose gloom the whole
> Horror of Popthink fastens on the soul,
> Harder to scrape off than bubblegum.

By and large, Merrill avoids Disneying up his story, but the cost is high. Great swathes of obscure "science" are delivered almost by dictation, set down in clumsy unrhymical lines of fourteen syllables (fourteen is one of the many numbers that struggle to assume significance in "Mirabell"). Merrill chooses to banish his poetic virtuosity in favor of hamhanded exposition ("BUT CAN U DOUBT THAT WE HAVE VERIFIED THE UFO'S / ON OUR SCREENS? THESE REFLECT EACH SMALLEST POWER SOURCE. BEING / AS YET SO FOREIGN TO THE DENSITY OF WORLD SCIENCE, / THE SAUCERS SHOW UP BEST IN A REALM OF SPECULATION"). Gasping for breath, one longs for the playful intelligence that introduced this section, the sheer bravura of Merrill's history of the Stonington room in which these meetings started:

So began
What must in retrospect be called the Age
—Some fifteen years—of the Wrong Wallpaper.
Still blue and white, still floral, in the shop
Looking unexceptionably prim,
No sooner on our walls, the buds uncurl
In scorn. Compulsively repetitive
Neuroses, full-blown and slack-lipped, then whole
Faces surely not intended, peer
Forth—once seen, no question of unseeing
That turbaned mongoloid, that toad with teeth . . .

In fact, on a level other than the expositional (or the psychological—Merrill scrupulously notes the parallels between this section's version of the creation and his own role as third child of a soon-to-be-broken home), *Mirabell* can be read as the struggle for a language. JM's and DJ's teacher, 741, is by exposure to human language and its emotional nuances transformed into a peacock. He eventually "more and more / Embellishes his text with metaphor. Some aren't bad; he likes to signal them / With a breezy parenthetic (m)." The numbing measures of instruction are also from time to time leavened by bits of Celestial gossip in earthly iambs, like this from WHA: "PLATO SAYS ATHENS WAS AT BEST HALF QUEER / What's Plato *like*? O YOU KNOW TATTLETALE, GRAY / NIGHTGOWN OFF ONE SHOULDER DECLASSEE, / TO QUOTE MM GAS, TO QUOTE CK"

Eventually, as 741 acquires the name Mirabell to go with his new plumage, the (m)s become more pronounced, the language—though it still marches on limping feet—richer and more allusive. By Book 9 ("Ephraim" was organized by the board's letters, *Mirabell* by its numbers), language has become THE LIFERAFT suggested in Book 1. And then, as the second section closes, the language is heightened once again, and rolling sonorities promise a third section:

I AM MICHAEL
I HAVE ESTABLISHED YOUR ACQUAINTANCE & ACCEPT YOU. COME
NEXT TIME IN YOUR OWN MANNER. SERVANTS WE ARE NOT.
I LEAVE NOW AS THE LIGHT LEAVES AND WIND MY PATH OVER ITS
TRACK ON EARTH I AM A GUARDIAN OF THE LIGHT . . .
LOOK! LOOK INTO THE RED EYE OF YOUR GOD!

Its promises of coming glories notwithstanding, reading *Mirabell* when it was first published in 1978 was more disquieting than satisfying. The parts one returned to for pleasure, even for instruction, were domestic—the love story that for all its charm is merely a subplot in the trilogy. Mirabell's words—and rhythms—monopolized the text, and it too often seemed that Merrill had lost control of his poem, had turned it over to a creature, however immortal, who wasn't much of a writer.

"Ephraim," though is surely came as a surprise, had been very much Merrill's; the heavenly instruction—perhaps 10 percent of the book in ALL CAPS—floated in a sea of wit, and of the focused particularity that had once seemed to make Merrill Richard Wilbur's heir. But *Mirabell,* more than twice as long as "Ephraim," is less than half Merrill, and too many of the fourteeners he produced from the dictated messages are murky or dull. Sandover, it seemed, was sliding rapidly downward, and it would take a virtual miracle to rescue it.

Miracles happen. Even without its content and its context, *Scripts for the Pageant,* which apparently completed *Sandover* when it was published in 1980, would be the most amazing American poem of the century. Released from the necessary tedium of *Mirabell*—which earned him, and us, the right to continue—Merrill soars. The most stylish of living poets pulls out all the stops and, without the slightest waver in control, produces one dazzling effect after another. Terza rima, villanelles, Spenserian echoes, sonnets, and schemes without familiar precedent succeed one another with awesome effortlessness. To the extent that poetry is music, *Scripts* is our (m) *Eroica.*

But words *mean,* and in the three sections of *Scripts* (their titles, "Yes," "&," "No," are a poem to ambiguity as well as the remaining marks on the Ouija board), Merrill dons masques to tell his truths. The subject is God's explanation of that 12 percent held secret even from his fallen children. These mysteries are revealed in dialogues among the four chief angels. Michael (Light, Air), Gabriel (Destruction, Fire), Emmanuel (Water, Reason), Raphael (Earth, Supply), and their mother—God's twin, Psyche (Nature)—meet, in what appears to be an English manor house turned school, with living and "dead" humans DJ, JM, WHA, MM, George Kotzsias (a scientist), and Robert Morse (a Stonington amateur of the arts). Buddha, Jesus, Mercury, and Mohammed make cameo appearances, as do the five immortal souls—Akhnaton, Homer, Montezuma, Nefertiti, and Plato—the nine muses, and (inter alia) Kirsten Flagstad, Mirabell, Robert Lowell, Wallace Stevens, Ephraim, Gertrude Stein, Pythagoras, Yeats, Alice B. Toklas. Throughout, the door is guarded by Unice, the only survivor of Atlantis and, as it happens, a Unicorn. Italic stage direction (provided *post facto* by Auden, we are told) sets each scene, and God Himself provides offstage commentary.

As this bald summary demonstrates, the pitfalls facing the poet/playwright (not to mention his secular audience) are legion. Merrill makes the whole thing work—makes us, for instance, fall in love with the unicorn—not simply by flash of style, but by the urgency of his matter. The question debated is our survival. Since Gabriel has already destroyed two thriving civilizations that had from time to time delighted their Creator, his doubts about us are chilling:

> OUR FATHER SAYS THERE IS GENIUS!
> & HE KNOWING, AH! CREATING ALL THERE IS TO KNOW, CREATED
> ME AS WELL.
> AND WHERE IS MY NATURE BUT IN HIS FIST?
> LISTEN: OUT OF THE PANTHEON OF GALAXIES FROM WHICH OUR
> FATHER COMES, I HAVE HEARD HIS VOICE:
> 'GABRIEL, MY DARKER SIDE, THERE ARE GALAXIES, GODS AS POWERFUL
> AS I. SON GABRIEL, WE ARE WARND. WE ARE HARD PREST.'
> YES, MADAME, ONE LIFE LOST BADLY MAKES ME GRIEVE. YES, POET,
> EACH GRAND SONG GLADDENS ME
> THERE AM I NOT ALMOST, ALMOST HUMAN?
> MORE SO, & YOUR WORLD WOULD LONG AGO HAVE VANISHT!
> I, OH I HAVE KNOWN FEELINGS! ALL BLACK RAGES AT IGNORANCE!
> DESPAIR AT THE FEELINGS THEMSELVES!
> YES, HAD A LIGHT HUMAN HEART BEEN MINE, I WOULD HAVE
> TURND TO MY LEFT AND SAID: HOW MUCH MORE, LORD, HOW
> MUCH? I WAS BENIGNLY SPARED THE BLINDING WHITE LIGHT SLY
> MICHAEL
> BATHES YOU IN.
> FOR, BURDEND WITH IDEAS, MICHAEL, YOU HEAP ON MAN PRIDE,
> AMBITION, A SENSE OF SENSE IN ALL HIS SENSELESSNESS. YOU
> CHUCK HIM UNDER THE CHIN WHO SHOULD SLAP HIS CHEEK.

The unfallen Gabriel has all the majesty of Milton's Satan, and as God's ally, greater power. But he is not unopposed. "Resistance," the book's great theme, surrounds him. GOD B holds out against the antimatter pressing on the panes of His Greenhouse, cell walls filter before they admit, human intelligence challenges the INGENUE'S TRUST IN FEELING. Nature (Psyche, Chaos) is herself at least a temporary agent of resistance. Pressing outward against the void, resistance is what holds the universe together.

It is also, we learn, an aspect of speech. In the final lesson of "Yes," DJ, JM, WHA, and MM travel far beyond the classroom and hear, for the first time, GOD B singing into the darkness:

> IVE BROTHERS HEAR ME BROTHERS SIGNAL ME
> ALONE IN MY NIGHT BROTHERS DO YOU WELL

I AND MINE SURVIVE BROTHERS HEAR ME SIGNAL ME
DO YOU WELL I AND MINE HOLD IT BACK I
ALONE IN MY NIGHT BROTHERS I AND MINE
SURVIVE BROTHERS DO YOU WELL I ALONE
IN MY NIGHT I HOLD IT BACK I AND MINE
SURVIVE BROTHERS SIGNAL ME IN MY NIGHT
I AND MINE HOLD IT BACK AND WE SURVIVE.

It is, Merrill thinks, the "Song of the blue whale / Alone in space." Then later, to Auden, "He's singing to the Pantheon. OR ALONE / KEEPING UP HIS NERVE ON A LIFERAFT." The implication in the reply: for all His endless power, God's last refuge, like ours, is language. And finally, in the lesson of "No," the flat wooden board containing letters and numbers, all we can ever have of knowledge, becomes the vehicle for what hope we have of—not salvation, perhaps, but survival. God, marking an X across the surface of the board: "POET FROM THIS MAKE A WORK / GIVING BOTH PAUSE AND HOPE TO THIS FIGURE / I SEE EMBLAZONED HERE"

And with the publication of *Scripts* Merrill did. By rights "The Higher Keys," the long Coda which now concludes *Sandover,* should be something of an anticlimax. Yet the title is no idle boast; it not only solves some of the trilogy's original mysteries, it contains a remarkable sequence on Robert Morse's rebirth that has never yet—drunk or sober—failed to make me weep.

Finally, in "The Ballroom at Sandover," it gathers together the Heavenly company in "the old ballroom of the Broken House" for a gala reading of the entire epic. Pope (the patron, surely, of Merrill's couplets), Goethe, Colette, Rilke, Proust, Eliot, and Jane Austen (whose heavenly job is to design new earthly lives for returning lab souls) are among the guests at a fete prepared by Alice B: "I shall study to ignore / Looks that more boldly with each session yearn / toward the buffet when steaming silver urn / Cucumber sandwiches, rum punch, fudge laced / With hashish cater to whatever taste. . . . For *their* ears I begin: 'Admittedly . . .'"

Now the manner of all this is, once one surrenders to it, VERY BEAUTIFUL, all 560 pages. But the *matter* forces a question: Is Merrill simply a more subtle version of the Times Square visionary? Or, worse, is *Sandover* the spectacular but sick effusion of a narcissism that makes *everything* merely its author's reflection?

The answer, I think, is not the ambiguous "yes and no" that the section titles in *Scripts* charitably offer us. Against all odds, the poem *is* believable (so much so that one wonders what Auden scholars will make of his posthumous work). Part of its success is a matter of tone: well into the final moments of the coda, Merrill is still supplying counterarguments to his senses, still bemusedly asking himself, and us, "What if all this is *true*?" The excruciating self-awareness isn't a hedge, but internal evidence that Merrill, aware that accusations of narcissism were inevitable, consciously risked allowing himself to be anointed by God. And whatever else it may be—like a storm-battered sailor grasping a gunwale, one relies again on tone—it is not a lie. No experienced reader can doubt that the cup moved, and that Merrill believes what it spelled out.

As would, I suppose, our placard-bearer. But subtlety does count for something, and the iron disciplines of form to which Merrill has subjected himself count as well. The inevitable elitism of Gnosticism notwithstanding, we are at every turn reminded by art that we are not dealing with brain-shattered ravings.

Okay. It is *true*?

"It's hard to speak of *the* truth," but power is among its measures. Like many of my generation, I have pursued the occasional Shaman. Drug-aided, I once sought (and believed I'd found) my Castaneda "spot." Don Juan was easy, though, the thrills technicolor, the adventures sugarcoated. There is nothing of the cartoon in *Sandover,* and I would not dare toy with it. It is a Holy Terror.

There are, even for the most diligent reader, too many good books, so I don't much believe in "must read" experiences. But to be literate and deliberately pass up *Sandover* is, I think, of a different order than never getting to *Emma* or to *Barbary Shore;* it is a kind of cowardice. The temptation is entirely understandable. Not only are the poem's technical demands as rigorous as anything in the *Cantos,* its bizarre content requires a reader to apply prodigious willpower as well as the intellectual gymnastics a generation in revolt from Eliot is loath to execute. To a reader with his skeptic's heels dug in, convinced that such a poem *must* be false, the effort can hardly seem worth making.

Dante was, as Mirabell points out, aided by the FIERCE CREDULITY of his age, and the polemicist in Milton had automatic allies. Merrill, whose *Sandover* launches him into that timeless company, is at loggerheads with our age. But with nothing going for him except language, our liferaft, he is inescapable: I WILL BE THE WOUNDED BLACK HOUND OF HEAVEN AT YR DOOR.

Afterword: Tradition and an Individual Talent

Neutral Ground

The centrally puzzling relationship in *The Changing Light at Sandover* entangles the living and the dead, earth and heaven, this world and the other one. But provocatively this mysterious bond is rendered in terms that relate a poet to his material. Questions of control—*who's* controlling, or in control of the poem—become its perhaps most resonant subject. Against W. H. Auden's buoyant, "ON WITH THE WORK! THRILLING FOR YOU JM," Merrill counters:

> And maddening—it's all by someone else!
> In your voice Wystan, or in Mirabell's.
> I want it mine . . . I'd set
> My whole heart, after *Ephraim,* on returning
> To private life, to my own words. Instead,
> Here I go again, a vehicle
> In this cosmic carpool. Mirabell once said
> He taps my word banks. I'd be happier
> If *I* were tapping them. Or thought I were.
>
> (261–62)

Although Auden shortly hushes JM's "SCRUPLES" with some vigorous couplets on the "MINOR / PART THE SELF PLAYS IN A WORK OF ART" such steadily entrapping questions about (and to) the sources of his inspiration spin their web until the very end of the coda, when Merrill circles back and reads the completed poem to an audience of the dead. Hesitations about his role as a "vehicle" or a medium propel the trilogy from section A of "The Book of Ephraim." There they travel in the guise of a familiar distinction between two styles of writing: one that in the customary lyric manner places the poet at the center of his story; and another, identified with the "kind of unseasoned telling found / In legends, fairy tales, a tone licked clean . . . serene anonymous," that acts out a ritualized self-effacement. The error that Merrill posits as a virtual initial premise for the poem ("Admittedly I err . . ."), together with his chafing against an uninvited interruption ("Here I go again . . .") that churns within it from the start, proceeds from his grudging persuasion that Ephraim, his primary interlocutor at this early stage, has conspired to deny him the form he elected as most evocative of his other-worldly theme. As he recounts in "The Will," a droll, pulsing shadow to "The Book of Ephraim" in *Divine Comedies,* the manuscript of the novel in which he planned a distanced recreation of Ephraim's revelations has been lost in a cab. "REMOVED THANKS TO MY COUP DE GRACE," Ephraim boasts. "BY THE WAY SINCE YOU DID NOT CONSULT / THEIR SUBJECT YR GLUM PAGES LACKED HIS GLORY."

Merrill's protests and discriminations in section A tighten the mainspring on so many convolutions to follow. With a first surprising turn of the screw, he stages himself not as a lyric poet inadvertently overwhelmed by volatile matters more reliably handled in prose, but as a novelist *manqué.* His "lost novel" is not only a jettisoned urtext, it also represents a forfeited narrative strategy that he regards as "beyond" him, even in the poem itself:

So my narrative
Wanted to be limpid, unfragmented;
My characters, conventional stock figures
Afflicted to a minimal degree
With personality and past experience—
A witch, a hermit, innocent young lovers,
The kinds of being we recall from Grimm,
Jung, Verdi, and the commedia dell' arte.

(4)

Individuals here are streamlined to types and archetypes, with a similarly depersonalized "narrative" that is not so much directed and shaped as passed on. In Merrill's original scheme his goals had been expressly mediumistic. As he argues for the novel in section S: "With just myself and D to set the scale / What could we learn? I needed neutral ground . . . Heights up there beyond the heights of self . . . so that (when the rains fell) would go / Flashing through me a perfected flow" (66). Yet, paradoxically, he's been blocked by what he dubs "word-painting," or precisely the overspicing of personality he's vividly condemning. And as the screw turns once more, the novelist talks himself back to lyric poetry:

The more I struggled to be plain, the more
Mannerism hobbled me. What for?
Since it had never truly fit, why wear
The shoe of prose? In verse the feet went bare.
Measures, furthermore, had been defined
As what emergency required. Blind
Promptings put at last the whole mistaken
Enterprise to sleep in darkest Macon
(Cf. "The Will"), and I alone was left
To tell my story. For it seemed that Time—
The grizzled washer of his hands appearing
To say so in a spectrum-bezeled space
Above hot water—Time would not . . .

(4)

On a later rereading we might be driven more to wonder just how "alone" this voice is, or how solidly his character should be distinguished from "Time's," when even his most impulsively exposed declaration slides by on a venerable double quotation, Job via Melville. But directly Merrill goes on to inhabit the solitary lyric disguise so absolutely that he almost compels us to apprehend Ephraim as only a mirror for himself, and the other world as an eccentric manifestation of his narcissistic will. An actual mirror supervises the sessions (as Merrill observes, "We saw each other in it. He saw us"). Likewise, a vocabulary that bristles with suspicion presides throughout the trilogy, but especially in the first half of "The Book of Ephraim," where the "affair" with the spirit seems inextricably embedded in Merrill's relationship with David Jackson. Ephraim tells them that their "FORTUNATE CONJUNCTION" set the stage for his entrance, and in sections A through M his evolving role in their lives all but reproduces the crosscurrents of their affection.

Thus when Ephraim announces that the lovers will not enter "eternity" at the same time or at the same Stage, Merrill responds first with a gust of upwardly mobile anger—"Why not *both* be reborn? Which at least spares one / Dressing up as the Blessed Damozel / At Heaven's Bar to intervene"; and, then, with a cautionary look earthward: "The cloud passed . . . Foreshadower of nothing, dearest heart, / But the dim wish of lives to drift apart" (25). Or when Jackson is placed under hypnosis, and Ephraim works through him, "using me, my senses, to touch JM who / this morning swears it was my hand stroking him," he candidly concedes, "I felt a stab of the old possessiveness" (27). Ephraim's sphere reflects DJ and JM's quotidian routine in other on-the-scene details that suggest the strokes of the counterfeiter. That the wily shade also issued from a broken home is advertised as the "first of several facts to coincide" (8). Their initial confusing glimpses of "appearances" in the other world replicate the dining room of their home in Stonington (16–17). When the couple impetuously assist Ephraim as he plots to have his "representative" born as Merrill's nephew, the poet denounces himself as "Narcissus bent / Above the gene pool" (20). An hour with his psychiatrist sums up this movement in the poem:

"There's a phrase
You may have heard—what you and David do
We call folie à deux.
Harmless; but can you find no simpler ways

To sound each other's depths . . .?"

(30)

The specter of folie à deux haunts even into *Mirabell.* If the "smiling Hellenistic lightness" of Ephraim's confabulations evokes the sensual iridescence of Merrill's lyric episode, then Mirabell, with his peacock regalia and incandescent metamorphoses, insinuates nothing less than a full-tilt, operatic intensification of moments in his earliest poetry (poems like "The Blue Eye," "The Peacock," and "Transfigured Bird"). Mirabell's very name circles Merrill's. As the latter sighs,

If only we were less free to reflect;
If diametrics of the mirror didn't
Confirm the antiface there as one's own. . . .

(162)

But his application of the mirror motif, fortunately for the poem, does not begin and end in reflection, at least in the sense of passively returning a likeness. Merrill tightens the screw yet again—and the spring rebounds with so much tension that the self-reflexive mechanism explodes. Mirrors in *The Changing Light at Sandover* are not so much looked at, as *through* and *beyond.* For the first time in his poetry Merrill approaches the world of appearances as a surface to be penetrated. As Judith Moffett has written, "With *Divine Comedies* Merrill has begun to move beyond his career-long commitment to the integrity of masks and surfaces, of sparkling appearances."[1] In *Sandover* mirrors function as they do in Cocteau's *Orphée:* they're rippling portals to another world.

Section K of "The Book of Ephraim" is emblematic of this realignment in his aesthetic. Merrill multiplies himself and Jackson in an ingenious array of reflecting surfaces: gems, a bronze gong, a polished bamboo dais, a glass phone booth. An allusion to Dante initially seems more of the glitter, but in fact interrupts it:

> Broad silver wings drone forth our own cloud-backed
> Features fainter than pearl
> On white brow (*Paradiso,* III, 14).
>
> (37)

The passage marks Dante's own calculated reversal of the Narcissus myth, specifying an instant when he also mistook real spirits for reflections.

The Changing Light at Sandover turns on such "meanings we had missed by simply looking" (83), as Merrill characterizes a recent X ray analysis of Giorgione's *La Tempesta,* "on the surface nothing less than earthly life in all its mystery" (76). Here, superficial mysteries give way to deeper enigmas, and the poem is layered with surfaces that must be passed through, with vessels that must be broken. In section L a flashy garden globe Merrill whirls into an extravagant, Elizabethan trope for his life with Jackson dazzles in itself, but even more for what it opens up:

> And what was the sensation
> When stars alone like bees
> Crawled numbly over it?
> And why did all the birds eye it with caution?
> It did no harm, just brightly
> Kept up appearances.
>
> Not always. On occasion
> Fatigue or disbelief
> Mottled the silver lining.
> Then, as it were, our life saw through that craze
> Of its own creation
> Into another life.
>
> (42)

In one of the spookiest exchanges in *Sandover,* Merrill is then guided by Ephraim to relive (as the film implacably runs backward) the death of his previous incarnation, Rufus Farmetton: "another life," but glowing like a "death's-head," behind the mirror. Much later in the poem, after hearing Mirabell compare himself to Mercury, Merrill again slips through the silver lining on a winding train of oxymorons:

Mercury!
With new eyes we confront the mirror,
Look *beyond* ourselves. Does he appear?
Never plainer, never more hidden, his glassy
Foyer, his permeable impasse.

(249)

As his language suggests, Merrill has set the poem on (as he christens it) "unsteady ground," at the interface of "Earth, Heaven; Reality, Projection" (46). The continually more volatile interdependence of the two worlds of *Sandover* is touched off by a recurrent crisscrossing of wires and, as Maria explains, the heat "COMES FROM BOTH SIDES OF THE MIRROR" (297). The silver lining steadily turns reflective with more animated implications, accruing attributes of thought and imagination. In *Sandover* imagination is defined as a "crossing" from one world to the other. Mirabell (or 741, as he is first known) is "an impulse" engendered "here at the crossroads of our four affections" (173); he's an imaginative spark fired at the juncture of the living and the dead. Auden enlarges on the process:

SHD WE NOT THINK ABOUT
THE IMAGINATION? IF MM & I
IMAGINE U, YOU US, & WHERE THE POWERS
CRISSCROSS WE ALL IMAGINE 741
& THEN TRANSFORM HIM! WHEN THE TIME COMES WILL
OUR KNITTED BROWS PRODUCE WHITE WINGS?

(159)

"WE ARE YOU YOU ARE WE EACH OTHERS DREAM" (117), discloses Mirabell, echoing Yeats on "concurrent dreams" in his essay "Anima Mundi."[2] Likewise, Auden will later remark of the angels, "THEIR POWERS ARE IN US QUITE AS MUCH AS OVER. / SO VERY BEAUTIFUL, WHICHEVER WAY" (345).

"Our own imagination working in the world" becomes embodied in the "SOURCE OF LIGHT," the centrally generative faculty that recalls that radiated point in the *Paradiso* on which, as Beatrice interprets, "the heavens and all nature are dependent" (XXVIII, 42). Containing "THE POTENTIAL OF PARADISE" (132), "THE PLACE OF GOD" (173), and the "UNIMAGINED CALM" that produces the angels (173), the S/O/L, in turn, is "ROOTED IN THE LIVED LIFE" (260). The unbeautiful underside of this reciprocity, and really the provocation for the whole of *Sandover,* preys upon the poem in the form of a distress signal about nuclear annihilation. As Ephraim and Merrill agitate the matter back and forth:

NO SOULS CAME FROM HIROSHIMA U KNOW . . .
Wait—he couldn't be pretending YES
That when the flood ebbed, or the fire burned low,
Heaven, the world no longer at its feet,
Itself would up and vanish? EVEN SO

(55–56)

This knotty collaboration of heaven and earth would only be the boldest of *Sandover's* "unverifiable epiphanies" were not Merrill so foxy in promoting it as an analogy for other imaginative transactions, such as those which result in poems, or enter into the composition of any human identity. As his examples of cross-worldly pollination proliferate, he cannily advances the mirror as an instrument for getting beyond the self. Just as the two worlds are mutually regarding and sustaining, identity in the trilogy depends upon the self being seen by others. But however persistently mirrored, otherness here is not so much a reflection of the self as its source. At every new crossroad Merrill flies from stability—and mercurially eludes self-definition. First, he distances his own lyric "I" through the conventions of novelistic characterization, thus becoming "JM" (even as he habitually mixes first- and third-person references); and then he skews his "characters," living and dead, fictional and real, human and abstract, such that it's impossible to trace where any one leaves off, or where his own starts. In section Q of "The Book of Ephraim" he cites Proust's "désir de mener la vie de tout le monde." Throughout *Sandover* Merrill lives *like* other people by living *as* other people.

Each of the characters from the "lost novel" who survives into the poem refracts splinters of his or her author's experience. The "hermit" Sergei is one evident sliver: he and the fire-breathing Joanna reenact opposite pulses in Merrill "vital to the psychic current's flow" (35). The poem goes on to establish this routine transformation of reality into fiction as a model for the more unpredictable "translations" that forge the psyche. Merrill's dead friend, poet Hans Lodeizen, terms these self-discovering acts of translation "TRANSFERRED EXPERIENCE" (24)—and the transfers are so fluid that charting them is like picking up a bead of liquid silver. On the one hand, personalities divide like protozoa; on the other, they blend like spices.

Viewed dramatically, *The Changing Light at Sandover* is a succession of recognition scenes. JM, for instance, uncovers aspects of himself by observing friends and mentors: Maya Deren, Auden, Maria, Hans. Maya is both an artistic and a personal guide. Her documentary about Haitian "ritual possession" instructs him on how to handle "gusts of material so violent / As to put out the candle held to them by mere imagination" (305). But more than in his work, it's in his life that he learns just how completely she's posessed him. When he visits her in the hospital after she's had a crippling stroke, it's almost as if *he's* been split in half:

> What light there was fell sideways from a mind
> Half dark. We stood and tried to bear
> The stroke *for* Maya, as her cats had done.
>
> The other eye, the one that saw, remained
> Full of wit, affection, and despair.
> When Ghédé mounted her. Brought his whip down.
>
> (63–64)

In *Sandover* the self jumps over its usual boundaries. Ephraim turns out to be the angel Michael; Nature is also Psyche and Chaos, each label conveying separate traits as well as distinctive habits of speech. The mysterious Mrs. Smith, herself linked with Nature, overlaps with Maya, St. Theodore, St. Lucy, Erzulie, Ephraim, JM's mother, and JM. What Maya whimsically offers as her new knowledge of Erzulie speaks for so many relationships in the poem: "ONE QUINTESSENCE CHANEL NO / 5 X 5 X 5 X 5 X 5" (64). *Sandover* teems with sets of complementary twins, recalling Otto Rank's argument in his essay *Der Dopplegänger* that the double was originally an insurance against destruction to the ego, an "energetic denial of death." As Ephraim asserts in a long hallucinatory speech in section Q, "NOTHING LIVE IS MOTIONLESS HERE." *The Changing Light at Sandover* catches up with any individual self just as it's about to metastasize into something other: the "clasping" of "dead selves," as well as "old lives made new."

Merrill's metamorphoses at once preserve and undermine identity. His methods are self-questioning in the related sense of continually renegotiating their own assumptions and choices. The poem sustains a revisionary attitude towards experience, as JM and DJ advance to successively higher levels of spirit-guides who then rework the conceits of their forerunners. Thus in the final sections of "The Book of Ephraim" Merrill returns to his opening gambits and amends them. A matching pair of second-thoughts in X addresses the modifications that writing the poem has prompted both in his understanding of his lyric voice and in the conjectures about the nature of the self that had grounded it:

> So Time has—but who needs that nom de plume? I've—
> We've modulated. . . .
>
> (85)

In his rejection of "Time" as an unnecessary pseudonym, the plural pronoun stands for all of his characters and their modulations, but zeroes in principally on Merrill's postponed acceptance of the degree to which his "I" is a synthesis or a consolidation. Much later he will ask Mirabell if Ephraim was a "composite voice," only to receive this pandemic reply: "HE IS THAT AS WELL AS AM I MY FRIENDS & AS YOU ARE" (266). This notion is acted out in the wheel-spinning rigors of "The Book of Ephraim" as self and other stage their intricate game of cat and mouse. *The Changing Light at Sandover* gains its main path only when the lyric note is no longer sounded. As Merrill writes at the conclusion of section Y:

> And here was I, or what was left of me.
> Feared and rejoiced in, chafed against, held cheap,
> A strangeness that was us, and was not, had
> All the same allowed for its description,
> And so brought at least me these spells of odd,
> Self-effacing balance. Better to stop
> While we still can. Already I take up
> Less emotional space than a snowdrop.
> My father in his last illness complained
> Of the effect of medication on
> His real self—today Bluebeard, tomorrow
> Babbitt. Young chameleon, I used to
> Ask how on earth one got sufficiently
> Imbued with otherness. And now I see.
>
> (89)

The Stripping Process and the God Within

Correlating this dwarfing of the ego ("what was left of me") and this expansion of the personality through contacts with otherness ("a strangeness that was us"), the metaphors that Merrill subsequently advances for the self in *The Changing Light at Sandover* spotlight a plastic receptivity that tallies with Keats's strictures about the "chameleon" poet.

In *Mirabell* JM interrupts the bat-angels' account of a crystal pyramid that Akhnaton and Nefertiti erected in Thebes:

> Earlier we'd been admiring an inch-high
> Prism set in noon light on the sill.
> Outflung, walls, us. DJ: It's really how
> His lessons flow through us. JM: And will

Forever be deflected by the grain
Of imperfection in that quartz capstone,
The human mind—Akhnaton's or our own.

(227)

That identities are intrinsically prismatic is an idea that first appears in "The Book of Ephraim" in connection with the human soul. After hearing Ephraim glumly disclose, "NO SOULS CAME FROM HIROSHIMA U KNOW," Merrill wonders:

If souls could be destroyed,
Colors disbanded of one's inmost prism—
Was it no more than human chauvinism
To care so helplessly?

(55)

The image rebounds in *Scripts* when Michael, during his "fete" for DJ and JM's twenty-fifth anniversary, confers "sense prisms" on Auden and Maria, with the result that they reexperience all of their past "psyches" and "personalities":

I WHO WAS WYSTAN SAW A YELLOW ME
AGED & WRY   A GREEN HILARIOUSLY
LAUGHING   A RED ME WRAUGHT   A BLUE
ME STARING STRAIGHT INTO MY OWN TWO EYES
While I WHO WAS MARIA IN THE FITTER'S
MIRROR SAW A RED ENRAGED MAMAN
A BLUE IN BLISS WITH FLOWERS IN HER HAIR
A GREEN TOO SHY TO SPEAK OF & MOST ODD
A YELLOW SELF I'D SEEN 100,000 TIMES
DOING MY FACE. TOO SIMPLIFIED, BUT THESE
WERE MERELY PSYCHES, PERSONALITIES,
THE UPPER CRUST OF A MILLEFEUILLES LAYER BY LAYER,
HABITS & LOVES & LIFETIMES, PEELED AWAY
FROM EPIDERMS OF HUMAN MEMORY

(357)

The special brilliance of the prism for Merrill's purposes is that it crystallizes the self as a transparent medium while allowing for individual differences. The characteristics of a prism materialize only when light passes through it, yet the glass also "deflects" or "changes" that light. In *Scripts* Robert Morse puts some body English on the metaphor when he compares the "LIGHT" that "HAS BEEN CONSTANT IN YOUR FIELD" to "A STAR WE ENTER / TO FIND OURSELVES" (498–99). Thus the prism encompasses both the uniquely Merrillesque "colorings" and "shadings" in the fable (as Auden says of Michael's fete, "TO EACH EPIPHANY / ITS OWN: FLAGSTAD & STRAUSS WDN'T AT ALL / DO FOR A BUTTERED SHAMAN IN NEPAL" [359]) and the forthrightly alien material that, as Merrill told Helen Vendler, "I climbed the walls trying to escape." The operations of the prism match up with Maria's impromptu definition of personality as "TECHNIQUE" (104).

"Technique is really personality," Oscar Wilde postulated in "The Critic as Artist." But for *The Changing Light at Sandover* Maria's crisp reversal prevails, as increasingly Merrill's cross-examination of the self is implicated in the techniques and technicalities of interworldly science. Perhaps the most crucial and resonant emblem that he propounds for the psyche is the atom, in "its outdated model by Neils Bohr—/ A quasi-solar system" (191).

Speaking to DJ near the midpoint of *Mirabell,* Merrill reactivates a figure that Ephraim broached some sixty pages earlier. "Suddenly I see my way—/ Wystan, Maria, you and I, we four / Nucleate a kind of psychic atom." As Merrill works through his metaphor, the individual takes on the properties of a chemical element that may spontaneously transform into other units by means of radioactive processes. On the one hand, "we are kept from shattering to bits / By the electron hearts, voices, and wits / Of our dead friends . . . in orbit around us"; and on the other, these friendly electrons "change our atomic weight."

As Merrill clinches his conceit:

all things alive
Or dead that touch us—Ephraim, the black dog
In Athens, Cynthia—but why go on?—
Are droplets in a "probability fog"
With us as nucleus.

(191–92)

Like the prism, the atom testifies to an idealization of the self that veers in contrary tracks: the individual retains an inviolable core (a "nucleus") even as he is entirely infused with otherness. But more forcibly than the prism tableau, atomic theory engages the instability and the precariousness that permeates the character alchemy in *Sandover.* The probability fog that Merrill's instructors atomize around all human life obscures the integrity of the self. There's hardly a facet of the cross-worldly network, whether scientific, theological, or literary, that is not imprinted with this self-effacing/self-enhancing pattern that at one point, describing the devolution of a star into a black hole, he terms "gassy expansion and succinct collapse" (85).

Ephraim, Mirabell, and the angels Michael and Gabriel all sedulously redesignate the most private or flamboyant exhibitions of personality as bargains with otherness. The arrangement of patrons and representatives downplays the significance of any individual life by locating it within a system of reincarnation that is defined as a collaboration between worlds. DJ and JM are told that every person is the representative of a spirit or patron; that patrons are promoted in heaven on the basis of their representatives' actions on earth; and that representatives ultimately can escape the round-robin of reincarnation and become patrons themselves. The actors get together between lives, anxiously planning for the next:

> Back
> To school from the disastrously long vac
> Goes the soul its patron crams yet once
> Again with savoir vivre. Will the dunce
> Never—by rote, the hundreth time round—learn
> What ropes make fast that point of no return,
> A footing on the lowest of NINE STAGES
> Among the curates and the minor mages?
> Patrons at last ourselves, an upward notch
> Our old ones move THEYVE BORNE IT ALL FOR THIS
>
> (10)

During *Mirabell* and *Scripts for the Pageant* this entr'acte swells until it is virtually the whole play. What had hummed along like a public school out of *Decline and Fall* reemerges as a bustling research lab directed by the bat-angels. The chief orientation of the bat-angels is "soul densities"; and Mirabell distinguishes two classes of souls: "run-of-the mill souls who / Life by life, under domed thicknesses, / Plod the slow road of earth," that are the province of their respective patrons, and an "elite" group of "at most two million relatively fleet / achievers" to whom densities are added between lives (139–40).

Merrill compares the bat-angels' enterprise to "marinade." But the word that Mirabell uses to indicate the annexation of soul densities is "cloning." The hit-or-miss commutations of patrons and representatives become for the R/Lab soul a manically methodical project of procreation through assemblage that has its closest literary analogue in Mary Shelley's *Frankenstein*. For the bat-angels in their lab, souls are a "raw material" they "process." The quality of their aggregates ranges from the "lowest human" soul to those of the "immortal Five," recurrent avatars who roam the corridors of history like the "thirty-six 'Just / Men' of the Jews" (143). The bat-angels aren't the only ones who tinker with the soul. The "12%," or the angels, also figure in the congerie. Something of the spellbinding precision of the venture—and the violence of its assault upon the individual—can be observed in this brisk summary from one of the "review" lessons in *Mirabell:*

> 10: SOUL WE HAVE LEARND IT EXISTS IT IS IN THE LAB WHEN
> OF A CERTAIN VALUE, IN THE BUREAUCRACY WHEN NOT.
> SOUL NEEDS A BODY TO BE USEFUL HENCE MAN IS NEEDED.
> SOUL IS AN INVENTION OF THIS 3RD WORLD MAN HAVING BEEN
> CHOSEN BY GOD TO EVOLVE FROM THE SUBSIDING WATERS
> HIS SOUL WAS PERFECTED, 12 P/C ENTRUSTED TO THE
> ANGELS, THE REST TO WORKERS SUCH AS WE. WE SET ABOUT
> MAKING THE SUPPORTIVE (M) BASE OF THE SOUL THIS WORK DREW
> ON ENERGY SOURCES U KNOW UNDER THE LOOSE HEADING:
> DENSITY. THEY STEM FROM THE 4 ELEMENTS BUT THE 5TH
> & RULING ELEMENT IS NOT OURS TO USE. WE USED (I
> SPEAK ONLY OF THE FIRST SIMPLE SOUL WE CONSTRUCTED &
> PLACED IN THE EARTHBOUND APE) WE USED THE ENERGIES OF SALT
> & OF (IN PARTICULAR CONFINED PLACES, WITH SAFEGUARDS)
> THE HEAVY ELEMENTS: TOUCHES GOD B PERMITTED US
> OF OUR ANCESTRAL POWER, BUT LOCKD INTO A STRUCTURE
> WHICH IF OPEND MEANS DESTRUCTION. WE PRODUCED IN A WORD
> A SERVICABLE SOUL.
>
> (236)

Within the "88%" of the soul that they superintend, the bat-angels' license to clone is unlimited, and there are frequent surprises. In their contrivance of the human composite they use animal, even plant souls. Mirabell tells JM that "ALL JAPANESE POETRY WAS / THE RESULT OF OUR EXPERIMENTS IN VEGETABLE CLONING" (151–52); his spelling out of JM and DJ's "Basic Formulas" includes the ratio of animal to human densities (143).

These freakish pronouncements might only be more of the wall-climbing silliness that Merrill once complained about to Helen Vendler[3] were not *The Changing Light at Sandover* so purposefully subversive of the traditional romantic and symbolist dualism between the self and the world. The poem's landscapes are rarely "externalizations of the poet's psyche" in the manner of Baudelaire's "Correspondences" or Stevens's "Auroras of Autumn."[4] Merrill's "I," and those of his assorted dramatis personae, evanesce "into the world of objects that bears the (imprint) of their presence." This tilt in his poetry recalls the self-dissolving landscapes of Rimbaud's *Illuminations* where, as Marjorie Perloff has observed, "the self no longer contemplates nature but becomes part of its operational processes"; and it's been a constant in his writing at least since *Braving the Elements,* where for poems like "Under Mars," "Yam," "The Black Mesa," and "Banks of a Stream Where Creatures Bathe," Merrill disperses his voice into a succession of talking vistas. As he intimates in "Log," the short lyric that serves as a prolegomenon to that volume: "I gasped and stumbled, and was less." Thus in "The Book of Ephraim," Joanna merges with "this entire / Parched landscape my lost pages fly her toward" (35). Or memorializing Isak Dinesen, Merrill notes:

selves in animal disguise

Light the way to Tania's goal:
Stories whose glow we seen our lives bathed in—
The mere word "animal" a skin
Through which its old sense glimmers, *of the soul.*

(53)

Mirabell similarly "explains" JM's poetry in terms of his "mineral densities": "SO WHEN FEAR THREATENS YR REASON, IMAGERY / DARTS FORTH WITH A GREAT SHINE OF REVOLVING FACETS TO THRUST / . . . ITS FLAMING BRAND / INTO THE PROWLER'S MUZZLE" (183). During *Scripts* Auden forces the fluidity of character and atmosphere to its natural conclusion when he announces that in his next life he is joining the elements: "BACK TO THE GLABROUS CLAYS / THE OILS & METALS MY FIRST LOVES" (303). Auden earlier had guessed that "WE FORETELL THE CLONE." This destination seems the inevitable denouement of his poem "In Praise of Limestone."

Cloning, contrary to what Merrill heard from Ephraim, can occur at any point in the R/Lab soul's circuit. Mirabell informs him that after the death of Hans Lodeizen their talents "intersected," and that HE NOW FEELS A GROWING PART OF YOUR WORK (221). The bat-angels clone for a myriad of purposes. Sometimes modifications are introduced—"THE NEW SOUL MUST BE FASHIONED / MORE RESISTANT TO THE ATOMIC ACID" (185). Or information may be transmitted—the idea of a "BENIGN GOD . . . HAS BEEN LATELY CLONED-IN TO ASSUAGE HUMAN FEARS" (137); and "PROPERLY CLONED ARCHITECTS ARE ON THEIR WAY" (194). Mirabell demonstrates to DJ and JM that "HEREDITY AND ENVIRONMENT ARE CLONABLE" (199). Poems are also eminently clonable. "HOMER WE HAD CLONED TO PROVIDE CATALOGUE & PROVIDE HIS ERA WITH A PANTHEON" (219). And what was true for the *Iliad* and the *Odyssey* also holds for Merrill's *Divine Comedies:*

"CLOSE YR EYES THINKING YOU SINK INTO OUR THOUGHTS A FORM OF / CLONING YR DC CAME IN THIS WAY THRU OUR INFLUENCE" (121).

Merrill labors at first to locate the bat-angel's industry within the romantic-symbolist tradition. Responding to the news of Auden's imminent exit into the earth, he deftly sidesteps the objectifying implications: "Like 'Adonais'—all of life imbued / With the dead's refining consciousness." Yet Auden's own prickly interruption indicates that he intends nothing so transcendent:

> MUCH MORE MUNDANE MY BOY WE I SHD GUESS
> WILL BECOME POWER STATIONS IN SUCH CRUDE
> TERMS AS OIL COAL WOOD WHEAT CORN WE'LL BE
> SOURCES QUITE LITERALLY OF ENERGY
>
> (310)

The scale of the bat-angels' intrigue also checks the individual ego. Since they speak at once from "WITHIN THE ATOM" (113) and as the "MEN B4 MANKIND" (56), their cloning swivels inward to "DEVELOPMENTS IN THE VERY NATURE OF MATTER" (115) and outward to history. All of the accounts in their ledger are, as JM recounts, "double-entry" (122). Mirabell begins to sketch in the connections between "microscopic particles" and the "Grand Design":

> SOUL IS THE KEY OUR COMPLEX SYSTEM OF INTERLOCKING
> DENSITIES OUR WAY OF TURNING IT, USING IT UNDER
> GOD B'S DIRECTION & WHERE DOES ALL THIS DIRECTED WORK
> MANIFEST ITSELF BUT IN THE HISTORY OF MAN'S REIGN?
>
> (239)

God B, in similar fashion, "IS NOT ONLY HISTORY BUT EARTH ITSELF" (187).

Cloning incorporates ingredients from Darwin, Stephen Jay Gould, Jung, and Freud, and scatters them in the blender with DNA and psychogenetic engineering. The self diffuses like linseed oil into the grain of the table—and that is exactly the bat-angels' point. "THIN OUT THE JOSTLERS FOR SELF REALIZATION," clamors one of their truculent spokesmen. The "Paradise" that they promise is as fluid as it is solid. "It's as we were told at the outset," JM paraphrases, "every grain / of dust, each waterdrop, to be suffused / with mind, with *our* minds. This will be Paradise" (308). The energies of non-Lab souls "WILL ENDOW BEINGS THEY CANNOT BE" (117). The "Alpha men" who will people this Paradise—"THE FUTURE'S FLESHLY

ROBOTS" (196), Auden tags them, "THAT RACE / USING US, EVOLVING FROM US" (308)—are celebrated for their marginally human virtues. Nature sums them up near the end of *Scripts:* "A SIMPLER, LESS WILFUL BEING. DULLER TOO? / IF SO, IS THAT SHARP EDGE NOT WELL LOST / WHICH HAS SO VARIOUSLY CUT AND COST?" (512).

But for all their quasi-scientific hanky-panky, the most sustained reverberations of the bat-angels' handiwork in *The Changing Light at Sandover* are, in fact, literary. Just as in their morphology the individual and the clone are identical (Akhnaton, for instance, is simultaneously the "1ST CLONED RULER" and "the first individual in History"), in their literary theory an individual talent becomes identified with tradition.

Otherworldly speculation about originality and inspiration, while preserving a hard biological gloss, spins off from refrains in the criticism of T. S. Eliot. (Even their scientism may ultimately stem from Eliot's employment of technical-sounding phrases like "objective correlative" and the images from the physical sciences that stud his essays.) In "Tradition and the Individual Talent," Eliot writes:

> we shall often find that not only the best, but the most individual parts of [a poet's] work may be those in which the dead poets, his ancestors assert their immortality most vigorously. . . . [T]he mind of the mature poet differs from that of the immature one not precisely in any valuation of "personality," not being necessarily more interesting, or having "more to say," but rather by being a more finely perfected medium. . . . The poet's mind is in fact a receptacle for seizing and storing up numberless feelings, phrases, images, which remain there until all the particles which can unite to form a new compound are present together. . . . [T]he poet has, not a "personality" to express, but a particular medium, which is only a medium and not a personality, in which impressions and experiences combine in peculiar and unexpected ways.[5]

Merrill's Ouija board method; the cloning of the dead that produced his *Divine Comedies;* the receptacle-like word banks that Mirabell taps in him—these are only three of the many literalizations of Eliot that back his poem like gold bullion. When Eliot argues that

> the historical sense compels a man to write not merely with his own generation in his bones, but with a feeling that the whole of the literature of Europe from Homer and within it the whole of the literature of his own country has a simultaneous existence and composes a simultaneous order,

Merrill's interlocutors do not disagree, they only collapse the corporeal metaphor. Mirabell tells DJ that Yeats is in his hand; and that the dead are in JM's

"GENES" (196), much as *Romeo and Juliet* was "IN THE GENES OF OUR BARD" (191). Homer speaks in Merrill's poem, and Auden addresses him as " IMMORTAL BARD, YOU WHO CREATED ME" (355). Again, Auden is not talking figuratively. Homer is one of the five immortals, in whom reside " THE MAXIMUM DENSITY IN EACH AGE" (142). Like "certain great scribes," their talents are infinitely divisible. The use to which they are put in heaven objectifies Eliot's maxim that the dead writers are "that which we know." Thus Maria sorts through Robert Morse's next life:

WE OF THE 5 ARE PARCELED INTO MORE
THAN ONE LIFE AT A TIME OUR ENERGIES
CONCENTRATE WITHIN THE PRINCIPAL LIFE
BUT EACH LEAST POWER IS USED. THE NEXT RM:
STRAVINSKY POWDER, A HALF CUP A TEASPOON
OF MOZART DOLLOP OF VERDI THESE AS U KNOW,
ASPECTS OF HOMER

(497)

The structuralist axiom that all books are about other books never seemed less like a clever turn of phrase than in this commentary on the "cooking" of great literature:

SINCE MID 19TH CENT SOULS OF THE GREAT SCRIBES
HAVE BEEN USED 1/9 ON EARTH REINCARNATED, 8/9
AS LET US SAY SAFETY DEPOSITS WE MINE THEM. MM
FINDS PLATO LIGHTWEIGHT & INDEED HE IS NEARLY A SHELL
BUT OUR HAUTE CUISINE IS STOCKD WITH HIS LIVE SOUL DENSITIES
WHICH SPICE & FORTIFY NUMBERLESS EARTHLY DISHES

(189)

Much earlier, Maria had wrapped up the exertions of the Five very Eliotically: "HOW SATISFYING. . . . ALL THIS LINKAGE WITH THE WORK OF EONS" (201).

Auden's great address in *Mirabell* about the minimal role of the self in a work of art translates strains in Eliot's thinking about poetry into impish slang. The infamously slippery theory of impersonality ricochets into court intrigue and toilet training:

CAN U STILL BE BENT,
AFTER OUR COURSE IN HOW TO SEE PAST LONE
AUTONOMY TO POWERS BEHIND THE THRONE,
ON DOING YR OWN THING: EACH TEENY BIT

(PARDON MME) MADE PERSONAL AS SHIT?
GRANTED THAT IN 1ST CHILDHOOD WE WERE NOT
PRAISED ENOUGH FOR GETTING OFF THE POT
IT'S TIME TO DO SO NOW

(262)

When he goes on to deprecate the self in favor of tradition, "THOSE GREAT GIVENS THE ROSEBRICK MANOR / ALL TOPIARY FORMS & METRICAL MOAT ARIPPLE," and speaks of the community of poets as a "FAMILY," with its "SWEET WILLIAMS & FATE-FLAVORED EMILYS," it's impossible not to think of Eliot's hierarchy of literary relationships in "Tradition and the Individual Talent." Eliot writes, "No poet, no artist of any art, has his complete meaning alone. His significance, his appreciation is the appreciation of his relation to the dead poets and artists." But there's a sequence in "The Function of Criticism" that Auden is shadowing still more closely:

> There is accordingly something outside of the artist to which he owes allegiance, a devotion to which he must surrender and sacrifice himself in order to earn and to obtain his unique position. A common inheritance and a common cause unite artists consciously or unconsciously: it must be admitted that the union is mostly unconscious. Between the true artists of any time there is, I believe, an unconscious community.[6]

The appreciable difference, once again, involves Merrill's literalization—his making what Eliot calls "unconscious" a calculated strategy. After all, in *Sandover,* it's a dead poet who is shouldering these claims about the past and tradition, and the community between Auden and Merrill is acted out in every one of his tart, uppercase speeches.

In *The Changing Light at Sandover* otherness and tradition displace the central authority of the self and the poet. Major poems are examples of what Mirabell calls "V WORK," or "WORK GUIDED BY HIGHER COLLABORATION" (162). His clarifying paradigm, suggestively, is *The Waste Land,* the West's one "PREWRITTEN POEM" since Homer (219). It's not Eliot's polyvocality that captivates Mirabell, but the fact that *The Waste Land* was "ghostwritten" by Rimbaud Allowing for the bat-angels' unrelenting psychobiology, his report is a textbook application of the principles in "Tradition and the Individual Talent." Along the way Merrill acquires supplemental analogues to his own prewritten poem:

YET RIMBAUD? IN HIS GENES WAS A V WORK CUT OFF BY LIFE
  Why? Did it offend Biology?
IT WAS PREMATURE A KIND OF ANTILIFE V WORK MORE
SUITABLE NOW IN THESE POP EXPLO DAYS. R SPOKE TOO SOON

BUT NO ACCIDENT FOR WHEN TSE WROTE HIS V WORK
THE TIME WAS RIPE: AR SAT AT HIS ELBOW
Rimbaud ghostwrote "The Waste Land"? You are *something*
THIS HAPPENS
IN VARYING WAYS. . . .
NO MAN CAN REACH US DIRECTLY TSE HAD
A NUMBER FROM OUR ORDERS AR HAD THAT SAME NUMBER
POINT ONE THUS YEATS & DJ TSE DOWN ON CERTAIN
SUPERSTITIOUS SCRIBES WE HAD TO APPOINT RIMBAUD HE WROTE
THE WASTE LAND WE FED IT INTO THE LIKE-CLONED ELIOT
And Uncle Ezra?
AS IN SHAKESPEARE WE LET THE CASE REST ON A POUND OF FLESH
Thank you, that will do.
NO JM FOR THE (M) OUNCE OF FLESH U CAN CLAIM AS YRS
LIVES BY THESE FREQUENT CONTACTS WITH YR OWN & OTHERS' WORK
(217, 219)

The Waste Land is hardly the oddest instance here of a maverick creation that turns out to be a composite. In the sparkling prologue to book 6 of *Mirabell,* which prefigures these revelations about Eliot and Rimbaud, the actress Sarah Bernhardt descends a spiral staircase that by degrees overlaps with a DNA molecule—"it's the theatre in our blood" (203). What David Kalstone remarks of this passage informs all of Merrill's accommodations of the self in *Sandover:* "the presence of Bernhardt is felt as if imprinted with that pattern at the basis of human life. The most exotically theatrical, individual, wilful, calculated, and idiosyncratic figure is identified with the most common, impersonal, and indwelling chemical force."[7]

The self-erasing mechanism that allows the individual to be "imbued with otherness" or a poet to fuse with tradition is styled the "STRIPPING PROCESS." In *Mirabell* Auden compares the later lessons to a "MASQUE" where, as in the court productions of Ben Jonson, successive maskings and unmaskings, disguisings and doublings, disperse and coalesce the identities of the masquers and courtiers, the actual monarch and the fictional player who represents him.[8] Each of the major character-actors in *Sandover* feels the pain of being used—and of being used up. As Mirabell describes Auden: "WHA IN OUR MASQUE EXPERIENCED WHAT? THE WIND LET OUT OF HIS BEING HIS PERSONALITY GONE" (211). Maria marks, but without complaining, "I AM BEING / USED USED UTTERLY TO THE VERY ASH / NO WASTE" (198). DJ initially resists the stripping process, which JM ultimately comes to regard as the condition of all art:

—It's what in any Quest, the heroes do—
But at the cost of being set apart,

Emptied, diminished. Tolkien knew this. Art—
The tale that all but shapes itself—survives
By feeding on its personages' lives.
The stripping process, sort of. What to say?
Our lives led *to* this. It's the price we pay.

(218)

The source once more is Eliot. The stripping process objectifies his famous pronouncement that "the progress of an artist is a continual self-sacrifice, a continual extinction of personality." As with all of the losses I've been describing, the stripping process also is a gain. Mirabell explains, in a line that echoes the triumphant dancing at the conclusion of the Renaissance masque, "ITS LOSS A COMPLETENESS IN THAT DANCE UNDER THE POWER-FUL LIGHT FLOODING THE LENS" (211). And Auden suggests that they are being "REDUCED TO ESSENCES / JOINED TO INFINITY" (209).

The immediate result for JM in the poem is that through his surrender to the stripping process he hears the voice of God. Mirabell, from the restricted perch of the bat-angels, speculated that these self-dispersals would reveal "THE DIVINE TRANSLATION":

JM THE STRIPPING IS THE POINT YR POEM WILL PERHAPS
TAKE UP FROM ITS WINTRY END & MOVE STEP BY STEP INTO
SEASONLESS & CHARACTERLESS STAGES TO ITS FINAL
GREAT COLD RINGING OF THE CHIMES SHAPED AS O O O O O

(211)

Almost 150 pages later those same resounding circles, or pinging zeroes—like the stripping process, they encompass nothing, and everything—introduce God B's forlorn dispatch, the "Pulse of the galactic radio / Tuned then to mortal wavelength" (360). Mirabell postulates that the bat-angels' challenge is to "MAKE MAN THE CLONE OF GOD" (269). Attuning himself to this ghostly signal, and serving as a vehicle for its transmission, JM modulates into God B just as earlier he had merged with Time. In the final stages of the poem he embraces the role that he had shrugged off in "The Book of Ephraim": "the good gray medium / Blankly uttering someone else's threat" (65). A haunting reprise of God B's bulletin has the last word in *Scripts for the Pageant:*

HERS HEAR ME I AND MINE SURVIVE SIGNAL
ME DO YOU WELL I ALONE IN MY NIGHT
HOLD IT BACK HERE ME BROTHERS I AND MINE

(517)

The Changing Light at Sandover peels back the laminae of the self to disclose what Merrill in an interview with the *Paris Review* calls "the god within."

> Well, don't you think there comes a time when everyone, not just a poet, wants to get beyond the Self? To reach, if you like, the "god" within you? The board, in however clumsy or absurd a way, allows for precisely that. Or if it's still *yourself* that you're drawing upon, then that self is much stranger and freer and more far-seeing than the one you thought you knew.

Merrill's qualification here points to another unconditional and verifiable gain—which is, of course, the poem itself. In *Sandover* this poet is "stranger and freer and more far-seeing" than the one *we* thought we knew. Delmore Schwartz cataloged the advantages of sibylline listening as "an immense energy and mobility," "an immediacy and a scope." Merrill's self-effacements and submissions have yielded an incalculable increase in his range and flexibility. As he notices in *Mirabell,* "putting it into words / Means also that it puts words into me" (172). Self-forgetting is self-discovering in this playful exchange from the coda, as Mirabell prepares JM for his reading of the completed poem to an audience of his dead friends and mentors:

> 'DEAR MR SECRETARY,
> WILL YOU BRING IN (VOICE MUSICAL & MILD)
> OUR POET?' Having long since brought him out.
> IS IT NOT JUST?
>
> (547)

Impersonality, at this level, can hardly be distinguished from personality. Ephraim's "bringing out" of the poet catches the crosscurrent in Eliot's theory that stirred him to explain the "greatness" of Yeats's poetry in terms of "personality."[9] At once autobiographical and rooted in otherness, self-canceling and self-amplifying, *The Changing Light at Sandover* is a stunning disappearing act that endows a still more spectacular return. It's "no accident," to adopt one of the bat-angels' shibboleths, that in *Sandover* Merrill overcomes his "chronic shyness / Vis à vis 'ideas'" (419), a volte-face that J. D. McClatchy during the *Paris Review* interview terms "a case of the return of the repressed," and Merrill "a *range* of metaphor, a depth of meaning, that hadn't been available to me in earlier poems." And no accident that by triangulating his own broken home into Sandover, and his own parents into the foster parents of Maria and Auden, Nature and God B, Merrill appears to have silenced the Oedipal horrors that agitated his strongest lyrics.

Schwartz had remarked that "the new [sibylline] method makes it possible to bring into the poem certain depths of experience directly and explicitly." It's precisely the immediacy (and the concomitant generosity) of Merrill's transmissions that distinguish *Sandover* from like-minded experiments in prior American literature. In "Song of Myself" Whitman also skirted self-dissolution as he identified himself as a receptive vehicle: "Through me the afflatus surging and surging. . . . through me the current and index . . . Through me many long dumb voices, / Voices of the interminable generations of slaves, / Voices. . . ." Yet Whitman did not relinquish any authority to his other vocalists: we only hear him *say* he's listening; and the pathos of his poem resides in his peremptory domination over what he's ostensibly hearing. From another angle, the sibylline listening for *The Waste Land* differs from Merrill's for *Sandover* in that Eliot palpably refused to direct his spinning shards toward a comprehensive (if unsteady) autobiography. What Ronald Bush evocatively labels the "nuggets of the objective world"[10] in *The Waste Land* emanate as the symptoms of a civilization in pieces: "These fragments I have shored against my ruins."

During the dinner that he shares with JM in Venice, Wendell Pincus ridicules what he calls "the representable self":

> "The self was once," I put in, "a great, great
> Glory." And he: "Oh sure. But is it still?
>
> The representable self, at any rate,
> Ran screaming from the Post-Impressionist
> Catastrophe . . ."
>
> (80)

The Changing Light at Sandover takes up this mocking challenge and represents the self by means of an unbridled polyvocality that Merrill, no less than John Ashbery, apprehends as naturalism. "Just as I love multiple meanings," he reports in the *Paris Review* interview, "I try for contrasts and disruptions of tone . . . / Poets will rediscover as many techniques as they need in order to help them write better . . . / Voice in its fullest tonal range—not just bel canto or passionate speech."

Resistance: Pressing Back against Eliot, Stevens, and Yeats

> Thank *you,* Unice. Tell
> Us more about your world? WELL I AND MINE
> RATHER RESEMBLE TALES WE WERE TOLD
> So do we. Tales shape us, of all kind.
> Myths. Novels. Awful books about "man's mind."
>
> (382)

The maneuvers Merrill devises in *The Changing Light at Sandover* for dramatizing the chameleon self can be pulled into sharper focus if we take stock of the use the poem makes of the modernist precursors in his word banks. The off-the-cuff appraisals by his otherworldly interlocutors convey anything but homage to his poetic masters, sustaining the tone that Auden associates with all exchanges between the young and their elders: "RESPECTFUL TOLERANT / HALF PITYING & GOODBYE TO U DEAR AUNT!" (308). Eliot emerges as a fussy clerk who "RESISTING THE FOSTER CHILD, ADDED TOUCHES OF HIS OWN: / THE SUBJECTIVE CORRELATIVE" (219). Mirabell dubs Stevens "THE INSURANCE MAN" (547), and Plato's acclaim of his poetry is automatic and thin: "NEITHER TOP / NOR BOTTOM, DEEP NOR SHALLOW" (429). Yeats and *A Vision* tap a wellspring of celestial merriment. Ephraim deadpans, "POOR OLD YEATS / STILL SIMPLIFYING" (14); and Auden expands this into "POOR LONG SUFFERING YEATS," criticizing the Irish poet as not so much misguided as self-deluding: "DEVOURED BY THE CHIMERA" (424). But even Auden must squirm through a catalog of the "FLAWS" in his later work.

These carping passages, which in fact resemble Yeats's cranky comments on other poets in *A Vision,* crackle with the high anxiety that Harold Bloom marks as the essence of all poetic relationships. Yet Merrill's own feelings inevitably run in wider and deeper channels than those of his spirit-guides who, fixated on their own message, are always evaluating from the perspective of V work.

Merrill's literalizations of Eliot point the way here. From *First Poems* and *The Country of a Thousand Years of Peace* through the trilogy, *Late Settings,* and *The Inner Room,* the habit David Kalsone calls "prospecting for ore" among dead metaphors and idioms has proved a potent device in his poetry.

> There is a special strangeness . . . to Merrill's colloquial style, a taut alertness to the meanings which lurk in apparently casual words and phrases. We may find this in all good poets, but Merrill raises it to a habit of vigilance, a quickened control and pose, sometimes bravado, which he clearly trusts as a source of power.[11]

For the *Changing Light at Sandover* Merrill sinks into what, for a poet writing near the end of the twentieth century, and raised on Yeats, Eliot, and Stevens, can only be called the commonplaces of modernism, which he views as submerged mines of latent signification that have to be exploded before they deliver up their riches. Thus in the critical sequences I cited earlier Merrill so thoroughly submerges himself in the implications of Eliot's familiar phrases—or they so thoroughly flow through his prism—that he distorts and inverts as much as he fleshes out and clarifies. Bolstering differences as well as affinities, his literalizations of prime moments in Eliot, Stevens, and Yeats are at once deferential and subversive.

Merrill's borrowings in *Sandover* elude systematic mapping because they're so serendipitous. He suggests in the *Paris Review* interview that the "mechanics of the board" might "embarrass the sort of reader who can't bear to face the random or trivial elements that coalesce, among others, to produce an 'elevated' thought. That doesn't bother me *at all.*" Merrill emerges as quite willing to reproduce inconsistencies and contradictions in his modernist sources—Eliot's theory of impersonality, for instance, or Wallace Stevens on the imagination:

> Stevens imagined the imagination
> And God as one; the imagination, also,
> As that which presses back, in parlous times,
> Against "the pressure of reality."
> Scholia discordant (who could say?)
> Yet coursing with heart's-blood the moment read.
>
> (66)

One powerful operating principle behind the trilogy springs from the literary opportunism that Merrill glances at here. He acknowledges in section A of "The Book of Ephraim" that "measures, furthermore, had been defined / As what emergency required" (4). *Sandover* persuasively makes do with what's available, locating a taproot of improvised mastery in the impromptu and the makeshift.

Maya Deren becomes Merrill's guiding star for a poetics of expediency. After Joseph Campbell comments on her Haitian film, *Divine Horsemen*—"such a theme, / He said, took all one's powers to 'document'"—Maya chimes in, "AS U ARE LEARNING, J?" (305). *The Changing Light at Sandover* is a late epic sweeping up of fragments, more Ovidian and Byronic than Dantean, and admitting to may varieties of influence. Merrill inhabits the shells of his literary progenitors only to crack them open.

The poem's application of Stevens is a preeminent instance of a sustaining influence that is ultimately shattered and shed. Merrill once again advances by means of telescoping literalizations and objectifications. A movement in Steven's "Adagia" ("Proposita: 1. God and the imagination are one. 2. The thing imagined is the imaginer.")[12] leads him to the S/O/L, and at length to the angels and God B. But an opposite inclination in "The Noble Rider and the Sound of Words" ushers in "Resistance," a concept that stitches together disparate sequences in *Mirabell* and *Scripts for the Pageant.* As Stevens writes in the "Noble Rider":

> the pressure if reality is, I think, the determining factor in the artistic character of an era and, as well, the determining factor in the artistic character of an individual. The resistance to this pressure or its evasion in the case of individuals of extraordinary imagination cancels the pressure so far as those individuals are concerned. . . . It is a violence from within that protects us from a violence from without. It is the imagination pressing back against the pressure of reality. It seems, in the last analysis, to have something to do with our self-preservation; and that, no doubt, is why the expression of it, the sound of words, helps us to live our lives.[13]

Resistance in *Sandover* echoes through many canyons. JM, for example, speaks of his "resistance" of the bat-angels, "for form's sake" (138). One formal consequence of this tension is the imagery that Mirabell ascribes to his mineral densities, in the passage I quoted above, where, to use Stevens's shuddering words, "a violence from without" is matched by "a violence from within." The five elements likewise claim that they "PRESS BACK" against antimatter (161). That is also the keynote of God B's song, "I AND MINE HOLD IT BACK" (360). As the poem presses on, Resistance becomes embedded in the opposition of universal forces that propel the atom, matter, the human soul, time, and all history:

> NOW IN THAT WHIRL IS A REVERSE WHIRL
> MAKING, AS IN THE BEATEN WHITE OF EGG,
> FOR THICKENING, FOR DENSITY, FOR MATTER.
> YES, FROM THIS OPPOSITION, WHICH HOLDS SWAY
> NO LESS WITHIN MAN'S SOUL, LORDS, CAME THE FIRST
> MINUTE PASTE THAT WAS GOD'S MATERIAL.
> IN SHORT: THE ELEMENTS FROM A 'WHITE' SOURCE
> RESISTED THOSE OF A 'BLACK' OR 'SHADOW' FORCE.
>
> (396)

Mirabell asserts that the "POWER" of man abides in his Resistance (262) and, as in Stevens, this concentrated stress is the agency of his preservation: the imagination "draws us / To, and insulates us from, the absolute" (84). The language that encodes this force for man becomes "THE ARK" and "THE LIFE RAFT" (119). But as Mirabell's pair of postdisaster metaphors suggest, Merrill's interlocutors believe that they speak with greater urgency, and under more literally apocalyptic pressures than Stevens.

Stevens delivered "The Noble Rider" at Princeton in 1941, and the uncertain "defeat or triumph of Hitler" was perhaps the gravest threat to the imagination that he was responding to:

> Rightly or wrongly, we feel that the fate of a society is involved in the orderly disorders of the present time. We are confronting, therefore, a set of events, not only beyond our power to tranquillize them in our mind, beyond our power to reduce them and metamorphose them, but events that stir the emotions to violence, that engage us in what is direct and immediate and real, and events that involve the concepts and sanctions that are the order of our lives and may involve our very lives; and these events are occurring persistently with increasing omen, it what may be called our presence.

Stevens's essay was published just as J. Robert Oppenheimer broke ground for his laboratory in Los Alamos, New Mexico. For *Sandover,* and the world as the poem sees it, atomic fission strips away the residue of the figurative in Stevens's charged phrases. The first words that DJ and JM hear from the other world are "HELLP O SAV ME" (6). Auden translates Stevens's grim fears about "society" and "order" into a planetary distress signal: "WE HERE TREMBLE ON A CRUST SO FRAGILE / IT NEEDS GOD'S CONSTANT VIGIL TO KEEP US AFLOAT." Resistance in "The Noble Rider" marks the imagination and reality as commensurate forces. But in *Sandover* nuclear power upends the balance. Not only does it destroy the human soul, it also tampers with the Resistance at the heart of matter. "ALL ENERGY SOURCES MUST BE KEPT COVERED / THAT IS OUR PRINCIPAL TASK . . . WHAT IS NUCLEAR ENERGY BUT DESTRUCTION / OF THAT SHIELD?" (126). The negative power of the atom is "A DISAPPEARANCE AN ABSOLUTE VOID" (119). Man's usurpation of the atom is a "PROMETHEAN OUTRAGE" (213).

Twice before, the bat-angels instruct JM, atomic fission had wrecked God B's Greenhouse. In our own era, Michael warns, "ACCIDENTS HAVE BEGUN":

> THIS ENIGMA, THIS IT, THIS EVENLY BALANCED X, THIS ANTIMATTER & ITS MONITOR GOD
> MATCHING WITS WITH HIS RIVAL TO SIEZE THE DAY AND MAKE OF US A CIPHER NIGHT, AN O
>
> (476)

For *Sandover* Merrill's otherworldly guides slip into the convenient glove of Stevens's rhetoric to employ it as a velvet fist. Although Stevens's suggestive terms permit Merrill to think about the pressures behind his poem and the issues of his world, a consoling account of the imagination is summoned principally—and reluctantly—to demonstrate its inadequacy to the present crisis. "The Noble Rider" informs and nourishes the poem. But in order to press back against *his* reality, Merrill must leave it behind.

Yeats similarly serves as a model at once cherished and cast away. Merrill dips into *A Vision* and the surrounding poems and essays before moving on to his own darker purposes. Auden tells DJ and JM that Yeats sits by them "FAINTLY IN THE DARK / A WORDLESS PRESENCE" (424), and so many lines in the two occult formations intersect that it's easy to lose sight of the points of departure.

Some of these correspondences proceed as coincidental echoes. When Merrill demands that his interlocutors "stop shifting ground" (122), the moment has a coordinate in *A Vision:* "They shifted ground whenever my interest was at its height, whenever it seemed that the next day must reveal what, as I soon discovered, they were determined to withhold until all was on paper."[14] One of Yeats's communicators informs him, "Remember we will deceive you if we can"; Ephraim and Mirabell periodically dissemble, descending to "PEARLGREY LIES." Yeats notes that his interlocututors often appeared to be "messengers"—and that is the bat-angels' favorite expression for their métier. Mirabell's tapping of JM's word banks seems a computer-age update of Yeats's claim that the "Spirit" of the dead can "tap the minds of the living." What Hans Lodeizen in *Sandover* calls "TRANSFERRED EXPERIENCE" Yeats terms "transferred thought" in "The Soul in Judgement" section of *A Vision.* During section U of "The Book of Ephraim" Merrill is instructed that he has six months to finish the poem, much as Yeats's controls were always setting deadlines for him: "*This* part of system *must* be finished by August next," huffs Ameritus, a spirit who participated in the sessions that generated thousands of pages of automatic script for Yeats in the period between 1917 and 1920.

Before they achieved an expedient form for their otherwordly encounters, both writers struggled through false starts. The dialogue between Robartes and Aherne that Yeats worked on from 1917 to 1919 circles *A Vision* from roughly the same orbit that the lost novel loops "The Book of Ephraim." The "yes and no" with which Merrill steadily enters into and shrugs off belief in his mythology matches the equivocation in Yeats. In 1929 Yeats wrote to Olivia Shakespear of "my conviction of the truth of it has grown";[15] yet a few years later he nonchalantly told Allan Wade, "Oh, I draw from it images for my poetry."

The thematic analogues are so extensive that Auden's guess that Yeats took dictation from the bat-angels seems cautious rather than histrionic. As in *Sandover,* the scale of *A Vision* simultaneously is individual and historical, and the internal and the external interwine. As Yeats wrote in 1937, shortly before he published the revised text of *A Vision,* in words that pointedly anticipate Mirabell's: "I begin to see things double, doubled in history, world history, personal history."[16] Throughout both schemes the dead depend on the living for a language in which to express themselves. Lacking that language, the dead drift in a state of suspended animation, shut off from even their own past lives. JM paraphrases Ephraim, "you see yourselves, then, in the mirror only / Of a live mind," while Yeats remarks of the dead's efforts to "relive" their earthly experiences, "the *Spirit* finds concrete events in the *Passionate Body,* but the names and words of the drama it must obtain . . . from some incarnate Mind." The prism effect also is prefigured in Yeats's perception of his role, and he periodically paused to acknowledge that the medium inescapably modifies what he receives. Perhaps his loudest statement of this motif is the brisk paragraph in "Per Amica Silentia Lunae" that commences, "Only in rapid and subtle thought, as in faint accents heard in the quiet of the mind, can the thoughts of the spirit come to use but little changed."[17]

Finally, the theory of the mask that Yeats conjured from the dialogues of Oscar Wilde loops through every sinuous reel of Merrill's pursuit of the self in otherness. The desire of the medium and the automatic writer to eclipse the boundaries of his own mind was implicated in the earliest psychic researches that Yeats undertook with the Hermetic Students of the Golden Dawn in the 1890s. The self retains dimensions grander than the individual in all of his later investigations—from the alliances with spiritualists in New York, London, and Dublin that led to "Per Amica Silentia Lunae," to the experiments with his wife, George, that produced the transcripts behind *A Vision.* In "Per Amica Silentia Lunae" Yeats quotes from his diary of 1909:

> I think all happiness depends on the energy to assume the mask of some other life, on a re-birth as something not one's self, something created in a moment and perpetually renewed. . . . If we cannot imagine ourselves as different from what we are, and try to assume that second self, we cannot impose a discipline upon ourselves though we may accept one from others. Active virtue, as distinguished from the passive acceptance of a code, is therefore theatrical, consciously dramatic, the wearing of a mask.

For their bird's-eye adaptation of this vocabulary of a divided and masked self, Merrill's spirit-guides reproduce intricacies from Yeats's later systematization of it into the twenty-eight incarnations of *A Vision.* The losses and dispersals that signify increase and elevation are adumbrated in Phase 17. Self-discovery through self-forgetting ("the joy of self-surrender") is the burden of Phase 24. The description of the Receptive Man in Phase 23, especially Yeats's warm account of the dramatist Synge, underlies the bat-angels' praise of Merrill's openness and receptivity in the poignant "WE MET ON THIS FAIR FIELD" interlude in *Mirabell.* The changes that Yeats rings on the Daimon parallel the transformations of the self in *Sandover.* Initially a spirit of inspiration who speaks to the poet from elsewhere, but using the poet's own voice, the Daimon subsequently is equated with memory in its most august and capacious sense, and with tradition: "co-existing in its eternal moment, all the events of our life, all that we have known of other lives." The activities of the Daimon "between lives" suggests a small-scale prototype of the bat-angels' Research Lab.

But the assumptions and goals of Merrill's project could hardly be more ruinous to Yeats's energetic, exhaustive system rearing. *Sandover* careers through *A Vision* flipping over even its most indispensable formulations. For Yeats, as for Wilde, the mask is a self-conscious construction fabricated by the poet in his progress toward the chief "good," which he identifies as "Unity of Being" and complete self-expression. Embracing a mask is a creative action designed to save himself from inner and outer fragmentation: the "stylistic arrangement of experience" in *A Vision* composes, as Yeats wrote to Edmund Dulac, "a last act of defense against the chaos of the world" that seeks to guarantee permanence beyond flux. "Hammer your thoughts into unity" is the sentence, he tells us in "If I Were Four-and-twenty," against which "for years I tested all that I did." For *A Vision* he externalized his fierce, synthesizing gestures in certain illuminated centers and ideal points of rest—Phase 15, the state called Marriage or the Beatitude, the Thirteenth Cone or the Phaseless Sphere, Byzantium—that endure outside of the blind alleys and fatal corridors of time.

Viewed from the bias of Merrill's communicators, Yeats was only the most organized of "THE JOSTLERS FOR SELF REALIZATION" that they are bent on eliminating. Burrowing into Yeats's lexicon, not to launch the performing self but to enact his own vanishing, Merrill offers his masks as found, not chosen; and as flickering, strobe-lit images of perpetual transformation, not stages to be passed through before the poet can cast off his disguise and reveal himself resplendent and whole. Any possible salvation in *Sandover,* moreover, far from transpiring in an idealized, timeless present, remains embedded in the ongoing temporal cavalcade. The Source of Light, which Mirabell consigns to the "LIVED LIFE," is set in motion by the diurnal routine, whose rhythms are intrinsically cherishable, irrespective of the eternal truths that may issue from them on the path to perfection. The masked dramas of *The Changing Light at Sandover,* the polymorphous clashes between light and dark forces, occur not once but over and over. As Michael recounts his struggle: "AND TWICE CHAOS RANG DOWN THE CURTAIN, AS HE WAITS TO DO AGAIN, / AND AGAIN OUR GREAT DIRECTOR CALLING: CURTAIN UP! LIGHT! LIGHT!" (326–327).

Sandover's mocking equivalent of Byzantium—and the great good place that JM and DJ sail to in both "The Book of Ephraim" and *Scripts*—is Venice, which advances not as an emblem of the fully realized individual but as more "unsteady ground." Like the self Venice was once a "great, great / Glory." But now? "The monumental / 'I' of stone . . . Each visit stands for less . . . A whole heavenly city / Sinking, titanic ego mussel-blue. . . . whose once fabled / Denizens . . . are dying" (75).

So much for Unity of Being. Merrill later renders his parody of Yeats's ringing resolutions still more particular and barbed. Venice emerges as

this drowning, dummy paradise
Whose nude, gnawed Adam and eroded Eve

Cling to their cornice, and September flies
Revolve above the melting tutti-fruiti.

(502)

Small winged insects have rendered recurrent surrogates for the self in Merrill's recent poetry. The mirrored ceilings that he encounters in section K of "The Book of Ephraim" impishly "reduce and multiply / The visitor to swarms of the same fly" (37). Michael says that his light is "ASWARM WITH GNATLIKE SELVES. . . . THROUGH AUTUMN DAYS" (347). In "The House Fly" (*Late Settings*), he observes: "Come October, if I close my eyes, / A self till then subliminal takes flight / Buzzing around me" And "Santorini: Stopping the Leak," from the same volume, presents Psyche in the form of "the peevish buzz / Of a wee winged one-watt" moth.

The casual yet abiding autumnal references in Merrill's catalogs of the diminished self ("September," "October," "Autumn days") suggest that it is too late for the grand personal dramitizations that Yeats encapsulated in the symbols of *A Vision*.

Of greater significance to the timbre and texture of *Sandover,* however, than Merrill's antisystematic dismantling of *A Vision* are the overlooked implications in Yeats's theory of the mask that the poem at once releases and terminates. Yeats's poetry hardly can be characterized as undramatic or untheatrical. Yet it's also true that Yeats did not differentiate his masked speakers by devising a distinctive language for each of them. While he often argued that "man can embody the truth but he cannot know it," his poems characteristically know rather than embody their truths. Thus in "A Dialogue between Self and Soul," "Ego Dominus Tuus," and "The Phases of the Moon," three of Yeats's dialogue poems that Merrill alludes to during *Sandover,* no particularizing turns of phrase or habits of speech distinguish "Self" from "Soul," "Hic" from "Ille," or Aherne from Robartes. Only *what* they say, the particular *knowledge* that they hold, serves to identify them. Yeats's claim that he wrote "The Phases of the Moon" as "a text for exposition" is especially instructive, as these dialogues are didactic summaries that represent rather than express principles in Yeats's evolving system. Although he once asserted that "I even do my writing by self-distrusting reasons," his conflicts and contradictions tend to manifest themselves from poem to poem and from period to period. His individual poems are in this specialized sense static and conclusive. The fragmentation of his personality (as well as the eventual synthesis and renewal) is described in gesture and symbol—the final stanza of "Byzantium," for instance, or the ending of "Leda and the Swan," or his account of the self-transforming divinities in "Whence had they come"—but they are not acted out in the diction. This proclivity also informs his plays where, as Helen Vendler notes, "dramatic indifference cannot be carried any further, and in fact one feels that Yeats would have preferred a single voice to speak all the way through, with the simplest indication of his changing persona."[18]

Merrill nails down the corners of Yeats's rhetoric, dramatizing his transcripts instead of paraphrasing them, accepting poems instead of "metaphors for poetry" from his guides.

Like Yeats, Merrill often limns his world as a rose. But his flower is imperiled, and rife with spikes:

Enough

To set the doomsday clock—its hands our own:
The same rose ruts, the red-as-thorn crosshatchings—
Minutes nearer midnight. On which stroke
Powers at the heart of matter, powers
We shall have hacked through thorns to kiss awake,
Will open baleful, sweeping eyes, draw breath
And speak new formulae of megadeath.

(55)

In *Scripts for the Pageant* James Merrill sets himself in—and against—a rose tradition. Although he does not refer to Yeats, it's not hard to surmise where the Irish poet would go in his sliding progression, the hinge linking Blake with Auden, who is being addressed here:

The lyrics may be changing. Dante saw
The Rose in fullest bloom. Blake saw it sick.
You and Maria, who have seen the bleak

Unpetalled knob, must wonder: will it last
Till spring? Is it still rooted in the Sun?
EXACTLY THEY CHOSE WELL IN U MY DEAR

(363)

Notes

1. Judith Moffett, *James Merrill* (New York: Columbia University Press, 1984), 150.
2. William Butler Yeats, "Anima Mundi," from *Per Amica Silentia Lunae,* in *Mythologies* (New York: Collier Books, 1969), 358.
3. "An Interview with Helen Vendler," in *Recitative,* ed. J. D. McClatchy (San Francisco: North Point Press, 1986), 51.
4. This paragraph adapts the language and arguments of Marjorie Perloff's *The Poetics of Indeterminacy* (Princeton: Princeton University Press, 1981), especially the chapters "Unreal Cities" and "'Trouver une langue': The *Anti-paysage* of Rimbaud," from which all the quoted phrases (though not intended as descriptions of James Merrill's poem) have been drawn.
5. All references to "Tradition and the Individual Talent" are to T. S. Eliot, *The Sacred Wood* (London: Methuen and Co., 1969), 47–59.
6. T. S. Eliot, "The Function of Criticism," *Selected Prose of T. S. Eliot,* ed. Frank Kermode (New York: Harcourt Brace Jovanovich/Farrar, Straus and Giroux, 1975), 68.
7. David Kalstone, "Persisting Figures: The Poet's Story and How We Read It," in *James Merrill: Essays in Criticism,* ed. David Lehman and Charles Berger (Ithaca, N.Y.: Cornell University Press, 1983), 140.
8. This discussion draws on Stephen Orgel's *The Jonsonian Masque* (Cambridge: Harvard University Press, 1965).
9. T. S. Eliot, "Yeats," *On Poetry and Poets* (New York: Farrar, Straus and Giroux, 1961), 295–308.
10. Ronald Bush, *T. S. Eliot: A Study in Character and Style* (New York: Oxford University Press, 1984), 58.
11. David Kalstone, *Five Temperaments* (New York: Oxford University Press, 1977), 80.
12. Wallace Stevens, "Adagia," *Opus Posthumous* (New York: Alfred A. Knopf, 1989), 202.
13. All references to "The Noble Rider and the Sound of Words" are to Wallace Stevens, *The Necessary Angel* (New York: Vintage Books, 1951), 1–36.
14. All references to *A Vision* are to William Butler Yeats, *A Vision* (New York: Collier Books, 1969).
15. William Butler Yeats, letter to Olivia Shakespear, 13 September 1939, as quoted by Richard Ellmann in *Yeats: The Man and the Masks* (New York: W. W. Norton, 1978), 266.

16. William Butler Yeats, as quoted by Helen Vendler, *Yeats's Vision and the Later Plays* (Cambridge: Harvard University Press, 1963), 16.
17. All references to "Per Amica Silentia Lunae" are to *Mythologies* (New York: Collier Books, 1969), 319–69.
18. Helen Vendler, *Yeats's Vision and the Later Plays,* 41.